TRADING BIBLE

4 BOOKS IN 1

*Day Trading Guide to Learn How Investing in Stock Market,
Options, Futures, Forex, Commodities, Bitcoin
With The Best Strategies to Make High Profits for a Living*

Alexander Taylor

THIS BOOK INCLUDES:

BOOK 1:
DAY TRADING GUIDE
Master Day Trading for a Living and create Your Passive Income with a positive ROI in 19 days. Learn all Strategies, Tools for Money Management, Discipline and Trader Psychology

BOOK 2:
DAY TRADING STRATEGIES
A Detailed Beginner's Guide with Basic and Advanced Trading Strategies to Achieve Excellent Results and Become A Successful Trader with A Positive Roi in 19 Days

BOOK 3:
DAY TRADING FUTURES
Learn how Day Trading and Futures Work to Build your Financial Freedom. How to Become a Smart Trader to Don't Lose Money and Earn Passive Income with a Positive ROI in 19 Days

BOOK 4:
OPTIONS TRADING FOR BEGINNERS
The Ultimate, Simple & Practical Options Trading Guide to Start Investing Consciously. Become an Intelligent Investor to Buy Options After Adequate Technical Analysis

Copyright 2021 - All rights reserved.

TABLE OF CONTENTS

DAY TRADING GUIDE

DAY TRADING STRATEGIES

DAY TRADING FUTURES

OPTIONS TRADING FOR BEGINNERS

DAY TRADING GUIDE

Master Day Trading for a Living and create Your Passive Income with a positive ROI in 19 days. Learn all Strategies, Tools for Money Management, Discipline and Trader Psychology

Alexander Taylor

Introduction

Before the advent of computers, only those people were involved in trading who had direct access to stock markets. These were mostly from financial institutions, trading houses, or brokerage houses. Short-term trading was considered gambling; day trading was not popular in those days, and stock markets were meant only for long term investing.

Once the internet became accessible to common people, day trading or short-term trading also rose in popularity. Online trading and brokerage houses emerged quickly and attracted a large customer base. The convenience of accessing stock markets from one's home; or sitting in a cafe, created a new, lucrative career for or those who were interested in financial markets. Suddenly investors became an old-fashioned word, and day trading became the buzzword.

With the rising popularity and concept of making money by just sitting at a desk, came some misconceptions. Before we proceed further into the mechanism of daily trading, we must clear these misconceptions.

Day trading is NOT some get-rich-quick scheme:

The biggest fascination, and the misconception, about everyday trading is that it is a money generating machine. It is not. People mistakenly assume that all you have to do is buy and sell every day, and you will be making big profits. This kind of thinking leads to huge losses for retail traders, who blindly jump into stock markets, listen to the advice of their friends, colleagues, TV experts, or even seamstress, and eventually lose their shirt. Trading in financial markets requires a thorough knowledge of the functioning of these entities, a disciplined approach, and considerable patience. Do not make the mistake of imagining day trading as easy as playing a lottery or gambling in the casinos. Money making, in any business, is not dependent on luck or chance. It is a calculated risk, which is taken after meticulous research of that field of business and knowledge. If you wish to enter the arena of day trading, make it your career, and earn your living by it, then learn its intricacies. Study all those aspects that impact the results of day trading. Take a step-by-step approach for acquiring the necessary skill sets to finally become a successful day trader.

After all, when you are spending money to earn money, you cannot afford to be unsuccessful in that venture.

Day trading is NOT a 9 to 5 job:

Another common misconception that causes a loss for many retail traders is that day trading is like their 9-to-5 job. They assume; you start trading as soon as markets open (reaching the workplace at a fixed time), trade through the day, and close your trades when the closing bell rings (leave the work workplace at a fixed hour). Workings of financial markets are not like a steady desk job. A plethora of factors that affect the functioning of financial markets and their entities, such as stocks, commodities, currencies, and indices. These are all instruments of day trading and are influenced by the happenings in business, finance, and geopolitical events. There is a very common term related to trading. It is called "market volatility." This term denotes the fluctuation in financial markets. While there are hardly any "fluctuations" or rapid changes in any 9-to-5 desk job, in the world of trading fluctuations happen in seconds! This volatility can be stomach-churning for new traders. One can only master these volatile fluctuations in stock markets by having an in-depth knowledge of how markets function and learning to use this volatility for trading. Remember, when you begin day trading, you put your money at risk. Your purpose should be to obtain every bit of knowledge, which will decrease this risk and improve the chances of reward.

CHAPTER 1

How Day Trading Works

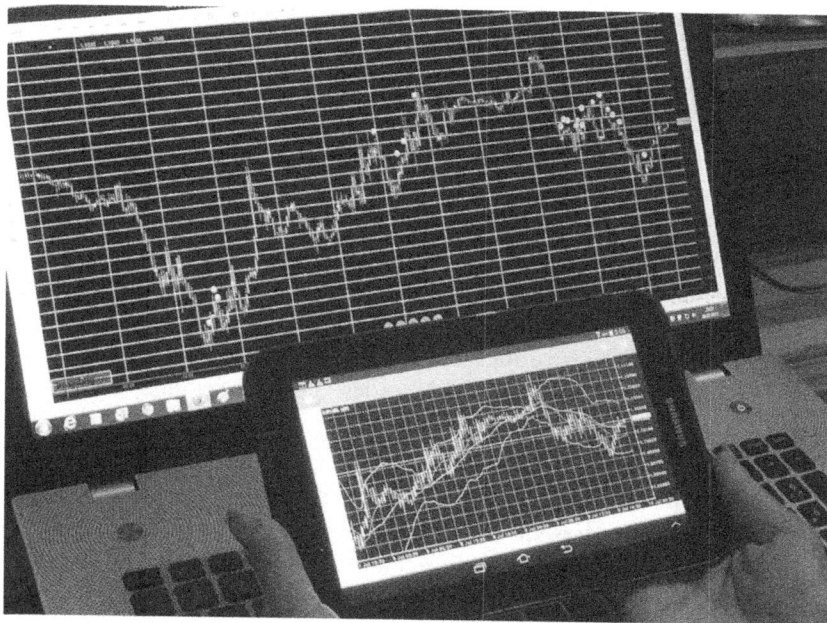

Always keep the primary rule of day trading in mind: never hold on to a position overnight, even if it means taking a loss on trades.

But why do you have to stick to this rule even if it means suffering trading losses? After all, isn't making money the point of day trading?

Yes, making money is the point of day trading. But given that the ideal securities to day trade are volatile ones, holding on to them overnight can put you at high risk for more significant losses the next day. It's ok to take small losses on day trades than large ones when you try to holding day trading securities overnight in the hopes that prices will recover significantly the next day.

By closing your position at the end of the day, even at a loss, you get to minimize day trading losses. And if you close positions at a profit, awesome! Don't feel like you could earn more by waiting until tomorrow. Remember, a bird in the hand's better than three in the bush.

You'll also need to remember that trading is a lot different than regular investing. While trading is a form of investing, regular investing usually refers to a more passive, buying-and-holding strategy that waits for months and years before taking profits. Trading has a much shorter time frame, which is only several hours for day trading and a couple of months at most for swing trading.

Buying Long and Selling Short

When you buy financial security, you take a long position on that security. When you hear a trader say that he or she's long 100 shares Intel stocks, it means that the trader bought and is currently holding a hundred shares of Intel's stocks. The point of taking a long position on financial security is selling them later on at higher prices. To close a long position, you sell the securities you're holding.

When you sell securities that you don't own yet, you take a short position on that security. When you hear a trader say he or she shorted or sold short 100 shares of Intel stocks, it means that the trader sold 100 shares of Intel stocks, hoping that its price will continue dropping so he or she can repurchase it at a much lower price. It's the same principle as buying low and selling high, except that the "selling high" part comes before the "buying low" part.

How can you sell something you don't have, and more importantly, why would you even do that?

First, let's answer why you should do that? And the answer is: to make money when prices of securities are dropping. As mentioned earlier, it's just a reversal of the general trading strategy of buying securities at low prices and selling them at higher ones. By selling securities while their prices are high and buying them later on at lower prices, you can trade profitably even during market downturns. Now, how can you do it? Depending on your broker and whether you're qualified, you can borrow the securities from your broker, sell them, repurchase them when prices drop, and return the securities you acquired from your broker. In the process, you profit from the short sell.

Keep in mind, however, that just like taking long positions, short selling also has its risks, which include that prices may actually go up instead of continuing to go down. In that case, you may also suffer trading losses.

You may be wondering, why would brokers or exchanges lend securities to their clients for short selling instead of selling the securities themselves? That's an excellent question. And the answer is: brokers usually want to take long term positions on securities. Why?

Why take risks with short-term trades on a downward trending market when they can make money with much lower risks by merely lending it to customers who want to short sell for a fee. This way, everybody wins. The long-term investors get to keep their securities and profit, even during bear markets, while those who don't own securities can have opportunities to make profitable trades via short-selling.

Retail vs. Institutional Traders

Retail traders are individuals who can be either part-time or full traders but don't work for a firm and are not managing funds from other people. These traders hold a small percentage of the volume in the trade market.

On the other hand, institutional traders are composed of hedge funds, mutual funds, and investment banks that are often armed with advanced software and are usually engaged in high-frequency trading.

Nowadays, human involvement is quite minimal in the operations of investment firms. Backed up by professional analysts and huge investments, institutional investors can be quite aggressive.

So, at this point, you might be wondering how a beginner like you can compete against the big players?

Our advantage is the freedom and flexibility we enjoy. Institutional traders have the legal obligation to trade. Meanwhile, individual traders are free to trade or to take a break from trading if the market is currently unstable. Institutional traders should be active in the market and trade huge volumes of stocks, regardless of the stock price. Individual traders are free to sit out and trade if there are possible opportunities in the market.

But sadly, most retail traders do not possess the know-how in identifying the right time to be active and the best time to wait. If you want to be profitable in day trading, you need to eliminate greed and develop patience.

The biggest problem of losers in day trading is not the size of their accounts or the lack of access to technology, but their sheer lack of discipline. Many are prone to bad money management and over-trading.

Some retail traders are successful by following the guerilla strategy, which refers to the unconventional approach to trading derived from guerilla warfare. Guerilla combatants are skilled in using hit-and-run tactics like raids, sabotage, and ambushes to manipulate a more prominent and less-mobile conventional opponent.

Remember, your mission is not to defeat institutional traders. Instead, you should focus on waiting for the right opportunity to earn your target income.

As a retail trader, you can make profits from market volatility. It can be impossible to make money if the markets are flat. Only institutional traders have the tools, expertise, and money to gamble in such circumstances.

You must learn how to choose stocks that can help you make fast decisions to the downside or upside in a predictable approach. On the other hand, institutional traders follow high-frequency trading, which allows them to profit from minimal price movements.

But for a brief overview, Alpha Predators are what retail traders are hunting for. These stocks usually tank when the markets are running, and they run when the markets are tanking.

It is generally okay if the market is running, and the stocks are running as well. Just be sure that you are trading stocks that are moving because they have a valid reason to move and are not just moving with the general market conditions.

Probably, you are wondering what the necessary catalyst for stocks is to make them ideal for day trading. Here are some catalysts:

- Debt offerings
- Buybacks
- Stock splits
- Management changes
- Layoffs
- Restructuring
- Significant contract wins/losses
- Partnerships/alliances
- Major product releases
- Mergers and/or acquisitions
- FDA approval/disapproval
- Earnings surprises
- Earnings reports

Retail traders who are engaged in reversal trades usually choose stocks that are selling off because there has been some bad press about the company. Whenever there's a fast sell-off because of bad press, many traders will notice and begin monitoring the stock for what is called a bottom reversal.

How can you identify the stocks that are alluring retail traders? There are some proven ways to do this.

First, you can use day trading stock scanners. Basically, the stocks that are significantly moving up or down are the stocks that are being monitored by retail traders.

Second, find online community groups or social media groups where retail traders hang out. Twitter and Stock Twits are often good places to learn what is currently trending. If you regularly follow successful traders, then you may see for yourself what everyone is following. There's a significant advantage to being part of a community of day traders.

Securities in Play

There's a reason why many investors, traders, and analysts focus on market movements or indices. It's because they know that, for the most part, most financial securities follow the overall trend of their respective markets unless they have an excellent reason not to. For example, the prices of most stocks in the NYSE tend to go up when the Dow Jones is trending upwards and vice versa.

However, there will always be outliers that will – for one reason or another – go against the general trend for some specific purpose. When their general markets are tanking, they're picking up. When their general markets are picking up, their tanking.

These securities are called securities in play (SIP). As a retail or individual day trader, these are the securities you should focus on within your chosen day trading market.

If you want to day trade stocks, these are stocks that buck the general trend of the NYSE or the NASDAQ. If futures contract, these will be futures contracts that go against the general direction of most other similar agreements.

You get the drift, right? Right!

What are some of the reasons that may account for the contrarian behavior of SIPs? These may include:

Unexpected results of earnings;

Surprise company or economic developments; and Major policy changes by the governing authorities.

So, just because a particular security bucks its general market trend doesn't mean you can consider it a SIP. There should be an underlying reason for the contrarian movement. If none, it's probably not a SIP.

Always remember another important day trading rule, particularly for choosing SIPs to day trade: Find out if a particular security's movement is due to general market sentiment or is it due to some unique fundamental reason? For this, you'll need to do your homework. As a beginner day trader, you may have to do a bit more research than what you're accustomed to. But as you become a more experienced day trader, you'll be able to easily distinguish when a particular security is just going with the general market flow or when it's trending based on a unique and specific reason. Professional day traders are those who do this type of trading for a living. While other forms of trading can sometimes be done as a hobby or a gambling high, day trading is often not included here. If you don't have a good understanding of the market and its fundamentals, you will most likely lose money.

CHAPTER 2

How to Think Like an Expert Trader

Know when to go off book: While sticking to your plan, even when your emotions are telling you to ignore it, is the mark of a successful trader, this in no way means that you must blindly follow your plan 100 percent of the time. You will, without a doubt, find yourself in a situation from time to time where your plan is going to be rendered completely useless by something outside of your control. You need to be aware enough of your plan's weaknesses, as well as changing market conditions, to know when following your predetermined course of action is going to lead to failure instead of success. Knowing when the situation really is changing versus when your emotions are trying to hold sway is something that will come with practice, but even being aware of the disparity is a huge step in the right direction.

Avoid trades that are out of the money: While there are a few strategies out there that make it a point of picking up options that are currently out of the money, you can rest assured that they are most certainly the exception, not the rule. Remember, the options market is not like the traditional stock market, which means that even if you are trading options based on underlying stocks buying low and selling high is just not a viable strategy. If a call has dropped out of the money, there is generally less than a 10 percent chance that it will return to acceptable levels before it expires, which means that if you purchase these types of options what you are doing is little better than gambling, and you can find ways to gamble with odds in your favor of much higher than 10 percent.

Avoid hanging on too tightly to your starter strategy: That doesn't mean that it is the last strategy that you are ever going to need, however, far from it. Your core trading strategy is one that should always be constantly evolving as the circumstances surrounding your trading habits change and evolves as well. What's more, outside of your primary strategy you are going to want to eventually create additional plans that are more specifically tailored to various market states or specific strategies that are only useful in a narrow band of situations. Remember, the more prepared you are prior to starting a day's worth of trading, the greater your overall profit level is likely to be, it is as simple as that.

Utilize the spread: If you are not entirely risk averse, then when it comes to taking advantage of volatile trades it's the best thing to do is utilize a spread as a way of both safeguarding your existing investments and, at the same time, making a profit. To utilize a long spread you are going to want to generate a call and a put, both with the same underlying asset, expiration details, and share amounts but with two very different strike prices. The call will need to have a higher strike price and will mark the upper limit of your profits, and the put will have a lower strike price that will mark the lower limit of your losses. When creating a spread it is important that you purchase both halves at the same time as doing it in fits and spurts can add extraneous variables to the formula that are difficult to adjust for properly. Never proceed without knowing the mood of the market: While using a personalized trading plan is always the right choice, having one doesn't change the fact that it is extremely important to consider the mood of the market before moving forward with the day's trades. First and foremost, it is important to keep in mind that the collective will of all of the traders who are currently participating in the market is just as much as a force as anything that is more concrete, including market news. In fact, even if companies release good news to various outlets and the news is not quite as good as everyone was anticipating it to be, then related prices can still decrease.

To get a good idea of what the current mood of the market is like, you are going to want to know the average daily numbers that are common for your market and be on the lookout for them to start dropping sharply. While a day or two of major fluctuation can be completely normal, anything longer than that is a sure sign that something is up. Additionally, you will always want to be aware of what the major players in your market are up to.

Never get started without a clear plan for entry and exit: While finding your first set of entry/exit points can be difficult without experience to guide you, it is extremely important that you have them locked down prior to starting trading, even if the stakes are relatively low. Unless you are extremely lucky, starting without a clear idea of the playing field is going to do little but lose your money. If you aren't sure about what limits you should set, start with a generalized pair of points and work to fine tune it from there.

More important than setting entry and exit points, however, is using them, even when there is still the appearance of money on the table. One of the biggest hurdles that new options traders need to get over is the idea that you need to wring every last cent out of each and every successful trade. The fact of the matter is that, as long as you have a profitable trading plan, and then there will always be more profitable trades in the future, which mean that instead of worrying about a small extra profit, you should be more concerned with protecting the profit that the trade has already netted you. While you may occasionally make some extra profit ignoring this advice, odds are you will lose far more than you gain as profits peak unexpectedly and begin dropping again before you can effectively pull the trigger. If you are still having a hard time with this concept, consider this: options trading are a marathon, not a sprint, slow and steady will always win the race.

Never double down: When they are caught up in the heat of the moment, many new options traders will find themselves in a scenario where the best way to recoup a serious loss is to double down on the underlying stock in question at its newest, significantly lowered, price in an effort to make a profit under the assumption that things are going to turn around and then continue to do so to the point that everything is completely profitable once again. While it can be difficult to let an underlying stock that was once extremely profitable go, doubling down is rarely, if ever, going to be the correct decision.

If you find yourself in a spot where you don't know if the trade you are about to make is actually going to be a good choice, all you need to do is ask yourself if you would make the same one if you were going into the situation blind, the answer should tell you all you need to know. If you find yourself in a moment where doubling down seems like the right choice, you are going to need to have the strength to talk yourself back down off of that investing ledge and to cut your losses as thoroughly as possible given the current situation. The sooner you cut your losses and move on from the trade that ended poorly, the sooner you can start putting energy and investments into a trade that still has the potential to make you a profit.

Never take anything personally: It is human nature to build stories around, and therefore form relationships with all manner of inanimate objects, including individual stocks or currency pairs. This is why it is perfectly natural to feel a closer connection to particular trades and possibly even consider throwing out your plan when one of them takes an unexpected dive. Thinking about and acting on are two very different things, however, which is why being aware of these tendencies in order to avoid them at all costs.

This scenario happens just as frequently with trades moving in positive directions as it does negative, but the results are always going to be the same. Specifically, it can be extremely tempting to hang on to a given trade much longer than you might otherwise decide to simply because it is on a hot streak that shows no sign of stopping. In these instances, the better choice of action is to instead sell off half of your shares and then set a new target based on the updated information to ensure you are in a position to have your cake and eat it too.

Not taking your choice of broker seriously: With so many things to consider, it is easy to understand why many new option traders simply settle on the first broker that they find and go about their business from there. The fact of the matter is, however, that the broker you choose is going to be a huge part of your overall trading experience, which means that the importance of choosing the right one should not be discounted if you are hoping for the best experience possible. This means that the first thing that you are going to want to do is to dig past the friendly exterior of their website and get to the meat and potatoes of what it is they truly offer. Remember, creating an eye-catching website is easy, filling it will legitimate information when you have ill intent is much more difficult. First things first, this means looking into their history of customer service as a way of not only ensuring that they treat their customers in the right way, but also of checking to see that quality of service is where it needs to be as well. Remember, when you make a trade every second count, which means that if you need to contact your broker for help with a trade, you need to know that you are going to be speaking with a person who can solve your problem as quickly as possible. The best way to ensure the customer service is up to snuff is to give them a call and see how long it takes for them to get back to you. If you wait more than a single business day, take your business elsewhere as if they are this disinterested in a new client, consider what the service is going to be like when they already have you right where they want you.

With that out the way, the next thing you will need to consider is the fees that the broker is going to charge in exchange for their services. There is very little regulation when it comes to these fees, which means it is definitely going to pay to shop around. In addition to fees, it is important to consider any account minimums that are required as well as any fees having to do with withdrawing funds from the account.

Find a Mentor: When you are looking to go from causal trader to someone who trades successfully on the regular, there is only so much you can learn by yourself before you need a truly objective eye to ensure you are proceeding appropriately.

This person can be someone you know in real life, or it can take the form of one or more people online. The point is you need to find another person or two who you can bounce ideas off of and whose experience you can benefit from. Options trading don't need to be a solitary activity; take advantage of any community you can find.

CHAPTER 3

Getting Ready for Your Day Trading Career

Welcome to the beginning of the rest of your life. This is the chapter where we talk about how to get your life ready for becoming a day trader, organizing everything you need to get yourself off to the best possible start. This will be a rather lengthy chapter because there's a lot to cover, including making sure you're cut out to be a trader, setting up your trading space, getting your finances in order, and getting ready to go. Here we go.

Is Day Trading Right for You?

This is an important question you need to ask yourself.

Using the questions detailed above, you need to make sure you're going to be committed to becoming a day trader. You must understand you're going to be working long hours, and you don't precisely get holiday breaks since you're your own boss and you're working for yourself. You will also need to make sure you're not an emotionally reactive kind of person. It's absolutely guaranteed that at some point during your career, you're going to invest in a stock, and you're going to lose money on it. That's just the way the game works, and it's inevitable. However, if you're an emotional person and you lose a significant investment sum that causes you to freak out, you can bet you're going to make some bad decisions in the future. Likewise, there are going to be times when you win big money, and it's easy to get excited and want to invest more and make more. This is called greed and can backfire just as badly. Being a day trader means being able to stand calm and relaxed in even the most stressful of situations, removing emotion from your decision-making process, sticking to your plan, and remaining grounded. If you're not this sort of person, or you can't cultivate this kind of mindset, then day trading is probably not for you.

Setting Up Your Finances

Being able to manage your finances is vital before you set into the world of day trading. If you have any kind of debt right now, you shouldn't even consider day trading until you've cleared it. If you have a loan or credit card, or both, where you're paying back interest rates of 20%, and you're only making a 5% return on your investments, then you're going to be losing money.

Instead, make sure you're paying off all your debts and then getting your capital ready. This way, you'll be minimizing how much interest you're paying on your credit and debt and then maximizing your profits when you start investing.

Once you're in the green, you need to start thinking about getting your capital in place. This is the starting amount of money you're going to be investing with. This can vary dramatically depending on your personal situation, so it's really up to you. You could start small, perhaps with $5,000 and then day trade part-time. As your capital grows over time, you can then begin transitioning over to becoming a full-time trader.

On the other hand, you may want to save up a lump sum that means you can quit your job and start investing straight away, although that's not recommended since you'll have no experience. Even if you have a lump sum, start small, so you can teach yourself the ropes of trading, and then start investing more and more once you start gathering experience.

Van Tharp, one of the top day traders in the world and author of Trade Your Way to Financial Freedom, recommends that if you're trading full-time, you're going to want around $100,000 to start with. If you're looking to day trade effectively, you're going to want approximately $10,000 in your trading account at all times.

The final financial aspect you'll want to consider is getting yourself a rainy-day emergency fund. This means creating a savings account where you put a recommended three months' worth of living expenses into an account and then leave it.

This means when you're trading, and if you ever come across a time in your life where you're suffering from financial difficulties, you'll have this fund to fall back on. However, you need to remember this is not an account you can ever use for trading or investment. If you have a hard-losing streak and you need money to live on to support yourself and your family, you don't want to end up with nothing. This is a financial crisis you'll want to avoid at all costs, which is why it's best to be as prepared as possible.

Learn About Stock Market Trading

This should go without saying, but if you want to become a day trader, you need to have some kind of passion or interest in the stock market world, or at least the drive to become educated about it. You need to learn when the stock market trading hours are and how the processes and systems within the stock market work.

You should have an interest in a particular niche or industry you want to trade in, and you better have some kind of passion surrounding it because you're going to need to be watching the news on this industry, reading articles and books on the subjects, and investing your time watching interviews and learning about these stock market companies in terms of how they work and what they're up too on a daily basis. You'll also need to learn about what stocks actually, as well as other potential trading options, such as ETFs, options, futures, and mutual funds. We'll briefly describe each one in the table below, but it's crucial you take time to develop a clear understanding of each other before you start implementing a trading strategy and investing in one.

Stocks When the ownership of a company or organization is broken down into all the shares, these are individually known as "stocks." Each stock represents a fractional ownership of a company relative to the number of shares it has in total.

ETFs The term shortened for 'Exchanged-Traded Funds,' ETFs are a type of investment fund that is traded identically to a stock on the stock market and exchanges of the world. ETFs are indexes made of other securities and assets, such as stocks, special funds, and commodity funds.

Options is the term given to a contract that gives a specific buyer a right to buy or sell any underlying asset, although it doesn't guarantee an obligation for sale. However, options will give the price that must be valid prior to or on a specified date stated on the option contract.

Futures are another type of contract that points to the legal agreement that contracts the buying and selling of something at a price, time, and date that has been predetermined. However, these metrics won't be known by the parties involved and is classed as an asset.

Mutual Funds Mutual funds are investment portfolios that are managed by professional financial services. These services bring in money from several investors to buy stocks, shares, and other securities, like the ones in this table.

Gold & Precious Metals Gold (and sometimes other precious metals) refers to the trading asset of the metal gold that is stored in banks around the US and around the world.

Eminis are another type of futures contracts that track the S&P 500 stock index market. It is also known as the E-Mini, ES, or just Mini.

Cryptocurrencies this is a broad term that refers to the trade of cryptocurrencies within the stock market. This can be done individually or via an exchange.

Forex is the trading of foreign currencies around the world by converting one currency into another and then continuing to trade in this manner.

Practice Your Money Management Skills

The last thing you need to do before you even start to think about getting ready to trade stocks is to consider how effective your money management skills are. If you're thinking to yourself, 'yeah, my money management skills are pretty good,' then take a step back and consider how you can improve. There's always room to be better, and as a day trader, these are improvements you're going to both want and need.

Consider this. If you're starting with $100,000 and you're using a tried-and-tested strategy that has a 60% success rate, how much are you going to invest to begin with? What happens if your first four trades fail and come out as a loss? How should you be allocating your capital?

With any kind of trading, it's always a good idea to start small and then expand over time. It's rather stupid to jump in on your first trade and buy $100,000 worth of stock and just hope for the best. Of course, it might pay off, but if you're this risky with your first investment, the chances are it's going to backfire dramatically later down the line.

Work on your money management skills and nurture the ability to step back and make decisions from a grounded state of mind. You need to be able to wisely select which opportunities you're going to invest in and how you're going to manage your investment capital. Even if you're using a strategy that has a 30% success rate, you can still make a large amount of profit from it when you have proper money management skills.

Once you've developed all these aspects of your life and you've got yourself ready, you're one step closer to starting your day trading career. Before we really jump into the meat of what you need to do and actually start investing, there's one more aspect we need to cover, and that's developing your day trading mindset.

Why Do You Trade?

Answer: It's simple—the only reason to trade is to make money! This question, why do you trade, is important and something to think about as we conclude this topic.While the answer "to make money" might seem obvious—a no-brainer—most losing traders actually trade for other reasons. They may think they are trading to make money, but their actions indicate that other motivations are driving their decisions. Remember, the most important indicator is you.

If you are truly trading to make money, then the next logical question to ask is how… How does a trader achieve that objective? The answer is by trading within the context and rules of a proven trade plan. A proven trade plan grows equity in your account, despite the random distribution of wins and losses. It includes rules to follow that you can prove to yourself.

Taking random trades that are not within the context of a proven trade plan is not trading to make money. It is something else. Why? Because we are traders. It is what we do. We take trades. If you win on a random trade, now what? There is still another trade to take, right? Making money comes from the edge that your proven trade plan gives you over time. Random trades are not going to reveal whether or not you have an edge—they're random—until after the fact, when you will most likely learn that the answer is no, you did not have an edge. And then it will be too late. This is how accounts get blown up.

If you are truly trading to make money, then your actions should reflect that. If they do not, then you are most likely trading for other reasons that you don't quite understand. You will need to address that if you truly want to internalize the correct reason to trade—to make money. Otherwise, the market will give you something else, and you probably will not like it.

CHAPTER 4

Risk and Account Management

Since the goal of every good trader is to make a profit, to be a good and successful one, you have to learn how to manage risks related to your trading and how to protect your profits. How well you manage your risks determines how successful you will be as a trader.
Prepare your mind because you are about to learn straightforward but powerful and practical techniques in risk management strategies and techniques.

Planning Your Trade

A Chinese military general, Sun Tzu, once said: "Every battle is won before it is fought," this implies that planning and strategy are essential in trading. Planning is inevitable. It is just like the famous quote says, "Plan the trade and trade the plan." This determines the success or failure of your trade; no successful trader goes into the deal without carefully planning out the trade, pointing out possible future losses, calculating risks, and listing out potential future profits in your trade. A plan should be written down clearly and concisely; your plan can change with changes in the market; risk tolerance should also be incorporated. Here are some steps you must follow for a successful trade plan:

Skill Assessment: here, you should be able to assess yourself very well to determine how ready you are to trade. You should ask yourself a very crucial question such as: are you prepared to trade? How much confidence do you have in a particular market? Have you tested your system by paper trading? (Paper trading is a way of practicing buying and selling without investing real money, it is usually done using online trading platforms such as paper Money and Investopedia) How sure are you that your system will work in a live trading environment? Can you spot and follow your signals without delaying? Mental preparation: As a good trader, you should be emotionally and mentally prepared for the upcoming tasks, you should be prepared for whatever situation that might arise and whatever changes that may occur in your market. Avoid distractions as much as possible in your trading area. If you are emotionally incapable, try taking a day off, take some rest, do some exercise. This keeps your brain ready for the upcoming task because trading has a lot of thinking associated with it.

Also, have a market mantra before the day begins; it is a kind of special quote or phrase that gets you ready for trading. Set Risk Level: this determines how much of your portfolio you should risk on a trade. Your portfolio includes all financial assets, such as bonds, stocks, and currencies, cash, commodities, and cash equivalents. This depends on how you choose to trade and the risks tolerance; It can vary, but it should be within the range of 1% to 5% of your portfolio on a given trading day. If you lose any of that amount of money in a day, leave that market immediately and save your portfolio for a better market.

Consider the One-Percent Rule

Most successful traders make use of what is called the one-percent rule; it merely states that you should never invest more than 1% of your capital or portfolio into a single trade or market. This means that if you have $10,000 in your trading account, the highest amount you would invest should not be above $100 per single trade. This technique is usually done by traders with accounts with less than $100,000. Some other traders may decide to go as high as 2%. It all depends on your position and the size of your account. The best thing to do is to keep the rule at least below 2%.

Setting Stop-Loss and Profit Points

Just like the name implies, a stop-loss point occurs when a trader decides to sell a stock and bear the loss, this situation usually happens when the market doesn't turn out well enough for the trader. The stock's in the market goes way below expected, hence before the stock's value could get any lower, the trader decides to sell it out. The take profit point is the price at which a trader will sell a stock and gain a profit from the trade. Traders usually sell before a period of consolidation takes place.

How to More Effectively Set Stop-Loss Points

Setting stop-loss points in order to have profit is usually made in technical analysis, although fundamental analysis can help out. A great way of setting stop-loss or take profit levels is by resistance trend lines; this can be done by connecting and comparing past highs or lows.

Diversify and Hedge

To diversify and the hedge is just like the famous phrase, "never put all your eggs in one basket." If you choose to put all your money in one stock, you are taking a significant risk. So spread your investments across different sectors. There may also be times when you need to hedge at a particular position considering stock and the market.

The Bottom Line

As a good trader, you should be able to know when to enter or leave a trade. By using the stop-loss, the trader can minimize losses. It is better to plan ahead of time.

Calculating Expected Return

Calculating expected returns is very crucial in managing risks, it helps you think through your trade, and it is a perfect way to compare trades in order to choose the most profitable and less risky ones. Returns can be calculated thus:

[(Probability of gain) × (take profit % gain)] + [(probability of loss) × (stop-loss % loss)]

The end of this should give the expected returns.

Day Trading Risks

To become a successful trader, you need to aware of the various risks that you are bound to face before getting into the trading world. There are three major categories of risks:

Market Risks

Understanding market changes in your trade is an essential aspect of your business. Understanding when the markets rise and fall, coupled with the possible risks associated with it, will help you to protect your profit more. Types of market risks include: Inflation risk: inflation occurs when there is uncertainty in the future value of an investment you are making. While deflation may mean more returns and profit for you. Rising inflation often reduces the returns and profit you'd be expecting from it. This also means that as prices of stocks and commodities increases, the demand for it decreases. Hence, you should prepare your plan for any market changes at all. Marketability risk: this tells how sellable your investment is. If there is any form of resistance or delay in selling or marketing your investment effectively, then your target market won't mean anything. For example, if you choose to invest in a small company whose stock isn't sold on one of the major stock markets, then you risk losing your investment for nothing. Currency translation risk: this usually occurs when you are trading with foreign countries when there are fluctuations between the values of your local currency and the currency of your international trading country. A piece of useful knowledge about currency trading risk would be very beneficial to traders because even if your stock or investment rises in price, you can still lose money depending on the currency exchange rate between the two countries. If the value of your local currency falls against the other currency, your investment can be far smaller when you convert it back.

Investment Risks

This suggests how you invest your money and manage how you enter into or leave trades. There are two major kinds of risks:

Opportunity risks: this kind of investment risk shuts or stops you from investing in other more profitable trades due to the fact that your money is already tied up in your current business. This type of risk makes you lose golden opportunities, all because your money is blocked by another one.

Concentration risks: this happens when you focus all your investment and capital in just one particular trade, perhaps because you think that you have found your dream trade that will make you a millionaire. Hence you invest all you've got, leaving yourself very vulnerable to any potential risks that might arise in that trade with the possibility of losing it all.

Trading Risks

Trading risks are common risks that swing traders usually encounter, and every trader needs to know about them, just as the saying "knowledge is power," you need to be knowledgeable about them, and this will give you leverage in managing the future risks that may arise. Some common risks that are associated with trading risks include:

Slippage risk: this risk gives attention to some hidden costs that may be related to every transaction the trader makes. Every time you enter or leave a trade, there is some very minor and little subtraction of money from your account. Also, every time you buy a stock at the asking price, which is the lowest price available for the stock that you want, and sells it at the bid price, which is the highest price someone is willing to pay for your shares, you have to know that it is always less than the asking price. At first, the amount for each trade may seem small, but as your trading increases, the amounts you also lose gains.

Poor execution risk: this risk occurs when your broker has a difficult time filling out your order, perhaps due to fast market conditions, inadequate availability of stock, and the absence of other buyers and sellers. When this happens, you risk having your stock trade going below than it should or not getting your order filled at all.

Gap risk: this occurs when there are price gaps in your transactions; sometimes, a stock opens at a significantly high or lesser price and sometimes may trade using your exit price. For example, a stock may close at $35 today and begin at $30 tomorrow. If your planned price is $34, your order is likely to be filled out at the opening price. Though these kinds of risks are infrequent, they can cause problems for most traders.

Other Types of Risks Include

BLACK SWAN EVENTS: these are the type of risks that comes up unexpectedly. They are tough to predict. It is a type of significant risk that has a substantial impact on the market.

UNDIVERSIFIED RISK: this is a type of risk that occurs when you 'put all your eggs in one basket.' This type of risk is usually tough to avoid and difficult to predict as markets can also influence this type of risk. This type is one of the primary reasons why investors and traders usually decide to diversify their stocks and money, avoiding the risk of losing everything at once.

CHAPTER 5

Psychology Discipline

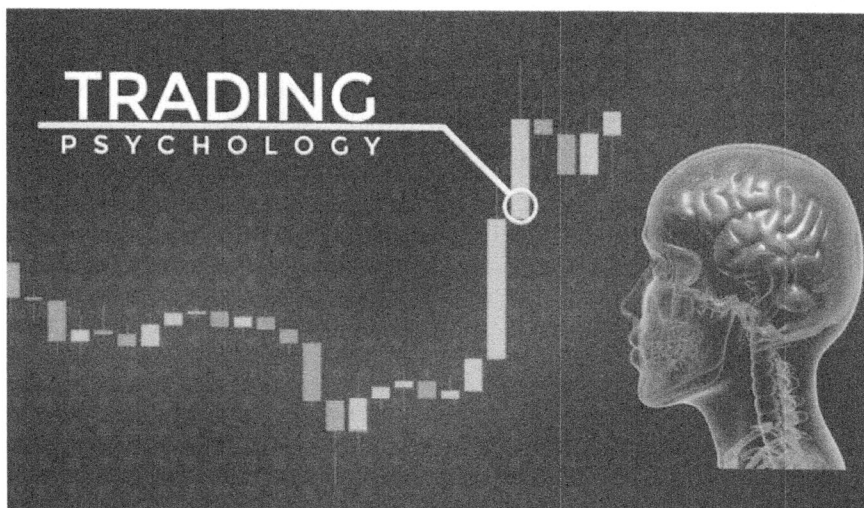

Trading with Emotions

It is common for traders to have their emotions and feelings jumbled up when day trading, from the highs and the lows they experience from the market. This is a far outcry from the confident self that a trader usually poses before the markets open, bubbling up with excitement over the money and profits that they intend to make. Emotions in trading can mess up and impair your judgment and your ability to make wise decisions. Day trading is not to be carried out without emotions, but rather as a trader. You should know how to work your way around them, making them work for your good. A clear level headed and stable mind should be kept at all times, whether your profits are on the rise or whether you are on a losing streak. This is not to mean that as a trader, you are to disconnect from your emotions.

Greed

A trader may be fueled to earn more money by checking their balances in their accounts and seeing it be as of a low level. While this may be a motivator to work hard, some traders take it too far, wanting to earn a lot of money right there and then. They make mistakes while trading that has reverse effects than the intended ones...

Taking Unnecessary Risks

Greed for more money will seek to convince the trader to take risks that are not worth so as to achieve a certain financial threshold in the trading account. These will most likely end up in losses. The risky traders may take risks such as high leverage that they hope will work in their favor, but at the same time may have them making huge losses.

Making an Overtrade

Due to the urge to make more and more money, a trader may extend over long periods of time trading. Commonly these efforts are in vain, for overtrading through the highs and the lows of the market put a trader in a position where their accounts can be wiped off as a result of greed. Not putting into account the time of trading and plunging into opening up trades without having done an analysis will most likely result in a loss.

Improper Profit and Loss Comprehension
Wanting to earn a lot of money within a short period of time will have a trader not closing a trade that is losing, maintaining the losses, and on the other hand, overriding on profit-making trade until a reverse in the market happens, canceling out all the gains made.

Fear
Fear can work in both directions, as a limit to an over-trade or also as a limit to making profits. A trader may close a trade so as to avert a loss, the action motivated by fear. A trader may also close a trade too early, even when on a winning streak in making gains, in fear that the market will reverse and that there will be losses. In both scenarios, fear is the motivator, working in avoiding failure and success at the same time.

The Fear to Fail
The fear of failing in trading may inhibit a trader from opening up trades and just watch as the market changes and goes in cycles when doing nothing. The fear of failing in trading is an inhibitor to success. It prevents a trader from executing what could have been a successful trade.

The Fear to Succeed
This type of fear in trading psychology will make a trader lose out his profits to the market when there was an opportunity to do otherwise. It works in a self-harming way in the market scenarios. Such traders in this category fear having too much profit and allow losses to run, all while aware of their activities and the losses they are going to make.

Bias in Trading
There are several market biases that a trader may tend to make that may be a result of emotional play, which traders are advised against. In the psychology of trading, these biases may influence a trader to make unwise and uncalculated trading decisions that may prove to be loss-making ones. Even when the trading biases are in focus, as a trader, you have to be aware of the emotions in you and come up with ways to keep them in check and maintain a cool head in your trading window.

Bias in Overconfidence
It is a common occurrence with traders, especially new traders, that when you make a trade with huge profits, you get in euphoria in the state of winning. You want to go on opening up trades with the belief that your analysis cannot go wrong, boiling down to the profits and gains you've made.

This should not be the case. One cannot be too overexcited and overconfident in the analysis skills that you believe you cannot make a loss. The market is a volatile one, and therefore the cards can change at any given time, and when they do, the over-excited and overconfident trader now turns into a disappointing one.

Bias in Confirming Trades
In trading psychology, the bias in confirmation of a trade you have already made, justifying it, is one of the factors that waste a lot of time and money for traders. This type of bias is mostly associated with professional traders. After making a trade, they go back to evaluate and analyze the trade they just made, trying to prove that it was the correct one, whether they sailed according to the market. They waste a lot of time digging for information that they are already aware of. They could also be proving that the mistake they made in opening a wrong trade and making a wrong move was a correct one.

Bias in Anchoring on Obsolete Strategies
This type of bias in the psychology of trading applies to the traders that rely so much on outdated information and obsolete strategies that do more harm than good to their trading success.

Anchoring on the correct but irrelevant information when trading might make the trader susceptible to making losses, a blow to the traders who are always lazy to dig up for new information on the market. Keeping up with the current events and factors that may have an impact on the market is one of the key aspects of having a successful trading career.

Bias in Avoiding Losses
Trading with the motive to avert losses usually boils down to the fear factor. There are some traders whose trading patterns and their trading windows are controlled by fear of making losses. Having gains and making profits is not a motivation to them when fear hinders them from opening trades that could have otherwise been profitable. They also close trades too early, even when making profits in a bid to avert the losses, their imaginable losses.

Psychology Affecting Traders' Habits

Psychological aspects affect habits in trading, the mistakes, and the winning strategies that a trader comes up with. Explained below are the negative habits that many traders make with the influence of psychology on their habits.

Trading Without a Strategy

With no trading strategy and plan, a trader will face challenges with no place to refer to the anticipated end result. A proper strategy should be drawn by a trader to be a referencing point when facing a problem in trading in the market. It should be a clearly constructed plan, detailing what to do in certain situations and which type of trading patterns to employ in different case scenarios. Trading without a strategy is akin to trading to lose your money.

Lack of Money Management Plans

Money management plans are one of the main aspects of trading, and without solid strategies in this, it is difficult to make progress in making gains in the trades opened. As a trader, you have to abide by certain principles that will guide you in how to spend your money in the account in opening up trades and ensuring that profits ensue from that.

Wanting to Be Always Right

Some traders always go against the market, placing their desire of what manner they would like the market to behave in. They do not follow the sign that the market points to, but rather they follow their own philosophy, not doing proper analysis and always wanting to be right.

Remedying the Effects of Psychological Habits

Coming Up with Clear Cut Goals

Drawing clear and concise goals and strategies to trade helps a trader in having a vision of trading and just not doing it for the sake of trading. Writing down goals also works to improve the confidence levels of the trader. Working with a well comprehensive strategy is a profit-making plan in the market.

Setting Up Rules for Trading

Rules for the trader work for the good in ensuring discipline in trading. As a trader, you should come up with rules that govern the time of the day that you start trading, the time that you close your trades, and whether or not you trade on a daily basis, or whatever your trading window is. Rules are the backbone of successful trading; when to close a losing trade and at the same time when to close a winning one.

Initializing Money Management Strategies

Coming up with money strategies is not enough, but also actualizing the strategies is equally important.

Money management strategies are of great importance in ensuring that a trader's profitability is put first, putting into consideration the risk of loss. Put the money strategy into action to avoid trading haphazardly and trading with emotions.

CHAPTER 6

Build Your Watch List

A Trading Watch List

As an active day trader, you must create a trading watch list. Basically, this is a list where you record the daily share prices of a group of stocks over time. It acts like a menu for the trading day. Based on the fundamental and technical new catalyst, a trading watch list should have active stocks that are ready to trade. It can either be done on the notepad, a spreadsheet, or even on paper. There are many software programs and other utilities that help in generating a watch list. It can also be provided by some brokerage houses where you pay a minimal charge, or for free.

A trader can have more than one watch list, but there are two specific watch lists that every active trader should never mess; a general watch list and a dynamic watch list. The general one may be composed of hundreds of stocks that are familiar to the trader. Every trader should also narrow down from the general watch list and come up with an active stock watch list every trading day before the market opening.

This watch list should have stocks that the trader has been watching for days or weeks that may be about to set up for a technical movement. Unlike the general list, the active trade list should not contain too many stocks. It should have a handful of ripe stocks that the trader is comfortable to trade. In other words, a general watch list may contain shares that the trader has already purchased recently or in the past, while the active watch list should contain stocks that the trader is considering to purchase.

For example, let's say that you are an active trader with ten positions on average at any given time. Usually, you will be tracking several stocks so that you can purchase another position from the watch list immediately after one position has been sold. This will help you avoid a situation where at any given time you have a lot of idle cash in your trading account. A watch list is convenient for many different reasons.

For example, let's say that you have done your research and found a company that you feel is sound and has promising potential, but the stock value seems to be currently high or overvalued. You decide to wait for a better convenient time so that you can buy. You will use the watch list to track the stock price and generate charts to monitor the stock trends. That way, you will be able to know the best time to purchase that stock.

Building Your Trading Watch List

Stocks in Play

When a stock is widely believed to be a takeover target, it is said to be in play. Day traders widely trade stocks in play because their volatility produces reasonable risks and trading opportunities. When company stocks have less volatility, they move slowly, and they only have a reasonable price change only when the company shows good or bad trading outcomes. This may occur only a few times in a year. Such companies are ideal for investors looking for returns in the long-term. Long term investors buy shares in these companies, which have good prospects, with shares moving slowly in the right direction, and it matters less to them if the share price doesn't move much intraday. But day traders buy and sell stocks during stock market opening hours and exit the trade before the day ends. Sometimes they even trade for a few minutes or an hour and exit the market. They, therefore, require more action than investors. They need stocks that move and produce price swings so that their trade becomes worthwhile. Such fluctuations in prices leave enough room for them to realize profits after paying the association fees charged by stockbrokers for buying and selling shares.

Stocks in play also have a large volume. Day traders are after quick entries and exits, and they want liquid stocks. That means they can buy and sell shares in the stock on demand. A stock that doesn't have good liquidity and my cost the broker time to strike a promising buying or selling deal. The broker is unable to negotiate the deal that the trader wants to buy or sell at. For day traders, this is a problem because it means the difference between a profitable trade and a non-profitable one. Day traders are guided by trade volumes of shares that are traded each day to arrive at what they consider good liquidity for them. For most traders, one hundred thousand shares traded per day would be their minimum, while some other traders may require a million shares.

Stocks in play will change in one day. An ordinary stock will be put in play by the company news, which is typically released early in the morning, and it will vary depending on the nature of the new, whether it is good or bad.

Sometimes good news for traders may be bad news for investors. Some of the big companies like Apple, Amazon, and Facebook have stocks that are always in play, and day traders will have these stocks constantly on their watch list. This is because they have large volumes of trades and traded shares. This is where a day trader looks for excellent trading opportunities and proper levels to trade from.

Other websites have free stock screening tools that help traders to find stocks that are in rapid movement, intraday, and break out pre-market. These are websites like Market watch and busy stock. Breakout shares and top lists for trending UK shares are produced by ADVFN. They also have apps like Seeking Alpha, with live news feeds that are accessible for you. Big company news and breaking news are quickly reported by news channels like CNN, BBC, Reuters, and Bloomberg. Up to the minute, relevant news for day traders is also provided by channels like Stock twits.

Float and Market Cap

As an active day trader, it is crucial to understand the link between company size, risk, and return potential. Such information is vital as you lay the foundation to pursue long-term trading goals. With such knowledge, you can build a balanced watch list that comprises different market caps.

Market cap means market capitalization. It expresses the stock value of all the company shares. To arrive at the market cap of an entity, multiply the entities' shares by the stock price.

An Entity with $50 million in shares with each share trading at $20, then $10 billion will be its market cap. Market cap is necessary because it helps traders to understand and compare the size of different companies. Market cap helps you to know the worth of different companies in the open market. It also helps you to understand how the market perceives a particular company and mirrors what investors and traders are ready to pay for its stock.

Large-cap stocks: $10 billion and over is their stock market value. Typically, these are reputable companies that produce quality goods and services. They experience steady growth and have a history of consistency in dividend payments to their shareholders. Their brand names are familiar to national and even international consumer audience. They are dominant players in their respective industries of the establishment. They are ideal for conservative investors since they pose less risk as they have less growth potential.

Mid-cap stocks: Typically, these are businesses with a minimum market value of $2billion and a maximum market value of 10$billion. In other words, their market value is between $2billion and $10 billion. They are medium-sized, established companies with growth potential. Such companies are experiencing rapid growth, or there is an expectation that they will grow rapidly in the near future. They are in the stage of boosting their competitive advantage and widening their share of the market. This is a crucial stage since it determines their ability to attain maximum potential. In terms of risk, they have less risk in comparison with new startups.

When it comes to potential, they offer more potential than blue-chip companies since they are expected to continue to grow until they reach full potential.

Small caps: their market stock value ranges from $300 million to $2 billion. They are growing businesses that are just emerging in the industry. They are the riskiest and the most aggressive and rely on niche marketing to survive in the industry. Due to limited resources, they are vulnerable to economic shocks. They are susceptible to intense competition and market uncertainties. Since they are new startups, they have high growth potential in the long-term, and they are ideal for investors who can cope up with volatile stock price swings in the short-run.

Float, on the other hand, is the number of shares, which are available for trading by the general public. Unlike the market cap that calculates the total stock value of all company shares, free-float does not include locked-in shares. Locked-in shares are those that are held by company employees and the government. Market cap can be affected by several factors. When there is a significant change in the value of shares, either up or down, this can have an impact on the market cap. Market cap can also be impacted when the number of issued shares changes. Market cap can be diluted when warrants are exercised on the stock of the company because the number of shares outstanding will increase. This is because such an exercise is often carried out below the shares market price, hence it has the potential to impact on the market cap. On the other hand, issuing a dividend or a stock split typically doesn't alter the market cap.

To build a stable watch list, comprising large-cap, mid-cap, and small-cap stocks, a trader will have to evaluate their time horizon, risk tolerance, and financial goals. A balanced watch list comprising all the market caps may be ideal in helping to reduce the investment risk.

Pre-Market Gappers

Pre-market trading refers to trading activities that take place between 8 am, and 9:30 am EST every trading day. This is usually before the regular market session begins. Traders and investors monitor the pre-market trading period to judge the direction and the strength of the market while waiting for the regular trading session. During the pre-market activity, there is limited liquidity and volume. Wide bid-ask spreads are a common thing during the pre-market period. The type of orders that can be used during this period is limited by many retail brokers, even though they offer pre-market trading. As early as 4 am, direct-access brokers begin to allow access to the pre-market activity to start. It is crucial to bear in mind that there is limited activity during this pre-market period. The most reliable types of stocks that are beneficial to trade during pre-market activities are gapper or dumper. They are usually viable during the seasons when earnings for various companies are reported. During such season, these stocks gap with the volume either up or down. They are usually triggered by a primary catalyst such as press releases, news, or earnings reports. They can also be reacting to rumors or analyst upgrades or downgrades. It is important to note that stocks tend to get more 'tradability,' follow-through, and consistent volume when they are gapped in reaction to earnings reports and guidance. As you trade during pre-market activity, you should always know that this period is characterized by fewer participants, wider spread, and thin liquidity. It is not advisable to trade pre-market unless there is a substantial volume gap that is being driven by a catalyst. Waiting for the market to open is the most suitable option for most traders.

CHAPTER 7

Why Most Day Traders Lose

With the numerous benefits that can be gained from day trading, it begs to question why most day traders fail. If the activity is as lucrative as it sounds, why do most of these traders fail? Understanding why traders fail gives you some insight into the common mistakes that traders fail, which makes them lose money. Accordingly, you will be better placed to trade wisely by avoiding common pitfalls in such trading. Here is a look at some of the reasons why traders fail.

Relying On Random

Let's assume we have a new trader in the market called John. John has some knowledge about the market just because he always watches the news more so on stock markets. However, John has never traded. Since he has some basic market knowledge, he feels that he can try out day trading. To this point, John has never sat down to write down some strategies which he could implement to trade on stocks. So, he opens up an account and purchases 400 shares without thinking.

Fortunately, to his advantage, the stocks rise during his lunch hour period. After lunch, John decides to sell off his shares. His first sale earns him a $100 profit. His second attempt also earns him $100. Now, John has the feeling that indeed he is a good trader. In just a day, he has managed to earn $200.

After a careful analysis of John's situation, an experienced trader would argue that John's day trading activity could easily be short-lived. In John's example, he faces the risk of losing money if he gains the perception that his strategies are working. Interestingly, he might be tempted to increase his shares because he knows that he will earn a profit. It is important to understand that John's strategies are untested. Therefore, there is no guarantee that his trading activity could earn him returns over the long-run.

The danger that John faces here is that he believes in his formulated and untested strategies. Consequently, he might overlook recommended trading techniques that would have helped him avoid common mistakes. In the end, when he loses money, he will be disappointed arguing that day trading is not lucrative. This is the trap that most newbies enter into. Their first luck in online trading blinds them from realizing the need for constant learning in this activity.

Abandoning Strategy

Assuming that John learned his mistakes and corrected them in his future trades. Now, he relies on a strategy that helps him find success in day trading for about a year or two. At this point, John feels that he has found the right strategy that works for him. However, there is another problem that ensues. John realizes that his plan has led him to losses for more than six times now. He is in a huge dilemma, wondering what to do since he cannot continue making losses. So, what does John do; he decides to adopt another strategy. Regardless of the success that he enjoyed using his previous plan, John now feels that it is time to switch to another strategy. Ideally, this is a new and untested strategy that he will be adopting. One thing that you should realize here is that John is going for a strategy that is not tested. He is abandoning a strategy that has worked for about two years now. The risk here is that John could find himself where he started. He could incur losses because of his abandoning strategy. Here, you should learn that randomness can lead to profits and that it can also drive a trader to incur losses. To ensure that such randomness is avoided, it is recommended for a trader to have a solid plan that they stick to. This is a plan that will define how they trade. A good plan ought to lay their entry and exit strategies. Also, the plan should stipulate the money management technique, which will help a trader use their money wisely.

Lack of Knowledge

A major reason why most traders fail is their lack of market knowledge. By failing to educate themselves about stock markets, they find themselves in a ditch. You cannot count yourself as a trader just because you buy and sell shares. Certainly not! You have to learn how to analyze the securities which you will be buying. Your broker might not give you all the information that you need to become a good trader. So, don't assume that reading magazines and newspapers will get you the market info that you need. A prudent trader knows the significance of working with a profitable trading plan. They understand why it is imperative for them to analyze stocks effectively to determine whether they are buying profitable stocks or not. More importantly, a wise trader should know of ideal strategies that they will employ to manage their finances shrewdly. Don't believe day trading myths circulating over the internet. Do your homework by researching and educating yourself about stock markets.

Unfitting Mindset

We are human beings with emotions. However, being overly emotional can be dangerous in an uncertain trading environment. To become a successful trader, you need to work on your emotions. The topic of trading psychology, which will be later discussed, will educate you on the importance of developing the right mindset in online trading. Dealing with your emotions will have a huge impact on whether you close your day with losses or profits. Hence, it is very important that you keep your emotions in check.

Rigidity to Market Changes

One thing that you can be sure of is that trading markets will always change. There is no guarantee that a particular market will rise steadily throughout the buying and selling period. If this were the case, then everybody would have been traders. The best traders will always adjust to market changes. They will know when to buy and when to sell. Before jumping to purchase a particular stock, it is advisable to conduct scenario analysis. Afterward, you should devise strategic moves that will ensure that you make profits while lowering the chances of incurring losses.

Learning from Mistakes

You often hear people say that failing is part of succeeding. Well, this is true. Unfortunately, it stands as one of the main reasons why day traders fail. Learning by making mistakes here and there will cost a day trader a lot of money. Engaging in trial and error is what discourages most traders from any attempt to put their money in stocks. Some even end up arguing that day trading is a form of gambling. To circumvent this problem, one should learn from other experienced traders. This way, you will reduce the chances of making losses. Equally, you will learn the tricks which can be utilized to take advantage of market volatility. Therefore, do not choose to learn how to trade through trial and error. You will only lose a lot of money beyond your expectations.

Unrealistic Expectations

Take a breather! Indeed, day trading is a profitable activity that can earn you a living. Nonetheless, this should not blind you from realizing that losses can also be made. You cannot get rich overnight with day trading. However, it is a slow and gradual process that will see your money multiply. Traders fail because they try to force returns to cover for the huge losses that they have made. Having the right plan and sticking to it will help you in toning down your expectations. Deep inside, you should have it in mind that you are trading for a living. Therefore, patience is important.

Poor Money Management

The effort that you put into finding a working strategy is the same effort that you should put in managing your finances. A trader should stick to a plan that defines the amount of money that they will risk on a regular basis. The money risked should give the trader the satisfaction that it is worth the rewards they anticipate. Having enough funds set aside for the trading activity should not give one the impression that they need to splash their money on stocks. As a matter of fact, the more you have as capital, the more you should preserve.

The bottom line is that traders can deal with their possibilities of failing by sticking to a plan. Sticking to a trading plan will mean that you are disciplined enough to know the exact amount of money you will risk. It also implies that you will employ a buying and selling strategy that works for you. Most importantly, you will also give yourself time to learn what there is to learn about day trading.

CHAPTER 8

Characteristics of Winning Traders

Anyone can indeed become a day trader, but to survive in the highly competitive market in the long run, you need to adapt yourself according to this business's requirement. You need to develop some qualities that will differentiate you from others and help you sustain as a day trader. Let's look at some of those characteristics of successful traders:

They Take Full Responsibility

Good traders accept their losses, and they do not dwell on or blame others or conditions. They learn from their failures and carry on their trade. There is a system for successful traders.

They adhere to their system of trade religiously. Many established traders are willing to take responsibility for their success; few are willing to take responsibility for failure.

There is no talk of the market-maker or broker somehow when they win, the market behaving strangely, the system, their risk management, or mind-affecting their trade. However, these bugaboos, all of a sudden, appear at the frontline of their thinking during a loss. There is a tendency, when things do not go your way, to look at someone other than yourself, the one who pushed the buttons. Having a responsibility to the gut-level does not distinguish winners from losers. They are identical. In the situation, they all came from the common denominator - you. Will you build up your ego when you excel, or do you draw on what you have done right to do more? Trading holds a mirror to oneself, sees what needs work, and works on it while seeing what works and increasing it. And it is your weakest trading skill that sets the height of your earnings and success. Fortunately, skill is a drill that can easily be molded to build your success's pillars.

They Have a Lot of Patience

Successful traders know most of the positions the minute that they are opened. They have to wait for their moment to come. They are patient enough to handle all the trading uncertainty. Most traders come up with a strategy that helps them decide when and where to enter a trade. That strategy should yield a profit if it is traded correctly. It sounds easy, but traders are facing a problem: when they see a fast-moving chart in real, their mind gets fooled into thinking that you enter a trade before the market structure is fully developed. You are afraid to lose out on a trade, so you enter early and usually end up losing.

Wait for the right setup and trigger your trade ultimately. You also need to be ok with missing an opportunity; take only trades that will give you the right setup and trigger your trade. There should be no trades unless the market causes this.

Have a brainstorming session about what you could do better if you are following your plan and still get into it a bit too early. If the price is higher and begins to go down, consider waiting for that to happen before considering getting in. When the price starts moving sideways, look for small clues that the price is beginning to rise again. If the movement lasts, waiting for the price to go high to cause the trade can help. If the price wiggles around during that pullback, consider watching those tiny price shifts inside the pullback for higher highs and higher lows.

These movements prove the buying pressure will build up again. When the price appears to shift opposite right before it moves in the direction you are expecting, you are waiting for the move to take place and then act. Do not trade until you are sure now is the time to get in. You do not have to capture every big move in prices to make a profit. When you miss a step, then you are missing it.

Be patient; the market takes longer than we would expect to move. By waiting for the right setup and trigger, you will begin to catch more of the price movements you anticipate and not waste your money on losing trades.

They Have Forward Thinking

Successful day traders cannot get trapped in the past. Although day traders are using past data to help them make trading decisions, they must be able to apply the information in real-time. Traders are also plotting their next moves, deciding what they will do depending on where the market is going.

The markets are not static. We cannot decide in five minutes we are going to buy at a certain amount and then forget all the market knowledge that is going on in those five minutes. Day traders are preparing their next move always, based on new market information they receive every second. They consider various scenarios that might be carried out and then prepare how they would execute their trading strategy for each of those different conditions.

They Do Not Overtrade

Overtrading is the unnecessary buying or selling of financial instruments. In many terms, getting too many open positions on a single trade or using a disproportionate amount of capital. There are no laws or regulations for individual traders against overtrading, but this can damage your portfolio. Overtrading can have significant implications for trading brokers, as they are controlled bodies. It is best to avoid overtrading and have a comprehensive trading plan and risk management strategy in place. Stop emotional trading: differentiate between logical and emotional trading decisions and provide sound reasoning for your decisions.

When you already have more than one open position, by spreading your investment through asset groups, you can help reduce risk. Using just what you have: determine how much you want to gamble but never use more money to trade than you can afford to lose. Good traders should not overtrade. They know that overtrading put their account at risk, and not everybody knows it is the day of the trade. They are waiting for an opponent with high probability.

They Are Adaptable

Successful traders are capable of adapting. They customize their trading methods and market-changing decisions. Successful traders understand what kind of dealer they are.

They do not force themselves to trade in methods or strategies; their personality does not fit. You are permitted to make small adjustments to your trading plan after a full month of trading, based on what you learned from your trading plan review sessions. Trades focused on these minor strategic improvements should be exercised for another month and evaluated afterward. Changes should not be made to the plan before the one month, because it is easy to make changes based on individual trades as opposed to overall results. The issues that come up in your self-review are being worked on every day. For the self-review, all you have to do is follow the trading strategy, whatever it might be. If the trading strategy evolves, so does your company, but it is always your job to follow the strategy. Your daily self-examination does not change the trading plan; instead, you are working on your personality traits to follow the plan. Strive to make minor improvements to the trading strategy weekly. The same concept applies to your day-to-day review of yourself. Work one thing at a time. Trying to solve a lot of problems at once means you are not focusing enough on each problem because your attention is spreading too widely.

They Take Action

Successful traders take action. They do not let them control their fear of their choices or interfere with their business. They use successful systems. Their methods of commercialization and metrics focus on high-probability, sound trades, managing money, keeping its strategies curve free of tying, and incorporating their program in their business plans. It is not enough to just watch videos or read. Day traders need to regularly practice what they are learning before becoming sufficiently determined to be useful in making trade decisions under ever-changing market conditions.

It is not just about putting in hours of action. Day trading is possible for years, putting in hundreds or thousands of hours and never seeing any progress because you are not focused on a particular activity. Focus on a particular activity to practice effectively.

Here's where the intention to exchange comes in. A trading plan is a document that specifies precisely how, why, and when a trader joins and exits trades, how they control the risk, and what the size of their position will be. It also specifies which markets are to be traded and when. The practice involves implementing a plan to allow tracking of progress.

Practice day trading in a demo account, one component of the trading plan at a time, until the strategy becomes second nature. You may go through charts, for example, and pick entry points for your strategy. Do this until you see all of the entry points your strategy provides. Day trading requires fast reflexes and accurate timing. Practice so entries occur precisely when they should, depending on the technique. Then move on to putting right the stop-loss. Then practice correctly positioning the target for income. Practice having the perfect size of position on each trade and every other trading element covered by the trading plan. While it may sound a little strange, you are also learning what not to do this whole time.

Your aim is not only to take action on your strategy and take all the trades you are told to make (when circumstances are favorable, based on your trading plan), but also to practice sitting on your hands when your strategy does not ask you to take a trade. Trading is about the deals you do not carry out as much as it is about those you do. When your plan does not deliver a trade incentive, then do not do it. Most new traders lack the patience needed to wait for a legitimate trade signal, but it can be learned through practice.

Where a legitimate trade opportunity occurs, practice being cautious and pouncing. The amount of time that traders will practice will differ for every item of their trading plan. You will usually work 15 to 20 days on every item of the trading plan. Using this method, a trader should have a clear understanding of their trading plan after about six months, have their strategy practiced for days, and have a reasonable idea of how to use it under all market conditions.

They Are Disciplined

Discipline is a key trait that every trader needs. The market gives you limitless possibilities for trade. Every second of the day, you will exchange thousands of different items, but very few of those seconds provide great commercial opportunities.

If a strategy provides about four to five trades a day and stop loss and goals for each trade are automatically set. During the day, there are just about five seconds of real trading activity.

CHAPTER 9

What Is Best to Trade?

When it comes to buying and selling stocks, it is entirely up to the investor to choose whatever he or she thinks will be a good investment. It is tough to generalize the type of stock that will suit everyone, as there is no one stock that fits all rule. However, here are the types of stocks that can be dealt with in the share market.

Company Stocks

Company stocks are those that are issued by the company to their employees and also to the public. Although top companies do not directly open up their shares for the public, employees who own the shares can sell them in the market. There are several multinational companies to choose from, including Microsoft, Coca Cola, Intel, Apple Inc., Nokia, etc. You can choose a company that you think will help you increase the value of your investment. You will have to research the companies which are doing well and which ones aren't and choose to invest in them accordingly. But don't be in too much of a hurry to find the best stocks for you. Take your time and observe the trend for a few months. Once you establish a pattern, you can start buying the stocks of that company.

Commodities

The commodities market is where several types of commodities are bought and sold. These commodities can be of the following types:

Agricultural

Agricultural commodities are food items such as vegetables, fruits, pulses, and other crops. Each commodity has a different price, and depending on which crops are doing well, you can decide to invest in them. These commodities are ideal for day trading as they generally rise in value by the end of the day. Some of the most preferred commodities include potatoes, pulses, rice, and sugar.

Metal

Metals are also a good market for investors. Metals such as copper, nickel, iron, and lead all have a good market value. It is possible for you to trade in these metals, and you will have to look for the ones that are currently doing well. You can choose to hold on to them for a specific period of time and then sell them before the deal's expiry date.

Industrial

Industrial solvents, chemicals, and other such liquid commodities are also quite popular. They are in constant demand and command high prices. You can choose the ones that you think will fetch you a good price and invest in them.

Energy

Energy resources such as crude oil, petroleum, paraffin, etc. are also traded. These are required to fuel your cars, used in cosmetics, etc. And so are in constant demand. You can choose the one that you think is in good demand and trade with them.

Livestock

Just like the other commodities, livestock is also traded on a daily basis in the stock market. These include pigs, sheep, etc. There are many factors that can affect their prices, including weather conditions, diseases, and also their market demand and supply. These form the various types of commodities that you can choose from, and you can purchase one type or diversify by purchasing several types.

Currencies

When it comes to day trading, it is possible for the investor to trade in currencies. As an investor, you have a lot of choices and flexibility to hedge your currency exposure to risk. FX options, as currency trading in the options markets is popularly known, allow the same core hedging and trading strategies used when trading options on ETFs, stocks, and indexes. The best and most straightforward way to remember what type of "option" you need to trade on is to focus on the base currency or the first currency in every currency pair. The second currency in the pair is the quote currency or the counter-currency. "Options" prices are typically derived from the base currency and are relative to the quote currency. A USD-based currency pair (per USD) is available for the ten FX pairs. For instance, when you expect the US dollar to strengthen against the Japanese yen, you purchase YUK calls. In the inverse situation, when you expect the yen to strengthen against the US dollar, you purchase YUK puts. It is up to you to decide what you think is best suited to trade with, depending on the resources you have at hand. You don't need to have extensive knowledge of these products, and only a little knowledge is enough for you to know if the products are worth investing in.

Index

Index trading refers to a type of trading where you bet on the index's rise and fall. Each sector of the stock exchange will have an index, which will take into account the prices of all the stocks that are listed under that index. Then by dividing it by the number of stocks present in the market, you will get a certain number. Now all of these indexes are pooled, and a final index is prepared, which is the entire share market's collective index. Now you can "bet" on where the index will reach by the end of the day. For this, you must study the individual indexes such as the IT industry index, the consumer goods index, etc. Once you think you know where the index will be by the end of the day, you can invest in it.

ETF

An ETF is also known as Exchange Traded Funds. These ETF's are like mini mutual funds that are traded in the market. Each ETF will have a combination of different underlying securities, and these will be split into several small pieces. You can buy these in bulk, and they can be traded on a daily basis.

The main idea is to buy them at a low price and then dispose of them at a higher price. You have to understand that they are slow movers, and you will have to buy them and wait for them to grow in value. These are much preferred as they will give you the advantage of a mutual fund but can be exchanged on a daily basis.

Bonds

Bonds are securities that are issued by companies and can be bought and sold to realize a profit. These bonds can come in several different forms and are explained below:

Government Bonds

Government bonds refer to those bonds that are issued by the government. As you may know, the government requires funds from time to time and will ask you to pay forward. Once you do, they will issue you a bond that is valued much lower than its actual value. After it matures, you can collect the amount you paid along with interest that they would pay you for it. If at any time you wish to sell the bond, then you can do so, and you will get paid a higher amount for it. The government might also agree to pay you a certain percentage of interest every month, and you can capitalize on this opportunity to keep your money safe and also earn a profit from it. This form of investment is extremely safe as the government will not default on paying you your due money.

Agency Bonds

Agency bonds are much like government bonds. They are run by companies that the government funds. So these can be counted as government bonds. They will pay you a great rate of interest on your investment. However, you cannot expect the same guarantee from them as you would from government bonds. You might have to invest a certain fixed sum as well. But given their success rate, they are a great option for all those looking to safeguard their money and also earn a certain rate of return on it. The same rules apply to agency bonds when you wish to liquidate them. You can sell them at a higher price or collect your sum and interest at the time of maturity.

Federal Bonds

Your local governments issue federal bonds. Just like how the central government issues bonds, your local governments will do the same. You can buy these bonds at low rates and then hold on to them. You can sell them whenever you like and earn a higher income from it. These bonds will pay you more than what your government bonds will, as your local government will not need a lot of money for a high scale project, and it will be slightly low key. This type of investment will be much better than saving in the bank, which will pay you much less interest.

Corporate Bonds

Corporate bonds refer to those that are issued by companies. As you know, multinational companies also require money for their projects. This money will raise by issuing bonds to the public. They will agree to pay you back after a while and until such time, pay you a fixed rate of interest. You can sell these bonds for a profit at any time. But you must understand that these companies will not provide you with a guarantee like your government and federal government bonds. So it will be a risk that you will be willing to take.

However, if you choose a big multinational company, then you might hit the jackpot. Not only will you get paid more but also win over their loyalty. They might be willing to give you shares in their company at a discounted rate, which will be a bonus for you. You can then sell these stocks at a later date and realize a big profit from it!

Zero-Coupon Bonds

Zero-coupon bonds are extremely popular owing to their ease of trade. They are extremely liquid, and there is always a lot of demand for them. Now suppose a zero-coupon bond is worth $500. When you buy it, they will issue it at $100 and ask you to exchange it for $500 in 2 years' time. So despite it being valued at $100 now, you will get back 4 times the value after exchanging it in 2 years' time. So not only will your money be safe, but you will also be able to increase its value several fold.

CHAPTER 10

How Much Do You Need to Day Trade?

Before you begin any business, one would want to know how much they need as capital. The same case applies to day trading. An important question that most investors would want to know is the amount of capital that is required from them. The amount of money that you need to day trade will depend on the market that you wish to invest in. Your style of trading will also have an impact on the amount of money that you need to raise. Different markets will require varying amounts of capital. Below is an analysis of the different markets that are at your disposal and the respective capital requirements.

Capital Requirements for Stock Traders

If you are going to trade in stocks, then you need to have at least $25,000 saved up for the trading activity. You are not limited to this amount of money. If you wish to trade more than three times, you should consider having more than $30,000. When your trading account falls below $25,000, it would not be possible for you to trade. You will have to top up your account to the minimum balance required. The account balance minimum here only stipulates to traders who would wish to invest in US stocks. You should realize that the minimum account balance required to invest in other stocks in global markets will vary. The country that you rise in might not have any minimum balance required. Regardless, it is advisable to deposit a reasonable amount that will see you earning good profits for every buying and selling activity that you engage in. Why are we saying this? There are instances where lower balances will only be eaten up by commissions and transaction costs. Therefore, you will not notice any changes in your account because of these deductions.

Lack of capital will always be a problem for most traders in the market. Insufficient capital will prevent you from taking advantage of market volatility. You might have incurred losses now, but later you could recover your money when the stocks unexpectedly rise. As such, having sufficient capital comes highly recommended.

Capital Requirements for Forex Traders

The forex market is somewhat different from the stock market. In this case, smaller amounts of capital are required. So, for a newbie like you, this should be good news. With the little capital that you have saved up, you can begin day trading in forex today. The advantage of forex is that you can exploit the leverage provided of up to 50:1. This could even go higher in certain nations. An increase in leverage implies that there is a higher risk that could be met with a remarkable reward.

Forex trading stands as an ideal choice for day trading due to its liquidity. The forex market is the largest market globally. Usually, the money in circulation on a daily basis goes up to $5 trillion. Therefore, the liquidity aspect of this market makes it quite appealing. So, how much money do you need to begin forex trading? With as little as $100, you can kick off trading. Nevertheless, a recommended figure is $500. This gives you the opportunity of buying currencies with ideal stop levels.

As you can see, this is a small amount of money which you will require to begin this activity. You cannot claim that you will make a living out of it. It is, however, important to remember that you can gradually raise capital with the daily incomes that you earn. In line with this, you should never overlook the importance of starting small simply because you are new to forex trading.

Capital Requirements for Futures

Besides investing in stocks and forex, you will also have the option of investing in futures. The good thing about futures is that you can invest in it with minimal capital requirements. There is no legal minimum balance that you should have so as to invest in futures. However, it is important for a trader to have enough capital to cover day trading margins within a particular day. A good number of brokers will require a trader to have a minimum balance of $1,000. If you are trading E-mini S&P 500 (ES) futures, brokers will demand a minimum balance of $400. This is the day trading margin that you will be limited to. Regardless of the fact that you are not limited to a specific balance, you should strive to begin with a realistic balance of at least $8,000. There are other futures that your broker will want additional margins for you to trade effectively. Hence, you ought to confirm with your trader before signing up for anything.

On a final word concerning the amount of money that you need, it is clear that different markets will require varying capital amounts. If you are running on a tight budget, trading in stocks is not advisable as it is capital intensive. On the other hand, forex gives you the flexibility of starting trading with as little as $1,000. Nonetheless, it is recommended for you to have more to warrant that you have a buffer. Futures is also a great option when working with limited funds.

It should also be made clear that it is never wise to trade with your capital at first. When working with a broker, make good use of demo accounts to trade with virtual money. Once you notice that your trading strategies suit you, you can move forward to use real money. The advantage gained here is that you can easily identify possible mistakes that you could make when using your money. As such, it saves you from risking with your hard-earned cash.

Defining Your Risk Tolerance

Aside from knowing the amount of money you will need to trade, you also should pause for a while and define your risk tolerance. What do we mean by risk tolerance? It refers to the degree of unpredictability in investment returns that a trader is willing to endure. As a trader, you ought to have an in-depth understanding of how much you can withstand the large market swings. There are times where you might panic when markets seem to be falling. In such cases, you might end up selling at the wrong time. Therefore, this is where you should be aware of your risk tolerance. How much can you stomach in day trading? To clearly define your tolerance capacity, you should assess your past performance. Find out the worst cases where you have been comfortable incurring losses. There are several factors that could affect your risk tolerance capacity. For instance, if you have high possibilities of earning increased income in the near future, this will influence how much you can stomach. Also, if you are looking to take advantage of future securities such as a pension, then your risk tolerance rate will also be high. Generally, you will be ready to face huge risks when you are sure that you have other assets that can earn you additional income. The forms of risk tolerance are detailed as follows.

Aggressive Risk Tolerance

Traders who have profound experience in day trading would find it easy to face the risk of investing in highly volatile securities. This is influenced by the fact that they are well informed about market trends. With their expertise, they can easily predict the next trend of a particular security. Often, they can tolerate any changes in the market. On a good day, they maximize returns with the greatest risks. This is what aggressive risk tolerance is all about.

Moderate Risk Tolerance

Moderate traders will accept some risks but will shy away from securities that are too risky. In this case, they will go to markets that are less volatile. Their main aim is to minimize the possible risks that they are likely to face.

Conservative Risk Tolerance

Conservative traders are quite different from aggressive and moderate traders. Just as the name suggests, these investors will try their best to minimize risks at all costs. Traders that fall into this category are mostly retirees.

From the information provided, where do you lie? How risk-tolerant are you? You should realize that your tolerance capacity will change with time as you will learn how to cope with losses. However, it is vital that you know what works best for you right from the get-go. The significance of this is that you will prevent yourself from giving up each time you incur losses that you never expected. Knowing your risk tolerance is part of your trading foundation, which will confirm that you grow to become a successful trader.

CHAPTER 11

Choosing What to Trade?

There are thousands of equities available for a trader to choose from, and day traders have no limit on the type of stocks they can trade; you can trade on virtually any stock of your choice. With all these available choices, it may seem like a difficult task to know the right stock to add to your watch list. This takes us to the first step in day trading, which is knowing what to trade.

Here are some tips that will help you to choose the best stocks for maximum profits:

High Volatility and Liquidity in Day Trading

Liquidity in financial markets refers to how one can quickly buy or sell an asset in the market. It can also mean the impact that trading has on the price of a security. It is easier to day trade liquid stocks than other stocks; they are also more discounted, which makes them cheaper.

Liquid stocks are bigger in volume, in the sense that one can purchase and sell larger quantities of stock without having any significant effect on the price. Because day trading strategies depend on accurate timing and speed, a lot of volume makes it easier for traders to get in and out of trades. Depth is also important, as it shows you the level of liquidity of stocks at different price levels below or above the current market offer and bid. Also, corporations with higher market capitalizations have more liquid equities than those with lower market caps because it is easier to find sellers and buyers for stocks owned by these big corporations. Stocks that have more volatility also follow the day trading strategies. A stock is considered volatile if the corporation that owns it experiences more adjustment in its cash flow. Uncertainty in the financial market creates a big opportunity for day trading. Online financial services like Google Finance or Yahoo Finance regularly list highly volatile and liquid stocks during the day. This information is also available on other online broker sites.

Consider Your Own Position

The stocks you decide to go for have to align with your goals and personal situation because there is no one-size-fits-all in the financial market. You have to put into consideration your capital, your risk appetite, and the type of investing you are going to take on. Let's not forget the role of research in all these. Your best bet is to read up on financials of different companies, study the market, consider the sectors that best reflect your values, personality, and personal needs, and remember to begin early. You need to be familiar with the market openings and time yourself to follow these openings. While day trading, ensure not to get emotionally attached to a particular stock. Don't forget that you are looking at patterns to know when best to exit or enter to minimize your losses and increase your profit. While you do not have to stay glued to your screen, you still need to know the earning season and what the economic calendar looks like. This will help you to pick the best stocks for day trading.

Social Media

This industry is also another attractive target for day trading as there are several online media companies like Facebook and LinkedIn that have high trading volume for their stocks. Also, there have been several debates on the capability of these social media companies to convert their massive user bases into a sustainable income stream. Although stock prices, in theory, represent the discounted cash flow of the companies that issued them, the recent valuations also look at the earning potential of these companies. Based on this, some analysts think that this has led to higher stock valuation than is suggested by the fundamentals. Regardless, social media is still a popular stock for day trading.

Financial Services

Financial services industries also offer great stocks for day trading. For example, Bank of America is one of the most highly traded stocks per trading session. If you are looking for company stock to day trade, stocks from Bank of America should be among your top consideration, despite the increased skepticism that the banking system is facing. The trading volume for Bank of America is high, which makes it a liquid stock. This also applies to Morgan Stanley, Citigroup, JP Morgan & Chase, and Wells Fargo. They all have uncertain industrial conditions and high trading volumes.

Going Outside Your Geographical Boundary

When trading in the financial market, you must diversify your portfolio. Look at stocks listed in other exchanges like the London Stock Exchange (LSE) or Hong Kong's Hang Seng. Extending your portfolio outside your boundary will grant you access to potentially cheaper alternatives as well as foreign stocks.

Medium to High Instability

A day trader needs to understand the price movement to be able to make money. As a day trader, you can choose to go for stocks that typically move a lot in percentage terms or dollar terms, as these two terms usually yield different results. Stocks that typically move 3% and above every day have a consistently large intraday moves to trade. This also applies to stocks that move above $1.50 each day.

Group Followers

Although some traders specialize in contrarian plays, most traders will rather go for equities that move in line with their index and sector group. What this means is that when the sector or index ticks upward, the price of individual stocks will also increase. This is crucial if the trader desires to trade the weakest or strongest stocks every day. If a trader will rather go for the same stock every day, then it is advisable to focus on that stock and worry less on whether it corresponds with any other thing.

Entry and Exit Strategies

After you must have picked the best stocks in the world, your strategies will determine if you will profit from them or not. There are several available day trading strategies, but to increase your chances of success, you need to stick to certain guidelines and look out for certain intraday trading signals.

Below, I will talk about 5 of these guidelines:

Trade Weak Stocks in a Downtrend and Strong Stocks in an Uptrend

Most traders in a bid to pick the best stocks for day trading prefer to look at EFTs or equities that have at least a moderate to high connection with the NASDAQ or S&P 500 indexes and then separate the strong stocks from the weak ones. This creates an opportunity for the day trader to make profit, as the strong stock has the potential to go 2% up when the index moves 1% up. The more a stock moves, the more opportunity for the day trader. As market futures/ indexes move higher, traders should purchase stocks that have more aggressive upward movement than the futures. With this, even if the futures pull back, it will have little or no impact/ pull back on a strong stock. These are the stocks you should trade in an uptrend as they provide more profit potential when the market goes higher.

When the futures or indexes drop, it becomes profitable to short sell those stocks that drop more than the market. The ETFs and stocks that are weaker or stronger than the market may change each day, however, certain sectors may be relatively weak or strong for weeks at a time. When looking for a stock to trade, always go for the stronger one. This same rule applies to short trades as well. As a short seller, you should isolate EFTs or stocks that are weaker so that when prices fall, you will have greater chances of having profits by being in EFTs or stocks that fall the most.

Trade Only with the Current Intraday Trend

The trading market always moves in waves, and it's your job as a trader to ride these waves. When there is an uptrend, your focus should be on taking long positions while you should focus on taking short positions whenever there is a downtrend.

We have already established that intraday trends do not go on forever, but you can carry out one or more trades before a reversal occurs. When there is a shift with the dominant trend, you should begin to trade with the new trend. It may be difficult to isolate the trend, but you can find simple and useful entry and stop-loss strategies from Trend lines.

Take Your Time. Wait for the Pullback

Trend lines provide visual guides that show where price waves will start and end. So, when choosing stocks to day trade, you can use a trend line for early entry into the next price wave. When you want to enter a long position, be patient, and wait for the price to move down towards the trend line and then move back higher before you buy. Before an upward trend line can appear, a price low before a higher price low needs to happen.

A line is drawn to connect the two points and then extends to the right. This same principle applies when short selling. Be patient for the price to move up to the downward-slope trend line, and once the stock starts to move back down, you can then make your entry.

Take Your Profits Regularly

As a day trader, you have limited time to make profits, and for this reason, you need to spend very little time in trades that are moving in the wrong direction or losing money. Let me show you two simple guidelines that you can use to take profits when trading with trends:

In a short position or downtrend, take your profits slightly below or at the former price low in the current trend.

In a long position or uptrend, take your profits at slightly above or at the former price high in the current trend.

Do Not Play When the Market Stalls

The market may not always trend. The intraday trends may reverse so often that it becomes hard to establish an overriding direction. If there are no major lows and highs, ensure the intraday movements are large enough to increase the chances of profits and reduce the risks of loss. For instance, if you are risking $0.15 per share, the EFT or stock should move enough to give you a minimum of $0.20 - $0.25 profit using the guidelines stated above. When the price is not trending (that is, moving in a range), move to a range-bound trading technique. During a range, you will no longer have an angled line but rather a horizontal line. However, the general concept still applies: purchase only when the price goes to the lower horizontal area (support) and then begins to move higher. Short sell once you notice that the price has reached the upper horizontal line (resistance) and begins to go lower again.

Your buying strategy should be to exit close to the top of the range but not exactly at the top. Your shorting strategy should be to exit in the lower part of the range but not exactly at the bottom. The chances of making gains should be more than the risk of loss. Place a stop loss just above the most current high before entry on a short signal or just below the most current low before entry on a buy signal.

Several traders find it hard to alternate between range trading and trend trading, and so they opt to do one or the other. If you choose to go for range trading, then you should avoid trading during trends but focus on trading EFTs or stocks that tend to range. On the other hand, if it is trend trading, avoid trading when the markets are ranging, and you should concentrate on trading EFTs or stocks that have the potential to trend.

CHAPTER 12

Have the Right Mindset

Day Trading can be a bumpy road if you feel that your mental energy is no more and that you cannot focus on the markets anymore. Luckily, you can resolve this problem and start enjoying trading once again by improving your mindset. Some people opine that stock markets are generally immoral, but the fact is that stock markets are neither immoral nor moral. Stock markets lack an emotion, that's why it is up to you how you perceive the stock market to behave. If you want to enter the business of the stock market for the long term and also establish yourself as a full-time day trader, you must develop a specific mindset that aids you in observing the stock market from an unemotional point of view. It is your mindset that will control your reactions to different transactions. It is your mindset that will help you define how you react to lost trades and big profits. Your mindset will define how you can stay calm during turbulent times and how you can avoid reacting based on emotions. A trader who is disciplined and who has a strong mindset will never let emotions meddle with his or her decisions regarding the stock market. If this sounds hard for you, don't worry because it should sound hard for every beginner. It takes a bit of effort to achieve that status. There is no way by which you can become a successful trader overnight. Trading is just like another business. As you cannot become a successful businessman overnight, you cannot become a disciplined trader overnight. You need to give yourself time to achieve the success that you are looking forward to.

Importance of a Positive Mindset

The stock market is void of emotions, but the participants of the markets are usually full of them. This is the reason reading chart patterns and trends work so well when it comes to trading. They show us some well-known patterns that humans possess. That's how as a trader you can take advantage of the market psychology. There is a notorious saying that 90% of traders lose 90% of funds in 90 days. This is wicked, to say the least, but still, this phrase is popular among traders. Before you take the leap in the stock market, you should ask yourself what are the psychological traits that 10% of the remaining traders have. What qualities they possess that make them different from the rest of the lot. If 90% fails, the money they have lost has surely gone to the 10% who succeeded. That's intriguing! Isn't it? When you lose, someone is earning your money. The people who are earning your money are humans just like you. They are a small bunch of traders who have found the secret of trading, which is nothing else but a trader's mindset. The term trading psychology refers to a specific state of mind that a trader usually has while he or she trades. If you don't have the right mindset, the odds will likely be turned against you.

Shape up Your Trader's Mindset

Day Traders can reshape their mindset by acting in a calm and relaxed manner. If you have proper knowledge of the subject and you have kept in place proper risk management guidelines, you need not be concerned about your trades at all. If a trade hits the stop-loss level, it doesn't mean that the world has ended for you. Traders lose trades all the time. It happens to even professional traders who have years of experience. Professional traders whose bread and butter rely on trading stocks have a winning rate of 50%. Even at this rate, you can bag sufficient profits on your capital if you trade with the right mindset. You should practice the habit of not taking a losing trade to heart. There is nothing personal in a lost trade, although the temptation to make it personal runs high. The thought may start spinning in your head that you have lost something you could have easily won, or you could have easily prevented. If you think like that, the need of the hour is to train your brain into thinking that markets tend to go upside and downside almost all the time. As a day trader, you should keep faith in the market analysis that you have already done. Just stick to the plan until the end of the day. Markets are void of emotions, and if you start succumbing to your emotions, you will not be able to compete with the traders who don't let their emotions meddle in their trading transactions over the day.

Try to nurture a morning routine for a more relaxed trading session. Try to wake up earlier, do some workout or a yoga session, and then sit on your desk with a heart full of faith in the homework you have done for the day.

Learn! Learn! Learn!

The education of the stock market is the key to success. It is one of the most important factors that play a key role in removing fear from your brain. This is what separates an average trader from a successful trader. Even if you have nurtured and developed the right mindset for trading, you cannot succeed until you have a solid knowledge base for the purpose. You must have a solid understanding of the reasons behind the price movements and market reactions. Similarly, I have hinted at how a market reacts to certain news and regular bonus reports. This will add more strength to your trader mindset.

There are lots of concepts that are worth learning. However, you cannot learn them in a single session. You should make it a habit to internalize a concept daily so that your brain gets enough time to understand the slight nuances in the concept and to use the same during trading without having to open a book. You also can prepare and keep notes in a small diary for reference. You can form a healthy routine by consuming an hour before going to bed a good book on trading to clear out your basic concepts and bring them into practice during trading. You also can enroll in trading courses to boost your knowledge about stock markets.

The Mindset of a Successful Day Trader

Your psychology is going to be the major determining factor in bringing about the trading results that you are aiming at. Each trader keeps a unique belief system, and it is their beliefs that determine how they trade and what results they get. The traders that have a weak belief system tend to fail even if they have the most profitable and seasoned trading strategy. What is a belief system? In simple words, it is called 'The Trader's Mindset.' When you go through psychological issues, it is in your best interest to track the issues in your brain, recognize them, and then find a cure for them. Otherwise, you cannot fix them. A psychologist recognizes the issues and then tries to cure the patient. The process of curing a problem can take longer because the patients take long to recognize the problem and accept it as the source of their downfall. As a day trader, you need to take responsibility for your problems if you want to heal yourself. Success in trading is directly proportional to a sound and operational tracking system of your brain. It also is directly linked to a successful money management strategy, sound psychology, and proper capitalization during the day. These need to be in proper sync if you want to be successful in your trading ventures. Mastering your psychology is very well an ongoing process that goes on end until you are in control of your thoughts and decisions.

Psychological Issues

The biggest psychological issue that day traders may confront is the fear of being stopped out or the fear of posting a loss and exiting a position. It is almost a nightmare for day traders, and it definitely weakens their nerves. The basic reason behind this behavior is that a trader is afraid of failure, and he feels as if he will not be able to bear the loss. His ego is well at stake. If you are getting out of a trade too early, you are losing profit if not capital. It becomes quite common for a trader to exit a position to relieve himself of anxiety and stress that an open position usually brings. The biggest fear in this sense is the fear of reversal. Traders succumb to it once it grows to an unprecedented level. They need gratification and a sense of security that their capital is safe now.

The biggest mistake that day traders make is adding on to the position they are losing. They just keep doubling down on it. This kind of act alludes to a mindset that doesn't want to accept that it has lost the game. Here again, ego won't let you close your position and save your capital. Your brain presses on winning out of the same position in which you have lost. The problem gets more intense if you have disclosed your positions to your colleagues and family members. You fear to become a laughing stock in front of everyone. Some traders don't want to take responsibility for their trades. They cannot accept the fact that the market went in the opposite direction than they had accepted it to move. This kind of mindset fogs their brain, and they try to create a reality that is aligned with their expectations. Sometimes traders enter the gambler's mindset. They fall prey to the euphoria of a bull market and get drowned in it by slipping into gambling. The gambler's mindset always tells you to ignore the indicators of the market and compels you to indulge in compulsive trading even when the odds are against it. Trading becomes your addiction. You keep losing until your capital is wiped out. This is very dangerous, and it needs a check.

Some people start getting angry after they lose a trading position. Their brain tells them that they are victims of the trade market. There are unrealistic expectations that when the shattered result in frustration and anger among traders. This condition can strike you if you are getting too much involved in a trade. You cannot control the market and turn it in your favor just by thinking that way. You might have expected the stock to rise during the day, but markets can take an ugly turn anytime, leaving you flabbergasted.

Too many expectations can lead to anger that can affect your future trading transactions. Not good for your profession. Just as excessive anger is bad for the health of your brain, excessive joy after you win a trading position is also bad. This indicates a mindset that makes you feel that you are unrealistically in control of the trade markets.

CHAPTER 13

How to Open an Account

Once you have your basics right and you feel primed and pumped up to invest in the stock market, you'll need your brokerage account to invest in the stock market. Without this account, you'll not be able to buy stocks or invest in other securities.

This system has got modernized, and with the coming of computers and the internet, you can make your trades in real-time through your brokerage firms. For this, you will need to open a brokerage account.

A brokerage account is an agreement between you and the brokerage firms to carry out the trades. The brokerage firm would give you software on which you'll be able to see the prices of the stock in real-time and bid on them at the price you want. You will simply need to deposit money in your brokerage account, and through this money, you'll be able to buy the securities you want. Although the securities are purchased through the brokerage firm, you will be the sole owner of the assets, and the brokerage firm will simply charge the brokerage fee on the trades executed through it. The process of opening a brokerage account is not very difficult, but there are several things you need to keep in mind. The cost, quality, and service are some of the things that would matter a lot for you in the end. You will also have to pay a lot of attention to the brokerage fee charged by the firm, as that can also be substantial for a small investor. You'll also need to consider the kind of securities you want to trade-in.

Choose the Kind of Brokerage Account You Really Need

As a beginner, it is not uncommon for people to get baffled by the kind of options available in front of them. The same can happen while choosing the kind of account you need.

For beginners, Robo Advisory services are the best option as they cost less, and they can help you in planning long-term based on your investment and waiting potential. The fees charged by Robo advisor services are low, and they have good algorithms to balance your funds as per your needs. Robo advisors are algorithm-based financial planning services that provide you an automated digital platform. Robo advisors would ask you detailed questions about your financial goals and also the kind of investments you can make, and based on that analysis, they will suggest the investments that can work for you. The best thing about Robo advisors is that they will do most of the work and planning for you, and hence you wouldn't need to track the market a lot. They will also carry out the rebalancing from time to time to ensure that the funds remain in good condition. They are very inexpensive, and you can open accounts with a very low balance. Popular Robo advisor accounts are Betterment, Wealth front, Personal Capital, Bloom, etc.

Alternatively, if you really want to get actively engaged in the stock market and want to invest your time in it, you can also open regular brokerage accounts where you can choose to trade in a variety of asset classes like stocks, ETFs, or Mutual funds. You can also get an option to trade regularly if you wish to. You will also have to pay attention to tax, and this brings us to the point of whether you would like to open a regular taxable account or an individual retirement account, as tax slabs vary in both. You should also consider the fact whether you want to own and operate that account solely, or you want others in your family also to have a role in it. Charles Schwab, Fidelity Investments, Merril Edge are some of the brokerage firms that provide such accounts that can be very helpful for beginners.

The Cost and Features

Brokerage firms charge fees and commissions, and there are many other costs involved that differ with every broker. The beginners should go for brokers that have low fees and more focus on educating the trader. A simple platform with better access to knowledge is always better for a beginner. Remember, you are going to invest your hard-earned money there, and you might not have much of it. This can make you feel overwhelmed when you are at the portal. At that moment, an interface that's educating and simple is always helpful. As a beginner, you should also look for brokers that have low fees.

Opening a Brokerage Account

Opening a brokerage account these days is not very difficult. Most of the things get done online, and hence there is very little paperwork involved.

However, this doesn't mean that the process of opening a brokerage account is not going to be extensive. You'll need to fill in a lot of information for opening your account.

From your personal information like your name, address, date of birth, and social security number to a lot of other details like your IRS Tax Id, signature, annual income, net worth, and employment status will be required. You should not hesitate to share this information as it is required. You must understand that opening a brokerage account is a detailed process, as you can be having short term and long-term holdings in this account, and such information will be required. Apart from these, you may also be asked about your investment objectives, financial goals, investment frequency, and risk appetite. This is done to do your risk profiling, and this helps in the assessment of your financial goals. Based on this, you can be provided with better advisory services. You may also be required to submit an acknowledgment of owning the account and an agreement that you'll provide the information the broker-dealer needs to obtain. You can then link your bank account with the brokerage account to transfer funds easily, and your account will be good to go.

Important Things to Consider

Commissions and Fees

There are various fees and commissions involved when you buy any stock. The cost that you bid for is not the actual cost of that stock. You will also have to pay brokerage fees, taxes, and settlement charges, and that should also be taken into consideration while calculating your actual cost.

The Brokerage Firms Will Charge You for Many Other Things Too

There are many costs involved with a brokerage account. For instance, you might get charged for inactivity fees, annual charges, fees for research and data, trading platform fees, as well as several other charges. You must have it clear in your mind the kind of charges you might have to pay at the end of the day so that there are no unpleasant surprises in the form of unexpected expenses.

Have the Frequency of Your Trades in Mind

This is also a very important thing to keep in mind. The people who wish to make trades very frequently would like to keep the commissions low. For them, even a slightly higher commission can raise the cost of the trade. Whereas, if you don't wish to trade frequently and would invest only occasionally, it might be a good idea to look at the kind of charges levied by the broker in the form of inactivity fees.

Good Support System is Helpful

As a beginner, give preference to brokerages that have a good support system as you can have frequent queries. If the brokerage firm doesn't have a good support system, you will have to rely mostly on the internet, and the advice you get there may not be very accurate or precise.

CHAPTER 14

Tools and Platforms

For you to carry out day trading successfully, there are several tools that you need. Some of these tools are freely available, while others must be purchased. Modern trading is not like the traditional version. This means that you need to get online to access day trading opportunities. Therefore, the number one tool you need is a laptop or computer with an internet connection. The computer you use must have sufficient memory for it to process your requests fast enough. If your computer keeps crashing or stalling all the time, you will miss out on some lucrative opportunities. There are trading platforms that need a lot of memory to work, and you must always take this into consideration. Your internet connection must also be fast enough. This will ensure that your trading platform loads in real-time. Ensure that you get an internet speed that processes data instantaneously to avoid experiencing any data lag. Due to some outages that occur with most internet providers, you may also need to invest in a backup internet device such as a smartphone hotspot or modem. Other essential tools and services you need include:

Brokerage

To succeed in day trading, you need the services of a brokerage firm. The work of the firm is to conduct your trades. Some brokers are experienced in day trading than others. You must ensure that you get the right day trading broker who can help you make more profit from your transactions.

Since day trading entails several trades per day, you need a broker that offers lower commission rates. You also need one that provides the best software for your transactions. If you prefer using specific trading software for your deals, then look for a broker that allows you to use this software.

Real-Time Market Information

Market news and data are essential when it comes to day trading. They provide you with the most recent updates on current and anticipated price changes on the market. This information allows you to customize your strategies accordingly. Professional day traders always spend a lot of money seeking this kind of information on news platforms, in online forums, or through any other reliable channels. Financial data is often generated from price movements of specific stocks and commodities. Most brokers have this information. However, you will need to specify the kind of data you need for your trades. The type of data to get depends on the type of stocks you wish to trade.

Monitors

Most computers have a capability that enables them to connect to more than one monitor. Due to the nature of the day trading business, you need to track market trends, study indicators, follow financial news items, and monitor price-performance at the same time. For this to be possible, you need to have more than one processor so the above tasks can run concurrently.

Classes

Although you can engage in day trading without attending any school, you must get trained on some of the strategies you need to succeed in the business. For instance, you may decide to enroll in an online course to acquire the necessary knowledge in the business. You may have all the essential tools in your possession, but if you do not have the right experience, all your efforts may go to waste.

CHAPTER 15

Charting

A chart is a graphical representation of the asset prices over a period. It exhibits properties like price point, price scale, and time scale. The day trader can find the price scale on the chart's right side. The scale goes from lowest to highest from top to bottom. Although it is such a simple concept, the price scale can have a complicated structure.

A linear price structure means that the space between the price points is of equal amount. If the difference between the first and second price points is 10, it will be the same for all price points. A logarithmic price structure has distances between two price points at equal percentage change. This means that if the price change is 25%, it will be the same for all the price points.

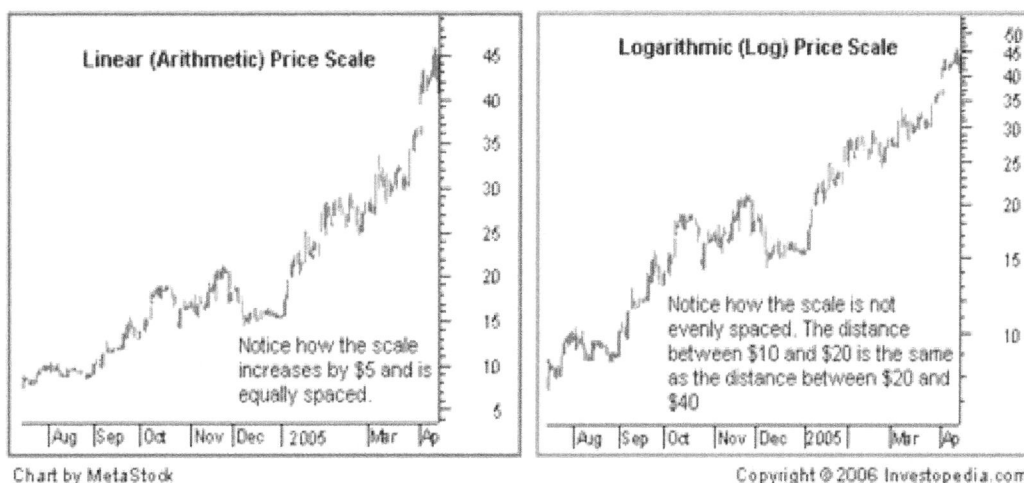

Chart by MetaStock   Copyright © 2006 Investopedia.com

The time scale is a date or time range located at the bottom of the chart. If he opts for a shorter timeframe, the day trader can expect a more detailed chart with each data point showing the asset's closing price. Some charts can also show the open, high, low, and close prices.

An intraday chart can show price movements within a particular period in one trading session. A day trader can expect to see a time scale as short as five minutes. A daily chart can have a series of price actions with a trading session represented by one point, which can be the open, high, low, or close price.

Types of Charts

Candlestick Chart

This is a charting method that came from the Japanese. The method fills the interval between opening and closing prices to show a relationship. These candles use color-coding to show the closing points. You will come across black, red, white, blue, or green candles to represent the closing point at any time.

Open-High-Low-Close Chart (OHLC)

These are also referred to as bar charts, and they give you a connection between the maximum and minimum prices in a trading period. They usually feature a tick on the left side to show the open price and one on the right to show the closing price.

Line Chart

This is a chart that maps the closing price values using a line segment.

Point and Figure Chart
This employs numerical filters that reference times without fully using the time to construct the chart.

Overlays
These are usually used on the main price charts and come in different ways:

Resistance – refers to a price level that acts as the maximum level above the usual price

Support – the opposite of resistance, and it shows as the lowest value of the price

Trend line – this is a line that connects two troughs or peaks.

Channel – refers to two trend lines that are parallel to each other

Moving average – a kind of dynamic trend line that looks at the average price in the market

Bollinger bands – these are charts that show the rate of volatility in a market.

Pivot point – this refers to the average of the high, low, and closing price averages for a certain stock or currency.

Price-Based Indicators
These analyze the price values of the market. These include:

Advance decline line – this is an indicator of the market breadth

Average directional index – shows the strength of a trend in the market

Commodity channel index – helps you to identify cyclical trends in the market

Relative strength index – this is a chart that shows you the strength of the price

Moving average convergence (MACD) – this shows the point where two trend lines converge or diverge.

Stochastic oscillator – this shows the close position that has happened within the recent trading range

Momentum – this is a chart that tells you how fast the price changes

Free Charts
An intraday trader can use free charts that are available online and offer the trader not only with tools for technical analysis, but also with advice, demonstrations, and guidelines about chart analysis. Different free charts provide various features such as delayed futures data, real-time data, and selection of frames of time and indicator accessibility. Furthermore, these charts enable a trader to participate in various markets like the forex, futures, stock exchanges, and equity markets. Free Stock Charts and the Technician are examples of free charts that an intraday can access and utilize without spending anything.

Heiken-Ashi
Heiken-Ashi outlines use candles as the plotting medium, yet take an alternate numerical definition of cost. Rather than the standard technique of candles deciphered from essential open-high-low-close criteria, costs are smoothed to all the more likely show inclining value activity as indicated by this equation:

Open = (Open of past bar + Close of past bar)/2

Close = (Open + High + Low + Close)/4

High = Highest of High, Open, or Close

Low = Lowest of Low, Open, or Close

Regular Terms
Average genuine range – The range over a specific timeframe, generally day by day.

Breakout – When value ruptures a territory of help or obstruction regularly because of an imminent flood in purchasing or selling volume.

Cycle – Periods where value activity is required to follow a specific example.

Dead feline skip – When value decreases in a down market, there might be an uptick in cost where purchasers come in accepting the advantage is modest or selling exaggerated. Be that as it may, when vendors power the market down further, the transitory purchasing spell comes to be known as a dead feline skip.

Dow hypothesis – Average. Advocates of the hypothesis express that once one of them drifts a specific way, the other is probably going to follow. Numerous traders track the transportation area, as they can shed understanding into the strength of the economy. A high volume of product shipments and exchanges is characteristic that the economy is on sound balance.

Doji – A flame type portrayed by close to zero change between the open and close value, demonstrating hesitation in the market.

Elliott wave hypothesis – Elliott wave hypothesis recommends that markets go through repeating times of good faith and cynicism that can be anticipated and, in this way, ready for trading openings.

Fibonacci proportions – Numbers utilized as a manual to decide backing and opposition.

Sounds – Harmonic trading depends on the possibility that value designs rehash themselves, and defining moments in the market can be recognized through Fibonacci arrangements.

Fibonacci Numbers

The Fibonacci number sequence develops by starting at 1 and adding the previous number. The sum is the new number, for example: $0 + 1 = 1$, $1 + 1 = 2$, $2 + 1 = 3$, $3 + 2 = 5$, $5 + 3 = 8$, and $8 + 5 = 13$. Therefore, Fibonacci numbers are 1, 2, 3, 5, 8, 13, 21, 34, 55, 89, 144, 233, and so on.

A Fibonacci number equals 1.618 times the preceding Fibonacci number. In turn, a Fibonacci number equals 0.618 times the following Fibonacci number.

Analysts anticipate changes in trends by using four popular Fibonacci studies: arcs, fans, time zones, and the most popular, retracements. On a Fibonacci scale of 0–100%, the retracement levels within that scale are 38.5%, 50%, and 61.8%. It's amazing how many creatures in nature, human beings included, are proportioned exactly to those ratios.

Those familiar with Elliott Wave Theory know wave counts adhere to the Fibonacci numbering sequence. Many trading software platforms offer Fibonacci studies as part of their charting features. Later, I will recommend you apply the retracements to your E-mini S&P futures chart.

"How fascinating," you mutter, scratching your head. "But what's this got to do with me making big bucks in the market?"

Plenty. Especially when it comes to the numbers 2, 3, and 5. From now on, we're going to keep the numbers 2, 3, and 5 in the forefront of our minds. These numbers crop up repeatedly on charts, and we use them to help predict price movement. We'll also talk more about Fibonacci levels in later chapters.

Stocks in strong uptrends tend to move up three days, then down (pull back) for two. Or they move up for five days, then retrace for three days. In a downtrend, reverse those numbers. A probable pattern is three days down, followed by two rally days, or five days down, and three days up.

If a stock moves down for four days, you can bet it will continue into negative territory into the fifth day. (This always happens, except when it doesn't.)

CHAPTER 16

Support and Resistance

Resistance levels are price levels at which selling pressure tends to overwhelm buying pressure during an uptrend, which can either interrupt or completely reverse an existing bullish trend. Resistance levels are usually drawn by a horizontal line that connects consecutive high prices, also called peaks or tops. Support levels are price levels at which the opposite happens: buying pressure overwhelms selling pressure to the point that an ongoing downward trend is either disrupted or reversed. Support levels are drawn by a horizontal line beneath consecutive low prices, also called bottoms or troughs. Significant support and resistance levels cause reversals of trends, while minor support and resistance levels only interrupt ongoing trends.

Here's how to use resistance and support levels for your day trades:

Identify your SIPs or stocks/securities in play.

Before markets open, check out the daily price charts of these SIPs and look for significant or critical resistance and support price levels for your SIPs. Always remember that support and resistance lines aren't still that obvious, and there'll be times when you may not be able to find clear lines. In such cases, don't force anything that isn't there. Just use other day trading strategies or look at your other SIPs to see if they have identifiable resistance and support lines.

When the market opens, observe your SIPs price movements using a 5-minute chart. Look for indecision or Doji candlesticks as signs for taking positions, whether long or short.

For long positions, buy at prices as close as possible to the support lines. For short positions, sell as closely as possible to

The resistance lines.

You can start closing or covering your long or short positions, respectively, when prices hit the next resistance or support levels. For optimal position management, close or cover half or a more significant portion of your open positions at the following levels. Then, close or cover the rest in the next resistance or support levels.

For long positions, set your stop-loss triggers at the support line, i.e., close your position and limit your losses when the price falls below the line. For short positions, cover your positions as soon as the price starts to go above the resistance line to minimize your trading loss.

If you're not yet very familiar with how to draw support and resistance lines, here are some tips to help you out:

You can identify support or resistance areas through the presence of indecision candles. It's because these candles indicate areas where buyers and sellers wage battles on an almost even keel.

In many cases, whole and half-dollar prices tend to act as resistance or support levels, especially for stocks priced at below $10 per share. Even if you don't see support or resistance lines on these price points, keep in mind that these numbers may serve as very subtle or even invisible support or resistance lines.

The best points for drawing these lines are the most recent.

Price points.

The more frequently support or resistance lines touch extreme price points, the more accurate or reliable those lines are. Prioritize such lines.

The only relevant resistance and support lines are those within the stock or security's current price levels. For example, it's useless to find such lines as far back when a $7.50-stock was still trading at either $13.80 or $2.45 prices. Given that you're day trading and not taking medium to long-term positions, the likelihood that the prices of your SIPs touching those levels are practically zero.

Resistance and support lines are more of estimates or areas rather than exact price points. If the support line runs through

$8.50, prices may start to bounce back within a few cents below or above this price level.

Solid resistance and support lines are those where stock or security prices have very clearly bounced back from. If you don't clearly see prices bounce back from such lines, the chances are that it's not a legit resistance or support line.

Particularly for day trading purposes, you'd be better off drawing these lines across extreme daily prices or wicks and not across places in daily charts where a significant number of price bars stopped. Why?

It's because past extreme low and high prices, i.e., tails and wicks, are influenced mostly by day traders while the price bars, i.e., the candlestick's bodies, represent daily open and closing prices that are influenced mainly by longer-term traders or investors.

CHAPTER 17

Classic Chart Patterns

Chart patterns tell the trader that the price is expected to move in a certain path or the other after the pattern ends. There are several patterns that you need to know – reversal as well as continuation. A reversal pattern tells you that the preceding movement will turn around when the pattern completes. On the contrary, a continuation pattern shows that the preceding pattern will maintain when the pattern completes. Before you go ahead and look at specific chart patterns, you need to understand a few concepts. The major one is the trend line that is drawn to show a level of support or resistance for the commodity. A support trend line is the level at which the process has difficulty going below. A resistance trend line shows the level at which a price has a hard time going beyond. Here are the different patterns that are used by chartists:

Head and Shoulders

This pattern is a popular one and also reliable for most traders that use technical analysis. As the name implies, the pattern resembles a head that has shoulders. This is a reversal pattern that shows that the price will possibly move against a preceding trend. The pattern signals that the price will most likely fall when the pattern completes. The pattern usually forms at the peak of the upward trend.

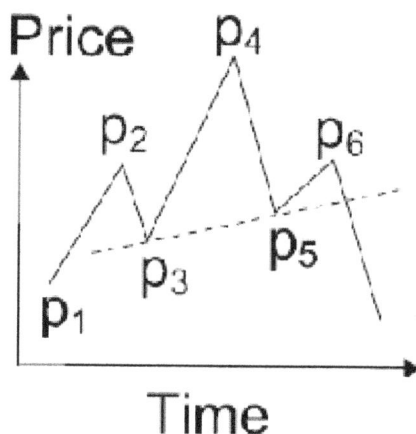

The pattern also has another form, an inverted head and shoulder facing down. It signals that the price might rise and usually forms during an upward trend.

Head and Shoulders Top

This tells the chart user that the price of a security will likely take downward trend. It usually forms at the peak of the upward trend and is a trend reversal pattern.

The pattern has 4 main stems to complete and show a reversal:

The formation for the left shoulder – comes about when the commodity hits a new peak then drops to a new low.

Creation of the head – after reaching the peak, the price retracts to the formation of the other shoulder.

Formation of the right shoulder – occurs when a peak that is lower than the peak in the head.

Neckline – the pattern finished when the price goes below the neckline.

Head and Shoulders Bottom

This is exactly the reverse of the previous pattern. This signal tells you that the scrutiny will make an upward move soon. The pattern usually comes when the downtrend ends and is considered a reversal pattern with the direction going high after pattern conclusion.

Steps include:

Configuration of left shoulder – happens when the price drops to a new minimum and then to a new high.

Head formation – when the price goes below the preceding low, then it jumps back to the previous high.

Right shoulder – this experiences a sell-off, ending at a low price but higher than the earlier one with a drop to the neckline.

Neckline – the return to the previous level forms the neckline.

This pattern is complete when the price goes above the neckline.

Cup & Handle

This looks like a cup on the chart. The pattern shows a bullish persistence pattern whereby the rising trend pauses and then traded downward, after which it continues in an upward trend upon conclusion of the pattern. It can run from numerous months up to a year, though the common form remains constant.

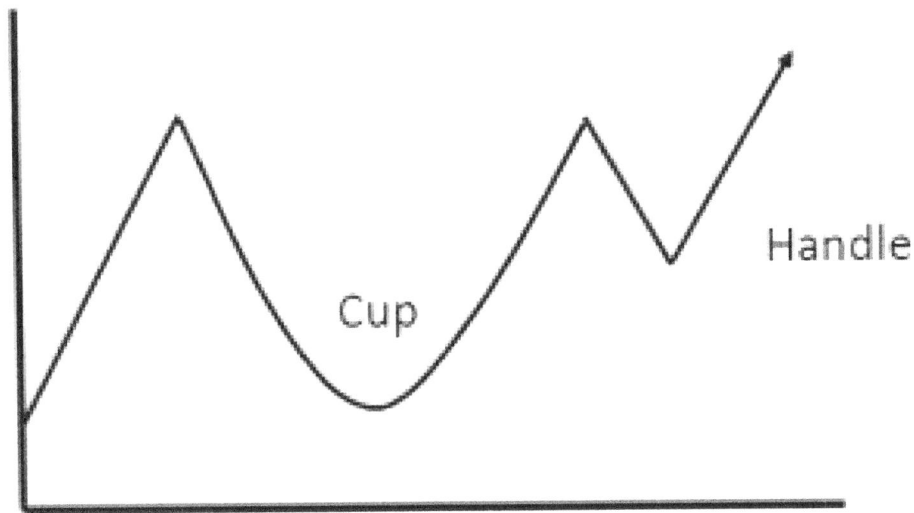

This is usually preceded by an increasing move, which then stops and sells off. This is the start of the pattern, after which the security trades flat for a long time without a definite trend. The final part of this pattern, called the handle, is a downward move that resumes the previous trend.

The Components

The cup and handle have several components that you need to know of. First, you need to know that an upward trend occurs before the trend forms. The longer the previous trend is, the lesser the possibility for a huge breakout after completion of the pattern.

The construction of the cup is vital – it ought to be nicely rounded, more of a semi-circle. The cup and handle pattern signals that weaker investors are leaving the market, and buyers are staying for the commodity. If the shape is too sharp, it shows a weakening signal.

You need to focus on the handle as well because it signals the completion of the pattern. The handle represents a descending move by the commodity after the increasing move on the right part. During the move, a downward trend line can be drawn to form a breakout. A move above the trend line shows that a prior upward trend is soon starting.

As with most of the patterns, you need to consider volume so that you confirm the pattern.

Double Top & Double Bottom

These indicate a reversal. They indicate the desire for security to continue with an existing trend. When this happens, especially with numerous attempts to run higher, the inclination reverses and begins a fresh trend all over.

Double Top

This occurs at the peak of an upward movement, and it shows that the previous trend is failing, and buyers aren't interested in the trend. Upon the conclusion of the pattern, the movement shows reversal, and the commodity is supposed to go down.

double top

The last phase of the pattern is the formation of new highs in the rising trend, after which the price starts to go towards the stage of resistance. The pattern completes when the price falls lower than the support level established in the preceding move, marking the beginning of a downward trend.

When using this pattern, it is vital that you wait until the price breaks below the key level before you place a trade. Doing this before the signal forms can lead to catastrophic results because the pattern is only setting up for a reversal. The pattern illustrates a pull between sellers and buyers. The buyers are trying so hard to shove the commodity through but are getting opposition, which prevents the rising trend from proceeding. When this continues for some time, the buyers decide to give up, and sellers take hold of the commodity, pushing it down on a new down trend.

Just like before, you need to consider volume before you make a decision as you need to look at the volume of the commodity when the price falls below a certain level.

Double Bottom

The double bottom shows a reversal to an uptrend. The pattern forms when the existing downtrend goes to a new minimum. The move finds all support, which then prevents the commodity from going lower. When the move finds the right support, the commodity will hit a new high, which in turn creates the resistance point for the commodity. The subsequent stage takes the commodity to a low. However, the commodity finds some support, and then it changes the direction. You confirm the pattern when the price goes over the resistance level it encountered before the move.

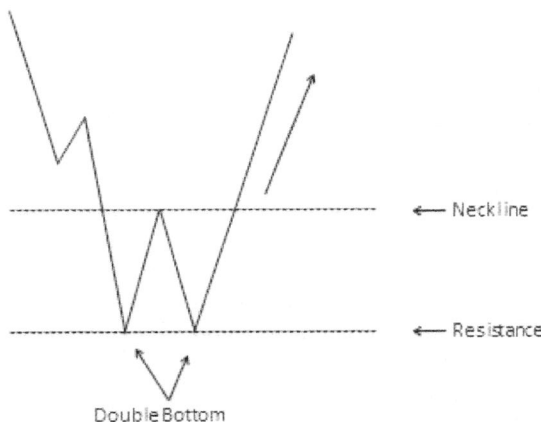

Double Bottom

For definite reversal, the commodity needs to get the support to show a reversal in a downward trend.

Triangles

As you see from the previous chart patterns, the names leave little to the imagination. As the name goes, triangle patterns form a triangular shape.

The essential design of the pattern is when two trend lines meet with the price of the commodity moving between the two trend lines.

The triangles come in three forms – the symmetrical triangle, ascending triangle, and the descending triangle.

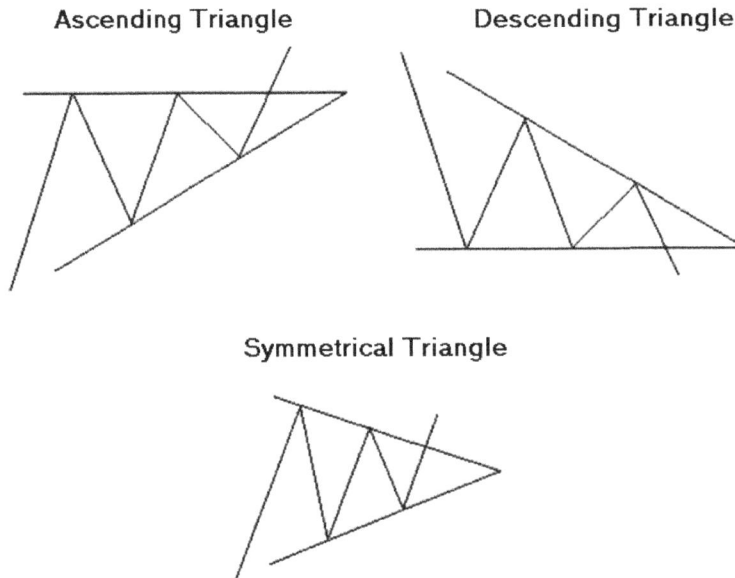

Ascending Triangle   **Descending Triangle**

Symmetrical Triangle

The Symmetrical Triangle

This presents a continuation pattern that signals a consolidation trend that is then followed by the continuation of a previous trend. The triangle is formed by the junction of a downward resistance line and an equally climbing support line. These converge at the apex. The price of the commodity usually bounces between the trend lines towards the apex then breaks out towards the preceding trend. To confirm the pattern, you need to look at various aspects depending on the direction of the pattern. If the pattern is preceded by a downtrend, focus on a break that happens under the support line. The pattern usually completes when the stock price finally leaves the triangle, therefore look for a volume increase in the direction of the breakout.

Ascending Triangle

This bullish pattern gives a hint that the price will close higher. The pattern forms from two trend lines, one flat line that forms the point of resistance and a rising line that acts as price support.

The most significant part of the pattern is the rising support line that shows that sellers have begun leaving the security. After the sellers leave the market, buyers go ahead to push the price past the resistance level so that it resumes an upward trend.

Descending Triangle

This is a clear bullish signal. It shows that the price will move downwards when the pattern completes. The pattern comes from a flat support line that meets a resistance line that is sloping downwards. The pattern tells you that the buyers are really trying to push the price higher, but they face a lot of resistance. After many attempts, they end up fading with the sellers overpowering them, which in turn pushes the price lower.

Flags and Pennants

These are a set of continuation lines that resemble each other closely. The only difference is in the consolidation periods of the pattern. The flag resembles a rectangle while the pennant resembles a triangle.

The patterns form when a spiky price movement occurs, followed by slanting price movement. The pattern finalizes when a price breakout occurs in a similar direction to the spike.

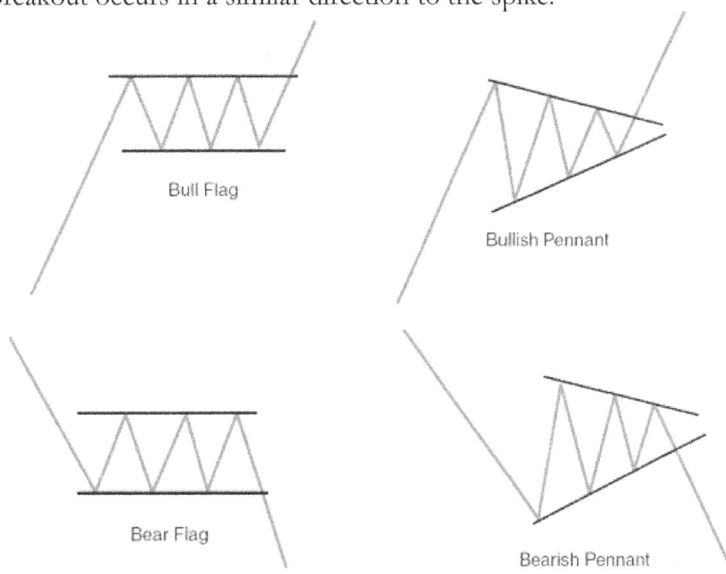

Bull Flag

Bullish Pennant

Bear Flag

Bearish Pennant

The cause of the movement is due to a huge price shift, market consolidation, or pause before the resumption of an initial trend.

The Flag

This part of the pattern forms a pattern that resembles a rectangle. This rectangle comes by due to 2 parallel trend lines that push the price until it breaks out.

The signal to buy or sell forms when the price goes through two levels, with the movement going in the previous direction. As always, consider the volume to justify the signal.

The Pennant

This is a sort of a triangle, where the lines form a convergence of sorts.

The Wedge

This chart pattern shows the reversal of the movement that forms inside the wedge. The construction is akin to a symmetrical triangle because it has two trend lines depicting resistance and support.

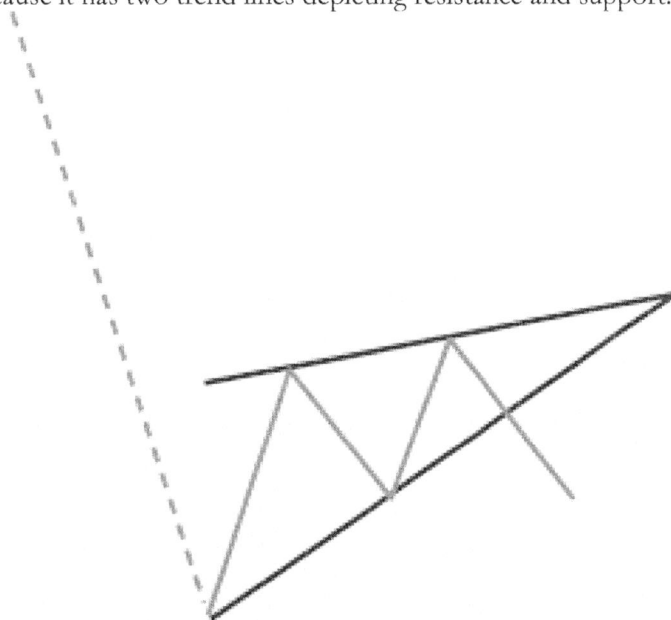

However, this pattern is different from the triangle in that it is longer, which usually lasts between 3 to 6 months. The converging trend lines incline upward or downward, different from typical triangles.

Wedges come in two types – falling and rising. The two differ due to the slant, with a falling wedge sloping downward and an easing wedge slanting upward.

Falling Wedge: this bullish pattern signals that you will probably see the price breaking through the wedge and adopt the upwards direction. You need to look at the resistance trend line, which ought to have a sharp slope than the support trend line. For this construction, the buy signal forms when the price goes through the resistance.

Rising wedge: this is the opposite of the falling wedge in that it has a bearish pattern that shows that the security might head in a downward direction. The trend lines that form this pattern usually converge, with all the trend lines slanting in an upward direction.

CHAPTER 18

Technical Indicators

Technical indicators are tools to help traders in technical analysis of stock charts. For day trading, learning about how to use technical indicators is a very essential craft, without which you cannot become a successful day trader. This is like learning to ride a bicycle if you want to win medals in competitive cycling events. Fortunately, the technical indicators are simple and easy to learn, and anyone can find several online resources that explain what technical indicators are and how to use them.

You can also join some offline workshops or lessons to learn technical analysis. There are dozens of technical indicators used in isolation or combination by day traders. The good thing is, all technical indicators help in some way to spot the price movement and hint at the right trade entry and exit points.

Day traders select technical indicators that they like and feel comfortable working with. It is possible to become enamored with too many technical indicators and try to use many of those for chart analysis. But the best practice is to use only a few indicators and stick with those for your trade analysis.

Using too many indicators can create confusion and make your chart a jumble of crisscrossing lines. Keeping it simple is the best when it comes to using technical indicators.

Many traders depend on finding support or resistance levels for trading in stock markets. Support levels are favored for buying and resistance levels for selling. This is also known as buying low and selling high.

These levels are the most important points you will need to know on charts for the right trading. Based on market trends, different methods are used for finding these levels. Mainly, there are three types of trends in the stock market: uptrend, downtrend, and sideways trend (also called range-bound trend). In the uptrend, the price continues to climb up; in the downtrend, the price falls regularly. But, in a sideways or range-bound trend, the price moves up and down within a horizontal range. In the up and downtrend, a slanting trend line shows the trading pattern.

Trend Lines

The first tool we will talk about is the trend-line. This is the most basic analysis tool that you will ever learn about. I can guarantee that you will find this tool in just about any trading software out there. So what is it?

Based on market direction, there are two types of trend lines: an uptrend line and a downtrend line. Let us take a look at each one of them.

An Uptrend Line

As the name suggests, this is a line that is drawn on an uptrend, such as the one shown above.

In case you forgot, an uptrend is basically an upward market movement. When a market goes up creating an uptrend, it does so in a zigzag manner, creating a pattern that is composed of small troughs and hills.

The troughs are commonly referred to as support levels. Support levels are also referred to as reactions or corrections. These are points where the market retraces back a bit before advancing in its original direction. These troughs offer excellent buy opportunities.

These troughs become the touching points when you are drawing an uptrend line.

One thing to keep in mind is that the touching points must be at least three for the line to be considered a valid trend line.

A Downtrend Line

Then we have the downtrend line.

Likewise, when a market is moving downwards, it will move in a zigzag manner, such as the one shown above, creating hills and troughs. However, unlike the uptrend line, this line is drawn across the hills. These points are also called points of resistance or resistance levels. And they offer excellent selling opportunities in a falling market.

Moving Averages

The Moving Averages are slanting indicators that move with the trend line and show major support and resistance areas. These indicators consist of different periods, such as the 20 days; 50 days; 100 days; and 200 days. Day traders use moving averages to find support and resistance points while markets are trending. On the other hand, the sideways trend is created by a horizontal movement of price. In such trends, traders require knowing horizontal support and resistance levels for buying and selling purposes. Day traders use pivot levels or Fibonacci levels in range-bound market conditions for spotting support and resistance. These are the simplest of indicators. Pivot levels are calculated by certain methods, and pivot calculators are freely available online. Fibonacci levels are drawn on technical charts from the highest and lowest price points. All trading charts provide facilities to draw Fibonacci levels. The third most important and simplest trading indicator is the RSI (Relative Strength Index). As the name suggests, this indicator shows the strength of any trend. RSI is plotted below the main charting area and keeps rising and falling with the price moment. A rising RSI shows the strength of an uptrend, and a falling RSI shows the strength of a downtrend. It has the top and bottom areas, respectively called overbought and oversold areas. Day traders look to sell from the overbought region and buy near the oversold area.

One can combine support and resistance indicators with the RSI and plan their trading strategies for buying and selling.

Momentum Indicators

Momentum indicators show the strength of a trend and whether a reversal is likely to occur. They are very useful in finding peaks and troughs. As such, they can be useful in knowing when or where to enter or exit a trade. Some examples of momentum indicators are the Average Directional Index (ADX), Relative Strength Index (RSI), and the Stochastic.

These indicators are leading.

Oscillators and Market cycles

These refer to indicators such as the Relative Strength Index (RSI) and the Moving Average Convergence Divergent (MACD) that reflect unclear price trends. The signals move between the upper bounds and lower ones, and the subsequent readings provide the day trader with feedback regarding the market conditions.

CHAPTER 19

Types of trades

There are different reasons some traders love to use forex instead of the stock market. One of them is the forex leverage. When it comes to forex trading, the entire system is totally different. Before you can trade using leverage, you need to have opened the forex trading account. That's the only requirement that is out there, nothing else. When you open a forex account, you can easily use the leverage feature. If you are trading in the United States of America, you will be restricted to a leveraging of 50: 1 leveraging. Countries outside of the US are restricted to leverage of about 200: 1. It is better when you are outside the US than in the US. Liquidity differences

When you decide to trade stocks, you end up purchasing the companies' shares that have a cost from a few dollars down to even hundreds of dollars. Usually, the price in the market tends to share with demand and supply.

Paired Trades

When you trade with forex, you are facing another world, unseen in the stock market. Though the currency of a country tends to change, there will always be a great supply of currency that you can trade. What this means is that the main currencies in the world tend to be very liquid. When you are in forex trading, you will see that the currencies are normally quoted in pairs. They are not quoted alone. This means that you should be interested in the country's economic health that you have decided to trade in. The economic health of the country tends to affect the worth of the currency. The basic considerations change from one forex market to the next. If you decide to purchase the Intel shares, the main aim is to see if the stock's value will improve. You aren't interested in how the prices of other stocks are. On the other hand, if you have decided to sell or buy forex, you need to analyze the economies of those countries that are involved in the pairs. You should find out if the country has better jobs, GDP, as well as political prospects. To make a successful trade in the Forex market, you will be expected to analyze not only one financial entity but two. The forex market tends to show a higher level of sensitivity in upcoming economic and political scenarios in many countries. You should note that the U.S. stock market, unlike many other stock markets, is not so sensitive to a lot of foreign matters.

Price Sensitivity to Trade Activities

When we look at both markets, we have no choice but to notice that there is varying price sensitivity when it comes to trade activities done.

If a small company that has fewer shares has about ten thousand shares bought from it, it could go a long way to impact the price of the stock. For a big company such as Apple, such number of shares, when bought from, it won't affect the stock price. When you look at forex trades, you will realize that trades of a few hundreds of millions of dollars won't affect the major currency at all. If it affects, it would be minute.

Market Accessibility

It is easy to access the currency market, unlike its counterpart, the stock market. Though you may be able to trade stocks every second of the day, five days weekly in the twenty-first century, it is not easy.

A lot of retail investors end up trading via a United States brokerage that makes use of a single major trading period every day, which spans from 9: 30 AM to 4: 00 PM. They go ahead to have a minute trading hour past that time, and this period has price and volatility issues, which end up dissuading a lot of retail traders from making use of such time. Forex trading is different. One can carry out such trading every second of the day because there are a lot of forex exchanges in the world, and they are constantly trading in one time zone or the other.

Forex Trading Vs. Options

A trader may believe the United States Dollar will become better when compared to the Euro, and if the results pan out, the person earns.

CHAPTER 20

Setups and Trading strategies

Anyone who wishes to make money with stock trading should have a better strategy on how to predict the trend in prices of the stock in order to maximize profits. The charts show the trends that have different patterns that a new person in the trade cannot easily interpret. The patterns in the trend have meanings that give signals to the trader on when to make a move by either buying or selling stock.

The ABCD Pattern

This is a harmonic pattern that is used to derive the other patterns of trade. This pattern is made up of three swings that are made up of the AB and CD lines, also known as the legs. The line BC is known as the correction line. The lines AB and CD are almost of the same size. The AB-CD pattern uses a downtrend that indicates that the reversal will be upward. On the other hand, the bearish pattern uses the uptrend, which means that there will be a reversal downward at some point. When using this pattern for trade, you have to know the direction of the trend and the movement of the market. There are three types of ABCD pattern: the classic ABCD pattern, the AB=CD pattern, and the ABCD extension.

When using this pattern, remember that one can only enter the trade when the price has reached point D. Therefore, it is essential to study the chart o at the lows and highs; you can use the zigzag indicator, which marks the swings on the chart. As you explore the chart, watch the price that forms AB and BC.

In a bullish trade ABCD, C should be at the lower side of A. The point A, on the other hand, should be intermediate-high after B that is at a low point. D should be a new point that is lower than B. as mentioned earlier, the entry is at point D, but when the market reaches point D, you should not be too quick to enter the trade, consider other techniques that would make sure that the reverse is up when it is a bullish trade, and down when it is a bearish trade.

Flag Momentum

In a trading market, there are times when things are good, and the traders enjoy an upward trend, which gives a chart pattern that represents a bull flag pattern. It is named as such because when you look at the chart, it forms a pattern that resembles a flag on a pole. The trend in the market is an uptrend, and therefore the pattern is referred to as a bullish flag. The bull flag pattern is characterized by the following; when the stock makes a positive move with a relatively high volume, the pole is formed, when the stock consolidates on a lighter volume at the top, the flag is formed. The stock continues to move at a relatively high volume breaking through the consolidation pattern. The bull flag momentum is a trading strategy that can be used at any given time frame. When it is used to scalp the movements of price, the bull is used only on two instances of time frame: the second and the fifth minute time frames. The trading bull flags also work well when using daily charts to trade and can also be used effectively when swing trading.

It is simple to trade, but it is challenging to look for the exact bull pattern. This problem can be solved using scanners that help to look for stocks on the upward trend and wait for them to be in a consolidation position at the top. The best and free scanners that can be used to locate bull flags are Finviz and chart mill. There are tips that can be used to indicate a bull flag. When there is an increase in stock volume that is influenced by news, and when the stock prices remain high, showing a clear pattern for a pullback. At this point, you can now check out when the prices break out above the consolidation pattern or on high volumes of stock. To make a move, place a stop order at the bottom of the consolidation. At this point, the ratio of risk to reward is 2:1, and it is the best time to target. The most substantial part of the pattern is the volume of the stock, and it is a good sign that there will be a significant move and a successful breakout. On the trend, it is also good to look at the descending trend as it gives a sign on the next breakout. This can be seen in the trend line that is found at the topmost of the flag.

When used well for trading, the bull flags are useful tools of the trade; however, things can go wrong, and therefore one must be ready with an exit strategy. There are two strategies, one is placing a stop order at a point below the consolidation area, and the second method is using a moving average that is monitored for within 20 days. Within 20 days, if the price of the stock is below the moving average, then it is time to close out the position and try out other trading routes.

Reversal Trading

Reversal trading, also known as a trend reversal pattern, is a trading strategy that indicates the end of a trend and the start of a new one. This pattern is formed when the price level of stock in the current trend has reached a maximum. This pattern provides information on the possible change of trend and possible value of price movement. A pattern that is formed in the upwards trend signals that there would be a reversal in the trend and the prices will go down soon. Conversely, a downward trend will indicate that there will be a movement of the costs, and it will be upwards. For you to recognize this pattern, you have to know where specific patterns form in the current trend. There are distribution patterns that occur at the top of the market; at this point, traders sell more than they buy. The patterns that occur at the bottom of the markets are referred to as accumulation patterns, and at this point, traders buy more than they sell. Reversal trends are formed at all time frames, and it is because the bank traders have either place trades are taking profits off the trades. The trend can be detected when there are multiple up and down formations that are fully formed; they should be at least two upswings and two downswings indicating a bearish pattern. The swing highs of lows on the trend line depend on which reversal pattern is formed. The highs or lows form at a similar price because the bank traders want to appear as if they are causing a reversal in the market by getting all their trades places at the same time. In the real sense, that is not the case because they appear at different points of the trend. Therefore, as a trader, you should wait for a bright and steady trend upward for you to sell in the case of a bullish trade and a steady trend downward for the case of a bearish trade for you to buy.

There are different types of reversal patterns. The double top reversal pattern is a pattern that has two tops on the chart. It looks like "M." The double top has its reverse type known as the double bottom pattern that resembles "W." The double bottom has two bottoms located either on the same support or at different supports. Another reversal pattern is the head and shoulders; this pattern resembled two shoulders and ahead. The two shoulders are tops that are slightly below the other top that is known as the head. The head and shoulders can also be represented in a descending pattern whereby the tops become bottoms.

VWAP Trading

VWAP is the volume-weighted average price. It is a trading strategy that is simple and highly Effective when you are trading in a short time frame. For it to work for you, you must use Different strategies and the most common approach is the waiting for a VWAP cross above and enter long. A VWAP that is across above gives signals to the traders that buyers would be joining the market, and there would be an upward movement of price. The bearish traders might short stock giving it a VWAP cross below, thus signaling the buyers to leave the market and take profits. VWAP can also be used as a resistance or support level for determining the risk of trade; when the stock trades above the VWAP, the VWAP is used as the support level, and when the trading is below the VWAP, the VWAP is used as a resistance level. In both cases, the trader is guided by the VWAP to know when to buy and when to sell.

When doing trading transactions, trading costs are determined by comparing the price of the transaction against a reference or a benchmark, and the most common benchmark is the VWAP. The daily VWAP benchmark encourages traders to avoid the risks of trading on extreme prices of the day by spreading their trades over time. This trading strategy favors those people who use market orders to trade rather than limit orders. This is because an opportunity cost arises from delays and passive trading.

CHAPTER 21

Step by Step to a Successful Trade

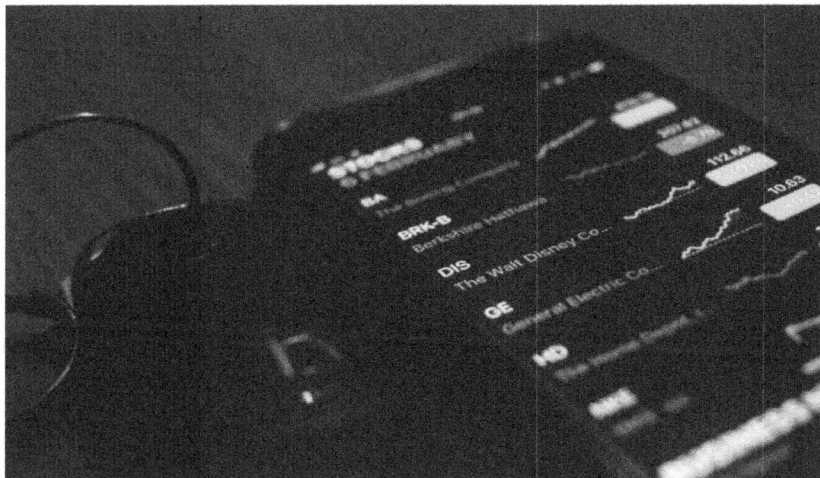

Usually, the US stocks have over 8,000 stocks on the list, but a typical day trader has access to only a fraction of them because they just fail to build a fortune due to lack of an effective trade strategy. They enter the market based on rumors and exit it empty-handed as a result. More often they play at the cost of their precious capital. Winning can be hard in the stock market if you lack discipline as a trader. You need to identify the right stocks to create a winning situation for you. Despite the presence of the learning curve, the effort to detect the right stock is worthwhile.

In this chapter, I will walk you through different steps that are involved in the completion of a successful trade.

Selecting a Broker

When it comes to selecting brokers, you have many options available. There is full service, discount, online, etc. Understanding the differences between them and selecting the ones best suited for your purposes is crucial if you wish to succeed. Another area that a lot of beginners ignore and then receive a rude lesson in is the regulations surrounding options trading. There are not too many rules to comply with, but they do have significant consequences for your capital and risk strategies.

This chapter will fill you in on all the details.

What Broker to Use?

Generally speaking, there are two major varieties of brokers: discount and full service. A lot of full-service brokers have discount arms these days, so you will see some overlap. Full service refers to an organization where brokerage is just a part of a larger financial supermarket.

The broker might offer you other investment solutions, estate planning strategies, and so on. They will also have an in-house research wing, which will send you reports to help you trade better. In addition to this, they will also have phone support in case you have any questions or wish to place an order. Once you develop a good relationship with them, a full-service broker will become a better organization to network. Every broker loves a profitable customer since it helps with marketing. A full-service broker will have good relationships in the industry, and if you have specific needs, they can put you in touch with the right people.

The price of all this service is you paying higher commissions than average. It is up to you to see whether this is a good price for you to pay. As such, you do not need to sign up with a full-service broker to trade successfully.

Order matching is done electronically, so it is not as if a person on the floor can get you a better price these days. Therefore, a full-service house is not going to give you better execution.

Discount brokers, on the other hand, are all about focus. They help you trade, and that is it. They will not provide advice, at least not intentionally from a business perspective, and phone ordering is nonexistent. That doesn't mean customer service is reduced. Far from it.

Commissions will be lower as well, far lower than what you can expect to pay for a full-service house. The downside of a discount brokerage is that you are not going to receive any special product recommendations or solutions outside of your speculative activities. A lot of people prefer to trade (using a separate account) with the broker they have their retirement accounts with, so everything is kept in-house.

So, which one should you choose? Well, if you aim to keep costs as low as possible, then select a discount broker. Only in the case where you are keen on keeping things in one place you should choose a full-service broker. These days, there's no difference between the two options otherwise.

An exception here is if you have a large amount of capital, north of half a million dollars. In such cases, a full-service broker will be cheaper because of their volume-based commission offers. You will pay the same rate or as close to what a discount broker would charge you, and you get all the additional services. Whatever additional amounts you need to invest can be handled by the firm through their wealth management line of business.

Building Up Your Watch List

There is a visible difference between a watch list and a portfolio. Before you head off to start, you should know that a portfolio is a collection of the stocks you own at a given time, while a watch list displays the securities that you own and also the ones that you have selected even if you don't have any investment in them. Watch lists give you insights into the stocks that you will eventually want to add to your personalized portfolio. You should create watch lists based on some current factors. You also need to use your previous watch lists if there are any. They would remind you of the searches that you have done in the past and would also help you fine-tune your future searches. Go through the list more often and also plan a personal schedule of how you will be able to comb through the list and see if the stock matches your criteria. In case of negative signals, delete the stock and save your time to focus on other stocks on your watch list. Start with the broader sets and then narrow down your stocks while you tailor them down as per your needs. If you know about your requirements, you can weed out the stocks that don't fulfill them. The key is to keep the list up to date. As the stock market reinvents itself each day each hour, you ought to reinvent your watch list in the same way. It is the best strategy to keep an eye on the stocks that seem to be popular. Keep an eye on the upward and downward trends in the popular stocks. When you keep an eye on the rise and fall of certain stocks, you will be able to trim and tune your watch list. You will no longer be needing to enter the stocks of only the big companies. Instead, you can prepare your watch list for small companies. While you prepare a watch list, you should keep an eye on the candlesticks, dojis, and charts. The fluctuation of prices is another element to watch for. You can build an effective watch list by collecting liquidity components in the stocks, adding scanned stock listings that meet general technical criteria. Rescanning the watch list to see which stock is ripe for investment and which should be discarded from the list after a while is also the key strategy to add to your skillset. For example, you can say that if a stock's volume has been unattractive for the past few days, the stock should be off of your watch list. Deletion is necessary to unburden a watch list. The shorter it is, the more you will be able to keep it into consideration.

Margin

Margin refers to the number of assets you currently hold in your account. Your assets are cash and positions. As the market value of your position fluctuates, so does the amount margin you have. Margin is an important concept to grasp since it is at the core of your risk management discipline. When you open an account with your broker, you will have a choice to make. You can open either a cash or margin account. To trade options, you have to open a margin account. Briefly, a cash account does not include leverage within it, so all you can trade are stocks. There are no account minimums for a cash account, and even if they are, they are pretty minuscule. A margin account, on the other hand, is subject to very different rules. First, the minimum balances in a margin account are higher. Most brokers will impose a $10,000 minimum, and some will even increase this amount based on your trading style. The account minimum does not achieve anything by itself, but it acts as a commitment of sorts for the broker.

Execution

We live in an era of high-frequency trading, and the markets' smallest measurement of time has gone from seconds to microseconds. Trades are constantly pouring in, and the matching engine is always finding suitable sellers to buyers. Given the pace of the market, it is important to understand that it is humanly impossible to figure out the exact price of an instrument. Therefore, within your risk management plan, you must make allowance for times of high volatility when the fluctuations will be bigger. For now, I want you to understand that just because the price you received was different from what was on screen does not mean the broker is incompetent.

How do you identify an incompetent broker? Customer service and the quality of the trading terminal give you access to be the best indicators. Your broker is not in the game to trade against you or fleece you. Admittedly, this is not the case with FX, but we are not discussing FX in this book. So, stop blaming your broker and look at your systems instead, assuming the broker passes basic due diligence. When it comes to placing orders with your broker, you have many options. There are different order types you can place, and each order has a specific purpose. First off, we have the market order. This is the simplest order to understand. When you place a market order, you are telling your broker to fill your entire order at whatever price they can find on the market.

A market order usually results in faster fills, unless there is a volatility event of some sort going on. The next type of order you can place is the limit order. The limit prioritizes order price over quantity. For example, if you want to enter 100 units of an instrument at $10, your broker will buy as much as possible under or equal to $10. If they can get just 90 units under $10, then that's it. A limit order works for a lot of traders looking to enter a position. Directional risk management depends a lot on the size of the position, so it is critical not to exceed the position limit. For such traders, this is a beneficial order. The last type of order you will encounter is the stop order. The stop prioritizes quantity over price.

Stop orders have a trigger attached to them, and once the market price hits the trigger, the entire quantity of the order is executed, irrespective of what the price is. Stop orders are very useful to get out of positions quickly. Indeed, the stop-loss order is a stop order with the 'losses in the name simply referring to the minimization of losses in case the trade goes south. Another order you should be aware of is the Good Till Cancelled or GTC. A cousin of the GTC is the Day order. These two do not order types as much as expiry conditions for the order. A GTC is valid until the trader explicitly cancels it, while the day the order cancels itself at the end of the market session.

All in all, there are over a hundred different types of order your average broker offers you. Do not get bogged down trying to figure them all out. Institutional traders use most of them for specific strategies. To trade well, you do not need to understand a single word of what those orders are about. Stick to the ones mentioned here, and you can trade successfully.

CHAPTER 22

Next Steps for Beginner Traders

Success in day-trading is largely based on three essential skills:

Critical Analysis - you have to assess the tension between sellers and buyers and place your money in the winning group

Financial Management - You need to practice excellent money management, or else you will lose your money in no time

Self-Discipline - You need to be highly disciplined and stick to your trading plan. You have to avoid getting overly depressed or excited in the financial markets and the temptation to make decisions based on your emotions. Now, after reading this book, you must be in a better position to decide whether or not day-trading is really the right career for you. Remember, day-trading requires a specific mindset, discipline, and a set of skills that you need to improve in the long run.

It is interesting to take note that many successful day traders are also avid players of poker. They say that they enjoy the stimulation and speculation that comes from this game.

But you need to remember that poker is a type of gambling. Day-trading is not because it dwells on the realm of science. It requires skill, discipline, and other skills that have nothing to do with luck like gambling. Selling and buying financial instruments is a serious business. You must be able to make quick decisions, with no hesitation or emotion. Doing otherwise could lead to a substantial loss of money and also depression in some individuals who don't yet have a formidable mind.

Once you have made up your mind and you have finally decided that you like to begin day-trading, the next step is to be properly educated. You must never begin your career in day-trading using actual cash. Look for brokers that will allow you to play with simulated accounts but are using real market data.

There are some day-trading brokers who will offer access to an account that uses delayed market data. This is not the best simulator to use. You have to work with real-time data so you can make actual decisions.

The majority of simulated data software are premium tools, so you have to save money for this software. Avoid free trials since many of them are cheap platforms. Remember, if you pay peanuts, you get monkeys. Invest in your education, and education in day-trading requires an upfront cost.

For instance, let's say that you want to get your master's degree. This goal will easily cost you around $40,000 or even more. Similarly, many diploma or post-graduation programs will cost a lot more compared to the education needed for your day-trading career.

When you have a simulated account, you need to develop your own strategy. Try the day-trading strategies we have explored in this book. Ideally, you should become a master of one strategy. Reversal Strategies, Resistance or Support, and VWAP are the easiest day-trading strategies.

You only have to master a few days of trading strategies, so you become profitable in this career. Keep it simple. Once you have mastered a strong strategy, make certain that you detach your emotions when you make the trade. Continue practicing with the level of money that you will trade in an actual account. It can be easy to purchase a position worth $50,000 in a simulated platform and watch 50% of it vanish in a matter of minutes. However, do you have the tolerance to lose this amount of money in real life?

If your answer is no, then you will probably become too emotional while you are trading and make quick decisions that will ultimately result in substantial loss. Therefore, always trade with the position and size that you will also use in an actual account. Otherwise, it makes no sense to trade in a simulator. You can move to a real account after training with a simulator and then begin with small real cash. Limit the number of your trades if you are still learning, or you feel that you are not emotionally prepared. Continue your self-education, and be sure to reflect on your trading strategy.

Do not stop learning about day-trading and the market you want to participate in - equities, forex, ETFs, or futures. These financial markets are quite dynamic. Day-trading is quite different from what it was a decade ago, and it will be different in the next decade.

So, continue reading and discussing your performance and progress with other day traders. Learn how to think ahead and keep a progressive attitude. Read as much as you can, but still keep a level of skepticism about everything you encounter, including this book, of course.

Ask important questions, and don't accept 'expert insights' at face value. Ideally, you should join a group or community of day traders. It can be extremely difficult to trade alone. It can also be emotionally overwhelming. It will help you a lot if you are part of a community of day traders so you can ask questions, discuss options, learn new strategies, and receive alerts and hints about the financial markets. But don't forget that you also need to contribute.

It is essential to take note, however, that if you are part of a community of day traders, you must not always follow the pack. Try to become an independent thinker.

In general, people do change once they become part of a crowd. They become more impulsive, unquestioning, and always looking for a 'guru' whose trades they can follow. They respond with the crowd rather than using their own minds. Day-trading groups may receive some trends together but could lose if the trends reverse. Don't forget that profitable day traders know how to think on their own. Learn how to use your judgment when to pursue the trade and when to get out.

CHAPTER 23

The Basic Tips for Beginner's Day Trading

It's time for you to look at how the day trading process works. You could just blindly jump in, but that is a recipe for disaster. Instead, let us get you started on how to smartly engage in day trading.

The first question to ask yourself is, how big an investment are you planning on making your day trading efforts? You need to think that not only how much money you are willing to invest, but also how much time. Many investors look at day trading as an escape from their normal jobs, others see it as an answer to the uncertainties of the job market. While you may hunger to day trade full time, people do succeed as part-time day traders while working a primary job. Beginners may also want to spend some time simulating investments to get a feel for how comfortable you are with the process and how much talent you may have. Simply jumping in is not a good idea. You need to understand the investment market, learn to look for indicators that give you an idea of stock movements, and make the most of your opportunities.

Infrastructure Concerns

While it may sound mundane, spending some time on your workspace and technology can be well worth it. Day trading can be stressful, so a work area that provides quiet and privacy can be helpful. Do not underestimate the importance of a reliable internet connection and a backup method of controlling your investments in case your network goes down. These days, it is not hard to have a fast land-based internet connection while also having the ability to use your smartphone as a wireless hotspot if your main connection goes down. It only takes one network failure when you have a big investment on the line to convince you of the importance of a backup internet access plan.

Understanding the Market

It's one thing to say you want to invest in stocks. It is another thing to find out what stocks you should be investing in. Investors break down the market into different sectors, such as "retailers," "manufacturers," "utilities," "airlines," "energy," "health care," and others. Day traders can choose to target all these sectors or choose to specialize in one or more. As a beginner, focusing on one sector may be advantageous, particularly if it is one you are already familiar with. Since as a day trader, you are interested in identifying opportunities for small changes in stocks, not long-term growth. This means you will need ample funding. U.S. based day traders need a minimum of $25,000 for their trading account, according to Securities and Exchange Commission (SEC) rules. This means you will really need at least $30,000 to have some flexibility. Keep in mind; in the U.S., you can currently leverage your trading capital by up to 400%. This means that you could control $120,000 worth of stock with your $30,000. As you learned earlier, this also means you could suffer four times the losses on your investments. Be aware that if you do not maintain your maintenance margin amount, you can receive a margin call too. In planning for your trading account, it would be better to have more funds available, since that would make more stocks available for your consideration. Remember, it is usually more cost-efficient to buy shares in multiples of 100, meaning a small investment kitty will either limit you to cheaply priced stocks or buying stocks in smaller increments than being less cost-effective too. If you can devote more funds to your trading account, you will be able to pursue more opportunities and have the wherewithal to recover from losses.

Calculating a Simple Moving Average

The moving average is a basic tool to invest or use to monitor a stock's behavior over a defined period. The investor simply adds the stock's closing price for a specific period (two weeks, a month, a quarter, etc.) And then divides that number by the number of trading days in that period. A trader will calculate a short-term moving average and a long-term moving average for a stock (actually, you will probably calculate a few more than this to get a better sense of the stock's behavior). A simple moving average can tell you whether a stock is on a rising or declining trend.

An important point for many traders is when the short-term moving average rises above or below the long-term moving average. A short-term moving average that crosses above a long-term moving average often indicates the stock is about to begin an upward trend. The opposite is also true.

One approach to using moving averages compares a specific short-term moving average (50 days) with a specific long-term moving average (200 days). If the 50-day average moves below the 200-day average, you have a bearish signal. This is known as the "Death Cross." If the 50 average moves above the 200-day average, it is a bullish signal and is known as a "Golden Cross." While it would be nice if you could rely solely on such a simple system, remember that relying only on a moving average approach is unreliable. It is better to use this information as another bit of information when making your trading plans.

Choosing a Broker

Once you have decided on your trading allocation, you need to choose a broker or brokerage. There are several online discount brokers available to the novice investor. Many will offer you their own electronic trading program. Do not be surprised to get offers for free trades and a bonus for picking their firm. Free trades and cash bonuses are nice, but make sure you choose a broker you feel comfortable with and one that checks out with your research. The biggest online brokerages include TD Ameritrade, Scott Trade, Fidelity Brokerage, Charles Schwab, Options Express, Merrill Edge, Robin Hood, Loyal3, Options House, E-Option, and others. Some like Robin Hood offers free trades, making their overhead on charging interest on margin accounts and using customer cash to earn interest. Others may offer more services or access to more investment exchanges. One thing you will not get from any of these discount brokerages, though, is personal advice. That is the purview of the traditional broker. In choosing a broker, consider the cost of trades, your comfort level with its trading program, and your ability to access the company's website. Furthermore, investigate what others are saying about the brokerage and whether it handles the investment vehicles you are interested in trading.

Buy Orders, Sell Orders, and Setting a Stop Loss Price

Not every move a trader makes must be executed immediately or at random. You can tell your brokerage you only want to buy or sell a stock when it hits a certain price. The risk, of course, is that the stock may not hit that price while you have money planned for it. You should also plan on setting a "stop-loss price," too. This is a protective move to make sure you do not get badly burned by the stock price moving in the wrong direction. Let us say you bought shares of XYZ Corporation when their price was at $4.50 a share. Based on your research, you expect an upward move by the share price and plan on selling when it reaches $4.75 a share (always have an exit price planned). Then something goes wrong. Bad news upsets the market (in general, or it affects your stock in particular), and your stock price starts dropping instead. Wisely, you left a stop-loss order with your broker, in effect instructing the broker to automatically sell your shares when their price drops to a certain point (perhaps in this example, $4.35) to limit your loss. You should know that stop-loss orders are not foolproof. Your broker still must find someone to buy the shares at that point. In times of crisis, share prices can fall so fast that they blow by the stop loss price and keep going before they finally sell, making your loss bigger than anticipated. While this is not a regular occurrence, unexpected events can cause them. The company selling the Epi-Pen recently saw its valuation drop $3 billion in a short period of time because of news about its price markup. No day trader could have anticipated this news, and even with stop-loss orders, traders who were expecting upward movement in this stock probably lost more than they expected.

Why Day Trading is the Best Way to Make More Money Investing

Day trading is one of the best methods that you can use to make money in the stock market and with other securities as well. Many people are interested in finding a way that will earn them a good profit, and none will find a better option than day trading. Not like some of the other methods that you can use out there, day trading is unique in that you can start earning profits on your very first day. While other traders may end up having to wait a few months too many years to receive a profit, a day trader is able to get into the market and earn a lot of profits in a short amount of time.

CHAPTER 24

Day Trading Do's and Don'ts

The blind approach to day trading is bound to failure. Knowledge on day trading is not a one-day event; it's a lifetime process. Profit making on day trading is a difficult thing to do, especially for starters, because they lack discipline and consistency. Despite the difficulty involved in this venture, some practices can help raise or reduce your profit margins. It is essential for the newcomers in this industry to learn to do's and the don'ts in day trading. Even though there is no guarantee these factors will assure you success in day trading, they will help you avoid trouble to some extent. Unlike other businesses, making the right decisions in day trading has an almost immediate impact since a slight mistake here will cost you dearly. Whereas human emotion is not an essential factor in other business ventures, the success in day trading depends a lot on human emotion. To succeed here, you will be required to mold your thinking or even let go of your old practices. Before getting into the trade market, it is essential to learn the risks involved in it. No amount of knowledge or research can make you guess the details of day trading. The best way of learning day trading tricks is by venturing into it. Whether you are in it or looking to venture into it, here are some of the Do's and the don'ts you should be aware of before taking on the trade.

Trading Do's

Have a Trading Plan

A trading plan is an important factor for both the experienced and the newcomers in the trade market. Your plan should have all the details and aspects of your trading plan. Well, without a well-constructed plan, your venture will be more of gambling than trading. To achieve this effectively, seek knowledge of how to create a good trading plan from experienced stock traders.

Be a Realist

Always be realistic about the kind of profits you expect from the trade market. Do not let greed make you lose your decent gains. Stock markets are tricky and competitive; it is, therefore, better for you to settle for small profits rather than losing out on everything. If you lose a chance, do not beat yourself up; instead, wait for the next opportunity to present itself. A slight gain or profit boosts your confidence in the stock market.

A Strict Routine Is Important

Trading is a lonely endeavor without a boss to tell you what to do or what not to do. Therefore, a strict routine will help put you overcome the challenge of self-discipline. If it is hard for you to follow a strict trading schedule, your career as an independent trader may be far from success. Therefore, self-discipline is an essential character that anyone looking to succeed in the day trade needs to have.

Never Stop Learning

Exhausting knowledge is something no human being can do or has ever done. Even though there are plenty of quick learning systems that have been put out there for new coming traders, learn the art of day trade from scratch. It will give you a better chance to succeed. It is essential that you learn the trade using your interpretation as opposed to learning it from anyone else. Even though different trading strategies that have worked for others can work for you, market conditions differ. By doing so, you will gain more confidence in your trading abilities.

Always Seek Professional Advice

It is essential to follow a given coaching program to succeed in day trading. By doing so, time for exploration will be minimized. Even though experimentation is a good practice in day trading, seek knowledge from experienced traders. Study shows that 90% of traders who lose money during their entry to the trade market do not end their careers well.

Set a Limit on Losses

Day trading is a game where profits and losses are two of the most critical factors. You cannot stay in a business where you are consistently losing your money. Therefore, it is essential for you to set your loss limit. Once you hit your limit, decide whether you want to continue trading or exit the market.

Apply Macro and Micro Idea Generation

A good marketer is quick in identifying opportunities in the market. Day trading is full of competition; therefore, it is important always to beat the biases.

Know the factors to look at when identifying a good opportunity. Macro and micro factors have direct effects on the trading market. Therefore, it is essential to correlate events, drivers, and indicators affecting the day trade market.

Concentrate On Fundamental Analysis

As a stock trader, it is vital that you learn and understand your company well. Factors such as financial information concerning your company should be at your fingertips. Through that, you will ascertain the capability and the health situation of your company. An excellent investment opportunity is that which has the stock price trading below the company's intrinsic value. The fundamental reason why most traders do not rely on fundamental analysis is that most traders spend a few days in the market.

Do the Technical Analysis

This is looking at the current stock price and currency. Analyze these factors to understand the direction the stock marketing may be taking. Also, look at the historical performance and the current stock price. These tools will help you in determining the market direction.

Do Action

Once you understand the market well and you feel confident about your next move, do not hesitate to make a move. Did you know that timing can make or break your chances of making it in the stock market? Regardless of the direction of the market, it is essential for you to set your targets to take your profits as you place your limits.

Always Control Your Emotions

The pace and events of day trading can be so tiring. Its experience can be intense and often draining mentally. A beginner will find this difficult, but once you learn to control your emotions, you will be a successful trader. The two most fundamental traits that are likely to take control of you are greed and fear.

If you are not keen, the two attributes will take control of you, and you are likely to fail. Do not exit too quickly when everything is going your way because of fear. However, do not also let it run too long, in case of a constant downfall, take out your profits before it all dries up.

Do Have a Limit

To maximize your profits, use the golden rule where you apply 'stop losses' and 'soft limits' policy. This means that your previous lowest point or highest point is close to stop losses. In a case where the market is moving to a position you anticipated, then it's your perfect chance to let your position move.

The most important thing here is that you maximize your gains. The number of commodities and stocks should be under control. Every stock is unique in its way. Therefore, with time, you will learn the tricks, and your judgment will improve with experience.

Mistakes Are Allowed

The moment you get into the stock market, failures, and setbacks is the norm of business. A perception that only the newcomers are bound to make mistakes is wrong; even the most experienced stock traders make mistakes. A common mistake made by most day traders is the time of entry or exit in the market. Through these mistakes, you will be able to predict and execute better. As discussed above, seeking knowledge from experienced traders will help minimize your mistakes in the market. Once you get into the market, you will realize that what you experience is different from what you learned from books. The best teacher in any stock market, therefore, is an experience.

Take Note at Every Mistake As You Improve

Losing a trade is not the end of the world in the stock market. Instead, use it as a learning process. Compare what you expected in the market to what you received. Identifying the mistakes you committed and the underlying factors that might have contributed to your failure.

Don'ts in Day Trading

Do Not Take Huge Risks

Avoid greed at all costs when it comes to day trading. Before taking any risk, look at the possibility of losing the money. If you cannot cope with the possibility of losing, then it is not worth investing your money. Always keep in mind that even with the best strategies, the chances of winning investment in a stock market is 50/50. Also, take time to learn the exact ratios that apply in the stock market since they fluctuate from time to time.

Don't Invest With The Intention Of Revenge

As a human being, you are likely to respond to an inevitable failure with a vengeance. Never approach day trade with such a plan since you are likely to fail terribly. In case of a failure, sit back and study to know the cause of your failures. Take time to strategize your next move. I can assure you that getting into the market with an intention of revenge will cause you more harm than good.

Do Not Trade Too Many Times

It is advisable for you to trade once in a while. Only put on an investment when an excellent opportunity presents itself. Proper analysis is important before putting your money on any stock market. However, you can spend as much time as you can analyze the market situation instead of doing the actual trading. Quit spending too much time trading since it is a recipe for disaster.

Do Not Scalp If You Are New In the Market

Scalping is merely taking a short cut by taking on trades that last only for a few seconds. Even though scalping is a good way of making good money, it is precarious. You need a certain level of skill and experience to understand and predict a sudden shift in market movements. In every trade you take, you are required to pay a spread fee notwithstanding the direction taken by any trade. Therefore, experience and knowledge are essential since you have got to achieve pips above the spread cost.

It is important to take notes as you try different strategies. Stock marketplace, experience, and knowledge are the two most important factors.

Do Not Trust Unreliable Sources of Information

Often you receive emails, text messages, or advertisements claiming a good profit on any stocks. Not that you shut down such sources, ensure the information they give is authentic and reliable. As a good trader, be careful not to fall into the hands of brokers who are hungry for commotions. These people can easily land you into bad trade hence losses.

Keep Away From Penny Stocks

As a starter in day trading, penny stocks should be the last thing you should do. Experienced traders will tell you that you should not engage in a trade that is difficult to exit. Also, penny stocks are highly illiquid; hence your chances of hitting huge profits are low.

Do Not Refuse To Take Out Your Profits

It natural for any human being to want more or never get satisfied with whatever they have since everyone is in business to make an extra coin. Moreover, a mistake comes in when you want to make quick money.

As a result, every trader wants to make unimaginable profits with their first trade. However, in the stock market what looks like a huge gain could end up being a huge loss. Well, expecting a huge gain from your trade is not bad. However, it is essential to be realistic about the kind of profits you expect from your investment.

CHAPTER 25

Common Day Trading Myths You Should Be Aware Of

In the digital world we live in, it is never wise to listen to everything that you hear. Some information delivered over the internet is simply meant to blind you from reality. Other facts are there to mislead you. With regards to day trading, there are certain myths that have been there for years now. Some of these myths are just stories meant to deter people from earning profits through this lucrative trading activity. If you are new to trading, it is essential for you to know some of these myths and ways in which you could distinguish them from the truth. This section unveils common myths that you might have heard about day trading.

Day Trading is Similar to Gambling

A huge misconception that most people have in mind about day trading is thinking that this activity is similar to gambling. If you mention this to an experienced investor, the chances are that they might punch you in the face. This is because this myth is far from the truth.

Day trading is not gambling. Gambling is purely based on luck. On the other hand, trading will depend on your rationality and reason. You have to set your emotions aside to ensure that you successfully trade.

Also, you should realize that with day trading, there are no fast profits to expect. Contrarily, this is what most gamblers expect from their gambling activity. You need to get it clear that trading is not similar to gambling. Don't be swayed to believing that this is true.

It Is a Man's Game

You shouldn't be surprised if you come across such a myth. Trading is not something that only men can engage in. Many traders out there are women. Just because you think that there is a huge risk tied to day trading doesn't mean that it's a man's game.

No! In fact, there are traders who often argue that the best investors in day trading are women. So don't make assumptions based on hearsay.

You Will Lose Everything

Honestly, how can you lose everything when you are using the risk management tips which have been discussed in this manual? Most people who fail in day trading enter the market without any plan. Also, a good number of them allow their emotions to get the most out of them. As a result, they end up making decisions that affect their finances terribly. It could also be that they lack disciple to stick to their strategies. Having a strategy is not just enough to guarantee that you limit your losses and grow your profits. You need to walk the talk by implementing the plan.

Stops Are Not Necessary

Some might lead you into believing that the idea of using stops only shows that you are too afraid to take risks. Well, this is also far from the truth. The truth of the matter is that stops are tools that help to save you from losing all your capital in a single mistake that you make. Sometimes it is better to live to fight tomorrow. Hence, you need always to embrace the idea of using stops at all times.

Trading All Day Makes Your Earn More Money

From the different strategies which you will be implementing, you will realize that there are good and bad times to trade. Hence, it is basically unreasonable to think that one could make more money trading all day. Most traders prefer to trade in the morning since they could take advantage of high market volatility during these periods. Others prefer to trade at different times. So, trading all day does not guarantee you make more money. As a matter of fact, you could feasibly take on more losses since there is no guarantee in day trading.

Allowing Your Wins to Run

Day trading newbies will believe that the best way of making a fortune from their good trades is by allowing them to continue running. One thing that should be made clear is that you can only make money once you sell the securities you are trading. Therefore, allowing your wins to run is not safe. Anything can happen when market prices fall drastically. It could be worse when you had stepped outside for a break waiting to make a fortune from your investments. For that reason, you should always acknowledge the importance of taking profits where necessary. Don't be greedy.

Leverage is bad

Some traders who have failed in the industry would argue that leverage is bad. Certainly, if you use leverage for all the wrong reasons, it will have a detrimental effect on your trading business. Essentially, leverage is a tool that helps you purchase more securities without funds. Therefore, if you employ a good strategy to trade, you could end up making a lot, thanks to leverage from your trader.

One Must Have a Huge Bankroll

Clearly, from what has been discussed, there are varying amounts of capital that you will require depending on the market you choose to trade. This means that the myth of having a huge bankroll for you to trade doesn't apply. With as little as $1,000, you can begin online trading. You should, however, be careful when limiting yourself to a certain amount. If you want to earn good returns, you have to be willing to risk.

You Don't Need Any Rules

Another misconception which you will come across is that you don't need to stick to any day trading rules. Picture a scenario where a soccer game is played without any rules. Undeniably, this would be utterly confusing. Day trading is just the same. Without rules, you will only incur losses. Ultimately, you will give up the perception that day trading doesn't work. Therefore, it is vital for you to have rules which help you to maintain your discipline. Knowing that there are several myths that could deter you from knowing the truth about day trading is significant. With some in-depth research into this topic, you will garner a deeper understanding of the possible benefits which could accrue as you trade. Don't believe anything that you hear. Always make sure you do your homework before entering any trading market.

CHAPTER 26

Common Mistakes to Avoid

Focusing on the Fundamentals

When you are first learning the basics of day trading, it is likely that you focused heavily on the fundamentals when it came time to learn which propositions were worthwhile and which were as likely to result in a loss as a gain. As you look to continue honing your skills, however, it is important to understand that the fundamentals don't matter nearly as much as the current trends the market is following. Regardless of the individual facts, if the market is trending downward, then this affects the good picks as well as the bad. The sooner you start seeing the forest for the trees, the sooner you will start making significantly fewer losing trades. Focus exclusively on the signs you see, not on whether or not they line up with what you expect to happen. Remember, trade mechanically whenever possible.

Walking Away from an Open Position

When you were only trading haphazardly, you might have been able to get away with walking away from the action in the midst of an open trade. If you ever hope to get past average, you need to train yourself to stop that habit now. Massive swings in price can happen in an instant once the major players decide to make a move. As such, if you choose to go and make a sandwich at the wrong moment, you could come back to find that those hunger pains just cost you dearly. Day trading is an extremely risky proposition, and you must learn to treat it as such if you ever hope to see any true success in the field.

Following Instead of Learning

When you first start trading regularly, you will most likely want to look for a mentor to show you the ropes when it comes to day trading with a purpose. This is a great idea and one that is highly recommended as long as you use the resources your mentor provides appropriately. This means that while you want to follow what your mentor tells you, you will want to take the time to learn the reasons why certain moves are a good idea, instead of blindly following in your mentor's footsteps. While both can often result in the same amount of financial gain, taking the time to understand the theory, as well as the practice, can ultimately lead you to a more prodigious output in the long run. You should set a limit on the amount of time you plan to spend with the potential mentor and strive your hardest to become self-sufficient by that time, any longer, and you may find the experience limiting instead of helpful.

Limiting Your Options

While focusing primarily on the short-term markets will likely result in the most consistent returns, thinking of yourself exclusively as a day trader is a good way to limit your overall investment potential. While it is perfectly fine to focus on day trading a majority of the time, having an unwillingness to go outside that time frame is only going to prevent you from turning a good trade into a great one.

In addition, if you are currently working with the 5-minute charts, you should consider trying the 30-minute charts instead. This does not increase your risk dramatically when compared to the 1 or 5 minute charts and actually decrease your risk as you are able to more clearly see where trends are actually developing instead of simply reacting to noise. If you feel that you have a real edge while trading in the 1-minute arena, do yourself a favor and try a weightier chart for a few days, you will be surprised at how much of a positive difference it can really make. As you improve your skills, you should be more and more interested in what the overall market trend is and less and less on individual scalping trades. While there is certainly money to be made in these scenarios, the odds are roughly the same as winning the lottery, not nearly what you can hope to see when you simply use a reliable system and choose the right times to use it. The higher probability is the right choice 100 percent of the time.

As you should not limit yourself to a specific time table, limiting yourself to a single market a recipe for lost profits. While it might initially make sense to stick to a single market as it is the one you know the best, if you ever hope to be more than a casual trainer, then you have to eventually step outside your comfort zone and start trading based on available opportunity, regardless of the market in question.

Remember, whatever program you are using is likely connected to all the markets at once, giving you an advantage that many more entrenched traders don't have. This goes along with learning to see the wide trends around the world, regardless of the market they occur in, if you follow a positive trend across multiple markets, there's no reason it can't continue to be profitable. Get the most from your research, follow your opportunities wherever they may happen to present themselves.

Using a Gimmick

Despite the perfunctory cautionary warnings related to the inherent volatile nature of the market, many people still think that they have the magic bullet that will separate them from the pack. Unfortunately, there are no guaranteed systems or gimmicks when it comes to day trading successfully. Don't waste your time looking for one and instead invest that time in finding the most reliable system you can track down. This still won't result in a guaranteed success rate, after all nothing is perfect, but it is guaranteed to be significantly more worthwhile than chasing a day trader fairy tale.

CHAPTER 27

The Rules of Day Trading

Let us turn our focus to some of the rules of day trading that every investor should follow. These rules are not necessarily set in stone. You can decide to take these rules with you on your investing journey or ignore them. However, they should be followed in order to give you the best day trading experience from the very first day of your investing career.

Day Trading is a Serious Business

When some people start day trading, they think that it is meant to be fun and games and do not take the profession seriously. This can be a grave mistake. While you want to enjoy what you are doing, you always want to remember that it is a serious business.

There are some types of investing that are easier to handle as a side career or on the weekends. If this is the type of investing you are looking for, you will not want to look at day trading. This type of investing is meant to be a daily business, and many people look at it as their day job. This means that once you decide to become a day trader officially, you need to treat it as you would any other career. You must get up in the morning, get ready for your day, and make sure you are ready to work by your set time, which could be as early as 7 in the morning.

While you will have some flexibility in your schedule from a regular job, meaning you could set a bit of a later start time in the morning, you will want to make sure to set a schedule you will follow at least Monday through Friday. Even working from home, you will want to make sure to limit distractions. For example, you will not want to focus on day trading and watching television at the same time. Set up an office for yourself and pay attention to your work. Get ready for your job as a day trader like you would for your job at any other office. Do not head into your office in your pajamas. You are more likely to feel like you want to put in 100% effort and succeed if you treat this as a career.

Day Trading Will Not Help You Get Rich Quickly

You should not look at day trading as a get rich quick arrangement. This is a common misconception and one reason people often turn to day trading. If you truly want to become a successful day trader, you will need to make sure you not only have the patience to build your investments, but also realize it takes time.

Day Trader is Harder Than It Looks

Day trading is not as easy as it looks, but this does not mean that you should set this book down and decide not to become a day trader. It just means that you will probably need to spend more time learning about day trading than you initially thought. You want to make sure you are well-versed in the field before you make your first investment. Luckily for you, this is one of the reasons I decided to write this book. I want to give you a comprehensive beginner's guide so you can learn as much as you can about day trading to start your journey in one location. In other words, I have done most of the research for you.

Trading is Different from Investing

One of the biggest rules that you should understand before becoming a day trader is this is different from investing. In order to help you understand the difference, here are a few basic differences between trading and investing:

As an investor, you need to have an idea where the stocks are heading in the future. However, as a day trader, you only need to concern yourself with which stocks will give you the best financial gain on that day. You look more closely at the minutes. In fact, you will not even pay much attention to the hours and will not worry about the next day, week, month, or year.

You Will Not Win Every Trade

It does not matter how experienced you become as a day trader, there will still be days that you lose on a trade. Many people create an image in their mind where they will become so experienced at trading that they will never make a mistake, and they will only gain capital. Every game has its rules and regulations, and day trading is not any different. In case you are new to the game, you must bear in mind the entire standard rules that have been put in place to control the game. That being said, it is important to note that these rules not unbreakable, but they can be instrumental in making decisions in regard to day trading. There are numerous rules of day trading that you have to familiarize yourself with irrespective of whether you specialize in forex, stocks, options, cryptocurrency, or futures. If you fail to abide by some of the rules, it can result in significant losses. In as much as some rules differ depending on where you are located as well as the size of your trade, this will focus on the most important rules. In addition, it will equally discuss the rules that novices can put into practice as they venture into the complicated field of day trading. These rules will also aid the experienced traders to improve their performance in trade, for instance, in the area of risk management.

Rules for Beginners

If you are new in this field, the rules of day trading that have been tackled below can help you harvest commendable profits and avoid incurring significant losses.

Get In, Exit and Escape

One major mistake that beginners make is jumping into the arena without a well thought out game plan. Do not dare to press the "enter" button if you do not have a plan of how to get in and exit. It is understandable that some elements of excitement can set in when you are new in the field. However, it is important to note that if you do not have a formidable plan, you will be thrown out of the game completely. Make use of the rules of risk management as well as stop-losses cut down losses.

Timing

I bet you usually wake up early and bright, ready to face the day ahead in the day trading arena. However, avoiding the first quarter-hour when the market is opened is arguably one of the most crucial trading rules to abide by. Most of the activity that takes place at this time involves market orders or panic trades from the previous night. You should instead use this period to follow up on reversals. The most experienced day traders also avoid the first quarter-hour.

Be Conscious of Margin

Do you remember the days when you started off, and you were looking for capital? It was very easy to fall for a margin.

However, you should keep in mind that it is a loan. A loan that needs to be repaid. In as much as it can greatly revamp your profits, it also has the ability to leave you nursing significant losses. Therefore, it is advisable to learn how to trade accordingly before resorting to the margin.

Demo Accounts

You have a lot to learn and absolutely nothing to lose by taking the initiative to first practice using a demo account. You can nurture your craft with a lot of time and space for trial and error because you are being funded by money that has been simulated. Very many brokers will give you free accounts so that you can practice because they are the best place to learn about strategies, patterns, and charts, as well as the quarter-hour day trading practice.

Learn to Accept the Loss

Virtually all the veteran traders have all achieved what they have achieved because they were willing to lose and learn from it. Losing is just the pathway to get more experience, embrace it. That being said, it is also important to say that cutting down your losses is very important.

Take in Everything

One veteran once said that a great trader is similar to an athlete, he might possess, but he has to train himself on how to use them. Complacency should not be something that great traders relate to because they should always be; I am searching for that edge. This means that they resort to a wide range of resources to boost their knowledge. They can use anything, ranging from videos, books, blogs, and forums.

Do an Evaluation of Tips

It is normal to get excited when you are given a tip that is thought-provoking. Nonetheless, unconfirmed tips from relatively undependable sources can result in significant losses. Jesse Livermore, a trader, said that experience had taught him a tip or a number of tips that will make him more money than what his judgment can. Therefore, ensure that you double-check any information that may affect your decisions as a trader.

Rules of Risk Management

The rules of money management and the risks of day trading are key determinants of how prosperous a trader will be. In as much as you do not have to follow these rules to the letter, they have proven to be indispensable to many.

1% Risk Rule

Here, the idea is to bar you from trading beyond your ability. When you put this technique into use, irrespective of whether a trade subsidy or not, you will always have some reserve I am stacked in the bank to help you correct your balance later on.

The idea is that you should never engage in trade with more than 1% of your total account on one trade. For example, if your account has $50,000, you will only use up to $500 on your trade.

CHAPTER 28

Power Principles to Ensure a Strong Entry into Day Trading Options

I cannot stress this enough - you need to have a plan if you want to be successful at day trading options. You are putting your money on the line every day. I am sure squandering those hard-earned funds is not the plan, but that is exactly what will happen without a proper plan in place.

Power Principle #1 – Ensure Good Money Management

Money is the tool that keeps the engine of the financial industry performing in good working order. It is essential that you learn to manage your money in a way that works for you instead of against you as an options day trader. It is an intricate part of managing your risk and increasing your profit.

Money management is the process whereby monies are allocated for spending, budgeting, saving, investing, and other processes. Money management is a term that any person with a career in the financial industry, and particularly in the options trading industry, is intimately familiar with because this allocation of funds is the difference between a winning options trader and a struggling options trader.

Below you will find tips for managing your money so that you have maximum control of your options day trading career.

Money Management Tips for Options Traders

Define money goals for the short term and the long term so that you can envision what you would like to save, invest, etc. Ensure that these are recorded and easily accessed. Your trading plan will help you define your money goals.

Develop an accounting system. There are a wide range of software that can help with this, but it does not matter which one you use as long as you are able to establish records and easily track the flow of your money.

Use the position sizing to manage your money. Position sizing is the process of determining how much money will be allocated to entering an options position. To do this effectively, allocated a smart percentage of your investment fund toward individual options. For example, it would be unwise to use 50% of your investment fund on one option. That is 50% of your capital that can potentially go down the drain if you make a loss in that position. A good percentage is using no more than 10% of your investment fund toward individual option positions. This percentage allocation will help you get through tough periods, which eventually happen without having all your funds being lost. Never, ever invest money that you cannot afford to lose. Do not let emotion override this principle and cloud your judgment. Spread your risks by diversifying your portfolio. You diversify your portfolio by spreading your wealth by investing in different areas, add to your investments regularly, being aware of commissions at all times, and knowing when to close a position.

Power Principle #2 – Ensure that Risks and Rewards Are Balanced

To ensure that losses are kept to a minimum and that returns are as great as they can be, options day traders should use the risk/reward ratio to determine each and to make adjustments as necessary. The risk/reward ratio is an assessment used to show profit potential in relation to potential losses. This requires knowing the potential risks and profits associated with an options trade. Potential risks are managed by using a stop-loss order. A stop-loss order is a command that allows you to exit a position in an options trade once a certain price threshold has been reached. Profit is targeted using an established plan. Potential profit is calculated by finding the difference between the entry price and the target profit. This is calculated by dividing the expected return on the options investment by the standard deviation. Another way to manage risks and rewards is by diversifying your portfolio. Always spread your money across different assets, financial sectors, and geographies.

Power Principle #3 – Develop a Consistent Monthly Options Trading System

The aim of doing options trading daily is to have an overall winning options trading month. That will not happen if you trade options here and there. You cannot expect to see a huge profit at the end of the month if you only performed 2 or 3 transactions. You need to have a high options trading frequency to up the chances of coming out winning every month. The only way to do that is to develop a system where you perform options trades at least 5 days a week.

To have consistently good months, you need to develop strong daily systems that keep your overall monthly average high. Therefore, creating a daily options trading schedule is key. Here is an example of an efficient options day trading schedule: Perform market analysis. This needs to be done before the markets open in the morning. That means that the options day trader needs to get an early start on the day. This entails checking the news to scan for any major events that might affect the markets that day, checking the economic calendar, and assessing the actions of other day traders to assess volume and competition. Manage your portfolio. The way that an options day trader does this is dependent on the strategies that he or she implements, but overall, it is about assessing positions that you already have or are contemplating for efficient management of entry and exits that day. It also allows for good money management. Enter new positions. After assessing the market and fine tuning your portfolio, the next step is to enter new trades that day. Research and efficient decision-making go into this step. The options trader who has already determined how the market was doing and forecasted for performance that day would have noticed relevant patterns. The key here is to enter trades frequently via a sound strategy. To narrow done which positions you would like to pursue, keep an eye on the bullish, bearish, neutral, and volatile watch lists, and run technical scans. Incorporate learning during the day. Continual learning is something that an options trader needs to pursue, but this does not always have to be in the way of formal classes or courses. You can up your knowledge of options and day trading by following mentors, reading books, listening to podcasts, reading blogs, and watching videos online. Such activities are easy to incorporate into your daily routine. Even just a few minutes of study a day can considerably up your options day trading game in addition to stimulating your mind. Being in regular contact with other options day traders is also a great way of increasing your information well.

Power Principle #4 – Consider a Brokerage Firm That is Right for Your Level of Options Expertise

There are four important factors that you need to consider when choosing a broker, and they are:

- The requirements for opening a cash and margin account.
- The unique services and features that the broker offers.
- The commission fees and other fees charged by the broker.
- The reputation and level of options expertise of the broker.

Let's take a look at these individual components to see how you can use them to power up your options day trading experience.

Broker Cash and Margin Accounts

Every options trader needs to open a cash account and margin account to be able to perform transactions. They are simply tools of the trade. A cash account is one that allows an options day trader to perform transactions via being loaded with cash. Margin account facilitates transactions by allowing that to borrow money against the value of security in his or her account.

Both of these types of accounts require that a minimum amount be deposited. This can be as few as a few thousand dollars to tens of thousands of dollars, depending on the broker of choice. You need to be aware of the requirements when deliberating, which brokerage firm is right for you.

Broker Services and Features

There are different types of services and features available from different brokerage firms. For example, if an options trader would like to have an individual broker assigned to him or her to handle his or her own account personally, then he or she will have to look for a full-service broker. In this instance, there minimum account requirements that need to be met. Also, commission fees and other fees are generally higher with these types of brokerage firms. While the fees are higher, this might be better for a beginner trader to have that full service dedicated to their needs and the learning curve.

On the other hand, if an options trader does not have the capital needed to meet the minimum requirements of a full-service broker or would prefer to be more in charge of his or her own option trades, then there is the choice of going with a discount brokerage firm. The advantage to discount brokerage firms is that they tend to have lower commissions and fees. Most internet brokerage firms are discount brokers.

Other features that you need to consider when choosing a brokerage firm include:

- Whether or not the broker streams real-time quotes.
- The speed of execution for claims.
- The availability of bank wire services.
- The availability of monthly statements.
- How confirmations are done, whether written or electronic.

Commissions and Other Fees

Commission fees are paid when an options trader enters and exits positions. Every brokerage firm has its own commission fees set up. These are typically developed around the level of account activity and account size of the options trader.

Broker Reputation and Options Expertise

You do not want to be scammed out of your money because you chose the wrong brokerage firm. Therefore, it is important that you choose a broker that has an established and long-standing reputation for trading options. You also want to deal with a brokerage firm that has great customer service, that can aid in laying the groundwork for negotiating reduced commissions and allows for flexibility. Options trading is a complex service, and your brokerage firm needs to be able to provide support when you are handling difficult transactions.

A list of reputable online brokerage firms includes:

- E*TRADE
- Options press
- Scottrade
- Ameritrade
- Train Station

Power Principle #5 – Ensure That Exits Are Automated

Even though I have stated that emotions should be set aside when trading options, we are all human, and emotions are bound to come into the equation at some point. Knowing this, it is imperative that systems be developed to minimize the impact of emotions. Having your exits automated is one such step that you can take to ensure that emotions are left out when dealing with options day trading. Using bracket orders facilitates this.

A bracket order is an instruction given when an options trader enters a new position that specifies a target or exit and stop-loss order that aligns with that. This order ensures that a system is set up to record two points – the target for profit and the maximum loss point that will be tolerated before the stop-loss comes into effect. The execution of either order cancels the other.

Glossary

Some common trading terms you will come across while day trading.

A

Ask

Ask price is what a seller offers to a buyer for selling any financial asset.

B

Broker

A broker can be an individual or a firm that acts as an intermediary between traders and exchanges and receives a commission whenever a trade is executed between these two parties.

Bid

In day trading, bid price is what a buyer offers to a seller for purchasing any financial asset.

Bear

Traders who have a negative outlook on markets, and expect the price to fall, are called bears.

Bear Market

In a bear or a bearish market, the price trend continuously declines.

Bull

Traders who have a positive outlook on the market, and expect the price to rise, are nicknamed bulls.

Bull Market

Markets with the rising price pattern are called a Bull market.

C

Cash Market

A market where actual stocks and commodities are traded.

Call Option

Options contracts that are bullish on markets. Popular among day traders.

D

Daily Trading Limit

Exchanges set the maximum price range each day for any contract. The daily trading limit does not mean that it will halt the trading, but only places a limit on the movement of price.

Day Order

An order placed during an intraday session, valid only for that session. It automatically gets canceled when the session closes.

Day Trade

Buying and selling of financial assets on the same day. These assets can be stocks, commodities, forex, or options.

Day Traders

Traders who buy or sell financial assets through a single session and close all their positions before the end of the day. They do not carry forward their positions for the next session.

E

Exchange

A regulated central marketplace where buyers and sellers trade financial assets.

F

Futures

Derivative contracts that cover the buying and selling of financial assets for future delivery. These trades take place on a future exchange.

Futures Contract

These are derivative agreements conducted through a futures exchange. These are legally binding on traders who buy or sell financial instruments for future delivery. Futures contracts have standard regulations based on quantity and delivery time.

G

Good till Canceled (GTC)

Open orders with buying or selling instructions at a specific future price and can remain open till the order is executed.

H

Hedge

The simultaneous buying and selling of a derivative contract of a later date. This is done to balance a loss and profit of open positions in derivatives and cash markets.

Hedger

When companies or individuals, who are holding positions in cash markets, make an opposite trade in the derivatives markets to balance any potential loss, they are called hedgers.

Hedging

The act of balancing any potential risk of loss in cash markets by taking an equal but opposite position in the derivative markets.

I

Initial Margin

To open a new position in derivative markets, such as in futures and options, traders are required to deposit a minimum amount of money in their trading accounts, called initial margin. This is to mitigate any risk of loss because of market volatility. The level of initial margin can increase or decrease according to the market volatility.

L

Last Trading Day

The last trading day is not the last day of the month, but the last trading day of derivative contracts (futures & options). On this trading day, the monthly derivative contracts are settled among traders.

Limit Order

An order, given to buy or sell a financial instrument at a specific price, beyond which the order is not filled. This shows that the buyer or seller will trade only at a specific price.

Liquidity

A characteristic of tradable financial instruments, which shows the ease of trading those. Traders and investors prefer to buy or sell highly liquid assets because these can be easily bought or sold.

Long

A trader is supposed to be 'long' if he has a bullish outlook for the market. A long position is taken when buyers expect the price to rise.

M

Maintenance Margin

This is the minimum value traders must keep in their trading account if they wish to keep a position open. The maintenance margin is usually lower compared to the initial margin.

Margin Call

If a trader's account falls short of the required maintenance margin, they receive a call from the brokerage firm, demanding to deposit the required amount. If a trader does not do so, the brokerage firm liquidates his positions amounting to the same value.

Market Order

An order to buy or sell any financial entity at the latest available price. Traders use this order when they want their trades to be executed quickly.

Market on Close

This order is used to buy or sell financial assets at the end of that trading session. The order price is typically within the closing range of market prices.

O

Offer Price

It shows the willingness of the seller to sell a financial asset at an agreed price. It is also called 'Ask' price.

Open Order

An order which is not executed. It can remain open till the specified price is reached or the order is canceled.

P

Pit

A specific place on the trading floor where traders conduct their buying and selling activities.

Position

A trade that has not been completed the process of both buying and selling. An open trade.

S

Settlement Price

This is the last price paid for any financial entity on a trading day. This is also called the closing price.

Scalp

A day trading method, where speculators trade for small profits. These trades are completed very quickly, within a few minutes. Scalpers trade multiple times through the same day.

Short

When a trader has a negative or bearish outlook on the market, he is said to be short on the market. Also, the selling side of an open derivative contract.

Speculator

Traders who try to anticipate market movements and price changes to earn profits.

Spot

Markets, where immediate delivery and cash payment is handled for financial assets.

Spread

Difference between the bid and ask price.

Stop Order

Also known as the stop-loss order. Traders use this order to limit the risk of loss or book profits at a certain price level.

Stop Limit

Like a stop order, but with a slight variation. Stop order with limit acts as a limit order in buying when the price is at or above the stop price. In selling, it becomes a limit order when the price is trading at or below the stock price.

T

Tick

In trading, the smallest increment in the price of any financial asset. Some scalpers use tick price for trading.

Conclusion

Day traders are technical traders. They rely on chart readings for executing their trades and ignore any other thing like the company's profitability, P/E ratio, debt-to-equity ratio, etc. For a day trader, technical charts are the only tools for making money. Usually, day trader's trade through a single session, and by the close of the day, they also close all open trades, not keeping any position open for the next day. Traders who keep their position open for the next session or overnight are swing traders. A day trader can use many time frames on technical charts for trading. These time frames can range from one minute or lower to 5 minutes; 15 minutes; 30 minutes; 45 minutes; 1 hour; 4 hours; or even weekly and monthly. If you are wondering how day trader can use weekly or monthly charts, know the difference between using various time frames. Day traders decide their trading style by looking at the charts and deciding which time frame will suit them the most. Many day traders can spend hours in front of their computer screens every day. But several day traders trade only part-time, are busy with other jobs or work, and cannot spend much time trading every day. In such situations, these traders can study weekly or monthly charts and decide at what price level they will buy or sell any stock. After deciding that, they wait patiently for that level to arrive and trade only at then. There are many ways to set an alert to know when a price level has reached. The brokerage platforms have SMS facilities to alert their clients about stock prices. Mostly, charting software also has facilities to alert about a stock price level. By trading this way, they save precious time and money, which they can use for pursuing other money-making activities like a regular job or doing some other work. There is another. Highly skilled type of day trading, call scalping. This is also known as micro-trading because the day trader focuses on a small timeframe (such as one minute or a few seconds) and trades for tiny profits. They keep the lot sizes higher so that small profits will also multiply into big money. Since the timeframe is very small, scalpers can trade several times throughout the day, sometimes even 20 to 50 times. But this is a risky type of trading and requires very fine trading skills. Otherwise, one can end up losing all the trading money within a single session. Day trading is also about buying and selling on the same day. But compared to scalping, day traders have a bigger time frame for keeping their positions open. This can range from minutes to hours. The Internet is full of articles that portray glamorous pictures of day trading, making you believe that you can get rich quickly by this trading method. But this trading method requires hard work, knowledge, razor-sharp focus, and high levels of patience, not to mention a big chunk of money to invest in the early stages. If you are day trading, then you should be completely focused, you cannot allow yourself to be distracted by other things. If you can afford to have this kind of discipline and dedication, then you will find day trading suits you. Another name for day trading is intraday trading. This term is a clearer definition of a day trader since it shows that buying and selling are happening within one day. Day traders can develop their style into other types of trading, such as momentum trading, positional trading, swing trading, or long-term trading. All these styles are specialization forms of trading, but usually do not fall under the day trading category.

DAY TRADING STRATEGIES

A detailed beginner's guide with basic and advanced trading strategies to achieve excellent results and become a successful trader with a positive roi in 19 days

Alexander Taylor

Introduction

The popularity of day trading started in the late 1990s, during the Dot-com bubble. For day traders, it was easy to book profits during those days; they did not need any skill. The stock markets used to make such big moments that it became easy to buy and sell internet stocks and make huge profits every day. That was a brief, but a very heady and profitable period for day traders, as they traded tech company stocks and made big money. The tech index NASDAQ was skyrocketing during that time, going up by thousands of points within a few months. Day trading was a booming business because it was a huge wave in the tech ocean, and traders were surfing on the back of that wave. Once the Dot-com bubble burst and markets came back to their normal trading pattern, day trading also became less profitable. However, it remained a lucrative career for many people. With the Dot-com era, online trading also saw rapid expansion. That brought day trading within the reach of common people. It made people realize, day trading was also a profession, like other professions, where one can achieve success by mastering the required knowledge and skill set. In day trading, stocks, or any other financial entity, are bought and sold throughout the day. For doing so they need to know various skills and tools, understand the right time to buy or sell stocks. Big financial companies cropped up overnight and started day trading on behalf of their clients. Banking institutions started opening their securities branches for common people, where they trained their clients to become skilled in trading. Since then, the popularity of day trading as an income-producing vocation has been increasing. If you are looking to become a successful day trader, here are a few things that you will need to learn:

Knowledge about stock markets: As a day trader, have at least the basic knowledge of stock markets. You should know which stocks or companies are popular in the stock market. They will trade with higher volume, and volumes play an important part in day trading. Basic principles of technical analysis: Unlike the fundamental analysis, the technical analysis tells how the price will move in a smaller timeframe, which is essential knowledge for day traders. So, if you are thinking about making day trading your career, this is a skill set that you must have. There are many online courses on technical analysis and chart reading. Various institutions also conduct offline workshops to teach this. You can join any of them and gain a basic knowledge of how to analyze charts and what tools to use for day trading. Money management skills: This goes without saying that you cannot spend an unlimited amount of money in stock trading. Before you start, you must set aside a fixed amount for your trading business and manage that money carefully. You should always know your losses and profits, so you will understand how your trading business is going: successfully or failing miserably. You can find many books online about money management in day trading. Reading a few popular ones will give you a good idea of how to manage your risk and reward ratio.

Learn about trading psychology: Emotions are terrible for day trading, and you must have some knowledge about controlling your emotions during trading. Many successful day traders have written books about trading psychology. It will be a good idea to read a few of them before you trade. No business can survive on emotion, and before you enter the trading arena, you should be able to control your emotions; whether you make profits and losses.

What Differentiates a Day Trader?

Day traders are technical traders. They rely on chart readings for executing their trades and ignore any other thing like the company's profitability, P/E ratio, debt-to-equity ratio, etc. For a day trader, technical charts are the only tools for making money. Usually, day trader's trade through a single session, and by the close of the day, they also close all open trades, not keeping any position open for the next day. Traders who keep their position open for the next session or overnight are swing traders.

A day trader can use many time frames on technical charts for trading. These time frames can range from one minute or lower to 5 minutes; 15 minutes; 30 minutes; 45 minutes; 1 hour; 4 hours; or even weekly and monthly. If you are wondering how day trader can use weekly or monthly charts, know the difference between using various time frames. Day traders decide their trading style by looking at the charts and deciding which time frame will suit them the most. Many day traders can spend hours in front of their computer screens every day. But several day traders trade only part-time, are busy with other jobs or work, and cannot spend much time trading every day. In such situations, these traders can study weekly or monthly charts and decide at what price level they will buy or sell any stock. After deciding that, they wait patiently for that level to arrive and trade only at then. There are many ways to set an alert to know when a price level has reached. The brokerage platforms have SMS facilities to alert their clients about stock prices. Mostly, charting software also has facilities to alert about a stock price level. By trading this way, they save precious time and money, which they can use for pursuing other money-making activities like a regular job or doing some other work.

There is another. Highly skilled type of day trading, call scalping. This is also known as micro-trading because the day trader focuses on a small timeframe (such as one minute or a few seconds) and trades for tiny profits. They keep the lot sizes higher so that small profits will also multiply into big money. Since the timeframe is very small, scalpers can trade several times throughout the day, sometimes even 20 to 50 times. But this is a risky type of trading and requires very fine trading skills. Otherwise, one can end up losing all the trading money within a single session.

Day trading is also about buying and selling on the same day. But compared to scalping, day traders have a bigger time frame for keeping their positions open. This can range from minutes to hours. The Internet is full of articles that portray glamorous pictures of day trading, making you believe that you can get rich quickly by this trading method. But this trading method requires hard work, knowledge, razor-sharp focus, and high levels of patience, not to mention a big chunk of money to invest in the early stages. If you are day trading, then you should be completely focused, you cannot allow yourself to be distracted by other things. If you can afford to have this kind of discipline and dedication, then you will find day trading suits you. Another name for day trading is intraday trading. This term is a clearer definition of a day trader since it shows that buying and selling are happening within one day. Day traders can develop their style into other types of trading, such as momentum trading, positional trading, swing trading, or long-term trading. All these styles are specialization forms of trading but usually do not fall under the day trading category.

CHAPTER 1

How Day Trading Works

There was a time when the only people able to trade in financial markets were those working for trading houses, brokerages, and financial institutions. The rise of the internet, however, made things easier for individual traders to get in on the action. Day Trading, in particular, can be a very profitable career, as long as one goes about it in the right way.

However, it can be quite challenging for new traders, especially those who lack a good strategy. Furthermore, even the most experienced day traders hit rough patches occasionally. As stated earlier, Day Trading is the purchase and sale of an asset within a single trading day. It can happen in any marketplace, but it is more common in the stock and forex markets.

Day traders use short-term trading strategies and a high level of leverage to take advantage of small price movements in highly liquid currencies or stocks. Experienced day traders have their finger on events that lead to short-term price movements, such as the news, corporate earnings, economic statistics, and interest rates, which are subject to market psychology and market expectations.

When the market exceeds or fails to meet those expectations, it causes unexpected, significant moves that can benefit attuned day traders. However, venturing into this line of business is not a decision prospective day trader should take lightly. It is possible for day traders to make a comfortable living trading for a few hours each day.

However, for new traders, this kind of success takes time. Think like several months or more than a year. For most day traders, the first year is quite tough. It is full of numerous wins and losses, which can stretch anyone's nerves to the limit. Therefore, a day trader's first realistic goal should be to hold on to his/her trading capital.

Volatility is the name of the game when it comes to Day Trading. Traders rely on a market or stock's fluctuations to make money. They prefer stocks that bounce around several times a day but do not care about the reason for those price fluctuations. Day traders will also go for stocks with high liquidity, which will allow them to enter and exit positions without affecting the price of the stock.

Day traders might short sell a stock if its price is decreasing or purchase if it is increasing. Actually, they might trade it several times in a day, purchasing it and short-selling it a number of times, based on the changing market sentiment. In spite of the trading strategy used, their wish is for the stock price to move.

Day Trading, however, is tricky for two main reasons. Firstly, day traders often compete with professionals, and secondly, they tend to have psychological biases that complicate the trading process. Professional day traders understand the traps and tricks of this form of trading. In addition, they leverage personal connections, trading data subscriptions, and state-of-the-art technology to succeed. However, they still make losing trades. Some of these professionals are high-frequency traders whose aim is to skim pennies off every trade. The Day Trading field is a crowded playground, which is why professional day traders love the participation of inexperienced traders. Essentially, it helps them make more money. In addition, retail traders tend to hold on to losing trades too long and sell winning trades too early.

Due to the urge to close a profitable trade to make some money, retail investors sort of pick the flowers and water the weeds. In other words, they have a strong aversion to making even a small loss. This tends to tie their hands behind their backs when it comes to purchasing a declining asset. This is due to the fear that it might decline further.

How to Start

People who want to start Day Trading should do several things to put themselves on the right path. Firstly, they need to step back and ask themselves whether this form of trading is really for them. Day Trading is not for the faint of heart. It requires a high level of focus and is not something people should risk their retirement plan to do. Actually, beginners should consider opening a practice account before committing their hard-earned money.

Reputable brokerage firms provide such accounts or stock market simulators to aspiring traders, through which they can make hypothetical trades and see the results.

In addition, aspiring day traders need to have a suitable brokerage account before they begin trading. Some brokers charge high transaction costs, which can erode the gains from winning trades. In addition, good brokers provide research resources that are invaluable to traders.

Aspiring traders who discover that Day Trading is not for them should do what smart investors do, which is engaging in long-term investing in a diversified fund or stock portfolio. They should regularly add more funds to their accounts and let the magic of growth expand their investment portfolio. This may not be as thrilling as Day Trading, but it is better than doing something that will clean out one's savings.

Consider Constraints and Goals

Before investing the time, energy, and effort in learning or creating and then practicing Day Trading, prospective day traders should consider their constraints and goals. For example: Traders need to determine whether they have enough capital to engage in Day Trading. If they lack the capital, they should wait until they have it while they are learning about and practicing different trading strategies.

They should understand that achieving consistent gains takes several months to a year, even when practicing several hours each day. For those who practice intermittently, it will take longer to achieve success; therefore, prospective traders should put in the time and effort required to achieve their goals. Once they start trading, they need to commit to trading for at least two hours a day, depending on their commitments.

Until their trading profits match or surpass their income, new day traders should not quit their day jobs. They also need to determine the ideal time of day to trade based on their other commitments. In addition, they should ensure that their trading strategy fits that time of day. Essentially, their trading strategy needs to fit their life.

People who want to venture into Day Trading need to determine whether they want to do it with the aim of quitting their regular jobs. To get to the point where they can replace their day jobs by Day Trading, prospective traders need to understand that they will probably need to practice and trade for a year or more, depending on their dedication.

Aspiring day traders should consider the factors above before investing their time and money in learning this line of trade.

Choose a Broker

While new traders are practicing and developing their trading strategies, they should set aside some time to choose a good and reputable broker. It may be the same broker they opened a demo or practice account with, or it may be another broker. Actually, choosing the right broker is one of the most important transactions day traders will make because they will entrust the broker with all of their capital.

Capital Needed to Start Day Trading

How much capital people need to start Day Trading depends on the market they trade, where they trade, and the style of trading they wish to do. There is a legal minimum capital requirement set by the stock market to day trade; however, based on the individual trading style, there is also a recommended minimum.

A day trader needs to have enough capital to have the flexibility to make a variety of trades and withstand a losing streak, which will inevitably happen. Traders also need to determine the amount of money they need, which requires them to address risk management. In addition, they should not risk more than 2% of their account on a single trade. Capital is the most important component when it comes to Day Trading. By risking only 1% or 2%, even a long losing streak will keep most of the capital intact. For day traders in the United States, the legal minimum balance needed to day trade stocks is $25,000. Traders whose balance drops below this amount cannot engage in Day Trading until they make a deposit that brings their balance above $25,000.

To have a buffer, U.S. day traders should have at least $30,000 in their trading accounts. Stocks usually move in $0.01 increments and trade in lots of 100 shares; therefore, with at least $30,000 in their accounts, day traders will have some flexibility. Day traders can usually get leverage up to four times the amount of their capital. A trader with $30,000 in his/her account, for example, can trade up to $120,000 worth of stock at any given time. Essentially, the trade price multiplied by the position size can equal more than the trader's account balance.

Day traders can trade fewer volatile stocks, which often require a bigger position size and a smaller stop loss, or stocks that are more volatile, with often require a smaller position size and a larger stop loss. Either way, the total risk on each trade should not be more than 2% of the trading account balance.

CHAPTER 2

Is Day Trading Right For You?

Now that you know a little about what day trading is and how day traders spend their days, you can start to decide if day trading is for you. There are emotional considerations, time commitments, your availability of funds, and of course, the question of if you can work alone. There is also the question of your other responsibilities if you have a backup plan, and what to do when the day trading world is especially difficult to navigate.

Emotions and Temperament

The first things you should consider are the emotions of the job. All jobs come with a certain emotional commitment to perform the job effectively. The effect of having your income tied to the uncontrolled ups and downs of the market can lead to a form of emotional mania and depression. When you are trading the market and have a profitable day, you can be floating in a euphoric-like place where nothing can affect you. Certainly this is a very positive emotion to experience, but as the markets reverse and your trading account shows losses, you could experience the opposite. Your emotions at these times could be just as low as the market is. This unmanaged emotional up and down of the market can become a thrill ride in itself, where you are always looking for the next wild swing of feelings. With this in mind, it is important to learn how to stand back and look at trading as a job and your trading account as your tools.

A mechanic would be excited when a customer brought in a Ferrari to be worked on, but he would engage the tune-up, carburetor adjustment, and engine rebuild with a cool, professional "separateness" apart from his love of Italian cars. He would not abuse his wrenches or gauges in such a way as to diminish their value or harm them in any way. This is a good way to start to think about trading and your trading account.

You will be "working on" very expensive, exotic things while using your precious tools of the trade, i.e., you will trade a particular sector using your precious trading account. This idea of trading as a professional or treating trading like a business is one of the key elements to a successful long-term day trading career. Your emotions can be tied to every trade before it is made. You can learn to use a cool head to plan entry points (the point at which you make your initial purchase of a stock, commodity, or currency), as well as using calm, calculated feelings to execute an exit from a trade to capture profits. There are many stories of day traders feeling elated with their unrealized gains on a trade (unrealized means the profits are still "on paper" and not yet in the day trader's account, as the trade has not been closed out yet) and not able to exit the trade in hopes of more gains.

With these stories the trade turns bad, and the profits are lost. These traders go on to tell stories of how they "should have taken the profits," and "what was I thinking?" If you can learn how to manage your emotions of trading, you can really be on your way to making money on good trading days and keeping your money on bad trading days. In day trading, good emotion management is important for good money management.

Time Commitment

The second thing to consider before you begin your day trading career is if you can make the time commitment. Depending on where you are with your personal overall market knowledge, it can take anywhere from one month to several seasons to get enough general knowledge to begin successfully trading. You have to commit yourself to a somewhat structured study period for a few weeks at the minimum to get acquainted with the markets by reading books and magazines designed for independent day traders, as well as skimming through the daily business newspapers such as The Wall Street Journal and the Financial Times. Often, people want to start placing trades and making profits immediately.

If you would like to be as successful as possible, it would be best if you took your time to learn the markets before committing any amount of money. There are stories of people opening an account online in a matter of minutes, depositing money, and hurrying to trade. There are also stories of day traders placing trades in fresh accounts when they aren't even sure how to use the trade input screens. They then made trades in the wrong direction and for the wrong amount. Such disasters can be avoided by taking your time while opening an account, learning how to operate it, and learning about what you would like to trade.

Trading also takes time once you are in full swing, as it takes time to sit in front of your computer to allow yourself to capture the gains of the market as it moves up and down. While some of the markets can be traded into the evening and overnight, most of them are open only during the mornings and early afternoons. This means that in order to day trade you would have to be available to follow news, read charts, and place trades during these hours. It is possible, however, to trade part-time. Some trades can be made on Sunday afternoons and after work during the week. If you would like to begin your day trading on a part-time basis, then this would be a good option for you. Just allow yourself enough time to learn the market on your shortened schedule.

Risk Tolerance

You should give some thought as to the amount of risk you are willing to take on before you begin a day trading career. Not only is there risk involved with the ups and downs of the market (and the possibility of the ups and downs of your fortunes), but there is the risk that comes from opportunity risk. This opportunity risk comes in the form of the possibility that you might be a day trader who makes a living day trading full-time, passing up the opportunity to earn a steady, relatively risk-free paycheck from working at your regular job.

Day trading by nature involves a certain amount of risk. You are risking money to make a living. It is as simple as that. Some careers offer very little risk of your money while in the process of earning a paycheck. This is not the case with day trading. You might have the opportunity risk of not earning your living working at your safe, steady job. You will need to learn that you will be putting up your capital — your money — in order to make more money. You will be taking on risk in an effort to gain a reward in the form of profits. It is said that risk leads to reward. This means that the more you risk, the greater the potential for reward. The key word here is potential for reward. You should know your risk tolerance before you begin day trading. You should re-evaluate your risk tolerance before every trading day and before every trade. Your goal should be to risk as small an amount as possible while gaining the greatest amount. Each trade should be set up with the knowledge that the trade will go bad. You should calculate ahead of time how much it is possible to lose on the trade, i.e., the worst-case scenario. You should keep in mind that you are trading money — money that might be put to better use than this particular trade. As with emotions, risk can be managed.

There is a whole science to risk management involving trade size, money management, and market knowledge. It is possible to make trades while day trading that is very risky. It is also possible to hedge all of your risk away, where as you are taking measures leading to very little risk during a trade, along with the possibility of gaining very little profit. You, as the day trader, must learn how to use a little math, market knowledge, and common sense to reach a happy, profitable balance between the two.

Available Funds

When work is done, some form of equipment is usually required. If you are a plumber, you might need a van to haul your plumbing equipment. If you are a painter, you might need brushes and ladders. If you are an accountant, you might need computers, adding machines, and tax software. When you are a day trader, your equipment is your trading account. Your trading account is usually filled with a combination of cash and margin. Just as a plumber needs a certain size van, you will need a certain amount of money to day trade with. To begin with, it doesn't have to be much. You can have a lot of fun and learn a lot with as little as $250 in your account.

For example, if you have $250 in your foreign exchange trading account, you could spend the night making small, quick trades while watching TV. It is possible to do this each night and to make enough money to pay for your breakfast doughnut, lunch, and afternoon coffee all on the profits you make from the night before. This can actually be a really good way to get used to the market lingo, software, and the process of order entry, all while building a positive trading experience. It can be a really rewarding experience to first begin to learn how to trade with smaller amounts. It takes a lot of confidence and willpower to place trades big enough to draw a salary against.

If you start small and get used to the feeling of winning a trade you actually planned, you can gradually add to your account and trade larger and larger amounts. You will, however, need to have enough money set aside from your normal household budget to trade with. It is not wise to trade with your rent or car payment money. You should trade with money that is earmarked for your trading account, i.e., it should be money that you are able to lose or at least use for a risky venture such as day trading. After you are up and running as a full-time professional day trader, you will be able to make bi-weekly or monthly withdrawals from your account as a salary draw. Until then, the money you trade with should be allowed to grow with each winning trade.

Can You Work Alone?

After you determine that you can temper your emotion, know your risk tolerance, and have disposable cash to trade with, the question will remain if you can work alone. Day trading is often done alone. Day traders often trade in an office in their homes, away from the business and financial districts of their hometowns or nearby cities. You might find that you miss the interaction of your fellow co-workers, the friendly chats with other commuters on the train going to work, or even the act of walking down to the corner coffee shop with an office friend for a much-needed afternoon break. You will basically be working alone all of the time.

Not only does this mean that you will not have co-workers to speak with about last night's game, you will also not be able to discuss your trading ideas with an office mate. You might even find yourself wishing that you could approach a manager or boss about a trade you are about to make with more than the usual amount of your money involved. In these cases, you might find it comforting to have a superior to help shoulder the burden of your decisions. This is not the case in day trading. All the cash, knowledge, skill, and risk taking are yours, and only yours.

CHAPTER 3

Risk and Account Management

Both account and risk management exercises are activities that coincide as you go through the Day Trading investment cycle. It is very important for you to ensure that you achieve your aims of making significant profits, while at the same time, mitigating losses from the capital in which you invested. Managing your account and the risks associated with Day Trading involves the responsible handling of the available equity in your brokerage account. You can perform account management through further investment in profitable stocks, ingenious trade maneuverability, or exiting from trade deals that stagnate.

On the other hand, your risk management strategies involve responding appropriately to alleviate prospective losses in an uncertain future and limiting the degree of your exposure to financial risks. The following are some of the primary strategies that you can apply to your Day Trading to ensure active risk and account management:

Hire a Stockbroker

As a beginner or a new investor participating in Day Trading, it could turn challenging if you went at it alone. You need advice on the right stock opportunities in which to invest, guidelines on how to handle probable financial risk exposures, and knowledge of technical analysis to keep track of your capital progress.

A qualified and registered stockbroker typically offers these financial services at a commission or flat fee. You need to seek the assistance of such stockbrokers to tap into their experience and expertise in Day Trading. Besides, the chances of attaining your profitable goals increase when you employ the services of a stockbroker.

Account management and risk management are strategies that are innate to a stockbroker, especially when given access to the account. Therefore, you need to open a brokerage account from which all your Day Trading activities take place. Maintaining liquidity in this account is as essential as making the right trade deals. Since you may not interact with the stock market all the time, running the trading account becomes the responsibility of your stockbroker. You need to give him or her freedom to make informed choices on long and short trades, however risky they might seem at first. Trust your broker to understand what he or she is doing with the account and hence the need to hire an honest stockbroker, preferably from a well-known brokerage firm.

In addition, it is usual for your stockbroker to have extensive experience with managing financial risks. Most of the strategies meant to combat potential financial threats such as spreads are somewhat complex to understand, let alone apply them effectively. The same levels of complications and fair sophistication apply to the tools used for technical analyses.

You need to follow these analytic tools to make informed choices based on their data. A stockbroker comes in handy at this point to assist in data interpretation. You also get to learn about the various management strategies of which you had no idea previously. Generally, account and risk management in Day Trading is often all about making the correct decisions from technical analysis.

Develop a Trading Plan

This document is a crucial tool for you as a new investor in Day Trading. If you do not possess such a program, then it may be time to develop one that tailors to your specific trading. Creating a trading plan is an activity that you need to perform with the help of your stockbroker. The broker typically has experience in the Day Trading sector, and so he or she can offer you pointers on the trading opportunities that have the potential of being productive. Based on this vital tip, you can create a comprehensive trading plan that contains an overall objective that is set out. Besides, the program should have tactical or short-term goals set at regular intervals during the cycle. The primary purpose of these operational targets is to enable you to keep track of the progress of your Day Trading activities.

Once you complete the creation of a trading plan, you must stick to its guidelines at all times. You and your broker need to have a chance at Day Trading's success. Hence, you both have to adhere to the rules of the trading plan.

It sets out instructions on how you should react and what measures to take with your capital under different situations. Since the future of Day Trading is often uncertain, it is essential for your plan to cover emergency financial responses. If you diligently adhere to your trading plan, your likelihood of attaining profitable returns eventually increases significantly. In addition, you will have a policy of intervention to potentially risky financial exposures.

Maintain Simplicity

In Day Trading, you may falsely believe that you need to overextend yourself on high-risk investments to make substantial amounts of return. This belief is a dangerous position for you to adopt when getting into Day Trading. Keep in mind the notion that the underlying stocks are often a more volatile type of security than other investments. Fluctuations in the value of the traded stock are frequent and typically occur over a relatively short period.

You must learn how to make small trade deals on the stock from the low-risk end of the trading spectrum. Beware of succumbing to the desire to stick your neck out for the riskier stocks. Greed and emotional influence are the leading causes of such irresponsible trading practices. In the case of a specific trade deal turning awful, you need to exercise restraint from the urge to make illogical trading decisions to try to cover your previous loss.

Besides, keep an eye out for volatile stocks and avoid trading in them as much as possible. If you can, distance yourself and your portfolio from such stocks. Ask your broker to let go of highly fluctuating stocks entirely due to their corresponding high levels of financial risk. All these missteps are easily avoidable when you stick to the simple trading practices laid out in your trading plan.

As a result, you will evade massive losses associated with complicated, high-risk trading that is subject to a high level of emotional influence. Proper and responsible account management demands that you avoid rash decisions that may lead to prospective losses and missing out on potential profits. Risk management also takes care of itself by minimizing your exposure to the high-risk end of the trading spectrum and keeping clear of volatile stocks.

Establish a Stop-Loss Level

To manage the amount of risk to which you are willing to expose your trading portfolio, you can issue orders that reverse potentially hurtful financial positions. A stop-loss order limits the amount of stock price that you can tolerate without taking a significant financial hit.

This order enables your stockbroker to cease all the Day Trading activities immediately. It allows him or her to instantly stop either buying or selling any further stocks based on the unfavorable prices. The order indicates the specific stock price beyond which you cannot risk either purchasing or offloading, respectively, because doing so would expose you to an apparent financial loss.

Getting into an apparent losing situation is an irresponsible practice on your part. Eventually, you will end up with a depleted brokerage account due to the mismanagement of the available capital that you previously had. Stop-loss orders are especially useful when conducting Day Trading on volatile stocks. It is advisable to set the stop-loss order to an amount that is as close as possible to your trading entry point.

Besides, close monitoring of the fluctuating price of your particular stock is a necessity to ensure the successful execution of the order when required. As you can realize, when used in this manner on volatile stocks, such stop-loss orders act as risk management tools that mitigate the financial downside associated with rapidly fluctuating stocks.

Determine Your Position Size

Position sizing involves making decisions on the amount of capital with which you intend to take part in a particular day trade. The size of your investment is directly proportional to the level of risk exposure. A high-volume trade will invariably expose you to more financial risks than a small number of trade deals. Your brokerage account will often get caught in the crosshairs of high-risk transactions and Day Trading practices. Exhaustion of the amount of available capital in your trading account becomes even more likely. Therefore, an early determination of your trading position is essential before engaging in any form of transaction. Your position size divides into an account and trade risk based on the number of shares of stock that you acquire on a particular trade.

For you to minimize any potential financial downfall resulting from the degree of your account risk, you must set a limit on the amount of capital to trade in each deal or transaction. A fixed ratio or small percentage is often the recommended format for this account limit. Maintaining consistency is vital in setting these account restrictions.

Do not keep altering the allocated portion for different trading deals. You should pick one value and apply it to all of your transactions during the Day Trading. A preferable limit should be one percent of your available capital balance or less. Make sure to adhere to the strategy of simplicity by making only small amounts of capital allocations to the low-risk stocks.

In addition to the risks to your trading account, the other financial exposure from position sizing concerns the trade risk. The best strategy to counteract trade risk involves the use of stop-loss orders. The gap between the entry point to your Day Trading and the specific numerical amount set as the limit on the order constitutes your trade risk. As earlier mentioned, this order enables you or your stockbroker to exit from a trade deal upon reaching the set limit of loss. This action results in capping further loss of capital; hence, it contributes to managing financial risk in this manner.

Consequently, you should execute stop-loss orders close to your trading entry point to minimize the likelihood of potential losses spiraling out of control. Be careful not to set it excessively tight to inhibit your ability to carry out any trading. Position sizing is responsible for both account and risk management. The evasive maneuvers described usually contribute towards minimizing risk.

Remember to allow for some flexibility when setting the restriction value on a stop-loss order. You need this leeway to give your stocks a chance to increase in value without encountering an obstacle in the form of the stop-loss order. Such moves enable you to maintain a healthy trading account. As previously mentioned, the number of shares needed for a potentially profitable trade relates to your ideal position size, as shown below.

The ideal number of shares required (Position Size) = Account risk / Trade risk.

Curb Your Emotions

Emotional influence on Day Trading practices can turn counterproductive very fast if you are not careful. The primary emotions to look out for are self-confidence and fear. Excessive confidence can cause you to have a false sense of self-belief in your trading abilities. As a result, you may end up making illogical trading choices and decisions based on your cockiness.

You should understand that you become more prone to develop a false sense of overconfidence whenever you are on a winning streak. The successive trade deals that end up panning out give you an air of self-belief that could be subject to abuse. You get to trust your super abilities in trading and dare to engage in more risky transactions. It is at this point that you will experience a massive financial catastrophe, especially if you overextend yourself financially. Beware of situations that seem too good to be accurate as well.

The other emotional input of concern is the fear of experiencing losses. Overcoming this fear is possible as long as you trade in amounts of money that you can afford to lose in case the transaction goes wrong. In Day Trading, you are bound to have trouble due to market fluctuations, especially when dealing with volatile stocks.

Losses are part and parcel of Day Trading, and you must learn how to bounce back after a particularly nasty run of successive losses. You may experience crippling fear that could render you unable to continue trading if you do not have a coping mechanism for potential losses. In addition, the fear of further losses may discourage you from taking risks resulting in missing potentially profitable opportunities.

Fear is responsible for holding onto a stock position for too long, as well. Instead of selling your shares at a reasonable profit, you may decide to wait on much higher prices leading to a loss if the trend in stock price undergoes a reversal. Another critical factor to consider in risk and account management is the tendency to chase after quick profits to cover for a recent run of bad trade deals and accompanying losses.

You must adhere to your trading plan guidelines and instructions even during such tough times. Do not modify or alter your response and come up with stupid decisions that you usually would not make. Remember that for you to ensure responsible management of your capital, you need to start making choices based on logic. Emotional corruption can hamper your ability to make significant profits and expose you to unnecessary risks.

CHAPTER 4

Psychology Discipline

To succeed in day trading, day traders require many skills, including the ability to analyze a technical chart. But none of the technical skills can replace the importance of a traders' mind-set. Discipline, quick thinking, and emotional control; all these are collectively called the trading psychology and are important factors for succeeding in the day trading business. On the surface, day trading is an easy activity; markets go up and down, and traders buy and sell with the price. Then how come 90% of traders make losses in day trading? The answer lies in trading psychology, where most of the day traders fail. You will see many online courses advertising to teach day trading or technical analysis, but it is unheard of any course that teaching trading psychology to traders.

It is a well-known fact that controlling emotions of fear and greed are two of the most difficult decisions a day trader can take. Even those who prepare a trading plan create trading rules; find it hard to stick to those rules and plans while trading in the stock markets. It is like dieting. When you are not supposed to think of ice cream, all you can do is think of ice cream.

Trading psychology identifies traders' mental and emotional state, which contributes to their success or failure in stock trading or trading any other financial security. Trading psychology is more important in day trading because here, traders must decide quickly and get to trade only for a few hours. It is like being boxed a small timeframe. For example, if a person is given two things to choose from and given a time limit of 3 hours, he will do it in a relaxed way. However, if he is asked to decide within 3 seconds, he will panic. In other words, he will get into an emotional state. Trading psychology involves two aspects; risk-taking and self-discipline. Traders know that emotions like greed and fear should not influence them, but they allow these emotions to affect their trading.

In greed, traders take more risk than is safe for them. Traders may try to place big trades in a hurry to earn profits. If their trades are profitable, they may refuse to exit these trades even if the exit point has come and continue holding positions hoping for bigger profits. This behavior ultimately ends with loss because markets do not keep trending in one direction. Eventually, the market trend changes, and the profitable position turn into a loss-making one. Fear has the opposite effect, but the same result for traders. In the grip of fear, traders may close their position prematurely and then trade again to earn profits. It becomes a vicious cycle of fear and greed, where the trader is afraid to keep the position open longer but keeps trading again in greed. This results in over trading and losses.

Fear and Day Trading

The technical progress has made it possible for news to travel quickly and reach far-flung places. This has created a unique situation for stock markets, where the positive news has a quick and positive reaction in the stock markets, but negative news causes sudden and a steep drop in stock prices as traders become gripped by fear and panic.

In situations leading to greed, traders still pause and think if they are being greedy. But under the influence of fear, traders usually overreact and exit their position quickly. This has a chain-reaction effect on markets. Prices fall, traders sell in fear, prices fall further, traders sell more in fear. This emotion creates bigger ripples in stock markets than greed. Traders exit from their positions fearing that they will lose their profits or make losses. The fear of loss paralyzes novice traders when their positions turn into loss-making. They refuse to exit such positions, hoping for a bounce-back in markets, hoping to turn their losses into profits. What should have been a small loss eventually turns into a big one for them, sometimes even wiping out their all trading capital. A rationally thinking person will quickly exit from such a position. But fear is such strong emotion in day trading that it stops even rational people from making correct decisions.

Rule-Based Trading

To protect yourself from psychological risks in day trading, you must take steps to eliminate this before you start trading. There is only one thing that can protect you from the emotional rollercoaster ride in stock markets, which is a ruled based trading system.

All aspects of your day trading must be governed by a set of rules, which will involve your trading plan and trading strategies. Every day, you must go over these rules and trade accordingly.

Before you trade, sit down and think, why will you start day trading? Are you going to do it for a side income? Are you going to do it for the excitement of stock markets? Or are you going to do it to prove any point to somebody? Many traders fall into the egotistical trap of proving themselves right in trading. They will keep trading against the market and expect the market to change its course instead of changing their trading style.

If you are starting day trading to earn a living, then this thought should always be uppermost in your mind. You cannot allow yourself to be distracted by small profits and losses and trade indiscriminately. This should be your goal, to earn a living, and it should be your aim of day trading every day. Before you trade, remind yourself that you are doing this for a living, not for the short-term excitement. Therefore, if you make any loss, remind yourself that in business, difficulties are a part of the cycle. Try to maintain a neutral mental state whether you make profits and losses. All your trades must be done according to your plans and strategy. Before you take any trade, know the risk-reward ratio, why you enter that trade, and when you will exit the trade with a profit or at a stop loss. Create rules about:

- How many trades will you make every day?
- What will be your loss tolerance limit for a single session?
- What will be your profit target for one session?

Stop trading when any of these three criteria are completed. For example, if you decided to take only two trades in a session, stop trading for that session once you have completed your two trades, whether your trades were profitable. If you have created a threshold of $20 loss for a single station, stop trading if you have reached that loss limit for the session. This will teach you disciplined trading, and you will consciously try to keep your losses to a minimum.

A similar rule should be applied for profit booking. Stop trading for the day if you have reached the profit target. This profit target could be in terms of a fixed amount or the number of successful trades. For example, some traders stop trading once they have made a profitable trade. This is one of the best greed management techniques. If you have made a profit in stock trading, even if it is tiny, just pocket it and run away from markets. Otherwise, greed will take over, and you will over-trade, trying to make more profit, and end up with losses.

Why Trading Psychology is Important

Most people fail in day trading because they start at the wrong end. They start by learning trading skills first and then move on to money and risk management techniques, and the last stop is to learn, superficially, about trading psychology.

In fact, the right sequence of learning day trading should be learning the trading psychology first and then money and risk management techniques, and the last part should constitute learning the trading skills. It is very easy to learn technical analysis and how to use technical indicators. But it is very difficult to control one's emotions like fear and greed while trading or astutely manage money while day trading.

If you look at people in different fields, you will find the mind-set is the main difference between those who reach the pinnacle of their chosen career and those who remain mediocre. Be it business, science, technology, sports, or any other creative pursuit, people who train their minds for success are the ones who win the race. In intraday trading also, hundreds and thousands of day traders use the same methods of technical analysis, however, only a few of them succeed in making profitable trade, and others go home with losses. It is the trading psychology that makes the difference between successful traders and those who failed. Every trader, who tries to learn day trading, knows that there are certain rules to be followed, and still the majority of them fail to do so find; therefore, if you want to succeed in day trading, you must pay attention to how you react to markets. Stock trading is nothing but watching the price rise and fall and trading off with the trend. But still, traders fail to follow this simple method of trading. Day trading happens 90% in the mind of a day trader, and only 10% in what happens in markets. A day trader takes a decision based on what he or she thinks is going to happen in stock markets and not on what is happening. This is the biggest mistake made by day traders, and the reason is their emotions.

To overcome this psychological hurdle, day traders must learn how to manage their trades without emotions. They can do so only with the help of technology and self-discipline. If they do not have self-control or do not follow a disciplined trading plan, they cannot make profits in stock markets.

CHAPTER 5

Why Most Day Traders Lose

With the numerous benefits that can be gained from day trading, it begs to question why most day traders fail. If the activity is as lucrative as it sounds, why do most of these traders fail? Understanding why traders fail gives you some insight into the common mistakes that traders fail, which makes them lose money. Accordingly, you will be better placed to trade wisely by avoiding common pitfalls in such trading. Here is a look at some of the reasons why traders fail.

Relying On Random

Let's assume we have a new trader in the market called John. John has some knowledge about the market just because he always watches the news more so on stock markets. However, John has never traded. Since he has some basic market knowledge, he feels that he can try out day trading. To this point, John has never sat down to write down some strategies which he could implement to trade on stocks. So, he opens up an account and purchases 400 shares without thinking. Fortunately, to his advantage, the stocks rise during his lunch hour period. After lunch, John decides to sell off his shares. His first sale earns him a $100 profit. His second attempt also earns him $100. Now, John has the feeling that indeed he is a good trader. In just a day, he has managed to earn $200. After a careful analysis of John's situation, an experienced trader would argue that John's day trading activity could easily be short-lived.

In John's example, he faces the risk of losing money if he gains the perception that his strategies are working. Interestingly, he might be tempted to increase his shares because he knows that he will earn a profit. It is important to understand that John's strategies are untested. Therefore, there is no guarantee that his trading activity could earn him returns over the long-run.

The danger that John faces here is that he believes in his formulated and untested strategies. Consequently, he might overlook recommended trading techniques that would have helped him avoid common mistakes. In the end, when he loses money, he will be disappointed arguing that day trading is not lucrative. This is the trap that most newbies enter into. Their first luck in online trading blinds them from realizing the need for constant learning in this activity.

Abandoning Strategy

Assuming that John learned his mistakes and corrected them in his future trades. Now, he relies on a strategy that helps him find success in day trading for about a year or two. At this point, John feels that he has found the right strategy that works for him. However, there is another problem that ensues. John realizes that his plan has led him to losses for more than six times now. He is in a huge dilemma, wondering what to do since he cannot continue making losses.

So, what does John do; he decides to adopt another strategy. Regardless of the success that he enjoyed using his previous plan, John now feels that it is time to switch to another strategy. Ideally, this is a new and untested strategy that he will be adopting. One thing that you should realize here is that John is going for a strategy that is not tested. He is abandoning a strategy that has worked for about two years now. The risk here is that John could find himself where he started. He could incur losses because of his abandoning strategy. Here, you should learn that randomness can lead to profits and that it can also drive a trader to incur losses. To ensure that such randomness is avoided, it is recommended for a trader to have a solid plan that they stick to. This is a plan that will define how they trade. A good plan ought to lay their entry and exit strategies. Also, the plan should stipulate the money management technique, which will help a trader use their money wisely.

Lack of Knowledge

A major reason why most traders fail is their lack of market knowledge. By failing to educate themselves about stock markets, they find themselves in a ditch. You cannot count yourself as a trader just because you buy and sell shares. Certainly not! You have to learn how to analyze the securities which you will be buying. Your broker might not give you all the information that you need to become a good trader. So, don't assume that reading magazines and newspapers will get you the market info that you need.

A prudent trader knows the significance of working with a profitable trading plan. They understand why it is imperative for them to analyze stocks effectively to determine whether they are buying profitable stocks or not. More importantly, a wise trader should know of ideal strategies that they will employ to manage their finances shrewdly. Don't believe day trading myths circulating over the internet. Do your homework by researching and educating yourself about stock markets.

Unfitting Mindset

We are human beings with emotions. However, being overly emotional can be dangerous in an uncertain trading environment. To become a successful trader, you need to work on your emotions. The topic of trading psychology, which will be later discussed, will educate you on the importance of developing the right mindset in online trading. Dealing with your emotions will have a huge impact on whether you close your day with losses or profits. Hence, it is very important that you keep your emotions in check.

Rigidity to Market Changes

One thing that you can be sure of is that trading markets will always change. There is no guarantee that a particular market will rise steadily throughout the buying and selling period. If this were the case, then everybody would have been traders. The best traders will always adjust to market changes. They will know when to buy and when to sell. Before jumping to purchase a particular stock, it is advisable to conduct scenario analysis. Afterward, you should devise strategic moves that will ensure that you make profits while lowering the chances of incurring losses.

Learning from Mistakes

You often hear people say that failing is part of succeeding. Well, this is true. Unfortunately, it stands as one of the main reasons why day traders fail. Learning by making mistakes here and there will cost a day trader a lot of money. Engaging in trial and error is what discourages most traders from any attempt to put their money in stocks. Some even end up arguing that day trading is a form of gambling. To circumvent this problem, one should learn from other experienced traders. This way, you will reduce the chances of making losses. Equally, you will learn the tricks which can be utilized to take advantage of market volatility. Therefore, do not choose to learn how to trade through trial and error. You will only lose a lot of money beyond your expectations.

Unrealistic Expectations

Take a breather! Indeed, day trading is a profitable activity that can earn you a living. Nonetheless, this should not blind you from realizing that losses can also be made. You cannot get rich overnight with day trading. However, it is a slow and gradual process that will see your money multiply. Traders fail because they try to force returns to cover for the huge losses that they have made. Having the right plan and sticking to it will help you in toning down your expectations. Deep inside, you should have it in mind that you are trading for a living. Therefore, patience is important.

Poor Money Management

The effort that you put into finding a working strategy is the same effort that you should put in managing your finances. A trader should stick to a plan that defines the amount of money that they will risk on a regular basis. The money risked should give the trader the satisfaction that it is worth the rewards they anticipate. Having enough funds set aside for the trading activity should not give one the impression that they need to splash their money on stocks. As a matter of fact, the more you have as capital, the more you should preserve.

The bottom line is that traders can deal with their possibilities of failing by sticking to a plan. Sticking to a trading plan will mean that you are disciplined enough to know the exact amount of money you will risk. It also implies that you will employ a buying and selling strategy that works for you. Most importantly, you will also give yourself time to learn what there is to learn about day trading.

CHAPTER 6

Characteristics of Winning Traders

While it can be fairly easy to make a few trades every day, if you are interested in taking your day trading to the next level, then there are a number of traits and characteristics you should strive to cultivate in your everyday life. While there is no one mold that all successful day traders fit into, they do tend to commonly embody a number of interesting characteristics in their own way.

Early riser: While trading in New York doesn't begin until 9:30 am, the most successful traders use the early morning hours to catch up on the international markets, so they have a broader idea of what the day is likely to bring. Having a strong macro view is crucial to taking advantage of micro changes. The Western economy is strongly influenced by global markets, and understanding one makes it easier to predict the other.

Dedicated: Common wisdom says that in order to truly master something complex, such as day trading, you need to put in 10,000 hours of practice time. This equates to 8 hours a day for roughly 3.5 years. This is to say that becoming an expert day trader is more akin to a marathon, not a race. While it is true that some people, such as those discussed in chapter 3, were able to see huge windfalls in short periods of time, they are without a doubt the exception, not the rule, and most people need countless hours of experience to understand when the perfect time to reap the greatest rewards really is.

Lifelong learner: The best day traders aren't the ones that are confident they've heard and seen it all before, they are the ones that understand that new and improved techniques are always coming along. Being constantly on the lookout for the newest advances in theory and strategy is what separates the true pros from the rank and file amateurs who will never be able to trade full time. The markets change every single day, which means that even analysis from 7 days ago can be hopelessly out of date. Don't curtail your earnings potential, make the choice to maximize it every day; remember, if you want to earn, you have to learn.

Intuitive: A great trader doesn't worry about what everyone else is thinking or doing, they do their own research and trust themselves when it comes to making trades outside of the mainstream. The best wins come from going against the mainstream and is what separates average earners from great ones. Understanding the difference between hype in the business world and cold hard facts will allow you to successfully discover good trades and avoid the sheep who are fond of listening to bad advice. If you are afraid of trusting your intuition, study more, and start with smaller trades, early success will bolster your confidence, and your future results, trust in yourself, and success should follow.

Always prepared: The most successful traders are those who have a precise plan and know to stick to it without fail. This doesn't mean blindly following a course of action that does not appear to be playing out as you expected, but it does mean that you prepare every day and know exactly what specifics you are looking for in the trades you pursue.

It is important to follow through on this plan as it can be easy for traders, even experts, to let their emotions influence trades that are then made without the benefit of prior planning. Learning to manage your emotions will be extremely helpful in maximizing your trading results each and every day.

Self-aware: Great traders are as familiar with themselves as they are with their preferred markets. This allows them to capitalize on their strengths and, perhaps more importantly, be aware of their weaknesses and how to ensure their importance is minimized during day-to-day trading. Understanding your weaknesses will help you to control risk to the greatest degree possible, which will ultimately lead to great profits every single time.

Decisive: The most effective traders are the ones that not only can do their research and plan ahead but have the ability to pull the trigger when the time is right. The market can change in a matter of seconds, and a major gain can be won or lost by the ability to strike at the exact moment the iron is as hot as it is ever going to get. This isn't about gut feelings or luck, it is about reading new situations and knowing the best way to react to them in the moment.

Self-motivated: The best traders are those that aren't motivated by a boss looking over their shoulder or even bills piling up in the mail; they are the ones who are motivated by a personal drive for success in whatever they endeavor to perform. Only by harnessing your personal drive to succeed will you be able to dedicate yourself to preparing to trade and trading properly with the discipline that it requires in order to go from good to great.

Financially secure: The best day traders know their limits and never make any trades they can't afford to lose. No trader can be right all of the time, sometimes loses happen. This fact alone means that you must have a stable enough financial situation that any one trade won't send you on a tilt and ultimately lead to more poor trades and a lost bankroll. Keep an emotional distance between the trades and yourself is crucial to always listen to reason and leaving emotion out of the equation entirely.

Measured: Expert traders know that there is nothing worse you can do than make split-second decisions without taking the time to think them through completely. Your goal should always be to make proactive decisions, never reactive ones. Understand all the possible outcomes of a given situation and know what you will do if each becomes a reality.

CHAPTER 7

Choosing What to Trade?

Stocks are perhaps the most common investment tool in the market. They are suitable for both beginners and professional investors. Let's figure out how to choose and buy suitable stocks.

Choose the Scope of the Company

The choice of the industry should be based on your interests and experience. For example, if you get the hang of interiors, pay attention to manufacturers of furniture and household goods. If you are into computer games - take a closer look at game developers and video card manufacturers. It is better to choose not one industry, but several, as you will need to distribute your investments. You will be better versed in companies that affect your personal or professional interests.

Explore Companies in the Chosen Field

Compare companies of the same industry: maybe right now dark horses demonstrate better results than recognized industry leaders. To do this, go to the website of the exchange you are interested in (MICEX, NYSE, or NASDAQ) and get acquainted with the list of traded assets.

Of course, to become a shareholder of a large company - this sounds good and more reliable. However, it is also impossible to deprive the attention of second-tier players, since their shares can rise at any time. Such ups can make shareholders wealthy. Make a list of companies that you find interesting. Each of them needs to be thoroughly studied.

Look Through the Company Profile

Work through all the available information about the company. How has it developed? How was it transformed? How did important events in the company's life in the past affect the movement of its shares? What are the plans for the future? Quite often, the vector of the company's movement in the past determines its future development. Pay special attention to profit and loss statements.

Pay attention not only to achievements but also to serious failures. It is important to understand how the company copes with difficulties and what happens to its shares at this moment. This will help assess your risks at the start. Do not forget about liquidity: the company and what it produces should be liquid, both now and in the future.

Learn Company News

The company's plans directly affect your income from investing in it. If the company plans to release a new product, if it has made a discovery, it can play into your hands. Everything brand new generates interest and, therefore, increases the likelihood of rising stock prices, although it is not a guarantee of quick returns. For example, a change of leadership can both positively and negatively affect the business of the company, and hence its value. Do not also think that companies always grow rapidly. Shares of many heavyweight corporations are growing slowly but confidently.

Explore Company and Industry Dynamics

Evaluate the dynamics of the company and the industry where it operates over the past few years. If the growth rate is falling or even worse negative, then looking in this direction doesn't worth it. Buying stocks after a period of sharp growth is like jumping into the last car of a running train.

The dynamics of such enterprises is generally healthier and more predictable, and predictability always reduces risks. Based on financial reports, predict its future and evaluate whether you are ready to be a shareholder of the company with such a future. Probable negative events should also not be forgotten, this will help to assess the risks soberly and your attitude to them.

Read Analytics

If you have not skipped the previous points, then you have already conducted some analysis. Now you can address the opinion of professionals and see what they think about the prospects of the companies you have chosen. Large investment banks regularly publish their own recommendations. The opinions of prominent experts and professional investors can be found on the Internet (including on their personal pages on social networks). Of course, analysts are not psychics, and they cannot predict the exact scenario. However, a professional view from the outside can open your eyes to the missing details. In addition, professional analysts often possess insider information. You can study analytics in previous years. This will help assess whether past forecasts have come true.

Build a Stock Portfolio

Some of the companies from the initial list are eliminated during the detailed review of the previous paragraphs. Some of them are in economic decline, some are already at the peak of their prosperity, etc. As a result, you will have a list of one, two, or more market players.

The stocks of a company having bigger prospects according to analysis carried out before should be bought. It is not necessary to dwell on one company from a field of activity. You can invest in the shares of two or three competitive enterprises and only then monitor whose performance will be better.

Try to have the stocks of 10-12 companies in your portfolio so that a possible drop in one asset is offset by others. As we mentioned earlier, you need to invest in different areas of activity. Investing in stocks and making profit out of them is not complicated, and do not be confused by the multi-stage process. In this case, multi-stage does not likely complicate the process, but it facilitates and improves the result. A rational approach takes time and your attention: warned means armed and with stocks. The main thing to remember is that you spend your time and effort on minimizing risks and generating income, and this stimulates.

CHAPTER 8

Do-It-Yourself Risks

Risks are part of stock investing or any investment. You cannot avoid these risks, no matter how knowledgeable you are. The only way to deal with these risks is by minimizing your exposure to them. Before you can develop strategies for minimizing your risks, understand them first. You need to know the different types of risks and what factors affect a risk to become a threat to your chances of earning gain.

The Different Kinds of Risks

Risk is losing part or all of the value of the investment. Some risks are directly related, while other risks indirectly affect stock investment and your purchasing power. Risks are inherent to any investment, so do not let these risks hinder you from investing your money in stocks.

Financial Risk

Financial risk is a concern even for established companies. This risk refers to the inability of a company to pay its investors. Remember, a company that declares insolvency pays first the creditors before paying shareholders and investors when the company is in the process of liquidation. More often, shareholders might not recover their investment value when the company declares bankruptcy.

Risk Related to Interest Rate

It is used to show the effect of a hike in interest rate after buying an investment. Oftentimes, this type of risk is directly related to investments that generate liability or investments that require payment of interest payout to investors. An example of liability-generating investment is bonds. Interest rate risk affects the financial condition of a company, especially for companies that rely on debt instruments to raise capitalization.

This risk affects stock investment. When a company issues bonds and other debts instruments and suffers from sudden increased interest rates, chances are their capacity to pay might be affected. Higher rates mean higher payment of interest. This means the company pays first the creditors before they could pay their investors. As a result, the value of stocks may decrease, or dividend payout may be postponed.

With a higher interest rate, stock investors tend to sell their shares, especially in the electric and financial industries. These investors may decide to invest in debt instruments instead of stock investment. To minimize interest risks, expert investors diversify their portfolio by investing in money market instruments that perform and still earn even during high-interest rates.

Market Risk

Market risk refers to the demand and supply movement in the market. When a type of share becomes in demand and its supply becomes limited its price increases. Conversely, when no investor wants a particular stock, its price decreases. Price and value of stocks increase or decrease depending on market demand. This is the reason stock is a risky investment in a short-term period. The stock market is unpredictable because of the millions of investors buying and selling stocks in a day. One minute, a stock's price increase. The next minute, the same stock's price crashes because no one decided to buy it. Aside from the demand, other factors may have affected the rise and fall of a stock's price, such as the financial condition of the issuing company, political and governmental situation, and inflation.

The point, do not invest your money in stocks if you do not know what you are dealing with. Ignorance can bring you massive losses.

Inflation Risk

Inflation risk refers to the decrease in purchasing power an investor has. You can't buy the same item at the same price and the same quantity as compared years ago. For example, you could buy 10 candies with a dollar five years ago. Today, you can still buy the same brand of candies with a dollar, but the quantity decreases. Perhaps today, you can only buy 5 or lesser.

How does this risk affect your stock investing approach? Suppose you buy a stock that yields 4% payout, and you invest the rest of your money in the bank that earns 4% interest. In effect, you are earning. Your first investment might be at risk with the increases in the interest rate and financial condition of the issuing company. Your second investment is safe and is not at risk with a higher interest rate. Since you have invested the rest in a bank, your money earns whatever interest that the bank uses. However, the inflation rate is around 5%. Your earnings are below the inflation rate. This means your investment in the bank is losing money.

Tax Risk

Tax risk is the decrease in what you can get. The purpose of stock investing is to build wealth. When there is wealth, a tax is present. You need to pay a portion of the tax obligations. This means you have to be knowledgeable on tax so that you can avoid paying more taxes than you earn.

Political Risk

Sometimes, when the government issues new rules and regulations, some companies are affected. Others may even become bankrupt because of a particular law, while some companies may profit from this same law. In a toxic and unfair political environment, companies may die or live. Thus, it does not hurt if you have a basic knowledge of how politics work in countries because political and governmental conflicts can affect a company's financial condition. In some countries, companies might become political targets.

Personal and Emotional Risk

Personal risk refers to your incapacity to increase your investment when an opportunity arises. This may also refer to your inability to maintain an investment because you need cash immediately. The first scenario arises when you have enough money to invest but are afraid to buy more. Alternatively, it could be that you do not have the money because you have spent it in an emergency. The second scenario arises when you do not have an emergency fund to pay for your emergencies. The first thing you need to do is ensuring that you have an emergency fund when you begin stock investing. If you skip that step, you are more likely to experience these scenarios sooner or later. Emotional risk refers to your inability to control emotions when you decide to buy or sell a stock investment. Most of the time, many investors let their emotions control their rational thinking. In stock investing, you are either greedy for more or be afraid to lose money. These are extreme emotions that you should learn to control when investing in stocks.

How to Minimize Risk

Stock market investing may involve so many risks, but minimizing such risks is easy and attainable. Don't let these risks hinder you from investing. Risks should not be your major criterion in deciding whether to invest or not.

Stop, Gather and Learn

Before investing your money in stocks, gather as much information as you can manage. Learn everything you need to know about stocks investing. The more information you know, the greater is your chance of making and choosing winning stocks. If it takes you years to understand even the basic language of stock investing, so be it. The important thing is minimizing the risks of losing money into a venture you know nothing about. Indeed, you might argue that the best teacher is experienced, but it does not mean you have to face a battle without preparing for it. If you think you are not ready, then don't start buying stocks even with the insistence of a financial adviser. Financial advisers may be experts in their field, but they are not the ones who will suffer the loss.

Remember the Basics

Whenever you feel strong enough to fight, always remember the basics. Make sure to keep yourself grounded and always go back to the basics of stock investing. These basic concepts can help you reach your goals without losing a large amount of money.

Diversification

This refers to a mix-and-match approach to stock investing. You don't concentrate on one investment. Your portfolio consists of short-term, intermediate, and long-term investments. The percentage depends on your personal style of investment. If you are an aggressive investor, the majority of your investment money is placed on short-term and intermediate investments. A lesser percentage is on long-term investment. If you are a conservative investor, most likely, a huge chunk of your investment money is placed on long-term investment. Only a small percentage is on short-term and intermediate.

Another way of diversifying is by investing your money in different financial instruments. Do not concentrate your investment money on stocks alone since the stock market is a volatile market.

CHAPTER 9

Opening Range Breakout

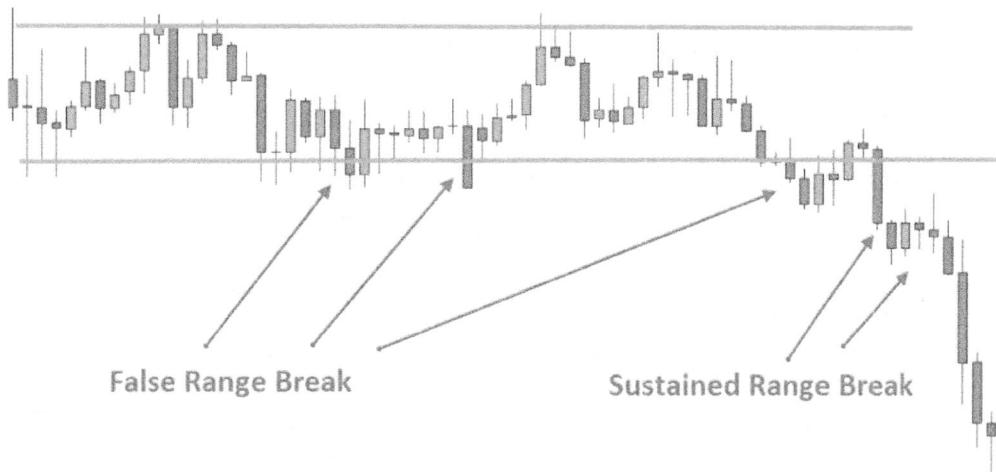

False Range Break   Sustained Range Break

N ow we will take a look at another trading strategy that is pretty well known, and it is called the opening range breakout, or ORB, strategy. This is a good strategy because it will signal an entry point, but it does not tell you the profit target. You will be able to pick out the best target for the profit based on some of the other strategies that we have talked about in this guidebook or by looking at some of the charts that are available.

The ORB will be used as an entry signal only, but to finish the trade properly, you need to make sure that you also define the stop loss exit, and the proper entry as well.

Right when the markets open, you will notice that the Stocks in Play will experience a very violent price action because of all the buy and sell orders that flood into the market right away in the morning. This trading will usually show up during the five minutes of the market day because o the loss or the profit that occurred for people who held their positions overnight. There are also going to be a lot of new traders and investors who want to get into the market and will want to do so right away in the morning.

There are some investors who will see that their position went down during the night, and they will panic, so they will sell off their stocks. There are also a lot of new investors who will see that a stock is low in price and will jump in right in the morning before the price goes up. Both of these will determine the price of the stocks and how they will do during the day.

As an investor, you will want to give this opening range a minimum of five minutes before you choose to invest. It is hard to figure out whether the buyers or the sellers will win out in the market when there is so much change going on in the market. It is best to wait at least five minutes before you make any trades with this strategy, but there are some traders who will wait up to an hour so that they have a better chance at identifying the balance of power that is available between the sellers and buyers.

Once the opening is done, the trader can work on their trade plan based on the thirty or sixty-minute breakout. There are some that will do even smaller time frames than this, such as a fifteen-minute breakout. The longer the time frame that you do with this, the less volatility that you will be able to find in the market, and it will change what you are doing.

Just like with many of the setups that you are working with, this ORB strategy will work the best with either large or mid-cap stocks, ones that are not going to have big price swings throughout the day. You do not want to go with this strategy when you have low float stocks. If possible, you will want to pick out a stock that will be able to trade inside a range that is smaller than the ATR, or the Average True Range, of this stock. You will be able to figure out this number by looking at the highs and lows of your candlesticks.

To work with the Opening Range Breakout Strategy, you will want to use the following steps:

After you have created your watch list early in the morning, it is time to monitor the stocks for at least the first five minutes of the market opening. You should identify their price action and the opening range. Look to see how many of the shares are being traded at that time and determine if the stock is going up or down. Are there a lot of orders that are going through here, or is there a high volume that has just a few large orders with it? It is important to look at the numbers of orders that are being sent in because this really shows how liquid the stock is.

You need to make sure that you can determine what the ATR is. In this step, you want to make sure that the opening range is much smaller than the ATR, so keep that number on hand.

After the first five minutes of the market are done, you may notice that the stock may still be traded in that opening range for a little bit longer. However, if you notice that the stock starts to break out of the opening range, it is time to enter into the trade. You will want to enter into the trade going in the direction of the breakout. You will want to go long for a breakout that is upward, and you will want to go short for a move that is downward.

You will want to make the stop loss below the VWAP for your long position and then have a break above the VWAP for a short position. You will want to make sure that you pick out a good profit target as well. You will first need to take a look at the daily levels throughout the day and then identify it in the pre-market. You can also look at the close from the previous day and the moving averages that are on your daily chart.

If there isn't a good technical level for your profit target and your exit, you will want to look for some signs of weakness in the stock if you are long. If you are doing a short position, you will want to exit when there is a strength in the stock. For example, if the price reaches a new low, this means that it is reaching a weakness, and if you are long, you will want to look at selling your stock. If you take a short position and the stock gets to a new high, then it is a good sign o a strength, and you may want to cover that position to help you out.

This is an example of working with five minutes ORB, but it is possible to use the same ideas when you are working with fifteen or thirty-minute opening range breakouts, depending on what you want to do with the market.

This is a great option to go with that will ensure that you are not going to be fooled by the changes that occur right at the beginning of the market, but you can still get a good look at how the market will go for the day. Make sure that with the ORB, you are not supposed to trade during the first five minutes or more in the morning because the whole market is just too volatile, but you can still use this information to help you get started on the right foot and can give you a way to make a lot of money with your trading strategy.

CHAPTER 10

Tools and Platforms

The main tools you'll need for day trading are an online broker and an order execution platform. It goes without saying that you'll also need a very good internet connection and a computer on which to execute your trades on the platform. And if you're not part of a day trading community yet, you'll also need a stock scanner.

The Broker

You'll need a very good broker, who'll be your access to the securities market you plan to day trade in, e.g., the stock market. Take note that your broker can't just be good: it has to be very good. Why?

Since you can't access the stock market or other securities markets directly, you'll need to go through a broker. Even if you choose your SIPs correctly, you can still lose money in your trades if your broker's slow to execute your order at your target price or if their system suffers from frequent glitches.

It can be challenging to choose a broker because there are many of them out there. Some offer top service but are expensive while some charge very low fees, but their service is crappy. Worse, some are both expensive and crappy! To help you narrow down your choices to quality brokers, I'll provide a list of really good ones at the end of this book in the appendix.

Minimum Equity Requirement

The United States Securities and Exchange Commission (SEC) and the Financial Industry Regulatory Authority (FINRA) enforce rules on people who day trade. They use the term Pattern Day Trader to qualify those who can engage in day trading with stock brokerage firms operating in the United States.

The qualify pattern day traders as those who day trades, i.e., takes and closes positions within the same day, at least four times in the last five business days. The SEC and FINRA require that pattern day traders must have a minimum equity balance of $25,000 in their brokerage account before they day trade. When the equity balance falls below this amount for one reason or another, brokers are compelled to prohibit pattern day traders from executing new day trades until they're able to bring their equity back up to at least $25,000.

Many newbie day traders, especially those who only have this minimum amount, look at this rule as more of a hindrance to day trading glory rather than a protective fence against day trading tragedies. They don't realize that it's mean to keep them from taking excessive day trading risks that can easily wipe out their trading capitals in a jiffy because of their brokers' commissions and fees.

While this rule is the minimum requirement under the law, many brokers and dealers may use a stricter definition of a pattern day trader for purposes of transacting with them. The best thing to do is to clarify this minimum equity requirement with your chosen broker to avoid confusion later on.

If you can't afford the $25,000 minimum equity requirement for day trading, you can opt to trade with an offshore broker instead. They're brokerage firms that operate outside the United States, such as Capital Markets Elite Group Limited, which operates out of Trinidad and Tobago. Because these brokers operate outside the jurisdiction of FINRA, they're not subject to the pattern day trader rule. This means you're also not subject to the same minimum amount.

Direct-Access and Conventional Brokers

Conventional brokers normally reroute their customers' orders, including yours, to other firms through some sort of pre-agreed upon order processing scheme. Thus, executing your orders through conventional brokers involves more steps and can take significantly more time. And when it comes to day trading, speed is essential.

Conventional brokers are often referred to as full-service brokers because they tend to provide customers with other services such as market research and investment advice, among others. Because of these "extras," their commissions and fees are usually much higher than direct-access brokers. Conventional or full-service brokers are ideal for long-term investors and swing traders because they're not as particular with the speed of trade executions as day traders are. Compared to full-service or conventional brokers, direct-access brokers focus more on the speed of trade executions than research and advisory services. And because they often skip the extra services to focus on providing fast and easy access to the stock market, they charge less commissions and fees. This has earned many of them the alias "discount brokers."

Direct-access brokers use very powerful computer programs and provide customers with online platforms through which they can directly trade the stock market, whether it's the NASDAQ or the NYSE. And while they provide the necessary trade execution speeds required in day trading, they're not perfect, and they have their share of challenges.

One such challenge is the imposition of monthly trading volume quotas. If you fail to meet their minimum monthly trading volume, they'll charge you an "inactivity fee," which often serves as their minimum monthly commission from your and all their other clients' accounts. However, not all discount brokerage firms impose inactivity fees.

Another challenge particular to direct-access brokers concerns newbie day traders, i.e., familiarity with direct-access trading. With conventional brokers, all a newbie trader needs to do is tell their broker the details of their orders, and the broker will be the one to take care of all things related to executing their orders in the market. With direct-access brokers, the day trader him or herself executes the orders through the broker's online platform or software.

This can be quite challenging for newbie day traders because apart from choosing their SIPs, they also need to know how to execute their orders on the platform properly. But since day trading is a more sophisticated form of stock market trading, the chances are high that newbie day traders have enough experience with direct-access trading already.

The Trading Platform

A trading platform pertains to the computer program or software that you'll use to day trade. This is different from the direct-access broker itself, but many traders make the mistake of thinking they're one and the same. The trading platform is what you'll use to send your orders to the stock exchange, which the direct-access broker will clear on your behalf. While it's different from the direct-access brokers, it's not unusual for such brokers to develop and have their clients use their own proprietary trading platforms to trade stocks in the exchange. The number and quality of the features of trading platforms influence the price direct-access brokers charge their clients for their services. The more features a platform has, the higher the commissions and fees may be and vice versa.

A very important feature that you should look for in a trading platform is the Hotkeys. Without them, you may not be able to execute trades fast enough to make them profitable. Considering that day trading focuses on stocks with relatively high volatility, being a second or two late can spell the difference of taking and closing positions at the ideal prices and missing out on profitable day trading opportunities.

Real-Time Market Data

Unlike long-term investors and swing traders who only need end-of-day price data that's available for free online, day traders need real-time data as the trading day unfolds because they need to get in and out of positions within a matter of hours, minutes, or even seconds. And unfortunately, access to real-time intraday price data isn't free, and you'll need to pay monthly fees to your direct-access broker or the platform owner (if different from the brokerage firm) for them. Just ask your direct-access broker for details on their monthly fees for access to real-time day trading data.

Two of the most basic types of data that you'll need to look at as a day trader are the bid and ask prices. The bid prices are the prices at which other traders and investors are willing to buy a particular stock. The ask prices are the prices at which other traders and investors are willing to sell a particular stock.

The bid and ask prices are arranged such that the best price is at the top. The best bid price is the highest one, i.e., the best price for sellers is the highest price at which buyers are willing to buy. It's considered the best price from the perspective of buyers. Bid and ask prices also indicate the number of shares that other traders and investors are willing to buy or sell them at specific prices.

The bid prices are usually listed on the left side while the ask prices are usually listed on the right such that the best bid and ask prices are right beside each other. If you want to execute your buy orders immediately, you "buy up" the best ask price. If you want to immediately execute your sell orders, "sell down" at the best bid price.

The Day Trading Orders

The three most important types of day trading orders are market, limit, and marketable limit orders.

Market orders refer to orders to buy or sell stocks at their current market prices for immediate execution. If you remember from earlier, these refer to buying up at the best current ask price or selling down at the best bid price. Depending on market conditions and subsequent price movements during the day, market orders may be the worst or best prices to trade in. For example, if you send a market order to sell when the bid-ask prices are $1.00-$1.05 and by the time your order hits the market, the bid-ask prices shift to $0.95-$1.01, your sell order will be done at $0.95. In this example, your sell proceeds get cut by a minimum of five cents multiplied by the number of shares you sold.

On the other hand, let's say you sent a buy market order when the current bid-ask prices are $1.10-$1.15. If the bid-ask prices change to $1.12-$1.17 by the time your market order reaches the market, you'll end up paying $0.02 cents more for every share of that stock.

Only market makers and professional traders with a lot of day trading expertise and experience can benefit from market orders. For retail day traders like you and me, we should avoid market orders as much as possible. Why?

Stock Pick Scanners and Watch lists

Because there are thousands of stocks that are eligible for day trading every single trading day, it's impossible to manually scan the market for SIPs fast enough to make timely day trades. That's why you'll need to use market-scanning software to short list your day trading choices.

CHAPTER 11

Charting

A chart is a graphical representation of the asset prices over a period. It exhibits properties like price point, price scale, and time scale. The day trader can find the price scale on the chart's right side. The scale goes from lowest to highest from top to bottom. Although it is such a simple concept, the price scale can have a complicated structure.

A linear price structure means that the space between the price points is of equal amount. If the difference between the first and second price points is 10, it will be the same for all price points. A logarithmic price structure has distances between two price points at equal percentage change. This means that if the price change is 25%, it will be the same for all the price points.

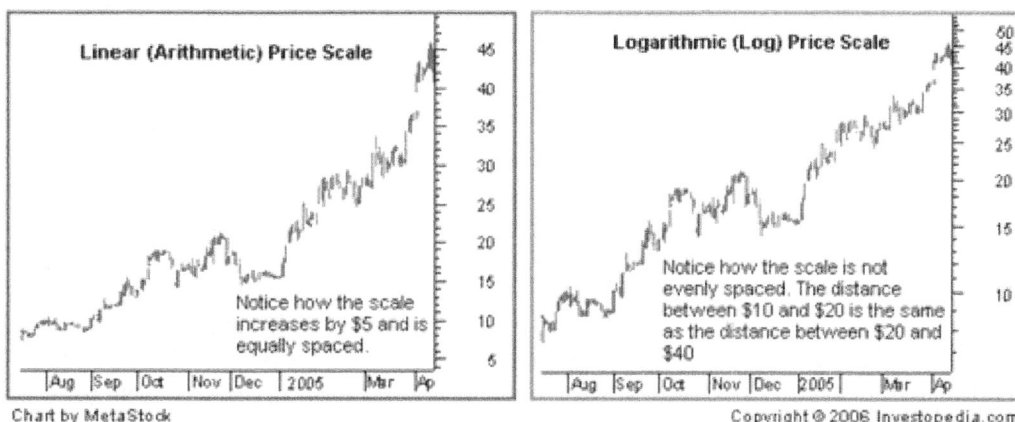

Chart by MetaStock   Copyright © 2006 Investopedia.com

The time scale is a date or time range located at the bottom of the chart. If he opts for a shorter timeframe, the day trader can expect a more detailed chart with each data point showing the asset's closing price. Some charts can also show the open, high, low, and close prices.

An intraday chart can show price movements within a particular period in one trading session. A day trader can expect to see a time scale as short as five minutes. A daily chart can have a series of price actions with a trading session represented by one point, which can be the open, high, low, or close price.

Types of Charts

Open-High-Low-Close Chart (OHLC)

These are also referred to as bar charts, and they give you a connection between the maximum and minimum prices in a trading period. They usually feature a tick on the left side to show the open price and one on the right to show the closing price.

Point and Figure Chart

This employs numerical filters that reference times without fully using the time to construct the chart.

Overlays

These are usually used on the main price charts and come in different ways:

Resistance – refers to a price level that acts as the maximum level above the usual price

Support – the opposite of resistance, and it shows as the lowest value of the price

Trend line – this is a line that connects two troughs or peaks.

Channel – refers to two trend lines that are parallel to each other

Moving average – a kind of dynamic trend line that looks at the average price in the market

Bollinger bands – these are charts that show the rate of volatility in a market.

Pivot point – this refers to the average of the high, low, and closing price averages for a certain stock or currency.

Price-Based Indicators

These analyze the price values of the market. These include:

Advance decline line – this is an indicator of the market breadth

Average directional index – shows the strength of a trend in the market

Commodity channel index – helps you to identify cyclical trends in the market

Relative strength index – this is a chart that shows you the strength of the price

Moving average convergence (MACD) – this shows the point where two trend lines converge or diverge.

Stochastic oscillator – this shows the close position that has happened within the recent trading range

Momentum – this is a chart that tells you how fast the price changes

Heiken-Ashi

Heiken-Ashi outlines use candles as the plotting medium, yet take an alternate numerical definition of cost. Rather than the standard technique of candles deciphered from essential open-high-low-close criteria, costs are smoothed to all the more likely show inclining value activity as indicated by this equation:

Open = (Open of past bar + Close of past bar)/2

Close = (Open + High + Low + Close)/4

High = Highest of High, Open, or Close

Low = Lowest of Low, Open, or Close

Regular Terms

Average genuine range – The range over a specific timeframe, generally day by day.

Breakout – When value ruptures a territory of help or obstruction regularly because of an imminent flood in purchasing or selling volume.

Cycle – Periods where value activity is required to follow a specific example.

Dead feline skip – When value decreases in a down market, there might be an uptick in cost where purchasers come in accepting the advantage is modest or selling exaggerated. Be that as it may, when vendors power the market down further, the transitory purchasing spell comes to be known as a dead feline skip.

Dow hypothesis – Average. Advocates of the hypothesis express that once one of them drifts a specific way, the other is probably going to follow. Numerous traders track the transportation area as they can shed understanding into the strength of the economy. A high volume of product shipments and exchanges is characteristic that the economy is on sound balance.

Doji – A flame type portrayed by close to zero change between the open and close value, demonstrating hesitation in the market.

Elliott wave hypothesis – Elliott wave hypothesis recommends that markets go through repeating times of good faith and cynicism that can be anticipated and, in this way, ready for trading openings.

Fibonacci proportions – Numbers utilized as a manual to decide backing and opposition.

Sounds – Harmonic trading depends on the possibility that value designs rehash themselves, and defining moments in the market can be recognized through Fibonacci arrangements.

Candlestick Charts

Candlestick charts are easy to understand and use, and they provide a trader with the most feedback by signaling where a price travels in a given period. They also enable him or her to incorporate information concerning frames of time. In this case, he or she can identify the highest and lowest price points, along with the last closing price that takes place in that particular period.

Candlesticks assist a trader in getting precise visual readings of the market by presenting only relevant information, such as the Heikin-Ashi chart that shows trends and reversals. Different candlestick charts also show various aspects of the market, such as time, volume, and price movements.

Some candlestick charts only use the movements of the price to help a day trader to identify the resistance and support levels. The resistance levels indicate the highest highs of trade, whereas the support levels show the lowest lows. Renko is an example of such a candlestick chart that employs colored bricks to reflect the trends of a trade.

When there is a downward trend, the blocks visible will be black, while white ones will be visible when an upward trend takes place. The bricks also move in terms of the price movement whereby a new white or black block appears in the following column if the price respectively moves above or below the previous one.

Other candlestick charts help a day trader to find points of reversals and sets of swing highs and lows. These charts enable him or her to determine areas and conditions of bias in the market, which assist him or her in making appropriate moves that give him or her gains. An example here is a Kagi chart that uses changes in price directions to signal reversals.

The intraday trader sets a particular reversal amount, and the price direction will shift to the opposite side once it reaches that predetermined percentage. It also indicates swings concerning high and low line signals, in that the lines become thinner as the market drops below the previous swing. Conversely, the line gets thicker as the stock increases above the prior swing.

Bar Charts

Bar charts provide a day trader with signals that are easy to read and interpret as they use color, horizontal, and vertical lines to reflect range or price in a given period. The horizontal lines show the closing and opening prices, whereas the vertical lines indicate the price range of a particular duration. Additionally, traders use them along with candlestick charts to reflect the trading actions in the market.

A bar with candlesticks uses the variation between the low and high to show the trading range. The top of the candle or wick represents the high state while the bottom of the candle signals the low one. Moreover, the chart uses different colors on the candlestick to indicate the opening and closing prices within a period of interest. A red candle could represent the closing price at the low end of a candle and have the opening price at the high end. Meanwhile, a green candle reflects its prices in reverse of the red candle.

Line Charts

Line charts indicate to an intraday trader the history of prices by showing a track of the closing prices in the market. The trader forms the lines when he or she links several closing costs in a given frame of time. He or she uses line charts along with other kinds of trading charts to get essential information for a successful Day Trading experience.

Charts Based on Time Frames

All the trading charts that a day trader utilizes contain frames of time that he or she set according to his or her aim or trading strategies. The trader can use intraday charts breaking down into 2-minute, 5-minute, 15-minute, and hourly charts. Each time interval indicates the price actions of trade of interest, and he or she can use the information represented to make relevant trading decisions and moves.

Free Charts

An intraday trader can use free charts that are available online and offer the trader not only with tools for technical analysis, but also with advice, demonstrations, and guidelines about chart analysis. Different free charts provide various features such as delayed futures data, real-time data, and selection of frames of time and indicator accessibility. Furthermore, these charts enable a trader to participate in various markets like the forex, futures, stock exchanges, and equity markets. Free Stock Charts and the Technician are examples of free charts that an intraday can access and utilize without spending anything.

Fibonacci Numbers

The Fibonacci number sequence develops by starting at 1, and adding the previous number. The sum is the new number, for example: $0 + 1 = 1$, $1 + 1 = 2$, $2 + 1 = 3$, $3 + 2 = 5$, $5 + 3 = 8$, and $8 + 5 = 13$. Therefore, Fibonacci numbers are 1, 2, 3, 5, 8, 13, 21, 34, 55, 89, 144, 233, and so on.

A Fibonacci number equals 1.618 times the preceding Fibonacci number. In turn, a Fibonacci number equals 0.618 times the following Fibonacci number. Analysts anticipate changes in trends by using four popular Fibonacci studies: arcs, fans, time zones, and the most popular, retracements. On a Fibonacci scale of 0–100%, the retracement levels within that scale are 38.5%, 50%, and 61.8%. It's amazing how many creatures in nature, human beings included, are proportioned exactly to those ratios. Those familiar with Elliott Wave Theory know wave counts adhere to the Fibonacci numbering sequence. Many trading software platforms offer Fibonacci studies as part of their charting features. Later, I will recommend you apply the retracements to your E-mini S&P futures chart.

"How fascinating," you mutter, scratching your head. "But what's this got to do with me making big bucks in the market?"

Plenty. Especially when it comes to the numbers 2, 3, and 5. From now on, we're going to keep the numbers 2, 3, and 5 in the forefront of our minds. These numbers crop up repeatedly on charts, and we use them to help predict price movement. We'll also talk more about Fibonacci levels in later chapters. Stocks in strong uptrends tend to move up three days, then down (pull back) for two. Or they move up for five days, then retrace for three days. In a downtrend, reverse those numbers. A probable pattern is three days down, followed by two rally days; or five days down, and three days up. If a stock moves down for four days, you can bet it will continue into negative territory into the fifth day. (This always happens, except when it doesn't.)

CHAPTER 12

Support and Resistance

Let's dive right into the meat of the material. Support and Resistance areas are the key to making profitable trades from the short-term fluctuations in the market.

Support

Support is an area where the stock has a hard time going below. It is an area where the stock price is being supported, and buyers are waiting for the stock to get to this area to purchase it. These are not arbitrary areas; they have special significance and are often based on areas that previously held up as a support (previously bounce and headed back higher) area. These support areas are areas we look to fail so that the position we take on the short side has a higher probability of being correct. This is where we want to participate for a downside movement. This is a bit counter-intuitive for most people as they would look at this area as a buy zone, which most people do. Being none biased with regard to the direction of the stock, we can take advantage of the up moves and down moves for security. This area of support will fail, and after it fails the probability of the short position being a profitable trade is extremely high. Here is an example of support on a stock chart:

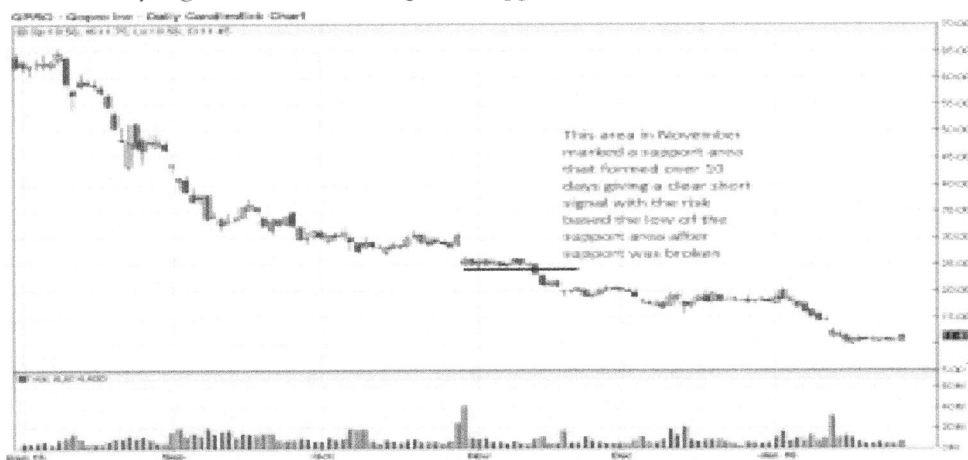

The above chart is a 6 month chart of GPRO. Pull it up on your trading platform to confirm the stock period. I have notated were a clearly defined support area broke. Under this point is a great place to short the stock and use that area as a place in which you get out if it crosses back above that level. This is a simple example of what support areas look like and what you should be looking for when trying to trade stocks after the support area breaks. To recap, an area of support is an area in which the stock has trouble going below. The more a stock touches a specific area on a chart, the more significant that area becomes in terms of support. The more significant area of support it becomes, the longer it holds, and when it breaks, the move down will be fast and extremely profitable. Areas that are of greater significance than breaks will have more meaning when and if it breaks, and thus more money can be made from them when trading in the direction of the break. This is an advanced technique but, a support area should be touched more than 3 times on the time frame you are looking at. If the support area is touched more than the size of shares trades should be increased to take advantage of the potential move that will happen when the break occurs.

Resistance

Resistance is the complete opposite of support. This is an area on the chart in which the stock has trouble going above. The resistance area is an area in which we look for them to break so we can buy the stock and participate in an upside movement. I know this is strange, most stocks that hit a resistance area like the word implies typically hit this area and turn back. The stocks that have the ability to break this area are the ones that we want to buy for the upside movement here. Below is a photo of a stock with a resistance point that is developing:

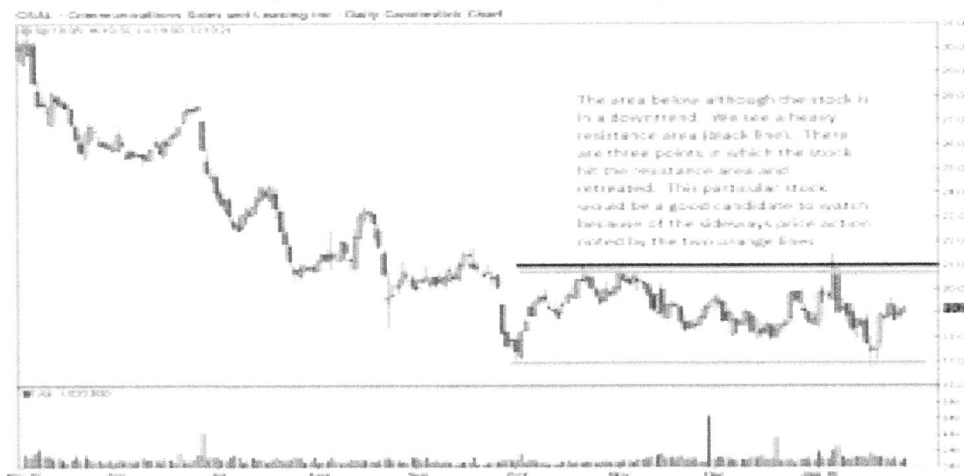

In the above chart CSAL we have a few things that we can note. We see the stock in a downtrend and creates a low and puts in a few resistance areas and then puts in another low, creating a *price* action channel. Within this price action channel, we typically look for another phase of the chart to start. We will get into this a bit later, identifying the charts we like to trade and the reason why, which is the key. What we are trying to identify here is the level at which the chart has had trouble breaking through. The visuals help when knowing what to look for.

How to Use Them in Trading

Support and Resistance areas allow us to ascertain the turning points with all stocks. These areas are trouble areas for the stock and should be given more weight when reviewing and preparing for the trade. Support breakdown should always be used for betting that the stock will continue in that direction until it hits another support area. Resistance breakouts allow a trader to participate in an up trending stock movement. Resistance breaks should be used for long trading, that is, betting that the stock is going to go up. We will get into where to set stops for these two simple types of trades. We are not concerned with candlestick patterns as they are too imprecise. Being able to look at how the chart is behaving in terms of price action gives us the ability to make informed decisions on the direction of the stock and whether or not the stock will continue its current course or reverse. Knowing this information is how a trader makes profits.

CHAPTER 13

Classic Chart Patterns

Chart patterns tell the trader that the price is expected to move in a certain path or the other after the pattern ends. There are several patterns that you need to know – reversal as well as continuation. A reversal pattern tells you that the preceding movement will turn around when the pattern completes. On the contrary, a continuation pattern shows that the preceding pattern will maintain when the pattern completes. Before you go ahead and look at specific chart patterns, you need to understand a few concepts. The major one is the trend line that is drawn to show a level of support or resistance for the commodity. A support trend line is the level at which the process has difficulty going below. A resistance trend line shows the level at which a price has a hard time going beyond.

Here are the different patterns that are used by chartists:

Head and Shoulders

This pattern is a popular one and also reliable for most traders that use technical analysis. As the name implies, the pattern resembles a head that has shoulders.

This is a reversal pattern that shows that the price will possibly move against a preceding trend. The pattern signals that the price will most likely fall when the pattern completes. The pattern usually forms at the peak of the upward trend.

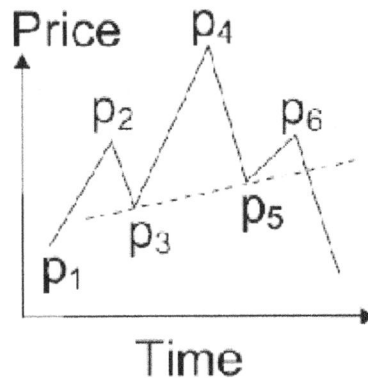

The pattern also has another form, an inverted head, and shoulder facing down. It signals that the price might rise and usually forms during an upward trend.

Head and Shoulders Top

This tells the chart user that the price of a security will likely take downward trend. It usually forms at the peak of the upward trend and is a trend reversal pattern.

The pattern has 4 main stems to complete and show a reversal:

The formation for the left shoulder – comes about when the commodity hits a new peak then drops to a new low.

Creation of the head – after reaching the peak, the price retracts to the formation of the other shoulder.

Formation of the right shoulder – occurs when a peak that is lower than the peak in the head.

Neckline – the pattern finished when the price goes below the neckline.

Head and Shoulders Bottom

This is exactly the reverse of the previous pattern. This signal tells you that the scrutiny will make an upward move soon. The pattern usually comes when the downtrend ends and is considered a reversal pattern with the direction going high after pattern conclusion.

Steps include:

Configuration of left shoulder – happens when the price drops to a new minimum and then to a new high.

Head formation – when the price goes below the preceding low, then it jumps back to the previous high.

Right shoulder – this experiences a sell-off, ending at a low price but higher than the earlier one with a drop to the neckline.

Neckline – the return to the previous level forms the neckline.

This pattern is complete when the price goes above the neckline.

Cup & Handle

This looks like a cup on the chart. The pattern shows a bullish persistence pattern whereby the rising trend pauses and then traded downward, after which it continues in an upward trend upon conclusion of the pattern. It can run from numerous months up to a year, though the common form remains constant.

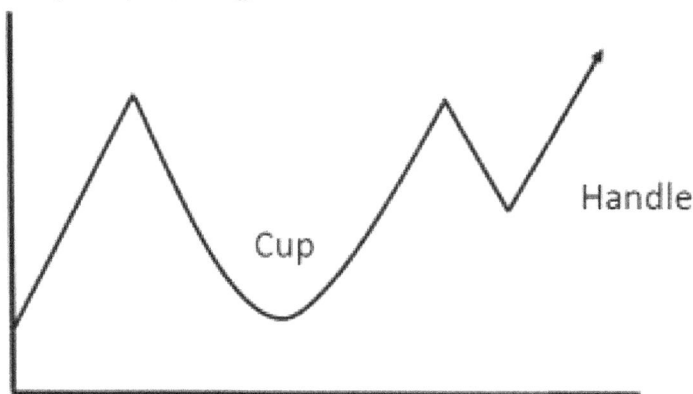

This is usually preceded by an increasing move, which then stops and sells off. This is the start of the pattern, after which the security trades flat for a long time without a definite trend. The final part of this pattern, called the handle, is a downward move that resumes the previous trend.

The Components

The cup and handle have several components that you need to know of. First, you need to know that an upward trend occurs before the trend forms. The longer the previous trend is, the lesser the possibility for a huge breakout after completion of the pattern.

The construction of the cup is vital – it ought to be nicely rounded, more of a semi-circle. The cup and handle pattern signals that weaker investors are leaving the market, and buyers are staying for the commodity. If the shape is too sharp, it shows a weakening signal.

You need to focus on the handle as well because it signals the completion of the pattern. The handle represents a descending move by the commodity after the increasing move on the right part. During the move, a downward trend line can be drawn to form a breakout. A move above the trend line shows that a prior upward trend is soon starting.

As with most of the patterns, you need to consider volume so that you confirm the pattern.

Double Top & Double Bottom

These indicate a reversal. They indicate the desire for security to continue with an existing trend. When this happens, especially with numerous attempts to run higher, the inclination reverses and begins a fresh trend all over.

Double Top

This occurs at the peak of an upward movement, and it shows that the previous trend is failing, and buyers aren't interested in the trend. Upon the conclusion of the pattern, the movement shows reversal, and the commodity is supposed to go down.

double top

The last phase of the pattern is the formation of new highs in the rising trend, after which the price starts to go towards the stage of resistance. The pattern completes when the price falls lower than the support level established in the preceding move, marking the beginning of a downward trend.

When using this pattern, it is vital that you wait until the price breaks below the key level before you place a trade. Doing this before the signal forms can lead to catastrophic results because the pattern is only setting up for a reversal. The pattern illustrates a pull between sellers and buyers. The buyers are trying so hard to shove the commodity through but are getting opposition, which prevents the rising trend from proceeding. When this continues for some time, the buyers decide to give up, and sellers take hold of the commodity, pushing it down on a new down trend. Just like before, you need to consider volume before you make a decision as you need to look at the volume of the commodity when the price falls below a certain level.

Double Bottom

The double bottom shows a reversal to an uptrend. The pattern forms when the existing downtrend goes to a new minimum. The move finds all support, which then prevents the commodity from going lower. When the move finds the right support, the commodity will hit a new high, which in turn creates the resistance point for the commodity. The subsequent stage takes the commodity to a low. However, the commodity finds some support and then it changes the direction. You confirm the pattern when the price goes over the resistance level it encountered before the move.

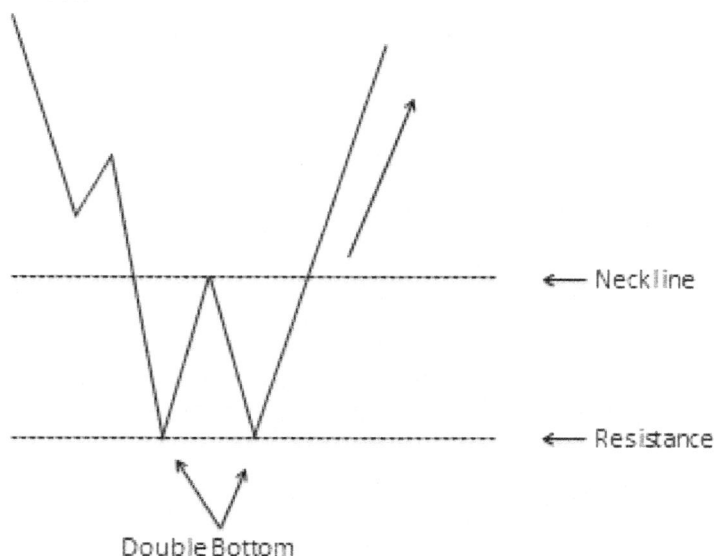

For definite reversal, the commodity needs to get the support to show a reversal in a downward trend.

Triangles

As you see from the previous chart patterns, the names leave little to the imagination. As the name goes, triangle patterns form a triangular shape. The essential design of the pattern is when two trend lines meet with the price of the commodity moving between the two trend lines.

The triangles come in three forms – the symmetrical triangle, ascending triangle, and the descending triangle.

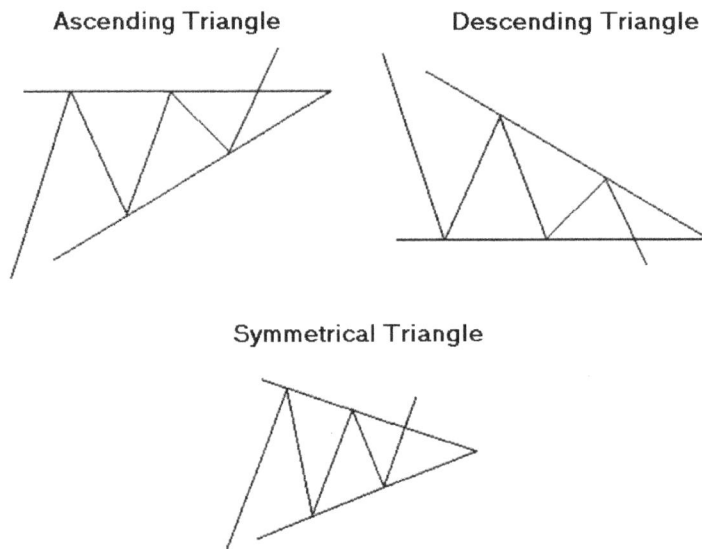

The Symmetrical Triangle

This presents a continuation pattern that signals a consolidation trend that is then followed by the continuation of a previous trend. The triangle is formed by the junction of a downward resistance line and an equally climbing support line. These converge at the apex. The price of the commodity usually bounces between the trend lines towards the apex then breaks out towards the preceding trend.

To confirm the pattern, you need to look at various aspects depending on the direction of the pattern. If the pattern is preceded by a downtrend, focus on a break that happens under the support line. The pattern usually completes when the stock price finally leaves the triangle, therefore look for a volume increase in the direction of the breakout.

Ascending Triangle

This bullish pattern gives a hint that the price will close higher. The pattern forms from two trend lines, one flat line that forms the point of resistance and a rising line that acts as price support. The most significant part of the pattern is the rising support line that shows that sellers have begun leaving the security. After the sellers leave the market, buyers go ahead to push the price past the resistance level so that it resumes an upward trend.

Descending Triangle

This is a clear bullish signal. It shows that the price will move downwards when the pattern completes. The pattern comes from a flat support line that meets a resistance line that is sloping downwards. The pattern tells you that the buyers are really trying to push the price higher, but they face a lot of resistance. After many attempts, they end up fading with the sellers overpowering them, which in turn pushes the price lower.

Flags and Pennants

These are a set of continuation lines that resemble each other closely. The only difference is in the consolidation periods of the pattern. The flag resembles a rectangle while the pennant resembles a triangle. The patterns form when a spiky price movement occurs, followed by slanting price movement.

The pattern finalizes when a price breakout occurs in a similar direction to the spike.

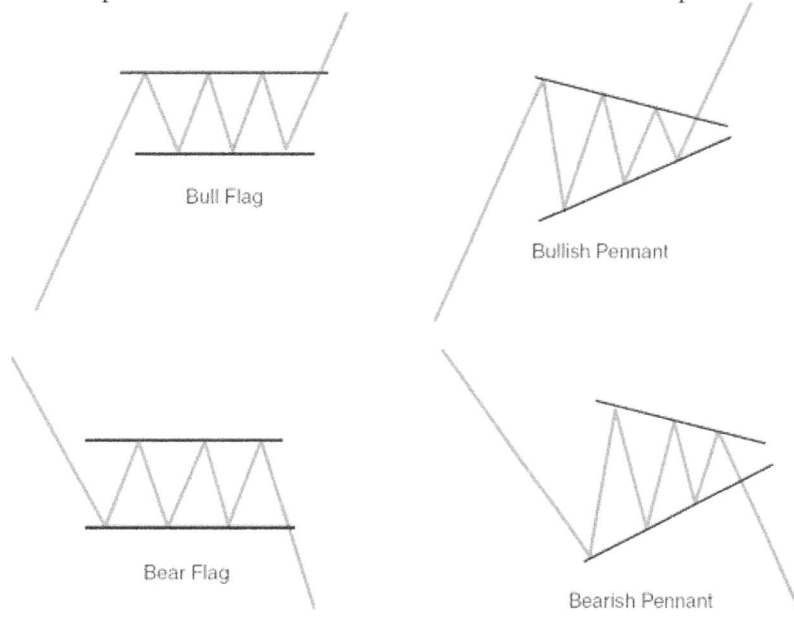

Bull Flag

Bullish Pennant

Bear Flag

Bearish Pennant

The cause of the movement is due to a huge price shift, market consolidation, or pause before the resumption of an initial trend.

The Flag

This part of the pattern forms a pattern that resembles a rectangle. This rectangle comes by due to 2 parallel trend lines that push the price until it breaks out. The signal to buy or sell forms when the price goes through two levels, with the movement going in the previous direction. As always, consider the volume to justify the signal.

The Pennant

This is a sort of a triangle, where the lines form a convergence of sorts.

The Wedge

This chart pattern shows the reversal of the movement that forms inside the wedge. The construction is akin to a symmetrical triangle because it has two trend lines depicting resistance and support.

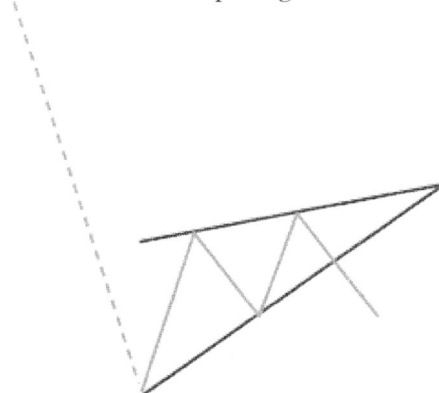

However, this pattern is different from the triangle in that it is longer, which usually lasts between 3 to 6 months. The converging trend lines incline upward or downward, different from typical triangles. Wedges come in two types – falling and rising. The two differ due to the slant, with a falling wedge sloping downward and an easing wedge slanting upward.

Falling Wedge: this bullish pattern signals that you will probably see the price breaking through the wedge and adopt the upwards direction. You need to look at the resistance trend line, which ought to have a sharp slope than the support trend line. For this construction, the buy signal forms when the price goes through the resistance.

Rising Wedge: this is the opposite of the falling wedge in that it has a bearish pattern that shows that the security might head in a downward direction. The trend lines that form this pattern usually converge, with all the trend lines slanting in an upward direction.

CHAPTER 14

Technical Indicators

S tochastics, Bollinger Bands, moving average, RSI, the MACD, and the list continues, but what are the best indicators when it comes to day trading? A day trader needs to act fast, so if you are trying to monitor too many indicators, it can take too much time. When it comes to day trading, things need to be kept simple. Follow only a couple of indicators max, or you could not follow any.

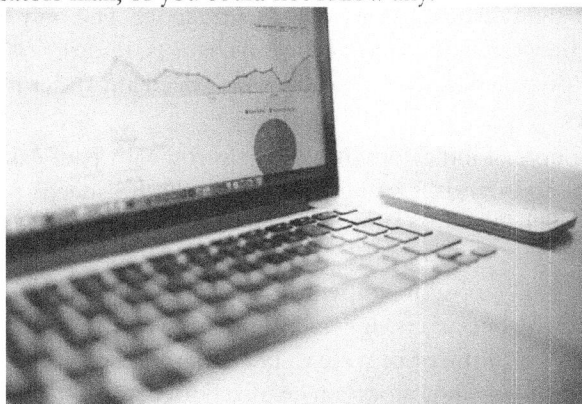

Consider the following to figure out the best day trading indicators for you.

To Indicate or Not to Indicate

Indicators are basically a manipulation of volume or price data. A lot of day traders won't use indicators. You don't have to use indicators to make a profit. You should practice trading based on price action, and then you will find that there isn't much need to use indicators. That being said, indicators can help certain people notice things that aren't obvious.

An example would be if the price is trending higher, but it starts to lose momentum. To a person that isn't used to reading price action, this could be hard to notice, but indicators will give them the ability to see them. Unfortunately, there are problems that come with indicators that include showing a reversal at the wrong time. Indicators aren't good or bad one way or the other. They are only tools, and therefore their usefulness depends on how you use them.

Redundant Indicators

A lot of indicators are pretty much the same thing with slight variations. One type could use percent movements, and another uses dollar movement. Indicators could also be a part of the same "family." RSI, MACD, and stochastics are all examples of this.

While they may look different on the surface, typically only one is good enough. Using all of them won't give you any extra information for your trades because all of them are going to provide you with the same info.

Even a MACD and a moving average can provide you with the same info. If you were to use a MACD indicator as well as a 12- and 26-period MA, they will both tell you the exact same thing. The only thing the MACD will show you is the distance the 12-period average is below or above the 26-period averages.

Once the MACD moves below or above the line of zero, the 12-period average has crossed below or above the 26-period. If both of these were on your chart, they would show the same thing.

If you are interested in using indicators, you should pick a single one from each of these groups. Even just having one indicator from each group could cause some redundancies and clutter and not provide you with any extra insight.

Oscillators: The oscillating indicators will flow down and up, typically between the lower and upper bounds. The most popular oscillators are MACD, Commodity Channel Index, Stochastics, and RSI.

Volume: These will normally mix together the volume along with price data to try to figure out the strength of the price trend. The best volume indicators are On Balance Volume, Money Flow, Chaikin Money Flow, and Volume.

Overlays: These are the types of indicators that show overlap in price changes. This is unlike a MACD indicator where it separates from the price chart. You can pick more than one overlay since the functions vary. The most popular overlays include Fibonacci Extensions and Retracements, Pivot Points, Moving Averages, Parabolic SAR, Keltner Channels, and Bollinger Bands.

Breadth Indicators: The last group of indicators includes those that deal with what the broader market looks like or trader sentiment. These typically only include stock-market-related information and include the Advance-Decline line, Trin, Ticks, Tiki.

You really don't need more than one indicator from each category. The only thing you could use more than once would be overlays because they can help to indicate trend changes, trade levels, and possible support or resistance. If you master overlays and price action, you probably won't need any other indicators.

Combining Indicators

It's best to choose only a couple of indicators that will help you with your exits and entries. And RSI is able to be used to find the entry point and trends. During an uptrend, the RSI needs to extend over 70 on rallies and stay over 30 on pullbacks. This will help you to confirm trends, see when the trend direction may change, and highlight trading opportunities.

Moving average envelopes, ATR stops, or a moving average can be added to the chart to aid in finding exits. An example would be you could use one as a trailing stock loss on trades that are trending. If you notice a trend going up, try to figure out when to exit if the price were to fall under the line.

This is only a single example of how indicators can be mixed together. The indicators that you choose will depend on how you trade and on your time frame. Make sure you calibrate your indicators to the specific strategy, timeframe, and asset that you are trading. An indicator comes with default settings, but they may not be in your best interest, so make sure you alter them to get the best signals for your trades that you take. Indicator settings could end up requiring adjustments on occasion as the market conditions start to change over time.

Unfortunately, there isn't a single indicator that will be perfect for day trading. These indicators are merely tools; they aren't going to give you profits. To make a profit, you have to use your price analysis abilities and your indicators the right way. This will take some practice. Whichever indicators you end up using, keep yourself to no more than three—even zero is okay. If you use more than three indicators, it becomes redundant and could end up costing you money.

Make sure you know everything about your indicators. Are there any drawbacks? When does the indicator normally produce incorrect signals? What are the good trades that it misses? Does it often give signals at the right time? Will the indicator trigger a trade or will it just tell you about a possible trade? It's important to know these things about your indicators, and you will be well on your way to making more productive use of them.

CHAPTER 15

Moving Averages

Using Moving Averages for Support and Resistance Trading

Moving averages are the most common indicator for finding support and resistance.

What is a Moving Average?

A moving average is a simple indicator, it is just a line that displays the average price for a certain period of time, which you input. For example, if you set your moving average to a 200 period moving average, it will show the line at the average price for the last 200 periods. It is important to remember that a moving average is a dynamic support and resistance, meaning it constantly moves with the trend.

There are different types of moving averages that use different calculations, but the two most commonly used being simple moving averages (SMA) and exponential moving averages (EMA).

EMA vs. SMA

A simple moving average is just the average price of the inputted amount of time. An EMA weighs the more recent periods higher, this causes the EMA to move more closely to the current price

Best Moving Averages to Use?

I prefer to use EMA's over SMA's for my trading style. EMA's tend to act as stronger support and resistance. It is also important to choose a good period for your moving average. Below are the most commonly used periods for moving averages.

Best Moving Average Periods

377 EMA
200 EMA and SMA
50 EMA and SMA
89 EMA
55 EMA
21 EMA
20 EMA and SMA
10 SMA

I recommend choosing only 2 or 3 to trade with at a time. My favorite combination is using a 21 EMA, 50 EMA, and 200 EMA. Probably the most commonly used moving average for support/resistance is the 200 day simple moving average (or also the 200 day EMA). Below the 200 day EMA is acting as support and bouncing the price (see figure 4.2). Many traders set their buy orders at both the 200 day simple moving average and 200 day exponential moving average.

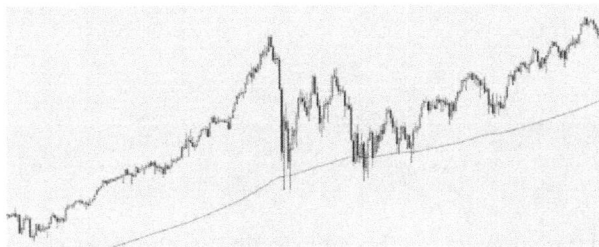

Figure 4.2

Moving Average Support Turned Resistance

Support can turn into resistance if broken through (and vice versa). Below is an example of the 200 day EMA being turned into resistance after being broken (see figure 4.3).

Figure 4.3

Signs That Moving Average Support Will Break

When making a trade it is important to understand that there is always a chance moving average support or resistance will break, that is why we use stop losses. These are warning signs we can look for to determine the chance of support or resistance breaking:

Repeated Touches

Price has repeatedly touched the support/resistance over a short period of time. If price touches support multiple times, then that will eat up the buy orders that have been placed there by traders. Sooner or later the bulls will run out of money to support the price, and support will break. We can see an example of this below (See figure 4.4), with price slowly moving sideways on a 21 EMA.

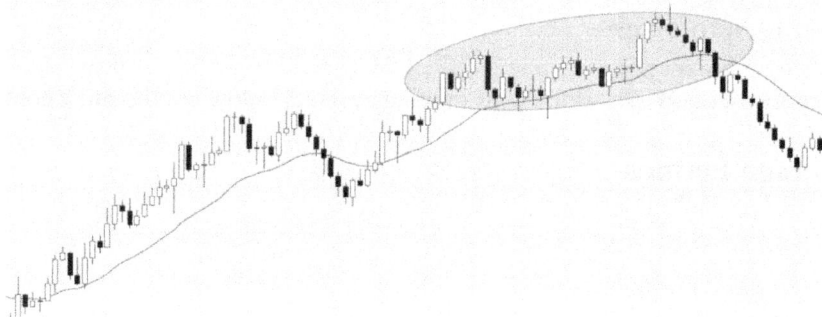

Figure 4.4

We do not want to see price slowly dribbling sideways along support, the longer price moves sideways at support or resistance, the higher the chances of it breaking. Indicators Turning the Other Way or Overbought/Oversold If you are using a momentum oscillator like a stochastic, and it is just starting to turn down at support, this is a warning sign that the support may not hold (vice versa for resistance). In the example below we see that the stochastic is showing a oversold reading at support (see figure 4.5).

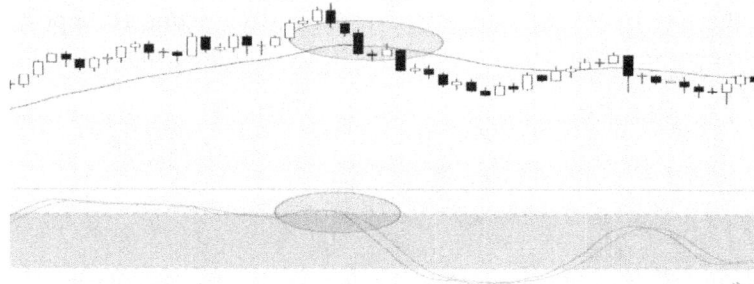

Figure 4.5

If you're using an indicator and it is showing overbought reading as it touches support, this can be a good red flag it may not hold. You can see in figure 4.5 the stochastic was also showing an overbought reading as the price was coming down to the moving average.

How To Confirm When Moving Average Support/Resistance is Broken

It is common for price to briefly move below support (or above resistance) for a short period of time and quickly move back above it. For support to be confirmed broken, you want to see a full candle open and close below (or above for resistance), and there should be a strong away under the support level like in the example below (see figure 4.6).

Figure 4.6

It is common when support breaks that it turns into resistance, which we can see in figure 4.6. This retest of former support turned resistance is a good method for placing a short trade.

Moving Average Crossover + Chaikin Money Flow Strategy

For this strategy will add a 12 EMA, a 35 EMA, and a Chaikin Money Flow (CMF) indicator on our chart. Once we added these indicators in our chart it should look like the example below (see figure 4.7)

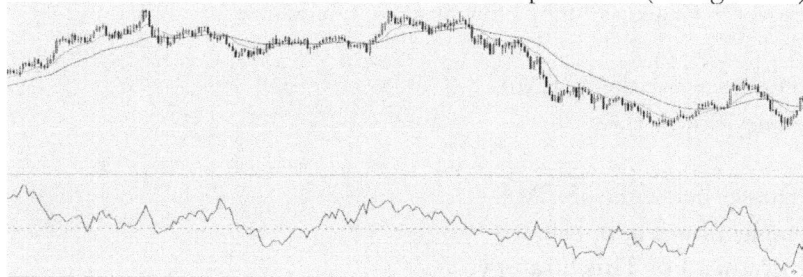

Figure 4.7

In this example, the 35 EMA is black, and the 12 EMA is blue. For shorting we want the 15 EMA to cross below the 35 EMA and the CMF to be below zero (See figure 4.8) For a buying this will be the opposite; the 12 EMA will cross above the 35 EMA, and the CMF will be above zero.

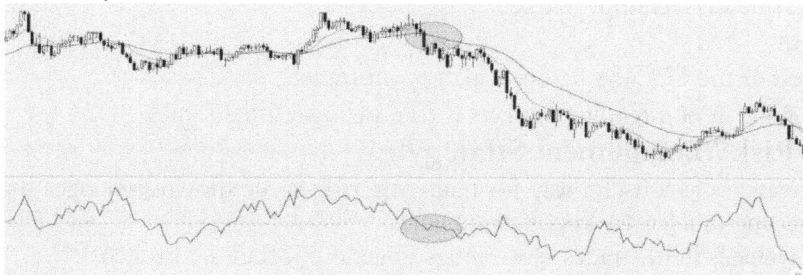

Figure 4.8

I recommend waiting for a retest of the 12 EMA before buying or selling! We want to see a retest of the 12 EMA, and in this example short when price tests this moving average while the CMF is still below zero, it's okay if hovering slightly above zero (See figure 4.9)

Figure 4.9

For exiting this short trade in this example, I will wait until the price breaks the 35 EMA. (See figure 5.1) The 35 EMA can also be used as a stop loss in case it breaks through on the retest.

Figure 5.1

As you can see, this crossover strategy can work well for getting in good trending moves.

Moving Average Crossover + Chaikin Money Flow Strategy Guidelines

Buy Signal:

- The 12 EMA crosses above the 35 EMA
- The Chaikin money flow is above 0

Sell/Short Signal:

- The 12 EMA crosses below the 35 EMA
- The Chaikin money flow is at or below 0

Recommended Timeframes For This Strategy:

- Any time frame will work with this strategy

Best Market Conditions for This Strategy:

- Strong trending markets
- Avoid using in sideways/choppy markets

Tips for This Strategy:

- Wait for a retest of the 12 EMA before making your trade
- This may be usable in non-tending markets if you use lower timeframes

Moving Average Risk Management Strategy

We can use moving averages as a useful way for managing risk, some moving averages that when broken may indicate a trend is reversing or a larger drop is imminent.

I usually use moving averages in my trades as warnings to get out if they are broken.

My favorite moving average for managing risk is the 10 simple moving average. If the 10 SMA breaks, then I use this as a red flag that the trend may be ending soon. It is important to note that I wait until I see a full candle *open and close* below this moving average before I consider it a red flag.

Below is an example of how I use the 10 SMA for risk management (see figure 5.2).

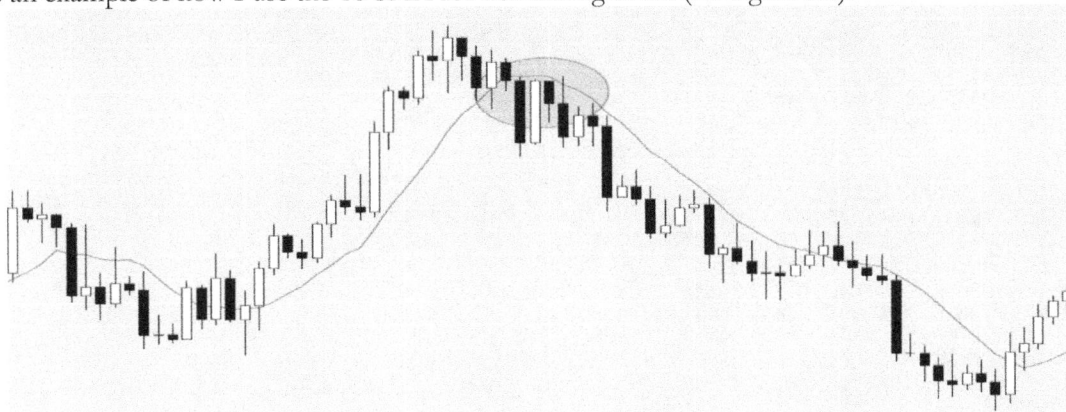

Figure 5.2

CHAPTER 16

Trading Order Types

Investors are utilizing a broker to buy or sell an asset utilizing their option of the order form. They initiate an order once an investor has decided to buy or sell an asset. The order gives guidance to the broker regarding how to proceed. Commercial securities are usually traded through a mechanism of bid/ask. A buyer is willing to pay the price of selling must be present to sell is meant by this. There needs to be a ready seller to offer as the price of the buyer to purchase. No deal happens when a buyer is there, and the seller is also there. The offer is the highest price advertised that someone is ready for asset pay, and the request is the lowest price advertised at which someone is ready to asset sell. The changes in the bid and the ask are constant, as each offer and bid represents some order.

The rates can change when commands are filled out. E.g., if a 25.25 bid is there and another bid of 25.26, the next highest bid is 25.25 when all 25.26 orders have been completed. This process of bid / ask is a key to remember when an order is placed, as the selected order type will affect the price at which filled the trade, when it is going to be filled out, or whether it is going to filled out at all.

Types of Orders

Orders are taken in most markets by the individual as well as institutional investors. Mostly by broker-dealers, individuals trade that requires placing many types of orders when doing business. Markets facilitate various types of orders, which provide some discretion to invest when planning a trade. Some basic types of orders are as follows.

Order of the market shall instruct the brokerage to complete the order at the price available next. Orders of the market have no fixed demand and are usually performed on all occasions when there is little competition in the exchange. Orders of the market are typically used when the trader wants the trades quickly in or out, and the price is not the concern they are getting.

The brokerage is instructed by the order cap to acquire at or less than a defined amount, the security. Limit orders make sure a customer just pays a certain security purchasing price. Limit orders may remain effective till executed, expired, or canceled. A broker is instructed by the sell limit order to sell at a price above the price currently, the asset. Such a form of order is used for long positions to gain gains as the price rises higher since purchasing. The brokerage is instructed by order of sell stop to sell if the asset is or reaches a price less than the price currently. An order of buy stop may tell the dealer to acquire an asset until it hits a level above the amount currently.

An order of the market is the stop order meaning that once triggered, and it can take any price or order of stop limit it can be and where it can be only executed within a given limit (price range) after triggering. Day order shall be conducted on the same business day on which set the order. Good until orders canceled remain effective till they have been filled or canceled.

If the order isn't an order of the day or good till the order has been canceled, the trader sets the order expiry typically. You must complete a kill or fill orders quickly and absolutely or not completed at all.

Trade results are affected by these kinds of orders. For example, a buy limit placing at a price lower than the asset is currently trading can give a better price to the trader if it decreases the asset in value (in comparison to now buying). But holding it so low will imply that never the price hits the limit value, so if it falls higher the price, the trader can lose out. One type of order is no better than the other. That order style serves a function which, in various cases, would be the correct alternative.

Order Usage for a Trade of Stock

A trader will think about how they are going to get in while purchasing a product and how they're going to get out on both a loss and profit.

This means that potentially three orders there are that at the beginning of a trade can be placed: one to enter, one to control the risk if does not move the price as expected (as stop-loss referred), and other to trade profit eventually if the price moves in the direction expected known as a profit target. An investor or trader should not position their orders of withdrawal at the same moment as they start a deal, but they will also be informed of how to get out (with a profit/loss) and what forms of instructions they should use for doing so.

Suppose a broker decides to buy AAPL (Apple Inc.). One configuration that can be possible is here that they use to place their orders for business and also control risk and have profit.

We track an exchange alert technical indicator and then put a trading order for buying the product at 124.15 dollars. The order will come in at 124.17 dollars. The disparity in the quality of the sales order and quality of the fill is known as slippage. They agree they do not want to gamble higher than 7 percent on the product, so they placed an order of sell stop at 115.48 dollars, 7 percent below the entry of them. That is power over defeat or failure end.

On their study based, they conclude that they should make a trade benefit of 21 percent, which implies that they intend to lose three times. That is a strong ratio of risk/ reward. They, therefore, place an order of sell limit at $150.25, which is 21 percent above their price of entry. This is the target for profit for them.

First, an order of selling will be there, by which the trade will be closed. In this scenario, the price first reaches the limit of selling, results in a profit of 21percent for the trader.

Market Order Definition

An investor's bidis and order of market – usually made through a brokerage or service of brokerage – for buying or selling a stock at a price best available in the present market. The most reliable and fastest way of entering or exiting a trade is considered widely and gives the best way to get in the trade or out of it quickly.

Business orders virtually instantaneously step in for other liquid stocks large-cap. Of all the orders, the basic most are considered market order. It is intended to be implemented at the existing selling price for defense as quickly as possible. That's why other brokerages have a button for Buy / Sell trading apps.

Typically perform a business order by clicking this switch. In cases, mostly market orders experience any type of order lowest commissions, since either broker requires very less work.

Key Takeaways

A market order is an investor's request for security buying and selling. Large price instruments like large-cap options, derivatives, or ETFs are well adapted. An order of market will be executed by the trader if he/she is ready at the requested price to buy or at the requested price to sell.

When Market Order be used

For securities traded in extremely high volumes like stocks of large-cap, ETFs or futures, market orders are well suited. For E-mini S&P, the orders are market. For example, a stock like Microsoft tends very quickly to fill without issue. Of stocks with weak floats or limited total regular value, this is a different matter. As such, stocks are traded thinly; the distribution of the asking bid appears to be large.

Due to this, market orders are sometimes slowly filled for securities like these and at prices unexpected often, which leads to significant trading costs.

Slippage of Market Order

It implies that if a dealer wants to fulfill a trading offer, the seller can purchase at the selling price or sell at the price of the bid. Thus, the market order executing guy leaves the asked bid spread immediately.

For reasons like this, it is the best idea sometimes to take a close look at the spread of the asked bid before an order of the market is placed– especially for securities traded thinly. Failure to do so could incur very high costs. It is doubly relevant to the individuals also who regularly deal, or whatever utilizes an electronic training program.

Market Order vs. Limit Order

The basic most buying and selling trades are market orders. Also, on the different side, limit orders allow the investors more extra price control of bid price or price of sale. It is achieved by specifying a maximum reasonable value of the sales price or an appropriate minimum acceptable price of sale.

The ideal is the Limit orders for trading thinly traded stocks are volatile highly or have larger asked bid spreads.

Market Order Example of Real World

Assume the asked bid production costs for Excellent Industries shares are respectively 18.50 dollars and 20 dollars, with hundred shares available on request. If the trader places an order for buying 500 shares on the market, at 20 dollars, the first hundred will execute.

Nonetheless, the upcoming 400 fill up the upcoming 400 securities at the highest selling price for sales. If traded the stock very thinly, the upcoming 400 shares could be executed around 22 dollars or greater. This is exactly why the usage of limit limits for such forms of shares is a smart idea.

The market orders trade-off filled at a dictated market price in opposition to restricting or stopping orders, which give more control to traders. Sometimes the use of market orders may result in unintended or significant costs in some of the cases.

CHAPTER 17

Trading Strategies

What Trading Strategy Do You Use?

Now that you have a better idea of choosing a brokerage and setting up your home office, let's learn more about trading strategies. No one-size-fits-all strategy for traders. Strategies depend on your personality and style. A strategy that works well for one trader may be meaningless to another. Besides day trading, you may want to try other trading strategies that worked well in the past. Naturally, past performance doesn't guarantee future results. Nevertheless, there may be times when you want a more lucrative approach to abandon day trading. Here are three of the most recognized trading strategies:

Position Trading

Position traders, unlike day traders or swing traders, hold positions for extended periods, usually several weeks or months, but possibly longer. However, unlike buy-and-hold investors, position traders won't hold indefinitely and will sell a position when profits (or losses are limited). Position trading is similar to swing trading in many ways, but with a longer hold.

Swing Trading

Unlike day traders rarely holding or keeping positions overnight, swing traders try to capture stock gains over a short period of time, typically two to five days. Although not locked into any specific time frame, swing traders usually buy early in the week but are back in the weekend cash.

Many professional traders use multiple trading styles. Therefore, they may switch from day-trading to swing-trading under certain market conditions. Swing trade, especially in short-term trend markets, could be the right strategy.

Scalping

Before decimalization, scalping was raging. That's when traders tried to capture a quick $0.25 per share or more in seconds or minutes, trading thousands of shares, and netting a fast $200-$500 per trade. It was much harder than it seemed. At that time, a few popular books about scalping were misleading— they made scalping sound like an easy strategy that anyone could do, when in fact it's very, very hard for most people. The practice may cost people a lot of money.

As a day trader, you'll probably occasionally scalp — that is, enter and exit a stock within seconds or minutes for a quick profit. The idea is to make many (five to hundreds) trades but aim for smaller profits. Keep in mind, however, that this is a stressful trading method that can end in commission losses.

After Hours Trading

The equities markets in the United States usually close down at 4.00 pm eastern time. Even then, traders continue to have access to the markets until 8.00 pm at night. Access is enabled via platforms such as ECN and exchanges such as the NYSE. Therefore, trading the markets any time after 4.00 pm till 8.00 pm in the night is referred to as after-hours trading, post-market trading, or extended hours trading. The problem with this trading period is that it is very illiquid as most trading specialists and market makers avoid trading at these times. The most outstanding feature of after-hours trading is the lack of liquidity in the market. A lot of experts consider this to be risky or even dangerous territory because there is often very little activity. Spreads are often very wide as most of the other traders, especially market makers, have left for the day. Therefore, the securities' activity is often very low. However, day traders know how to benefit from such situations. For instance, if breaking news is announced during this period, then related stocks could have significant action that can be traded. Trading after hours is tricky due to the illiquid nature of most securities as well as the large spreads. The best time to trade after hours is only when there is a significant news item that affects a particular company or an industry. Such news is best if received during the earnings periods, which occur mostly during quarterly earnings reporting times. This kind of trading should, therefore, be left to seasoned traders only.

High-Frequency Trading

High-frequency trading, also referred to as HFT, are essentially programs that execute complex algorithms that can generate superfast trades across different markets. The purpose of these rapid trades includes arbitrage and market making. The outstanding feature here is the thin profits that accrue from the large volumes of trades initiated. Trades initiated can number in their millions on any given day. It is said that about 50% or half of the volume trades initiated in US stock markets are HFT.

These trades rarely hold a position for long. One of the most useful ingredients in any HFT operation is low latency in order to keep the speed advantage over other traders, such as retail traders. It is a modern computer algorithm that power HFTs. If well executed, such programs can generate modest to average profits for a long period of time without incurring any significant losses. There are reports of HFT firms running for 1000 profitable days without any losses. When everything works as required, then HFT offers a great opportunity to earn plenty of money with very little risk over a long period of time. Latency: This term actually refers to the time taken for data transmitted between two points to get to its destination. Basically, low latency refers to high speeds, while high latency means low speeds. Most investment companies invest a lot of resources in acquiring the latest cutting edge infrastructure and hardware necessary for processing trades at high speeds. Algorithms: These are basically instructions set out, which are to be executed once certain conditions are met. A sophisticated algorithm, such as the HFC algorithm used in trade has millions of lines of code. In recent years, algorithms have become commonplace, and most traders make use of one type or another to execute their trades.

Momentum Trading

Day traders choose momentum trading simply because all the action is on the stock market momentum. This type of day trading aims at profiting from stocks that experience a price gain, especially with huge trade volumes. In momentum trading, stocks and securities are affected by factors such as margin calls, short squeezes, and stop losses, so they move in an excessive and extreme manner. The typical approach by day traders on momentum trading is to scalp profits as quickly as possible and with as much leverage as possible. Day traders who prefer momentum trading usually trade any security that has large volatility and significant volume. These include securities that have sustained a significant rise in price and are known as high-flyers or momentum stocks. Most of the stocks suitable for this kind of trade strategy are more volatile than those of major blue chip companies. It is this volatility that attracts momentum traders to these trades. Volatility provides a great option to capitalize and benefit from price movements and volume. Securities with large volumes and high volatility that feature in the news are usually the best suited to momentum trading.

Price movement: This is the hallmark of momentum day trading. Traders often make use of shorter time frame charts like the 15-minute, 5-minute, and even the 1-minute charts. In order to manage risk, the focus should be on the immediate action with large share volumes. It is important for momentum day traders to have precision when entering and leaving the market. Executions and charts will, in this case, carry significantly more weight compared to the fundamentals of the underlying company. Also, stories in the news carry more weight as news is often the main driver of momentum. Also, chart patterns and essential signals will help determine the best times to initiate trades.

- Things momentum traders should look out for
- High probability chart patterns
- Intraday setups
- Volume
- The reasonable risk to reward ratios

Options Day Trading

A stock option is yet another trading option commonly used by day traders. Options contracts ideally offer the holder a right with no obligation to sell or purchase an underlying security at a certain price. Options actually are derivatives. This means that their price is derived from an underlying security or even commodity. Therefore, like other derivatives, stock options enable the holder to enjoy the benefits of the price movement of the underlying security, yet the losses they can incur are capped on the option. A stock options trader basically enjoys the benefits of stock ownership without the obligation or financial implication of having to buy the stock. They only incur costs that are a fraction of the total cost of buying or investing in the stock. Each and every options contract has about 100 shares of the underlying security attached to it. So a trader holding 10 call or put options basically has control of 1000 shares of the underlying stock.

Many exchanges accept and trade in options contracts. These include exchanges such as the International Securities Exchange, Chicago Boards Options, and many others. This is also due to the fact that their prices move up and down in tandem with the underlying stock. However, options are unlike stocks because they can lose most of their value should their time expire. All options come with an expiry date, as this is an inherent aspect they all possess.

Penny Stocks Trading

What are penny stocks? These are stocks trading on the markets that are worth less than $5 each. They constitute some of the most speculative shares in the market, and most of the time are priced at less than $3 and even $1. There is always the concern about fraud, speculation, and even pump and dump tendencies. However, things have improved, and so penny stocks are now viewed as a less expensive option for investing in stocks at the markets. The essential ingredients when trading penny stocks are volumes and liquidity. These two ingredients make it easy to enter and exit trades. It is also essential that any day trader dealing in penny stocks have direct access to a brokerage to execute any trades fast and seamlessly. Penny stocks have a tendency of increased volumes, then peaking eventually and leaving plenty of traders trapped with expensive shares. Before entering such trades, it is important to perform exhaustive research and make use of all tools and leverage in order to have the best information possible. With penny stocks, the essential point to remember is that price is key, so always have an exit plan way before commencing any trade.

Pre-Market Trading

Another type of day trading strategy is pre-market trading. Trading in these markets begins as early as 4.00 am EST, even though the normal pre-market trading hours start at 8.00 am EST. It is during the normal trading hours that liquidity and high volumes begin to stream in. regular trading starts at 09.30 am EST. Pre-market trading is generally accessible via dark pools and ECNs. This is very similar to after-hours trading. While there are generally no specialists or market makers in the market at such hours, it is possible that they may be participating in the markets via certain ECNs.

Pre-Market Trading Versus After Hours

Generally, the risks of trading the pre-market are much lower compared to the after-hours session. This is because action continues within the markets after 09.30 am EST as compared to after-hours where activity just shuts off. Many traders are likely to be trapped in after-hours trading because it ends at 8.00 pm. Such traders will have no option but to wait until pre-market hours the following morning. Also, trade can resume with a sharp gap against positions taken by the traders.

CHAPTER 18

Basic Strategies

A dhering to the following tips, you will succeed in your day time trading.

Invest in Knowledge

Having basic knowledge in daytime trading procedures is essential. However, it is crucial as a daytime trader to stay updated with news, developing events in the market that could affect the stocks they are trading in. This may include the economic outlook or the Fed's interest rates, among others. As a trader, you must do your homework keenly, list your preferred stocks to trade in, and stay informed about your companies of choice and general market trends. Follow business news and read from financial websites that are reliable.

Set Aside Your Trade Capital

You must assess the amount of capital you feel you need to use for each trade. Most of the successful traders take a risk with not more than 2% of their account on each trade. For instance, if your trading account has $50,000, and you decide to have a capital of 0.5% risk per trade, your expected loss per trade is $250 (0.5%*50,000). Always have extra capital to trade with and are willing to lose. However, one doesn't have to lose.

Create Time

To be successful in day trade, you must set aside time. Most day traders give most of their day time to trading. If a person does not have enough time to spare, day trading is not yours. The process of trading needs the trader to keep track of the markets and identify any opportunities. Constant monitoring is important because opportunities can arise at any time, and moving with speed is essential.

Start Small

Do not overwhelm yourself when you are a newbie. Start with two trades, not more at a time, because it is easier to monitor and identify opportunities with few stocks. In recent times, traders have started to trade with fractional shares. This enables a trader to specify smaller amounts to invest.

What this means is that if a particular company stocks are selling at $200, you want to purchase shares amounting to $50, you can do this directly. However, through a broker, it may be difficult because many brokers do not allow a person to buy one-fifth of a share.

Stay Away from Penny Stocks

As a trader, you may be in search for low prices or deals, however, keep off penny stocks. The reason is these stocks are often illiquid, and the chance to hit a jackpot with them is rare. Many of the stocks that trade under $5 per share often get removed from the main stock platforms and can exclusively be traded across the table. However, if you have not identified a genuine chance and carried a thorough analysis, it is advisable to stay away from them.

Know How to Time Trades

When traders and investors place orders, they start to trade just as the markets open first thing in the morning. This is a main contributor to the volatility of prices. A seasoned trader or player must be able to recognize the patterns and pick the best time to make profits. However, if you are a beginner, it is best to monitor the market for at least 15 to 20 minutes before making any move. In the middle of the day, prices are less volatile, and trading starts to intensify again towards the closing time. The rush hour offers various opportunities, but, as a newbie, it is best to avoid the rush hour trading.

Minimize Your Losses with Limited Orders

As a player, it is essential for you to know the kind of orders you will begin with and end with the trade with. What type of orders do you want, market, or limited ones? If you decide to use a market order to trade, you must keep in mind that it will be traded at the right time and at the right price available then. On the other hand, if you decide to use a limit order, you will be guaranteed to get the right price but not on how it is carried out. This kind of order allows you to trade with a specific target of price to trade at for both buying and selling. It is important as you set the trade price to be realistic so that it can be executable. With day traders that are more sophisticated and experienced, they may opt to use options strategies to enhance their position.

Have Realistic Expectations in Profits

As a trader, you must understand that having a good strategy doesn't guarantee profitability at all times. Statistics show that most day traders will win not more than 60% or less than 50% of their trades. It is also worthwhile to note that they make more on their winners as opposed to what the losses they would make on their losers. A trader must make sure to cap their risk for every particular transaction with a precise percentage of their capital. They should also ensure that they write down the time they make an entry and the strategies for their exit.

Be Calm and Cool

Sometimes trading in stocks can become frustrating. As a business person, you must not allow greed and fear far from you. Make your decisions based on logic but not on emotion.

Keep to the Plan

Moving fast is a trait of successful day traders, but that should not be confused with thinking fast. To be successful, think, and develop your strategy way before and cultivate the discipline to stick to the strategy. Following your set strategy and formula is more important than chasing after profits. Chasing profits is driven by emotions, and if not checked, they can take the best of you and cause you to abandon your strategy. Always ensure you plan beforehand how to trade and trade based on the plan.

Even with these strategies, day trading is not easy and can be challenging if not executed well. Here, we discuss why it is challenging to do day trading.

Why is Day Trading Challenging?

This type of trading requires building consistency and expertise. However, several factors make the process challenging. You need to be aware that you are up against professionals that have their careers revolving around trade. They have access to excellent connections in the industry and technology such that should they fail, they will still succeed eventually.

The government also expects you to pay taxes for any profit you make. Whether the gains are short-term or long-term, any investment you hold must be paid for taxes. However, if you have made any losses, they will offset the gains. An individual trader is also prone to psychological and emotional biases. Professional traders, on the other hand, are able to disengage emotionally while trading. This happens because they are not trading with their money directly as does an individual trading directly.

How to Decide What and When to Buy

People in day trading make profits through the exploitation of how assets fluctuate in pricing, and they do that by leveraging huge amounts of capital. In order to decide what to focus on in trading, a day trader will normally look at the following:

Liquidity – liquidity ratio allows a trader to start and finish a trade at a favorable price. For example, you can take advantage of the difference between the quoted offer and the price the stock is being sold for or of the lower spillage, which is usually the variance from the price expected of a stock and its real price.

Volatility – this simply is the indicator of movements in prices. It is the level where traders feel comfortable operating. If the movement in prices is more than usual, it typically indicates prices for the stocks increase.

Trade Volume – this is the measure of the number of times the stock has been purchased and resold in a particular period, often referred to as the daily average trading volume. If the volume of trade is high, it indicates that the stock has many traders interested in it. When the interest in a certain stock happens, it may end up increasing the price of the said stock.

Establishing Your Entry Point

When as a trader you know the assets or stocks that you want, you must learn how to establish the entry points. This means the precise moment to make your investment. Some of the tools that will enable you do this will include:

Intraday Candlestick – they give unedited price trends of a stock.

Real-Time News Service – information affects how stocks fluctuate. Enroll for services that will update you on news that will move the market comes out.

Ecn/Level 2 Quotes – this is also known as Electronic Communication Network. It is a computer system that shows the available best bids and asks for quotes from various participants in the market, and it automatically matches the orders and executes them. Level 2 is also a service that you must enroll for. It provides live access to the NASDAQ order book that has indicators of prices that are registered with NASDAQ. These two used together will be able to give you an idea of orders on trade as they happen.

Once you have decided on your rules to enter, analyze various charts, and establish if the same outcomes are produced daily and if they produce an anticipated price movement direction. Once you have done this, it will mean you have a probable strategy for entry and will have to establish how you will sell or your exit point.

Establishing your Exit point

Multiple ways exist that facilitate exiting in a winning position that may include profit targets and trailing stops. The most common exit methods are profit targets. This involves taking a profit at a level that was previously predetermined. Price target strategies commonly used include:

Fading – this is about bringing down stocks after they had rapidly shot up. This is based on the belief that the stocks have been overbought, those that bought them early are ready to make profits, or the current buyers may be scared. This strategy is risky but equally rewarding. The price target in this case is when buyers start stepping up again.

Scalping – this strategy is very popular. It entails selling immediately a trade has become beneficial. The targeted figure is that which will allow you to make good gains out of the deal.

Momentum – with this strategy, a trader bases his transaction on the news release. This involves identifying strong trending moves that support a high volume of stocks. A momentum trader may opt to buy on news release and wait until there is an exhibition of signs of reversal. Another type of momentum trader may decide to fade the surge in price. With this strategy, the exit is when the volume starts to decline.

Daily Pivots – this strategy involves a trader making profits daily out of the stocks being volatile. This is done when a trader buys when it is at its lowest and decides to resell when highest in the day.

Ideally, a trader will want to leave from trading in an asset when interest on it has decreased. At this point, the targeted gains must provide for more gains from profitable trades than the loss experienced in losing trades.

CHAPTER 19

Effective Methods for Manage Your Money

The truth is that many traders, especially novices, started with a lot in their trading accounts, and at the end of the day, they had little or nothing to boast. Many of them lost their funds because of thoughtless actions or not following a well-crafted strategy. There are some things that you have to do to manage your money well.

Choose the Right Lot Size Based on Your Capital

When you start at forex training or financial market trading, you will tend to learn about trading lots. What we mean by a lot is the tiniest trade size available that can be placed when you decide to trade currency pairs on the foreign exchange market. Usually, brokers tend to talk about lots using increments of a thousand or a micro lot. You have to understand that the lot size determines directly, as well as shows that risk among that you are willing to take. Using a risk management calculator or a top like that can help you know the right lot size, based on what your trading account assets are currently. This can be used when you are trading life, or you are merely practicing. It allows you to know what amount that can be risked.

The trading lot size affects how the market movements can affect the accounts. Let's use an example.

When a 100-pip move occurs, it won't have so much effect on a small trade like a similar 100-pip move on a trade size that is quite massive.

As a trader, you will see several lot sizes.

We will explain the lots as follow:

Trading with Micro Lots

The tiniest tradable lots that can be used are called mini lots. A micro lot has a thousand units of the currency that is in your account. If you have funded your account with USD, a micro-lot of that has a value of a thousand dollars as the base currency.

If you have decided to trade a dollar-based pair, a pip means ten cents.

As a beginner, it is favorable to use micro-lots to reduce your risk while you practice trading.

Mini lots have ten thousand units of the currency that you use to fund your account. If you are making use of an account with dollars as its base currency, then every pip in the trade would be valued at around $1.00.

As a beginner that wants to begin with mini lots, you should be adequately capitalized.

A dollar per pip may seem quite tiny, but the market sometimes gets to a hundred pips daily. Sometimes, this may happen in one hour.

If the forex market isn't moving in your direction, this means that you have made a loss of a hundred dollars.

It is you that will choose your ultimate risk tolerance. Before you can trade a mini account, you shouldn't mind using at least two thousand dollars.

Using Standard Lots

A standard lot has a hundred thousand units of the base currency in a trading account. If you have a base currency of dollars, this is a hundred thousand dollar lots. The normal pip size for a standard lot is ten dollars for every pip. When the trade is against you by ten pip, this is a loss of hundred dollars. Institutional-sized accounts use this type of lot. What this translates to is that you should possess at least $25,000 to be able to carry out trades using standard lots. A lot of forex traders tend to make use of either micro-lots or mini lots.

To a novice, this may not seem glamorous, but when you keep the lot size proportional to your account's size, your trading capital will be preserved, and you can easily trade with it for a long while.

Let's use an illustration:: Using a small trade size compared to what you have in your account can be likened to strolling on a sturdy bridge with a shelter to prevent any issue from worrying you. It doesn't matter if heavy rain occurs; you will be sheltered.

If you place a big trade size compared to the account funds, it can be likened to walking on a narrow bridge. In this case, the bridge is fragile and narrow, meaning that you can fall. A tiny movement in the market could toss you away and lead you to a spot that you can't return from.

Below are some things you should consider before you begin.

Do Not Let Your Gain Become a Loss

One thing that has been noticed is that many forex traders tend to turn their profit into a loss. The forex market worldwide does at least $5 trillion daily. This has made it the most significant financial market globally.

The fact that Forex is lucrative has made it popular amongst many traders, from novices to experts in the field. Since it is quite easy to get involved in Forex because of the little costs, round-the-clock sessions, and so on, it is also straightforward to lose your capital as you trade Forex.

To ensure that your gain doesn't turn to a loss as a forex trader, you should try and avoid some mistakes.

Learn, Learn and Learn

The fact that it is quite easy to get involved in Forex has led many people to get involved without bothering to learn. To succeed in Forex or any financial market for that matter, you need to learn. You should learn from live trading, experience, as well as reading up on forex literature. Don't forget the news. You spiel find out about economic and geopolitical factors that affect the preferred currencies of a trader.

The world of Forex is ever-changing, meaning that you must keep yourself abreast of these changes in the regulations, market conditions, as well as global events.

While you undergo the research process, you should also consider creating a trading plan.

This plan should involve a method where you can screen and analyze investments in a bid to determine how much risk should be expected when creating investment goals.

Use Only a Reputable Broker

The truth is that the forex world isn't so regulated, unlike others, meaning that you may end up carrying out business with unscrupulous brokers. It is advisable that you only open an account with a National Futures Association (NFA) member if you want your deposits to be safe. You are interested in the integrity of that broker. Use only brokers that are listed as futures commission merchant with the regulatory body of your country. If the broker isn't registered, avoid them.

It is also advisable that you study the brokers' account offerings like commissions, leverage amounts, spreads, account withdrawal, funding policies, and so on. You can find these out by talking to a customer service representative.

Utilize a Practice Account

Almost every trading platform out there has a practice account. This is also called a demo account or a simulated account. The account permits traders to carry out hypothetical trades that do not need a funded account. Using a perceive account allows the trader to get used to order-entry techniques quickly. Using a practice account allows the trader to learn, thereby avoiding a lot of mistakes in their trading account. We had seen cases of when a novice trader erroneously adds to a losing position when he intended to close the trade. Several errors in the order entry could worsen to a big losing trade. Losing funds is not the only issue; you have to also battle with a stressful and annoying situation. There is nothing wrong if you decide to try out order entries before you start to place the real money on live trading.

Keep Your Charts Clean

When a forex trader creates an account, he or she may be tempted to use every tech assessment tool available on the trading platform. Many of these indicators are high in the foreign exchange market, but you should reduce the hunger of analysis methods you use to be efficient. You are making use of several similar indicators like three oscillators, or as three volatility indicators may come off as unnecessary. Sometimes, you may even get opposite signals. You should try and avoid this. If you aren't using an analysis technique well, consider taking it out of your chart. It is also essential that you look at the total appearance of the workspace.

The hues, kinds and fonts of price hard such as candle bar, line, range bar, and so on that you use should craft out an easy-to-read-and-interpret chart, permitting you to respond to the ever-changing conditions in the market quickly.

Stop Loss Order Is Not Just for Preventing Losses

Stop-loss orders are used a lot in preventing losses, but it does more than that. It can also be used in locking profits. If used for this, it is sometimes called a "trailing stop." At this point, the stop-loss order is being set at a percent height that is beneath the current market price and different from the price that it was bought. The stop loss's price fluctuates the same way the price of the stock adjusts.

This means that if the price of a stock increases, you may have to battle with an unrealized gain. This means that you won't have the money with you until after the sales. Making use of trailing stop permits you to allow your run and still guarantee you an amount of realized capital gain.

You must note that the stop-loss order will always be a market order, meaning that it would lie low until the trigger price has been reached. This means that the price your stock may sell for may end up being a bit different from what you specified as your trigger price.

Benefits of Stop-Loss Order

One thing that we all love about stop loss is the fact that we don't have to pay a dime to implement it. The normal commission is only charged when you have reached a stop-loss price and your stock has been sold. What you should see it as is a free insurance policy.

Using a stop loss ensured decisions are made based on facts and taking out any form of emotional influence.

Many people end up crushing on their stocks, feeling that if they allowed the stock to stay on, it would surely succeed, even when the facts are saying another story. This leads to delay and procrastination on the part of the trader, and before you know it, he is raking in unimaginable losses.

It doesn't matter what kind of trader you see yourself as; there must be a reason you have decided to own a stock. The criteria listed by a value investor is usually different from the one listed by a growth investor and an active trader.

CHAPTER 20

Advanced Strategies

Whenever you are looking forward to capitalizing on the small frequent price movements, day trading strategies are the best for you. Any effective strategy that you will choose must be consistent and must rely on in-depth technical analysis that utilizes charts, market patterns, and price indicators predicting future price movements.

It is your responsibility to choose the most appropriate strategy that best fits your requirements. As a trader, it is good that you know the average daily trading volume.

Fallen Angel

A Fallen Angel is a strategy that involves a bond that has been reduced to junk bond status from an investment-grade rating as a result of the issuer's weakening financial conditions. In terms of stock, a fallen angel refers to a stock that has always been high and now has fallen considerably. Fallen angel bonds can be a sovereign, corporate, or municipal debt that a rating service has downgraded. The main reason for such downgrades could be attributed to revenue decline that generally jeopardizes the capabilities of issuers to servicing debt. The potential for downgrade often experiences a dramatic increase when expanding debts are combined with expanding debt levels. The securities of fallen angels are at times so attractive, particularly to contrarian investors who seek to capitalize on the potential. This enables the issuer to recover from the temporary setback.

Example:

Due to the ever-falling oil prices over several quarters, an oil company has reported sustained losses. The company, therefore, can decide to downgrade its investment-grade bonds to junk status as a result of the increasing risk of default. This will result in a decline in the prices of the company's bonds and, in addition, increase yields, which will make the contrarian investors to be attracted to the debt as they only see the low oil prices as a temporary condition. However, there are conditions where you are likely to go at a loss, especially when the fallen angel bond issuers do not recover. For example, if there is an introduction of superior products by a rival company, the issuers may fail to recover.

ABCD Pattern / Reverse ABCD Pattern

The ABCD pattern is a pattern that shows perfect harmony between price and time. ABCD pattern usually reflects the common and rhythmic style in the market movements. The geometric price/time pattern consists of three consecutive price trends with a leading indicator that can guide a trader to determine when and where to enter and exit a trade. As a trader, ABCD Pattern can be very important in identifying the available trading opportunities in any market (be it futures, forex, or stock) on any timeframe (be its position, intraday, or swing), and in any market condition (be it range-bound, bullish or bearish markets). Before placing a trade, ABCD Pattern can help you determine the reward and the risks of trade.

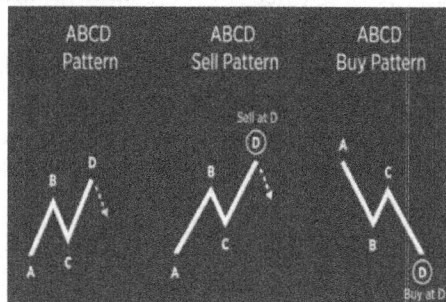

Fig. 1: A representation of the ABCD Pattern (Above)

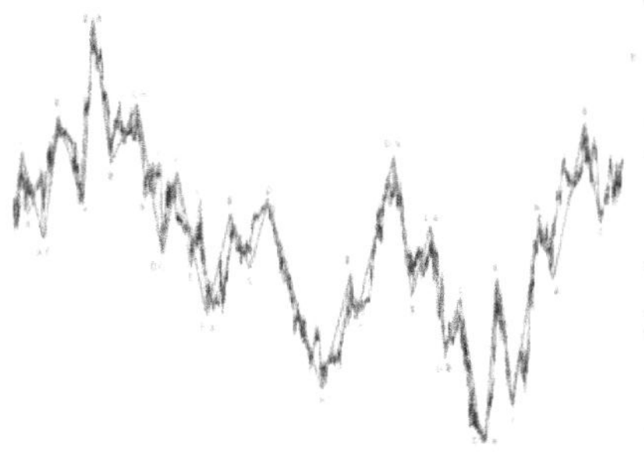

Fig. 2: ABCD pattern on a trading chart

Bull Flag and Bear Flag

With technical analysis, a flag refers to a price pattern that can explode and move within a shorter timeframe to the prevailing price trend that has always been observed in longer time frames on a price chart. With the flag patterns, a trader can identify the possible prevailing trend that is continuing from a given point where the price has drifted against the same trend. Therefore, in the case that the trend resumes, by noticing the flag pattern, there will be a rapid price increase, and this makes the timing of a trade advantageous. Flags are areas of tight consolidation in price actions, and they show a counter-trend sharp directional movement in price. This pattern has 5 to 20 price bars.

Bullish Flag Formation

These are formation patterns observed in stocks that have a strong uptrend. Bull flags got their names from the fact that the pattern closely resembles a flag on a pole. A vertical rise in-stock results in a pole, and a period of consolidation results in a flag. The flag is usually angled down away from the trend that is prevailing but also can be a horizontal rectangle. The bullish flag pattern starts with a strong price spike that is almost vertical. The prices then peaks and forms an orderly pullback where the lows and the highs become almost parallel to each other, making them almost to form a tilted rectangle.

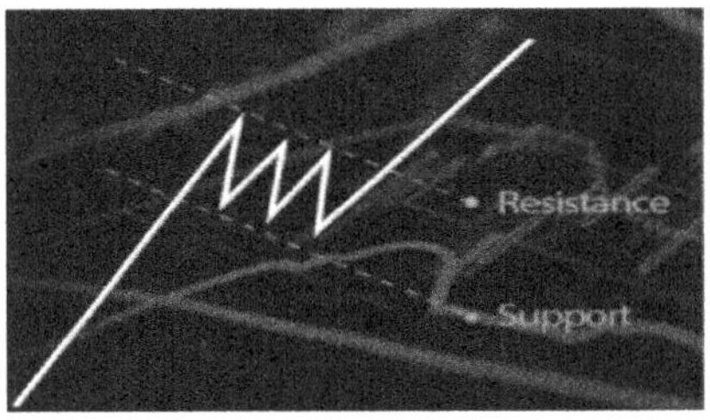

Fig 3: Bullish Flag Formation

The parallel diagonal nature is reflected by the plotted trend lines (both lower and upper trend lines). The breaking of the upper resistance trend line forms the first breakout. Another uptrend move and a breakout are formed when there is an explosion of the prices, causing prices to surge back towards the high of the formation.

Bearish Flag

Comparing to the bullish flag, this flag is an upside-down version of the bull flag. The bearish flag is an inverted version of the bull flag. In this case, an almost vertical panic price drop is formed by the flagpole because the sellers make the bulls to get blindsided and, as a result, there is a bounce having parallel lower and upper trend lines, forming the flag. The panic sellers are triggered when the lower trend lines break.

This flag is similar to the bull flag in that the severity of the drop on the flagpole will determine how the strength of the bear flag can be.

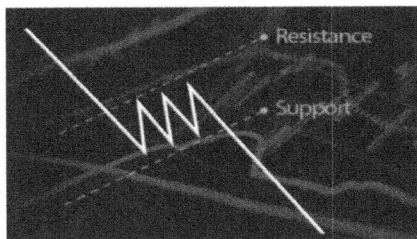

Fig. 4: The Bearish flag

Develop Trading Skills

To become a trader, you are required to not only know about just finance or business, but also hard science or mathematics. You must be an individual who can do deep research and analysis that can mirror the economic factors from a broader perspective, as well as the day-to-day chart patterns impacting different financial markets. As a trader, it is crucial that you need to sharpen your ability to concentrate and focus, especially in a fast-moving environment containing different people with different goals and ideas. You must also be able to practice self-control and regulate your emotions even when in situations upsetting you. Lastly, you should always be able to keep an accurate record of your trades to check on your account and to provide you with a learning opportunity that will help you become a better trader.

CHAPTER 21

Rules of Day Trading

Let us turn our focus to some of the rules of day trading that every investor should follow. These rules are not necessarily set in stone. You can decide to take these rules with you on your investing journey or ignore them. However, they should be followed in order to give you the best day trading experience from the very first day of your investing career.

Day Trading is a Serious Business

When some people start day trading, they think that it is meant to be fun and games and do not take the profession seriously. This can be a grave mistake. While you want to enjoy what you are doing, you always want to remember that it is a serious business. There are some types of investing that are easier to handle as a side career or on the weekends. If this is the type of investing you are looking for; you will not want to look at day trading. This type of investing is meant to be a daily business, and many people look at it as their day job.

This means that once you decide to become a day trader officially, you need to treat it as you would any other career. You must get up in the morning, get ready for your day, and make sure you are ready to work by your set time, which could be as early as 7 in the morning. While you will have some flexibility in your schedule from a regular job, meaning you could set a bit of a later start time in the morning, you will want to make sure to set a schedule you will follow at least Monday through Friday.

Even working from home, you will want to make sure to limit distractions. For example, you will not want to focus on day trading and watching television at the same time. Set up an office for yourself and pay attention to your work. Get ready for your job as a day trader like you would for your job at any other office. Do not head into your office in your pajamas. You are more likely to feel like you want to put in 100% effort and succeed if you treat this as a career.

Day Trading Will Not Help You Get Rich Quickly

You should not look at day trading as a get rich quick arrangement. This is a common misconception and one reason people often turn to day trading. If you truly want to become a successful day trader, you will need to make sure you not only have the patience to build your investments, but also realize it takes time.

Day Trading is Harder Than It Looks

Day trading is not as easy as it looks, but this does not mean that you should set this book down and decide not to become a day trader. It just means that you will probably need to spend more time learning about day trading than you initially thought. You want to make sure you are well-versed in the field before you make your first investment. Luckily for you, this is one of the reasons I decided to write this book. I want to give you a comprehensive beginner's guide so you can learn as much as you can about day trading to start your journey in one location. In other words, I have done most of the research for you.

Trading is Different from Investing

One of the biggest rules that you should understand before becoming a day trader is this is different from investing. In order to help you understand the difference, here are a few basic differences between trading and investing:

As an investor, you need to have an idea where the stocks are heading in the future. However, as a day trader, you only need to concern yourself with which stocks will give you the best financial gain on that day. You look more closely at the minutes. In fact, you will not even pay much attention to the hours and will not worry about the next day, week, month, or year.

You Will Not Win Every Trade

It does not matter how experienced you become as a day trader, there will still be days that you lose on a trade. Many people create an image in their minds where they will become so experienced at trading that they will never make a mistake, and they will only gain capital.

Every game has its rules and regulations, and day trading is not any different. In case you are new to the game, you must bear in mind the entire standard rules that have been put in place to control the game. That being said, it is important to note that these rules not unbreakable, but they can be instrumental in making decisions in regard to day trading.

There are numerous rules of day trading that you have to familiarize yourself with irrespective of whether you specialize in forex, stocks, options, cryptocurrency, or futures. If you fail to abide by some of the rules, it can result in significant losses.

In as much as some rules differ depending on where you are located as well as the size of your trade, this chapter will focus on the most important rules. In addition, it will equally discuss the rules that novices can put into practice as they venture into the complicated field of day trading. These rules will also aid the experienced traders to improve their performance in trade, for instance, in the area of risk management.

Rules for Beginners

If you are new in this field, the rules of day trading that have been discussed below can help you harvest commendable profits and avoid incurring significant losses.

Get In, Exit and Escape

One major mistake that beginners make is jumping into the arena without a well thought out game plan. Do not dare to press the "enter" button if you do not have a plan of how to get in and exit. It is understandable that some elements of excitement can set in when you are new in the field. However, it is important to note that if you do not have a formidable plan, you will be thrown out of the game completely. Make use of the rules of risk management as well as stop-losses cut down losses.

Timing

I bet you usually wake up early and bright, ready to face the day ahead in the day trading arena. However, avoiding the first quarter-hour when the market is opened is arguably one of the most crucial trading rules to abide by.

Most of the activity that takes place at this time involves market orders or panic trades from the previous night. You should instead use this period to follow up on reversals. The most experienced day traders also avoid the first quarter-hour.

Be Conscious of Margin

Do you remember the days when you started off, and you were looking for capital? It was very easy to fall for a margin.

However, you should keep in mind that it is a loan. A loan that needs to be repaid. In as much as it can greatly revamp your profits, it also has the ability to leave you nursing significant losses. Therefore, it is advisable to learn how to trade accordingly before resorting to the margin.

Demo Accounts

You have a lot to learn and absolutely nothing to lose by taking the initiative to first practice using a demo account. You can nurture your craft with a lot of time and space for trial and error because you are being funded by money that has been simulated. Very many brokers will give you free accounts so that you can practice because they are the best place to learn about strategies, patterns, and charts, as well as the quarter-hour day trading practice.

Learn to Accept the Loss

Virtually all the veteran traders have all achieved what they have achieved because they were willing to lose and learn from it. Losing is just the pathway to get more experience, embrace it. That being said, it is also important to say that cutting down your losses is very important.

Take in Everything

One veteran once said that a great trader is similar to an athlete, he might possess, but he has to train himself on how to use them. Complacency should not be something that great traders relate to because they should always be; I am searching for that edge. This means that they resort to a wide range of resources to boost their knowledge. They can use anything, ranging from videos, books, blogs, and forums.

Do an Evaluation of Tips

It is normal to get excited when you are given a tip that is thought-provoking. Nonetheless, unconfirmed tips from relatively undependable sources can result in significant losses. Jesse Livermore, a trader, said that experience had taught him a tip or a number of tips that will make him more money than what his judgment can. Therefore, ensure that you double-check any information that may affect your decisions as a trader.

Rules of Risk Management

The rules of money management and the risks of day trading are key determinants of how prosperous a trader will be. In as much as you do not have to follow these rules to the letter, they have proven to be indispensable to many.

1% Risk Rule

Here, the idea is to bar you from trading beyond your ability. When you put this technique into use, irrespective of whether a trade subsidy or not, you will always have some reserve I am stacked in the bank to help you correct your balance later on. The idea is that you should never engage in trade with more than 1% of your total account on one trade. For example, if your account has $50,000, you will only use up to $500 on your trade.

Why Use It?

You will have to lose over 100 trades simultaneously to clear your bank account balance completely. This is important to safeguard your earnings when market conditions are volatile as you get good returns in the process. I bet you are worried that you will not be raking in maximum profits if you trade so meagerly. Calm down. You can make good profits. If you stake 1%, you should expect a profit of about 1.5%—2%. If you trade several times a day, the profits will definitely make themselves evident. It is arguably the best approach for the people that are starting off. In as much as you get to experience through trial and error, losses can come fast and thick. However, if you are consistent, it will teach you the tricks of the game until you become a veteran in trading with an arsenal of techniques for making maximum profits in daily training.

Variations

As soon as you have created an efficient technique, you can make changes to your risk tolerance. You can upgrade it to 1.5% or 2%. However, it is important to note that traders with $100,000 in their accounts should not risk more than 1% in one trade because even a 1% loss could have a massive impact.

Basically, it is about finding an area that you and comfortable with, and it also connects with your style of trade.

CHAPTER 22

Steps to Success on Trading

A higher percentage of individuals fail in day trading because of ignoring crucial steps. If you have made up your mind to do day trading, there are specific steps that you ought to follow to make huge profits.

Have a Trading Plan

A trading plan is a set of guidelines that need to be followed by most traders to guide them in their activities. A trading plan helps you in proper money management to avoid losses. Before executing a trading plan, you need to back test and ensure it has positive results. Most of the trading brokers provide back testing tools in their software. A working and an affirmative trading plan will guide you on how to do your things the right way for you to succeed.

Set an Entry and Exit Price

To survive in this game, you ought to have knowledge of the entry plus that of exit prices. Day trading, like any other business, has worst-case scenarios. The entry price will help you understand when to get in, while the exit point will help you to know when to get out. With the prices, you will able to plan yourself on how to handle things in terms of market disasters with no worries.

Do Not Rush to Trade When the Market Opens

Have a schedule for your trading. Do not rush to trade immediately when the market opens. These are risky moments since the trades might be of the nights, and the market is not stable at that moment. You should know the best time to make your trade.

Different market securities have a different time to trade.

Do not be overexcited and do things anyhow. Have a timing plan for your trades.

Have Limit Orders

You are highly recommended to use limit orders in trading. What is a limit order? It is a trading order which gives you the capability to make sales and purchases in market trade at a specific price. Limit orders, unlike market orders, enable you to be in control of the maximum price you will pay for and also the minimum amount you will sell.

A market order allows traders to purchase or sell orders at the current prices in the market. A market order usually is concerned with the execution of the order made rather than the price. It will execute the order so fast with the current market price, unlike a limit order. A limit order checks on the amount and makes sure it is within the parameters of the limit order. If it does not fit within the settings, no trade executions will take place.

Shun from Losses

Losses usually are part of the game in all businesses, but try your best to avoid them. Small losses are sometimes not a big deal, but watch out for the losses not to be continuous. You might fail terribly. Be disciplined enough, and follow your trading plan strictly. Learn the mistakes you make that lead to failures and correct them. If the losses are still there, yet you followed your trading plan, change your strategies as quickly as possible or get out of trading. To be successful in trading, you need to cut off losses, which will lower your profits.

Accept Losses

Losing in trading is part of learning. Do not panic when losses occur in trading; accept them. Learn from the failures and find a solution. Do not despair or anything. Even pro traders experienced losses once or twice and worked things out.

Take Advantage of Technology

Day trading is all about competition. You should choose methods or techniques that are efficient for an excellent performance. You can implement some of the means by the use of modern technology tools in trading.

The technology tools may include simple charting platforms and back testing tools. Most of the charting platforms have simple user interface features that make it easier to read prices on the market. Back testing tools furthermore help traders to test their trading plans and strategies for better performance in trading. Technology speeds up trading transactions and enables you to stay up to date. Staying up to date keeps you alert on any changes in the market like price fluctuations.

Be Focused

Being a focused and self-disciplined trader will save you from lots of trouble. If you want to be successful, get yourself together, have strategies and plans on how to do trading. Know when is the right time to make trades so as not to miss the golden time to make your trades.

Having a schedule will keep you organized and managed. You have to follow this rule for success in day trading.

Trade with Money You Can Afford to Lose

The risks involved in day trading are huge. The money to be used for day trading should not be capital or your savings, which are essential aspects in all businesses. You should instead trade along with cash specifically for trading, which will not be a big deal when you lose it, and you can recover it so fast. Do not ever think of trading with your child's school fees, you will be all messed up.

Manage Your Risks

You need to have ways on how to handle your trading risks. Do not ignore them, or else you want to be a failure in trading. Be familiar with the dangers, or your day trading will be out of control. Make trades according to the trading plan and strategies, and you will ace it.

Have a Mindset of Steady Growth

You should possess a mindset of steady growth in day trading. Most of the traders have the mentality of getting higher profits all at once after starting day trading. Rushing for huge benefits when you are not even stable will give you lots of stress. Relax; everything will work out well with time. Do the right thing at the right speed, and everything will eventually work out.

Avoid Using Margins

Margins enable you to leverage your funds and even extra cash that you borrow from brokers. It can also increase your borrowing power. Operating on margins is sometimes risky in trading. Margins can increase or decrease in the market. The significant risk involved in margins is its big loss that occurs when the margin falls. It makes it worse when you lose the funds that you have borrowed.

Have Big Goals

You need to have stringent goals for yourself. Goals will assist you in working towards something that you need to accomplish. Visualize your goals so good and perform day trading towards them. Work hard, and you will succeed in day trading.

Bear the Business Kind of Mindset

Businesses are involved with pretty much of things. They include profits, losses, expenses, risks, stress, and so much more. Normally, it is highly recommended that that in-depth research about your business has to be undertaken, and good strategies have to be laid so as to improve the potential of the business. Well, this is much similar to day trading, lay out a good plan with set strategies and learn more about your day-to-day trading occurrences in a bid to excel and acquire large chunks of profits.

A Student of the Markets

Trading markets are quite dynamic. As a trader, you ought to discover what actually used to happen, what is happening, and master all the facts involved in day trading as much as possible. This makes you really informed, educated, and improves your rates of managing risks. With all these outcomes, undertaking day trading becomes quite easier, and chances of incurring day-to-day losses become limited.

Developing and Implementing the Trading Methodology

A day trading methodology is a system of methods that are laid down so as the trader can implement them in their day-to-day trading activities. This discourages hesitation that is mostly experienced by most traders that just try out their luck during trading without any plan and really expect the best out of it. Day trading is not a "get rich overnight" kind of engagement but a certain activity that calls for intelligence and several tactical skills.

Frequently Using Stop Losses

A stop loss is basically a predetermined amount of risk that a day trader is willing to accept with each trade. It is normally in the form of a particular percentage or a certain trading amount that limits the trader from exposure during trading. Most importantly, using stop losses ensure that risks and losses are limited.

Knowing When to Stop Trading

There exist two reasons why you should most probably stop trading; the presence of an ineffective trading plan and an ineffective day trader. Major amounts of losses are expected in an ineffective trading plan, probably due to the fact that markets may have changed, market volatility may have much lessened, or perhaps the trading plan is just not working out as expected. This does not necessarily imply that trading has to be terminated, but the fact that a new trading plan had to be laid and strong trading strategies set.

On the other hand, an ineffective day trader is an unwanted day trader. So as to excel in day trading, there has to be a rule; be disciplined, follow your big plan, work hard and learn, be patient, and so much on. If this does not entirely define you, then the chances are that day trading is not really your kind of engagement.

Keep Trading in Perspective

It is advisable to focus on the bigger picture during trading. Setting realistic goals is one of the ways of keeping trading in perspective. For instance, if a trader happens to have a smaller trading account, he or she should not expect some huge returns. Always work with what you have on your plate and really try to remain sensible. It is a step to step income-generating engagement that requires much patience and a variety of day trading skills. Also, winning and losing in day trading is really going to be such common events. When winning, enjoy and celebrate your good efforts but do not lose too much control and during the sad moments, remember that losing trade is not afar off. Stay put and focused.

Trading is Not Entertainment

The word has been clearly misunderstood by most traders, especially beginners. The novice should realize that day trading is an income-generating engagement and also a capital diminishing kind of activity. Remember that failing to plan is also planning to fail. Plan your strategies, learn, and get your day trading journey shining all the way with just a little loss occurrence.

Learn to Trade Options

With trading options, a trader has to wait for a single day before money settles after a trade. The day trading options rules are T + 1. Read several blogs describing these and most preferably check the kind that is not really advanced to avoid making it hard to implement several kinds of strategies at the early day trading stages.

CHAPTER 23

Average Income of a Day Trader

You can go to a reliable gauge of what an informal investor can make dependent on their area, beginning capital, and business status. Let's face it, a significant number of people are thinking about going out without anyone else and are not hoping to find a new line of work.

Anybody that discloses to you a conclusive range for a day exchanging pay is likely pulling your leg. I may as was well be conversing with one of my children about Yo Gabba (it was one of their preferred shows on Nickelodeon). The reason being, there is a large group of outside variables that play into how a lot of cash you can make. In this article, we will tear through all the lighten on the web and get down to cold hard certainties. Sit back, unwind, and get some espresso.

A Decision You Should Not Take Lightly

You ought not to trifle with this choice, and you should gauge the upsides and downsides. First of all, exchanging for another person will permit you the chance to use the devices and systems of an outfit that is ideally beneficial. A portion of the positives exchanging for another person is evacuating the weights of distinguishing both a triumphant framework and a tutor that can help you end route.

It is On the off chance that you are not beneficial "enough," be set up to have a more significant number of rules tossed at you than when you were in sixth grade. This degree of administration over your exchanging action is because of the reality you are utilizing another person's cash, so profit or become acclimated to somebody revealing to you how to relax.

The one significant upside for day exchanging for another person is you will get pay. This pay is likely insufficient to live on; however, you do get a check. At the point when you go out alone, there is no pay. You are a financial specialist wanting to make payments. We will go into this theme a lot further. Later on, however, I needed to ensure I express this forthright.

Licenses

On the slim chance that you choose to work for the firm and are exchanging customer's cash or conceivably interfacing with clients, you will require your Series 7 and perhaps your Series 63 permit.

Arrangement 7

The Series 7 will give you the permit to exchange. Last I checked, the test cost $305, and relying upon the outfit will be secured by the firm.

Arrangement 63

The Series 63 is the following test you should take after the Series 7. This test licenses you to request orders for stock inside a point of view state. A straightforward perspective about this is the 7 gives you the privilege to exchange on a government level, and the 63 enable you to work inside the limits of state laws.

I don't anticipate covering the theme of day exchanging for somebody finally because I haven't lived it. From what I do know, you are required to finish some in-house preparing programs for the firm you speak to. For venture houses, you will get a not too bad base pay, enough to keep you at the lower white-collar class extend for New York.

Know the Best Part

Your base stock merchant pay could go from 50,000 - 70,000 dollars in the US, which is only enough for you to take care of your link tab, feed yourself and perhaps take a taxi or two. In any case, this not the slightest bit covers meals, vehicles, excursions, tuition-based schools, and so on.

In this way, I surmise you can rapidly observe that for you to be fruitful, you're going to need to make your reward. There is only one catch; you need to profit day exchanging. Superficially, this sounds sensible because you bring down your hazard profile by having another pay stream of a base compensation; in any case, you need to perform to remain utilized and will just get around 10-30%% of the benefits you get from your exchanging movement. In light of these numbers, you would need to make about 300k in exchanging benefits to break a 100k in compensation. Most likely about it, the advantage of exchanging with an organization is, after some time, your purchasing influence will increment, and you have none of the drawbacks dangers since it's the organization's cash. The key is ensuring you have a lot of money under administration.

As should be evident in the infographic over, the way to making genuine cash is to begin dealing with different assets. You, in one way or another, draw that off, and you will make by and large 576k per year. Indeed you read that right.

I realize the 576k looks engaging; however, recall it is out and out hard labor to get to the highest point of the mountain. The other brings up to get out from the infographic is that the usual reward is beginning to drift higher and if things go as conjecture will surpass the downturn top not long from now. Along these lines, on the off possibility that one of your objectives is to profit, you are looking in the right business.

Regular Income Trading for a Company

The widely appealing individual can hope to make somewhere in the range of 100k and 175k. In conclusion, it is on the off chance that you are beneath normal, hope to get a pink slip.

In any case, pause - there's additional. Certainly, if we broaden our exploration past New York, you will see the regular pay for a "Merchant" is $89,496.

Open Trading Firms

Be that as it may, I can consider many employments where you can make near $89k, and it doesn't require the degree of responsibility and hazard taking required for exchanging. You might be thinking, "This person just revealed to me it could go as high as $250k to $500k in case I'm better than expected, where $89k becomes an integral factor."

What I have talked about so far are the pay rates for traded on an open market organization—good karma attempting to get precise information for the first-class universe of private value brokers. What you will discover are regularly the top brokers from the Chase and Bank of America's endeavor out to flexible investments, as a result of the opportunity in their exchanging choices and the more significant compensation potential.

Here's the most significant part, with the general population firms, corporate objectives will frequently drive a segment of your other targets. The magnificence of the multifaceted investment world is while there are still organization objectives, you have the chance to eat a more significant amount of what you slaughter.

It's nothing for a top broker to out-acquire their chief on the off chance that they carry enough an incentive to the firm. What amount do you figure you could make?

Advantages of day exchanging for an organization:

- Pay
- Medical advantages
- The renown of working for a venture bank or fence investments
- No danger of individual capital
- Climb the corporate positions to deal with various assets
- A drawback of day exchanging for an organization
- Must connect with customers
- Office legislative issues
- By and large, you get 20% of benefits (Public Firm)

Day Trading for a Prop Firm

Day exchanging for prop firms can feel similar to living on the edge. Like exchanging for an organization, you will get some preparation before the prop firm enables you to trade with their cash and approach their frameworks. From that point forward, all likenesses between exchanging for a prop firm and an organization contrast. Try not to expect any human services of paid downtime. You won't have a base compensation or yearly audits. The prop firms will expect you to store cash to begin utilizing their foundation.

The advantages are the prop firm will part benefits with you anyplace from a third and up to half. The drawbacks are again no compensation, and you bear a portion of the torment with regards to misfortunes. However, here's the rub, the explanation prop firm merchants make not precisely those for the speculation houses is access to capital. Since you are likely exchanging the exclusive firm proprietor's cash, the pool of assets you approach is constrained.

I would state a better than an expected broker for a prop firm can make about 150k to 250k every year. The typical broker will do somewhere in the range of 60k and 100k, and underperformers will have such huge numbers of position limits set for them, they are fundamentally rehearsing and not profiting. These underperformers will probably expel themselves from the game because rehearsing doesn't take care of the tabs.

Advantages:

- Split benefits with Prop Firm
- Low commission rates
- No Boss
- Increment Margin
- Utilize your cash-flow to begin
- Loss of individual riches
- Constrained preparing
- No medical advantages or paid downtime
- No vocation movement
- Just cause cash off what you to acquire

Day Trading Salaries State by State in the US

Notwithstanding the information showed in the infographic from the Office of the New York State Comptroller, I needed to make it a stride further to distinguish the beginning pay for a passage level exchanging work the country over. I arrived on a passage level to give a counter to the middle national normal of $89k for an exchanging work. Keep in mind that $89k is normal of junior exchanging employments - right to the most senior.

Along these lines, in the situation that you are genuinely beginning and are offered $50k, you don't get disheartened. We, as a whole, need to start somewhere! True to form, the New England and Pacific districts of the nation have the most significant pay. Presently, these can be just ascribed to the standard average cost for essential items. However, you can discover your state to perceive what you can hope to make as a lesser dealer.

The Myth

A large number of the online articles are explicit about the benefit proportion you can expect when you become an informal investor. For instance, an article by Cory Mitchell that shows up on the Vantage Point Trading site spreads it out in detail and expects to start exchanging capital of $30,000:

"Accept your normal five exchanges for every day, so if you have 20 exchanging days a month, you make 100 exchanges for every month. You make $3,750; however, despite everything, you have commissions and perhaps some different charges. Your expense per exchange is $5/contract (full circle). Your bonus costs are: 100 exchanges x $5 x 2 agreements = $1000."

In Mitchell's model, your net after bonuses is $2,750. Since you began with $30,000, that is a month to month return of a little more than 9 percent, if you reinvest those benefits on a month to month premise, toward the finish of one year, you'll have an interest of $55,944 and change. Not awful, and the best news is, you don't have to get dressed for work.

CHAPTER 24

Common Pitfalls You Can Avoid When Day Trading

No matter which strategy you use, which market you participate in, or which assets you choose to trade, there are some basic tenets of day trading that you'll need to follow. When day traders fail, it's generally because they fell into some very common and easy to avoid traps. Before you even get started with your trading career, as you're making your trading plan, take a look at these mistakes and make sure you're protecting yourself from them.

Starting Big

As a new day trader, it is likely that you're bubbling with enthusiasm as you look forward to starting your trades. You have read up on all the theory, including the trips and tricks, and believe that you are ready for the game. If you have managed a sizeable capital portfolio from an investment, you may be keen to start big and make big profits.

Learn the Basics

Day trading is not something that you can simply teach yourself and then start excelling at. You need to get some hands-on advice from people who are seasoned day traders. To do this, you should find an experienced trader and spend some time observing them, asking questions, and listening to advice. Learn how to play the game of trading, to build up the confidence to give it a go yourself. Realize that this will require patience on your part so that it is done right. With proper determination, you'll find that your efforts are enough to lead to big profits.

Planning to Fail

Failing to plan is planning to fail, and this is especially true for day traders. Trading is about making a profit and not about experiencing feelings of exhilaration by taking chances with money. Considering the outcome that is expected, it's important that all traders have a plan of action. A plan is particularly of value because of the speed and emotion that affect day trading. Day trading is likely to be backed into corners where they need to make instant decisions, or during a volatile day of trading, they could get caught up in the events of the day and make decisions that will negatively affect their bottom line. Have a plan in place, especially when it is in writing, is an important step to controlling day trading.

Missing Discipline

An aspect of discipline includes stop-loss orders. These orders are triggered based on certain conditions within the day-trading market. They help investors to save money, particularly if the trade is taking place automatically. It's imperative that all traders have a plan that will help them to manage their risks, as well as their possibilities for success or failure.

Manage your Expectations

Day trading is not a get rich quick scheme. Neither is it a magic wand that will help relieve all your problems. It is challenging, and there is the constant pressure that you could lose it all. Rather than expecting to rake in dollars, expect to put in a significant amount of work into perfecting the method in which you trade. The reason for this is that success in trading requires a considerable amount of planning, along with hard work.

Keeping Too Busy

Being busy is good, and many people want to be observed as being busy, as this is a way that they can validate the amount of work that they have had to do. In trading, being too busy is not good for a trader. It indicates the possibility of letting things slip through their fingers. A new trader may attempt to manage at least 10 trades in a day. The assumption is by trading more, you can make more.

This may not actually be the case. Some professional traders insist on trading just two trades through the day. They may complete the trades early in the day, but then they can spend the rest of the day following up. By having fewer day trades to monitor, it becomes easier to see when there is a change in the market.

Watch Out for Losing Streaks

There is nothing that can be as disheartening as repeatedly losing when you're day trading. If you aren't careful, it may reach the point where you end up being clinically depressed, especially if you're always losing more progressively. That is why even though you may have the enthusiasm to day trade on your own, you need to seek out counsel from a professional who has been successful. Over time, you will pass the phase of losing streaks, and the moments that you were demoralized will be distant memories.

Thinking Anyone Can Do It

Should you ever be in a car accident and needed life-saving surgery, would you allow a teenager in high school to operate on you? Your answer is most likely, "Absolutely Not!"

If you had a large sum of money which you wanted to see grow, would you pass it to the first person that you walk by on the street and say, "I'll wait to hear from you." Of course, it's highly unlikely.

Keep an Eye on Your Risk Capital

Your trading capital is money that you are willing to risk. This is money that should be solely dedicated to day trading and nothing else. That way, you lose it all, your life won't start to fall apart all around you. It's also noteworthy that a day trader is required to keep a certain amount in their account as equity, and the minimum must be maintained if there is any day trading to take place.

Messing up Your Margin

Your capital as a day trader is likely to fluctuate up and down throughout the day. Sometimes, it is on the lower side, and you need an extra boost. So, you choose to borrow from a broker so that you can purchase securities. This is meant to be a facility that gives day traders some wiggle room if it's used correctly. Although some people have used this support in the wrong way or have abused it. This could occur when one borrows much more than they can pay back, and the result is an empty trading account and the mounting of debt. Day traders should trade within their means as long as possible.

Ignoring Important Resources

Perhaps the most valuable asset that you can get that will lead you to success when day trading online is an excellent high-speed internet connection. Next is an investment in state-of-the-art software that is specialized and fully loaded with a range of analysis tools. Then you should make sure that your trading wallet is well stocked, as you need a significant amount of capital to get you started. As part of your resources, you should have direct access to an expert in the field so that you can get advice when you need it and get input on your equipment and its specifications. Finally, hire yourself a coach. This will be a great investment, allowing you to learn what is necessary to master day trading for the long haul.

Forgetting About Mental Health

Having the right state of mind could be the difference between winning and losing. In order to come out on top as a winner, one who is competent and can trade on instinct, you need to learn how you can manage your emotions.

So, you cannot allow the intense thinking and mental energy that goes into day trading bring you down and drain your energy. You must be ready for action. This is like having a jerk reflex. With this as a trick up your sleeve, you will be able to gain competence and win consistently. It will build up your intuition so that you always aim for and attain trading success.

Improper Education and Research

Not understanding the markets is the first mistake newbies often make. Before you get out your wallet or bank card, make sure that you understand the basics before you start buying. That means having a good idea of what all the index funds mean, some basic stock market jargon, and knowing the different ways you can buy stock. It's also important to understand the markets on another level.

Letting Emotions Rather Than Facts Govern Decisions

Emotions have a nasty way of injecting themselves into stock market investing. It's exciting and can be filled with fear if you're looking at losing your shirt. Of course, the real problem is that people overestimate the dangers.

Lack of Planning

The common mistake made by beginners is not planning their trades. To be an experienced trader, you need to work smart for it. You cannot make up a mind map for how you think you can carry on the trade. Proper working and research are called for. You need to jot down the risks, the potential gains, and the cost-to-revenue ratio.

Not Having Up to Date Technology

Day trading is a game of inches, and the changes that can happen in the blink of an eye can be enough to make or break the success streak that you have been courting all day long. Remember, even if you think the technology that you are using to trade is good enough, you aren't just trading against the market, and you are trading against other traders, both big and small, who are all trying to one-up one another with the best technology on the market today. While this doesn't mean that you need to go out and buy a $3,000 computer, it does mean that you'll want to have a rig that can compete with the current generation of hardware if you hope to make the sorts of split-second trades that ultimately lead to profit in the long run.

Getting in at the Wrong Time

Starting out, it can be difficult to get your bearings, which means that when you do happen upon a specific trend, it can be easy to jump on it now and ask questions about it later. While this might lead to success from time to time, the fact of the matter is that spotting a trend at the right time is much better than spotting it in the first place. The most profitable time to spot a trend is right as it is beginning; in this way, you will have a good timeframe to turn a profit as it matures. When it comes to finding trends early, it will help to have an idea of who the major players are in the types of stocks that you tend to favor. Big time players are the ones whose movement alone is enough to alter the state of the market and to get to know them, and watching them like a hawk, is key to your long-term success as a day trader.

Not Balancing Research with the Current Truth

New day traders typically fall into two camps, those who do too much research before starting out and those that don't do enough research before starting out. Those that do too much research tend to consider every aspect of the companies that they are thinking about purchasing stock in and only purchase when the fundamentals appear to be completely on the up and up.

Not Treating Day Trading as a Job

If you ever hope to day trade full time, the first thing you will need to do is to treat trading as though it were already a job. What this means is committing to it for the same period of time every day, no matter what. If day trading is a job, then it means you are your own boss, and that means you will need to keep tabs on your comings and goings and ensure you dedicate the time you need to trading each day to reach your goals.

CHAPTER 25

Common Day Trading Mistakes to Avoid

Aside from doing the right things, you'll also need to refrain from certain things to succeed as a day trader. Following are some of the most common day trading mistakes you should avoid committing.

Excessive Day Trading

By excessive, I mean executing too many day trades. One of the most common mistakes many newbie day traders make is assuming that they can become day trading ninjas in just a couple of weeks if they trade often enough to get it right. But while more practice can eventually translate into day trading mastery in the future, it doesn't mean you can cram all that practice in a very short period of time via very frequent day trading. The adage "the more, the merrier" doesn't necessarily apply to day trading. Remember, timing is crucial for day trading success. And timing is dependent on how the market is doing during the day. There will be days when day trading opportunities are few and far between, and there'll be days when day trading opportunities abound. Don't force trades for the sake of getting enough day trades under your belt. Even in the midst of a plethora of profitable day trading opportunities, the more, the merrier still doesn't apply. Why? If you're a newbie trader, your best bet at becoming a day trading ninja at the soonest possible time is to concentrate on one or two day trades per day only. By limiting your day trades to just one or two, you have the opportunity to monitor and learn from your trades closely.

Can you imagine executing 5 or more trades daily as a newbie and monitor all those positions simultaneously? You'll only get confused and overwhelmed, and worse, you may even miss day trading triggers and signals and fail to close your positions profitably.

Winging It

If you want to succeed as a day trader, you need to hold each trading day in reverence and high esteem. Plan your day trading strategies for the day and execute those strategies instead of just winging it.

As cliché as it may sound, failing to plan really is planning to fail. And considering the financial stakes involved in day trading, you shouldn't go through your trading days without any plan on hand. Luck favors those who are prepared, and planning can convince lady luck that you are prepared.

Expecting Too Much Too Soon

This much is true about day trading: it's one of the most exciting and exhilarating jobs in the world! And stories many day traders tell of riches accumulated through this economic activity add more excitement, desire, and urgency for many to get into it.

However, too much excitement and desire resulting from many day trading success stories can be very detrimental to newbie day traders. Let me correct myself: it is detrimental to newbie day traders. Why?

Such stories, many of which are probably urban legends, give newbies unrealistic expectations of quick and easy day trading riches. Many beginner day traders get the impression that day trading is a get-rich-quick scheme!

It's not. What many day traders hardly brag about are the times they also lost money and how long it took them to master the craft enough to quit their jobs and do it full time. And even rarer are stories of the myriad number of people who've attempted day trading and failed. It's the dearth of such stories that tend to make day trading neophytes have unrealistic expectations about day trading.

What's the problem with lofty day trading expectations? Here's the problem: if you have very unrealistic expectations, it's almost certain that you'll fail. It's because unrealistic expectations can't be met, and therefore, there are zero chances for success.

One of the most unrealistic expectations surrounding day trading is being able to double one's initial trading capital in a couple of months, at most. Similar to such expectations is that of being able to quit one's day job and live an abundant life in just a few months via day trading. Successful day traders went through numerous failures, too, before they succeeded at day trading and were able to do it for a living.

If you decide to give day trading a shot, have realistic expectations. In fact, don't even expect to profit soon. Instead, take the initial losses as they come, limiting them through sensible stop-loss limits and learning from them. Eventually, you'll get the hang of it, and your day trading profits will start eclipsing your day trading losses.

Changing Strategies Frequently

Do you know how to ride a bike? If not, do you know someone who does? Whether it's you or somebody you know, learning how to ride a bike wasn't instant. It took time and a couple of falls and bruises along the way.

But despite falls, scratches, and bruises, you or that person you know stuck to learning how to ride a bike and with enough time and practice, succeeded in doing so. It was because you or the other person knew that initial failures mean that riding a bike was impossible. It's just challenging at first.

It's the same with learning how to day trade profitably. You'll need to give yourself enough time and practice to master it. Just because you suffered trading losses in the beginning doesn't mean it's not working, or it's not for you. It probably means you haven't really mastered it yet.

But if you quit and shift to a new trading strategy or plan quickly, you'll have to start again from scratch, extend your learning time, and possibly lose more money than you would've if you stuck around to your initial strategy long enough to give yourself a shot at day trading successfully or concluding with certainty that it's not working for you.

If you frequently change your day trading strategies, i.e., you don't give yourself enough time to learn day trading strategies, your chances of mastering them become much lower. In that case, your chance of succeeding in day trading becomes much lower too.

Not Analyzing Past Trades

"Those who don't learn history are doomed to repeat it," said writer and philosopher George Santayana. We can paraphrase it to apply to day traders, too: "Those who don't learn from their day trading mistakes will be doomed to repeat them."

If you don't keep a day trading journal containing records of all your trades and, more importantly, analyze them, you'll be doomed to repeat your losing day trades. It's because by not doing so, you won't be able to determine what you're doing wrong and what you should be doing instead in order to have more profitable day trades than losing ones.

As another saying goes: if you always do what you always did, you'll always get what you always got. Unless you analyze your past day trades on a regular basis, you'll be doomed to repeating the same mistakes and continue losing money on them.

Ditching Correlations

We can define correlations as a relationship where one thing influences the outcome or behavior of another. A positive correlation means that both tend to move in the same direction or exhibit similar behaviors, i.e., when one goes up, the other goes up, too, and vice versa.

Correlations abound in the stock market. For example, returns on the stock market are usually negatively correlated with the Federal Reserve's interest rates, i.e., when the Feds increase interest rates, returns on stock market investments go down and vice versa.

Correlations exist across industries in the stock market, too. For example, property development stocks are positively correlated to steel and cement manufacturing stocks. This is because when the property development's booming, it buys more steel and cement from manufacturing companies, which in turn also increase their income. Ignoring correlations during day trading increases your risks for erroneous position taking and exiting. You may take a short position on a steel manufacturer's stock while taking a long position on a property development company's stock, and if they have a positive correlation, one of those two positions will most likely end up in a loss. But caution must be exercised with using correlations in your day trades. Don't establish correlations where there's none. Your job is to simply identify if there are observable correlations, what those correlations are, and how strong they are.

Being Greedy

Remember the story of the goose that lay golden eggs? Because the goose's owner was so greedy and couldn't wait for the goose to lay more eggs immediately, he killed the goose and cut it open.

Sadly, for the owner, there were no golden eggs inside the goose because it only created and laid one

When it comes to day trading, greed can have the same negative financial impact. Greed can make a day trader hold on to an already profitable position longer than needed and result in smaller profits or, worse, trading losses. That's why you must be disciplined enough to stick to your day trading stop-loss and profit-taking limits. And that's why you should program those limits on your platform, too. Doing so minimizes the risks of greed hijacking your otherwise profitable day trades

CHAPTER 26

Do's and Don'ts of Day Trading

Do's of Day Trading
Risk Capital

You have to understand that the stock market is a very volatile place, and anything can happen within a matter of a few seconds. You have to be prepared for anything that it throws at you. In order to prepare for it, you have to make use of risk capital.

Risk capital refers to money that you are willing to risk. You have to convince yourself that even if you lose the money that you have invested, then it will not be a big deal for you. For that, you have to make use of your own money and not borrow from anyone, as you will start feeling guilty about investing it. Decide on a set number and invest it.

Research

You have to conduct a thorough research on the market before investing in it. Do not think you will learn as you go. That is only possible if you at least know the basics. You have to remain interested in gathering information that is crucial for your investments, and it will only come about if you put in some hard work towards it. Nobody is asking you to stay up and go through thick textbooks. All you have to do is go through books and websites and gather enough information to help you get started on the right foot.

Diversification

You have to stress diversification in your portfolio. You do not want all the money to go into the same place. Think of it as a way to increase your stock's potential. You have to choose different sectors and diverse stocks to invest in.

You should also choose one of the different types of investments as they all contribute towards attaining a different result. Diversification is mostly seen as a tool to cut down on risk, and it is best that you not invest any more than 5% in any one of the securities.

Stop-Loss

You have to understand the importance of a stop-loss mechanism. A stop-loss technique is used to safeguard an investment. Now say, for example, you invest $100 and buy shares priced at $5 each. You have to place a stop loss at around $4 in order to stop it from going down any further.

Now you will wonder as to why you have to place the stop loss and undergo one, well, by doing so, you will actually be saving your money to a large extent. You will not have to worry about the value slipping further down and can carry on with your trade.

Take a Loss

It is fine to take a loss from time to time. Do not think of it as a big hurdle. You will have the chance to convert the loss into a profit. You have to remain confident and invested. You can take a loss on a bad investment that was anyway not going your way.

You can also take a loss on an investment that you think is a long hold and will not work for you in the short term. Taking a few losses is the only way in which you can learn to trade well in the market.

These form the different dos of the stock market that will help you with your intraday trades.

Don'ts of Day Trading

No Planning

Do not make the mistake of going about investing in the market without a plan in tow. You have to plan out the different things that you will do in the market and go about it the right way. This plan should include how much you will invest in the market, where you will invest, how you will go about it etc. No planning will translate to getting lost in the stock market, which is not a good sign for any investor.

Over-Rely on Broker

You must never over-rely on a broker. You have to make your own decisions and know what to do and when. The broker will not know whether an investment is good for you. He will only be bothered about his profits.

If he is suggesting something, then you should do your own research before investing in the stock. The same extends to emails that you might receive through certain sources. These emails are spam and meant to dupe you. So, do not make the mistake of trusting everything that you read.

Message Boards

You have to not care about message boards. These will be available on the Internet and are mostly meant to help people gather information. But there will be pumpers and bashers present there. Pumpers will force people to buy a stock just to increase its value, and bashers will force people to sell all their stocks just because they want the value to go down. Both these types are risky, as they will abandon the investors just as soon as their motive is fulfilled. So you have to be quite careful with it.

Calculate Wrong

Some people make the mistake of calculating wrong. They will not be adept at math and will end up with the wrong numbers. This is a potential danger to all those looking to increase their wealth potential. If you are not good at calculating, then download an app that will do it for you or carry a calculator around to do the correct calculations. The motive is to make the right calculations and increase your wealth potential.

Copy Strategies

Do not make the mistake of copying someone else's strategies. You have to come up with something that is your own and not borrowed from someone else. If you end up borrowing, then you will not be able to attain the desired results. You have to sit with your broker and come up with a custom strategy that you can employ and win big.

Glossary

A
Ask
Ask price is what a seller offers to a buyer for selling any financial asset.
B
Broker
A broker can be an individual or a firm that acts as an intermediary between traders and exchanges and receives a commission whenever a trade is executed between these two parties.
Bid
In day trading, bid price is what a buyer offers to a seller for purchasing any financial asset.
Bear
Traders who have a negative outlook on markets, and expect the price to fall, are called bears.
Bear Market
In a bear or a bearish market, the price trend continuously declines.
Bull
Traders who have a positive outlook on the market, and expect the price to rise, are nicknamed bulls.
Bull Market
Markets with the rising price pattern are called the Bull market.
C
Cash Market
A market where actual stocks and commodities are traded.
Call Option
Options contracts that are bullish on markets. Popular among day traders.
D
Daily Trading Limit
Exchanges set the maximum price range each day for any contract. The daily trading limit does not mean that it will halt the trading, but only places a limit on the movement of price.
Day Order
An order placed during an intraday session, valid only for that session. It automatically gets canceled when the session closes.
Day Trade
Buying and selling of financial assets on the same day. These assets can be stocks, commodities, forex, or options.
Day Traders
Traders who buy or sell financial assets through a single session and close all their positions before the end of the day. They do not carry forward their positions for the upcoming session.
E
Exchange
A regulated central marketplace where buyers and sellers trade financial assets.
F
Futures
Derivative contracts that cover the buying and selling of financial assets for future delivery. These trades take place on a future exchange.
Futures Contract
These are derivative agreements conducted through a futures exchange. These are legally binding on traders who buy or sell financial instruments for future delivery. Futures contracts have standard regulations based on quantity and delivery time.
G

Good till Canceled (GTC)

Open orders with buying or selling instructions at a specific future price and can remain open till the order is executed.

H

Hedge

The simultaneous buying and selling of a derivative contract of a future date. This is done to balance a loss and profit of open positions in derivatives and cash markets.

Hedger

When companies or individuals, who are holding positions in cash markets, make an opposite trade in the derivatives markets to balance any potential loss, they are called hedgers.

Hedging

The act of balancing any potential risk of loss in cash markets by taking an equal but opposite position in the derivative markets.

I

Initial Margin

To open a new position in derivative markets, such as in futures and options, traders are required to deposit a minimum amount of money in their trading accounts, called initial margin. This is to mitigate any risk of loss because of market volatility. The level of initial margin can increase or decrease according to the market volatility.

L

Last Trading Day

The last trading day is not the last day of the month, but the last trading day of derivative contracts (futures & options). On this trading day, the monthly derivative contracts are settled among traders.

Limit Order

An order, given to buy or sell a financial instrument at a specific price, beyond which the order is not filled. This shows that the buyer or seller will trade only at a specific price.

Liquidity

A characteristic of tradable financial instruments, which shows the ease of trading those. Traders and investors prefer to buy or sell highly liquid assets because these can be easily bought or sold.

Long

A trader is supposed to be 'long' if he has a bullish outlook for the market. A long position is taken when buyers expect the price to rise.

M

Maintenance Margin

This is the minimum value traders must keep in their trading account if they wish to keep a position open. The maintenance margin is usually lower compared to the initial margin.

Margin Call

If a trader's account falls short of the required maintenance margin, they receive a call from the brokerage firm, demanding to deposit the required amount. If a trader does not do so, the brokerage firm liquidates his positions amounting to the same value.

Market Order

An order to buy or sell any financial entity at the latest available price. Traders use this order when they want their trades to be executed quickly.

Market on Close

This order is used to buy or sell financial assets at the end of that trading session. The order price is typically within the closing range of market prices.

O

Offer Price

It shows the willingness of the seller to sell a financial asset at an agreed price. It is also called 'Ask' price.

Open Order

An order which is not executed. It can remain open till the specified price is reached or the order is canceled.

P

Pit

A specific place on the trading floor where traders conduct their buying and selling activities.

Position

A trade that has not been completed the process of both buying and selling. An open trade.

S

Settlement Price

This is the last price paid for any financial entity on a trading day. This is also called the closing price.

Scalp

A day trading method, where speculators trade for small profits. These trades are completed very quickly, within a few minutes. Scalpers trade multiple times through the same day.

Short

When a trader has a negative or bearish outlook on the market, he is said to be short on the market. Also, the selling side of an open derivative contract.

Speculator

Traders who try to anticipate market movements and price changes to earn profits.

Spot

Markets, where immediate delivery and cash payment is handled for financial assets.

Spread

Difference between the bid and ask price.

Stop Order

Also known as the stop-loss order. Traders use this order to limit the risk of loss or profits at a certain price level.

Stop Limit

Like a stop order, but with a slight variation. Stop order with limit acts as a limit order in buying when the price is at or above the stop price. In selling, it becomes a limit order when the price is trading at or below the stock price.

T

Tick

In trading, the smallest increment in the price of any financial asset. Some scalpers use tick price for trading.

Conclusion

Y ou can pair it up with your current job or you can adopt it as a full-time profession. The point is that you can work when and where you want if you opt to be a day trader. You get the freedom to structure your day as you need, and you can work from home or even when you are traveling.

It is a small business, and it doesn't need a large amount of investment to get started. The initial investment in the equipment that is a computer, a couple of monitors, a fast and reliable internet connection, and trading software. They are relatively inexpensive.

As an active trader, you have no commitments of any kind to anyone. You work as an independent person, hence you answer to no one except yourself. You don't have a nasty boss who is always glaring from his office to check if you are working or not. When you are ill, you have the liberty to stay in bed for the day.

The best thing about day trading is that you get to develop your style that is compatible with your nature, your disposition, and is easy-going. When the market appears to be too volatile to handle, you can take the day off and do the pending tasks such as household repair, cooking, or visiting a family member or a friend. You can play with your kids, run errands, or go shopping with the money that you have saved by keeping out of a tricky market. The top upside about choosing day trading as a field of earning money is that you don't need a degree or a specialized level of skills for the purpose. You will have to absorb plenty of knowledge before you could declare yourself fit for active trading, but you don't have to get some kind of certification in this field. The internet is loaded with several free resources that can help you upgrade your knowledge base in the field of investing. You can enroll in them. The best approach is to pair up the study of online resources with the study of a good book. Another best thing about day trading is that you get the chance to be your boss. You work from the comfort of your home, sipping your coffee. You don't need to seek permission from any higher authority to execute your trades. You are responsible for profits and accountable for the way the trade goes on.

One of the top advantages of being a day trader is that you get to sleep peacefully. All of your trades close when the day ends. There is no risk of an overnight loss. There is no risk that your stock value will drop to zero while you are lost in the valley of dreams. Day trading offers you the security of your profit and greater control over your trading business. If it went well during the day and you bagged sufficient profits, you can go to sleep soundly overnight.

Even if the market is taking a bad turn, you can take advantage of that. While it struggles, you can short sell and bag profits while it dips to the bottom. If you can make money off bearish conditions in the stock market, you get a competitive advantage over traders. Long term investors have to focus on the fundamentals of a company like its overall health, information about who is in the management board and how they are running the company, the past reports about the company, the record of the profits it posted, its contracts with government and non-government agencies, its tradition of awarding dividends to shareholders and its financial statements.

DAY TRADING FUTURES

Learn how Day Trading anad Futures Work to Build your Financial Freedom. How to Become a Smart Trader to Don't Lose Money and Earn Passive Income with a Positive ROI in 19 Days

Alexander Taylor

Introduction

Futures are financial agreements or contracts in which the parties involved agree to trade an asset at a future date with a fixed price. It can either be on buying an asset or selling of an asset at a future date and a fixed price as agreed by the trading parties. Futures are not subject to market or price fluctuations, irrespective of the market conditions or price of the asset on which the future has been agreed over; the trading parties must fulfill their obligation to sell the tradable asset or buy the tradable asset as at when due. It is made use of leverage, which requires the parties to deposit a percentage of the total price agreed on with a broker.

To invest in futures, you need the services of a broker whose role is to process access to the market for you. Choose only credible futures brokers to avoid getting dumped and abused. The various types of futures include commodity futures, currency futures, stock index futures, US Treasury futures, gold futures, ETC.

The advantages of futures include speculation purposes, protection of price against price instability and market volatility, the compulsion of contract, and deposit of a percentage of the contract. Futures are used by investors for speculation purposes. For example, it is used by investors to speculate on the path or direction in which the price of a given asset or security is going to take.

Another advantage of futures is that prices are protected and secured. Futures lock down prices for the duration of its existence. It does not matter if the price of the underlying asset or commodity goes up, remains the same, and the price falls; the price that is set at the signing of the future remains. Individuals use it to protect themselves from possible price instability, while corporations use it to protect the prices of what they sell from violent and unfavorable price movements.

Futures are obligations binding on the parties that are signatories to it. Futures are a compulsory contract and cannot be dissolved until the terms of the futures are met. With futures, you can rest assured that the other party, even though it does not want to fulfill the terms of the contract any longer, will be forced by the legal implications. Futures allow for a deposit of a percentage of the contract with a chosen broker. This payment is used to show and assure the other party of seriousness to go through with the terms and conditions of the futures.

Some of the disadvantages of futures include: it is not suitable for day trading, loss of margin, missing out on favorable price changes, and losses. Futures are not suitable for day trading as they have a future date in mind, which exceeds the trading window of a day trader. Futures are more suited to long term trading.

Futures make use of leverage, which means the trader is not obliged to deposit a hundred percent of the contract. In cases where the terms of the future do not favor the investor, the investor ends up losing his margin advantage. Futures are useful when the price of the asset to be traded is favorable with the terms of the future. Investors can miss out on exciting and favorable price changes due to his or her obligation to the terms of the futures. It also applies to companies also involved in futures.

Futures have their prices fixed no matter the condition, rain, or sunshine. Futures can be a disadvantage to investors and corporations when instead of recording profit, the corporation or investor records losses caused by an unfavorable price movement. Futures are like a legendary two-edged sword; on one side, it can bless the investor or corporation with favorable price movements and result in bargain deals while, on the other hand, it can result in unfavorable price movements for the investor or corporation and result in losses and misses.

Futures contracts are a type of derivative in which the underlying asset of the contract is paid for in advance of its delivery. Futures deal almost exclusively in commodities though there may be futures contracts in other assets such as currency. Futures are generally traded on all major stock trades around the world. Therefore, futures are not just limited to one specific trade.

Since futures deal with assets whose price fluctuates according to market conditions, keeping open positions for a more extended period may expose investors to sudden market fluctuations. For instance, oil futures tend to be the riskiest of all.

Since day trading implies opening and closing positions on the same day, investors can avoid the ups and downs that come with leaving positions overnight. Besides, futures are often traded after the close of markets in the

United States. That implies that fluctuations in Asian markets will have a direct impact on futures traded in the United States.

So, if oil futures fall during trading in Asia, an investor in North America may wake up to an unpleasant surprise. By cashing out at the end of the day, day traders can ensure there will be no surprises at the beginning of the next trading day.

Advanced day traders may choose to keep positions open overnight. However, derivatives are the riskiest type of investment vehicles. This is why investors need to be clear on the advantages and disadvantages that come with dabbling in these markets.

The trades facilitate trading between buyers and sellers. To trade futures, traders need to put up cash, which is commonly referred to as margin in futures trading. A proper margin must be maintained for the life of the trade. Traders need to have a sufficient margin to trade futures. This will usually depend on the kind of future that is being traded and how many contracts.

CHAPTER 1

Understanding Day Trading?

Day trading is regularly associated with its traders exiting their positions before the market closes. The main aim of this act is to avoid risks that cannot be managed and price gaps that are negative. The negative price gaps can result from the closing one-day prices and opening of the following day prices at the open.

Day trading often involves the use of margin leverage. A good depiction of this phenomenon can be used in the United States of America. Regulation T has the potential to permit initial maximum leverage of up to 2:1. However, many brokers go to levels of promoting up to 4:1 leverage during the moments the leverages are reduced to 2:1 or even less. This is mostly done near the end of the trading day.

The market of United States terms traders who trade for more than four days as pattern day traders. These forms of traders have an obligation to maintain a minimum of twenty-five thousand dollars in their accounts as equity. Traders in the day can end up not fees for interests that are charged for margin benefit. It is because margin interest is a typical charge for the balances that are accrued at midnight. However, this does not brush away the risks of a margin call that are experienced sometimes.

A broker is a person who is the determinant of the margin interests because of his or her call. There are several financial instruments that are commonly traded in the modern era day trading. These financial instruments include currencies, stocks, contracts for difference, hosts for future contracts, and options. The common future contracts that are traded include interest rates futures, commodity futures, and equity index futures.

There was a time day trading was an exclusive activity. It was a form of trade that was associated with professional speculators and financial firms. A large portion of day trading individuals are the employees of banks and other financial institutions. This group of employees tasked with such roles is always good specialists in managing funds and equity investment.

The year 1975 saw the popularization of day trading with several parties joining the trade. It was because the commissions in the United States were deregulated. The rise of electronic platforms for trading was witnessed in the years of 1990s. The volatility of stock prices was also seen during the periods of the dot-com bubble, as represented in Figure 1 below. Scalping is a new intraday trading technique that is used by traders in the day trading. It involves holding the trading position for a couple of minutes or seconds. Day trading is basically the purchasing and selling of securities within a single trading day in any marketplace at commonly stock markets and foreign exchange (FOREX) for the purpose of obtaining a compound of short-term loans.

How Day Trading Works

Day trading is a career that you have to invest time into. If you have decided to try it out, you have to spend time practicing it before you start live trading. As you practice, you improve your strategies. Only then do you use live money to try it out? All these need you to invest your time. Day trading isn't something that can be done successfully only when you have the urge for it. You must spend your time and energy on it if you want to succeed. If you have decided that trading is something that you want to consider, you should think of starting up as little as possible. Go for a few stocks or currencies initially, instead of trying to enter the market with a boom, and at the end of the day, you thin yourself out. If you go all out initially, you will end up confusing yourself, and this could lead to a large number of losses. It is advisable that you are calm while you trade. Shut off your emotions while you trade. Use only facts and don't try to make use of emotions because they could mislead you.

The more you are able to take out the emotional aspect, the more you can be true to the plan that you have laid out. When you are calm, it permits you to be focused.

Characteristics of a Day Trader

Being a day trader does come out naturally; a specific personality and traits are duly required. Below are some of the characteristics of a day trader.

Disciplined

This is a major trait that day traders really need to input. Day traders should always be disciplined to remain input when no opportunities emerge and really act so fast when opportunities avail. Acting fast also includes strictly considering the step by step rules and obligations initially formed in their big plans.

Open-minded

Day trading is a learning kind of income-generating engagement, implying that there are going to be happy times and downfalls. Save yourself and learn from all that. Improve the happy times and completely discard the downfall of wrong moves. Being exposed to the winnings and the failures makes you open-minded, master of all possible win moves.

A Fan of Technology

Day trading is carried out in various trading platforms and systems that a trader should be familiarized with. This should not scare you. Getting to know how they work does not, in any case, require you to be a computer whiz. Get to learn the basic moves and grow technologically with time.

Mentally Tough

Losing market trades are constant; most successful traders will have losing trades every single day. They typically win slightly more times than they lose. It is so important to stay focused and rational during a losing period and do not let in the basic fact that money has been lost too. Focus on the future day trading activities by implementing some of the strategies outlined in a big plan.

Independence

Independence is striving to build your own toolbox that is, and willy forever lead you. Reading trading books to trading books, watching each and every video, interacting with one mentor after the other, can be a total miss. What if different books have one confusing point on a particular field? What is your YouTube subscriber who decides to quit vlogging? Always grasp the basics after in-depth research and day stay put. Dare to yourself that you got you and get the large chunks of benefits. However, when you feel you are so lost, do not hesitate to get assistance. Most importantly, master and analyze successful moves and let them be part of your big plan.

Patience

Good things do take quite some time. In every strategical move you try to make, think about it carefully, but this should not make you paranoid. Act accordingly with many disciplines to reduce the number of losses likely to be incurred during various day trading activities.

Also, a patient day trader is a learning day trader. Day trading is not going to be easy at first, but with time, where you will be equipped with lots of skills and experience, things are expected to flow very smoothly. Hey, be patient.

Future-oriented

Getting stuck in the past makes you much of a prisoner. Forward-thinking lets you see the possible moves and gives you the decisive air when the next trading activity will occur considering the set protocols set in the day trader's plan. Being future-oriented incites forward-thinking, which is basically clearly involves mental thinking and knowing your next possible moves after a considerate examination. Being future-oriented hastens and simplifies the day trading operation moves, and the chances are that they are going to be successful.

Financial freedom

Day trading does not require you to be a tycoon necessarily, but you are required to have a specific amount of money that has been precisely selected to begin day trading with. Remember, the first times are always a win or lose situation as you continue to learn and grow. This particular set of money can be lost too. Be careful about how you handle your finances in day trading. Not every story is a good story.

Enthusiasm

A great interest in something is a pending successful goal. A great enthusiastic inclination to stocks, securities, commodities, markets, the business gives you the thirst to learn and master what day trading is all about. These are signs of a future successful day trader.

Experience and Familiarity

Experience comes with pretty much of downfall lessons and learning. Expose yourself to different learning sources and master every profitable move during day trading so as to squeeze the best out of that. Getting the actual experience and familiarity of the trading platforms and various strategies needed to be successful at day trading is worthwhile.

Profit and Risks of Day Trading

The process of day trading involves sloppy financial leverage, and speedy returns are probable. This phenomenon makes the trade to either be extremely profitable or extremely unprofitable. Those people who are described as high-risk profile traders are also greatly impacted by such a phenomenon.

These groups of traders have the probability of making enormous percentages of profit or, on the other hand, undergo massive amounts of parentage loss. Day trading trader's individuals are sometimes referred to as bandits or gamblers by other traders or investors. It is because these traders can either make huge amounts of profits or losses during the trade. There are several factors that can make this form of trade to be very risky while an individual is trading. They include individual trading on trade with low odds instead of trading on a trade that has high odds of winning; the presence of risk capital that is inadequate, which is tied together with overload stress of surviving and presence of poor management of funds which entails poor execution of the trade.

Gains and losses are mostly amplified by the popular usage of buying on margin. The process of buying on margin can be described as the use of borrowed funds. This action usually results in a trader experiencing a substantial loss or gain in a short span during the day. Brokers have the common tendency of allowing bigger trade margins for day traders.

Short Trades and Long Trades

The terms regarding short trades are common terms to an individual who is participating in stock trading. These terms are majorly used in situations where a trader is either buying or selling first. There are several expectations that a trader always has in mind if he or she is either doing short trade or long trade. When a trader is participating in a short trade, he or she purchases the financial instruments with the aim of selling them at a higher price in the future to make profits. On the other hand, short trade involves a trader selling financial instruments with the intent of later buying them at a lower price so as to make his or her profits.

Long Trade

Some day traders are common participants in the long trade. They are purchase financial instruments with hopes that they will increase in value. This makes their prices to increase in turn. The term that is mostly used by day traders always buys and long, which are interchangeable. Software developed to help long trade, with buttons that are either marked long or buy. These buttons are used to represent an open position entered by a trader. This position simply means an individual has shares in a certain firm or trade. When a trader decides to go long, he or she is always interested in purchasing a certain financial instrument. If the decision for such is perused, the potential for profit levels is always unlimited. It is because the prices of the purchased financial instruments can get higher indefinitely. This is despite a day trader participating in small moves. The risks in this form of trade have a lower risk potential of the purchased instruments to fall to zero. It is because profits and risks are always controlled by the multiple small moves that are made.

Short Trade

Day traders in short trades always sell their financial instruments before purchasing them. During moments they buy the financial instrument, they hope the prices will have gone down. This the moment they are able to realize their profits because they will be buying the financial instruments at a lower price from that which they had sold. Short trading is one of the most confusing forms of trade because people across the globe are used to buying first before selling. However, one can sell and buy in the financial markets.

There are common terms that are used by traders participating in short trades. These terms include short and sell, which are used interchangeably. Software developed to aid short trade also has buttons marked short or sell. The term short usually means a trader has an open position to shorting some financial instruments.

Profit levels are always limited in this situation when compared to the initial amount that was used to purchase the financial instruments. Various traders are used to taking short positions to reduce or minimize risks.

Difference Between Day Trading and Swing Trading

The main aim of traders in business is to be able to generate profit. There are several forms of trading that can be used. For an individual to understand what day trading is about, he or she is supposed to also have insight about swing trading. Having this knowledge and knowing the difference between swing trade and day trade will help them have a clear line of how to perform the trade to impeccable standards.

The first step to understanding swing trading is by getting what its definition is. This is the form of trade that involves a trader to buy or sell financial instruments and hold them for a varied time of a few days. The holding on time of financial instruments can go on to an extended period of several weeks.

There are several factors that can make a trader practicing swing trade to be in a sell or buy position. These circumstances are based on technical, quantitative, or fundamental valuations by the trader. Such occurrence may mean that a swing trader may take longer working periods than the day trader.

Most people who practice swing trade have a common set of beliefs amongst themselves. They mostly go for the thought of accumulating gains or losses. This process is done in a swift manner that is very slow and smooth compared to day trading.

However, there are certain instances where a trader practicing swing trading can experience swings in his or her trades. The results of these swings are always too extreme in two ways. He or she can either gain large percentages of profits or experience huge percentages of loss in a very short time. Individual trading as a swing trader usually does not take part as a full-time trader in the market.

There are four key differences between swing trading and day trading. They include:

An individual practicing day trading sells or buys financial instruments and liquidates his or her position on the same day. On the other hand, a swing trader upholds his or her position for a variation of days or even weeks. A person in day trading is meant to invest a huge number of hours in a day so as to be able to monitor the flow of prices in their portfolios. However, a swing trader is estimated to use few hours in trading as he or she can maintain his or her position for days or weeks. Day trading is involved with several sessions of being fast-paced and having adrenaline rushes. It is because there are quick decisions to be made, and the trade is fast-paced. This is the exact opposite of people who practice swing trading. It is they are required to be calm when making decisions because they focus more on the long-term return.

Day trading involves the usage of an advanced system of charting. The charting system is designed to accommodate short intervals of trade. These intervals can be programmed to track one to up to thirty minutes. However, swing traders are prone to using a less complex charting system. These charting systems can be programmed to monitor the market for a varied time of about one to four or five hours.

Retail vs. Institutional Traders

In the world of trading, there are basically two forms of traders: institutional and retail. The difference between them dictates the way they approach their trades. For example, institutional traders usually make large trades as compared to retail traders. But what are they exactly?

Their names might just give you a clue as to what you can understand about them.

The term "Retail traders" refers to individual traders. These traders can be anyone in the world who has the ability to get in on a trade. On the other hand, institutional traders are those who represent large financial institutions, hedge funds, banks, or other big firms that manage money. You could say that institutional traders are "corporate" traders, whereas retail traders are "home" traders.

So, does the amount invested in the trade dictate the type of trader one becomes? Is that the only point of distinction?

Not quite.

Analysis

A retail trader usually prefers to use some sort of technical analysis system for their trades. They utilize price patterns and behaviors in the past or indicators in the present that dictate future price scenarios. On the other hand, institutional traders do not usually refer to only technical patterns or systems to show them opportunities in their trade.

Focus

As institutional traders have been dealing with the system for a long time, their experience has led them to hone their skills well. They make use of market sentiments and fundamentals. They make use of trading psychology (which is a firm grasp on their emotions and keeping an analytical mind despite the situation) and understanding of overall responses towards a currency. They are keeping a close eye on the news to see if there are certain trends or reactions that they can pick up on.

Retail traders are not experienced in managing risks or having a proper psychological mind for trading. However, this is a situation that happens to everyone who gets started in Forex trading. No one can be prepared for what they will experience. They have to experience it first before they can decide how to keep their minds sharp.

Leverage

Institutional traders do not usually use leverage. Their main attention is spent on risk management. Even if a situation were to occur where they had to make use of leverages, they would be careful about how much leverage they are going to use.

On the other hand, retail traders make the mistake of looking for brokers that provide them with high leverages. While that act in itself is not wrong, it does pose a problem to those retailers who choose their brokers solely on the criteria of how much leverage those brokers provide them.

Now that we have understood more about the Forex market and its players, it is time we look at the most essential component of the market, currencies. More importantly, we are going to look at some of the major players in the Forex market.

High-Frequency Trading (HFT)

This trading technique entails high-frequency trades. It is perhaps the riskiest, most complex, and involved style of trading, which demands speed and attention on a 24-hour basis. Traders using this technique rely on analyzing multiple markets concurrently for profits. Successful traders in this segment are able to evaluate their composite and trademarked systems of trading. Usually, a beginner, perhaps working from home, is usually not competitive in this market. This trading approach differs from day trading since day trading follows a one market approach. Essentially, day trading differs from all these trading mechanisms because of the holding period of the stocks bought. Remember that trading mainly entails buying low and selling high. Also, remember that day trading entails entering and exiting the market within the same day. Day trading is often like a full-time job, where you have to identify and ensure that all requisites are in order. Any disruptions of the working space can make traders miss the intraday price fluctuations and hence miss their best trading opportunities. However, it is not as complex, intensive, or risky as scalp trading, which takes less trading spans and stricter conditions.

CHAPTER 2

Futures Trading

What happens when you buy futures is one of the most frequent questions about futures trading. When you buy futures, you are accepting to purchase products or service the company from which you bought futures has not produced yet. In comparison to stock trading, futures trading is much riskier because you deal with products and services that are not yet produced. With such characteristics, future trading is very popular among the producing companies and individuals and customers and speculators. While stocks or shares are being traded on stock markets, futures are being traded on futures markets. The idea of future markets developed from the needs of agricultural producers in the mid-nineteenth century, where often happened that the demand was much bigger than supply. The difference between the futures markets and futures markets today is that today's futures markets have crossed the borders of agricultural production and entered many other sectors, such as financial. As such, future markets today are used to buy and sell currencies and other financial instruments. What future markets made possible is the opportunity for a farmer to participate in the goods with customers on the other end of the world. One of the biggest and most important future markets is the International Monetary Market (IMM), established in 1972. Futures are financial derivatives that obtain their value from the movement in the price of another asset. It means that the futures price is not dependent on its inherent value. Still, on the amount of the asset, the futures contract is tracking. One of the advantages of the futures market is that it is centralized and that people from around the world electronically can make future contracts. These future contracts will specify the price of the merchandise and the time of delivery. Every future contract contains information about the quality and the quantity of the sold goods, specific prices, and the method in which the goods are to be delivered to the buyers.

A person who buys or sells a futures contract does not pay for the whole value of the contract. He pays a small upfront fee to trigger an open position. For example, if the futures contract's value is $350,000 when the S&P 500 is 1400, he only pays $21,875 as its initial margin. The exchange sets this margin and may change anytime.

If the S&P 500 moved up to 1500, the futures contract would be worth $375,000. Thus, the person will earn $25,000 in profit.

However, if the index fell to 1390 from its original 1400, he will lose $2,500 because the futures contract will now be worth $347,500. This $2,500 is not a realized loss yet. The broker will also not require the individual to add more cash to his trading account.However, if the index fell to 1300, the futures contract will be worth $325,000. The individual loses $50,000. The broker will require him to add more money to his trading account because his initial margin of $21,875 is no longer enough to cover his losses.

History of Future Trading

The history of futures trading began on the Midwestern frontier of the United States of America in the early 1800s. Chicago's strategic location, at the base of the Great Lakes and close to the Midwest's fertile farmlands, contributed to the city's rapid growth and development as a grain terminal. In 1848, 82 merchants formed a central marketplace, the Chicago Board of Trade. Their purpose was to promote commerce in the city by providing a place where buyers and sellers could meet to exchange commodities. Growing use of contracts that specified delivery of a particular commodity at a predetermined price and date made the CBOT increasingly popular as a central marketplace. These early forward contracts in corn were first used by river merchants. They received farmers' corn in late autumn and early winter and needed to ship it to grain producers such as flour mills, bread manufacturers, etc. Often the corn needed to be stored all winter.

Definition of a Futures Contract

The best futures contracts you will find in the market.

S&P 500 E-mini

Most traders will fancy the idea of trading in the S&P 500 E-mini because of its high liquidity aspect. It also appeals to most investors because of its low day trading margins. You can conveniently trade in S&P 500 E-mini around the clock, not to mention that you will also benefit from its technical analysis aspect. Essentially, the S&P 500 E-mini is a friendly contract since you can easily predict its price patterns.

10 Year T-Notes

10 Year T-Notes is also ranked as one of the best contracts to trade in. Considering its sweet maturity aspect, most traders would not hesitate to trade in this futures contract. There are low margin requirements that a trader will have to meet when trading in 10 Year T-Notes.

Crude Oil

Crude oil also stands as one of the most popular commodities in futures trading. It is an exciting market because of its high daily trading volume of about 800k. Its high volatility also makes the market highly lucrative.

Gold

This is yet another notable futures contract. It might be expensive to trade in gold; however, it is a great hedging choice, more so in poor market conditions.

Why We Need Futures Markets

Let's take a simple example. A farmer is planting his crop and wants to be certain he will obtain a particular price for his crop of corn. He feels comfortable with the current corn price and wants to protect himself from a falling price. Suppose he wants to be able to obtain $4 per bushel for his crop, which is due for harvesting and delivery in October, regardless of what happens to the market price. The market price can fluctuate as a result of weather conditions or supply and demand between now and harvesting time in October. One corn contract consists of 5,000 bushels, so he sells a sufficient number of contracts to cover his entire October crop at $4 a bushel through his broker on a commodity exchange like the Chicago Board of Trade.

After a spell of good weather, the predicted bumper crop materializes in October, and because of this, the cash price for one bushel of corn drops to $3.

The farmer is not concerned because he has guaranteed himself a price of $4, so he buys contracts at $3, which offsets against the contracts he sold for $4, giving himself a profit of $1 dollar per bushel. This profit offsets the loss on the cash price when the crop is harvested, and he ends up with $4 per bushel.

This is known as hedging.

Conversely, a bread manufacturer will use this technique to protect him from rising prices. The manufacturer will buy enough October contracts at $4 as a hedge against rising prices. If the price jumps to $6 per bushel because of floods or drought, he will profit from the increased value of his contracts, offsetting the increased cash price he has to pay for wheat.

Where Do We Fit in?

There are many people like you and me who trade simply to make money. Some are big institutional investors, but the majority of the market consists of small investors or speculators.

All of the speculators, large or small, provide a vital function to the futures market by buying or selling millions of contracts every day, and by doing so, provide liquidity to the markets.

Without liquidity, the markets cannot function.

Futures Market Categories

There are similarities in all futures contracts. However, each contract may track different assets As such, it is essential to study the various markets that exist.

Categories of Futures Markets				
Agriculture	Grains	Livestock	Dairy	Forest
Energy	Crude Oil	Heating oil	Natural gas	Coal
Stock Index	S&P 500	Nasdaq 100	Nikkei 225	E-mini S&P 500
Foreign Currency	Euro/USD	GBP/USD	Yen/USD	Euro/Yen
Interest Rates	Treasuries	Money markets	Interest Rate Swaps	Barclays Aggregate Index
Metals	Gold	Silver	Platinum	Base Metals

You can trade futures contracts on different categories and assets. However, if you are still a new trader, it is important to trade assets that you know. For example, if you are into stock trading for a few years already, you must start with futures contracts using stock indexes. This way, you won't have a hard time understanding the underlying asset. You only need to understand how the futures market works.

After choosing a category, decide on the asset that you want to trade. For example, you want to trade futures contracts in the energy category. Focus on coal, natural gas, crude oil, or heating oil. The markets trade at various levels, so you must understand relevant things, likes the nuances, liquidity, margin requirements, contract sizes, and volatility. Do the necessary research before trading in futures contracts.

How to Trade Futures

The safest way to trade a futures contract is with Stop-Loss orders. They are just what they sound like—instructions to staunch the bleeding at a predetermined level. They can also be used to lock in profits, so Stop-Loss orders are good to have in an investor's toolbox.

Stop-Loss orders are placed at the same time a trade is entered. For instance, take Frozen concentrated orange juice contracts, Dan Aykroyd was waving around for sale at $1.42. The price would eventually fall to 29 cents. That would spell ruin for anyone buying those contracts, as it did for Ralph Bellamy and Don Ameche. But if they had bought Aykroyd's contract with a stop-order of $1.40, they would have parachuted out of the position automatically when the price fell below $1.40, saving most of their fortune.

On the other hand, if the price rose to $1.50, Bellamy and Ameche could move their original stop-order from $1.40 to $1.48 and ensure they would profit by at least eight cents should the price of frozen concentrated orange juice begin falling back down.

Of course, safety in investing often comes with a price tag. Using the example of a stop-order at $1.40, let's say that the price dropped briefly to $1.38 and then shot quickly up over $1.50. Those profits will not be padding your bank account because you are automatically moved out of the contract as soon as the price hits your Stop-Loss order limit.

Never cancel a Stop-Loss order once you place it. You initiated the order—hopefully—as part of a sound investment strategy, and you do not want to bid it farewell due to an emotional reaction to later events. And never change your position in a market without sound, rational motives. If you are the type who likes to work without a net, you can avoid using Stop-Loss orders but always realize that you can lose significantly more money trading futures than may sit in your account.

The reason a Stop-Loss order is critical is the margin call. Since you are investing only a small percentage of the value of the contract, you must maintain a minimum amount of money in your account, called the maintenance margin. If the price of the commodity tumbles below that level, a margin call is issued for you to bring the amount of your account back up to its initial level. If a margin call is issued, you must pay up immediately, or the brokerage has to right to liquidate your entire position to cover the losses. That is why people were jumping off buildings when the stock market crashed in 1929.

As with your entire investment portfolio, diversity can be the key to minimizing risk in trading futures. The best traders in the world limit their position in a single commodity to between 3 and 5% of their trading capital. You should certainly do the same. Build positions in as broad a selection of markets as you feel you have knowledge. That may include positions in corn, gold, crude oil, and the Nasdaq, for instance. But never enter a market without judgment to support your move—do not try to build a diversified futures portfolio for diversity's sake.

When searching for new markets to flesh out a portfolio, look beyond the big exchanges like the Chicago Board of Trade or the Chicago Mercantile Exchange and investigate other exchanges where you can take on much smaller contracts—as much as 80% smaller. This way, you can ease your way into the vagaries of commodities. You can also engage in paper trading (using make-believe trades and following real-market results for a period of time) if you find that way of learning about new investments helpful, but it is never like trading with real money.

Find a Good Broker

One of the critical decisions that you will make when you first get started in trading is who you will hire as your broker. There are many brokers out there, so this can be a hard decision to choose who will be the right one.

The first thing to determine is how much time you plan to put into your investing and how much help you will need. Some people like to do the work all on their own, and others will need some hand-holding to get them started at least. There are brokers out there that can help with both situations; you just need to know what your situation is before you start looking.

Then, you need to take a look at some of the fees that the broker is going to charge. If the fees are too high, then they will start to eat into your profits, and that is never a good thing. All brokers are going to charge you some fees to invest and use them, so that is something you should expect right from the beginning. However, the way they charge these fees and the amount that you spend on these fees over time is going to depend on each broker.

Decide How Much You Can Spend

This is a tricky one to work with because the amount will depend on your budget. Any amount can be used to make trading profitable. You have to keep in mind never to trade more than you can afford to lose.

One way to make sure that you follow this rule is to set up a separate account that you would like to use just for trading money. Each month, add in the amount that you can safely invest without hurting your other finances, and that is all that you can trade on. That way, if you make a few bad trades, you have not lost all of the money that you need for making the house payment or something else that needs to be paid that month.

Choosing to Buy Long or Sell Short

The price of a stock is going to do one of three things at a given time. It will go down, go up, or it will move sideways. When you enter into the market as a swing trader, you are expecting that the stock is going to go up, or it will go down. If you think that the stock will see an increase in its price, then they will purchase the stock. This move is going to be considered "going long" or having a "long position" in that stock. For example, if you are long 100 shares of Facebook Inc., it means that you purchased 100 shares of this company, and you are making the prediction that you will be able to sell them at a higher price later on and earn a nice profit.

How to Enter a Trade

If you are brand new to trading, you are probably curious about how you would sell or purchase security. Any time that the market is open, there are going to be two prices for any security that can be traded. There will be the bid price and the ask price. The bid price is what buying or purchasing traders are offering to pay for that stock right then. The ask price, on the other hand, is the price that traders want in order to sell that security. You will quickly notice that the bid price is always going to be a bit lower simply because the buyers want to pay less, and the asking price is always going to be higher because sellers want more for their holdings. The difference between these two prices is known as the spread. The spreads that are found will vary for each stock, and they can even change throughout the day. If a stock doesn't have a ton of buyers and sellers, then there could be a bigger spread. When there are more buyers and sellers, then the spread between these two prices will be much lower.

Investment and Margin Accounts

There are two types of accounts that you can choose to open in order to trade stocks. The two main options include the margin account and the investment account. With a margin account, you can borrow against the capital that you have placed in your account. The investment account, on the other hand, will allow you to buy up to the dollar value you hold in that account. You are not able to spend more than what you have put in that account at a time.

When you decide to open up a margin account, you may be able to borrow money from the investment or brokerage firm to help pay for some of your investment. This is a process that is known as buying on margin. This can provide you with some advantages of purchasing more shares that you would be able to afford if you just used the capital in your account, and it can help you leverage to get more profits with your money.

However, there is a catch with this one in the form of more risks. When you borrow the money to make your investments, there will come a point when you must pay the loan back. If you earn the profits that you think you will, it is easy to pay this back. But, if you lose out and make the wrong predictions, you are going to have to find other ways to pay the money back. Making investments with leverage can magnify the percentage losses on your money.

As a beginner, you should stick with a regular investment account. Trading on margin can increase the amount of risk that you are taking on in your trades. This may be tempting because it can increase your potential profits, but there is a lot more risk that comes with it as well. You will do much better going with an investment account instead. This way, you can just pull out the money that you are comfortable with rather than hoping that you make a good prediction in the beginning when you are learning.

Picking out How Much You Want to Invest

Finally, before we move into talking about some of the different swing trading platforms that you can work with, we need to discuss some of the basics of how much you are going to invest in your account. Since we have already discussed the importance of working with an investment account rather than trying to do the trading on margin, you will need to decide how much money you would like to put into your account. First, talk with your brokerage firm and decide how much you need to put in to meet their requirements. Some brokerage firms will ask you to spend a certain amount or keep a certain amount in your accounts at all times in order to trade. If your chosen firm has that kind of requirement, then make sure that you put in at least that much. Putting in more is up to your discretion.

Do Some Research

Research is your best friend when you go through this process. The more time you can spend researching and look at charts, the more you will understand how the market works and how much you can make on it in the process. There are a few other resources that you can spend your time on to make sure that you see the best results and that you can take your trading to the next level. Sources from the news are an excellent place to start because they can provide you with some great information that the company is releasing or what other analysts are saying as well.

Know What Good Futures Contracts Look Like

You should be aware of what a good futures contract is. Before commencing any trade, you should obtain as much information as possible to make sure that you do not come across any unexpected situations. A significant point to note is that there may be several significant differences between futures contracts that need to be taken into account before moving ahead. You should be aware of the particular contract unit because each prospective futures contract will depict the size and the units it is trading in. A specific currency will always be used to denote forex futures, whereas those that depend on stock indices usually consist of a reference point on the index multiplied by a given price per share. The details of this measurement are generally not very significant as they are only critical at the moment to enable you to comprehend precisely what you are becoming involved in.

Choosing Right Contract

You should ensure that you choose the correct contract. Before selecting the appropriate agreements, you should comprehend the different degrees of insecurity that are occurring within the market in comparison to the possibility of a severe payout in case everything works out well. This is important because there is a significantly higher variance in the futures market compared to other markets because they include a much higher variety. When such kinds of decisions are to be made, a significant point to note is that in this case, the previous results are not going to forecast future outcomes accurately. This indicates that even though the price has stayed constant for many days, it does not need to remain so in the future.

Look for the Right Signals

You need to determine the correct signals. When carrying out day trading of futures, you should remember that you will be able to achieve the best outcomes when you use three indicators that do not particularly have a link with each other. You should observe the sine wave as a way of identifying the price concerning resistance and support, the momentum to determine the volume in comparison to the supply, and the pro-am to identify the particular trade size, which will help you find out the degree to which the market is interested in the trade at that point.

Factors that Should Be Taken into Consideration

Before you go into an exchange, there are a few key factors that you should take a gander at other than the pattern and exchange arrangements, and they are:

Margins

When you enter into a trade, the exchanges will require a margin to be paid as your insurance that you will fulfill the terms of the contract. The size of margins can differ substantially from one commodity contract to the next. For example, an index contract margin like the S&P 500 can be as high as $25,000, whereas some of the grain contracts can be as low as $400. The amount of margin depends on the size of the contract and the volatility of the commodity. Make sure that you have enough money in your trading account to cover your margin. If your contract position makes a profit, you will get back your margin plus your profit. If your contract position is making a loss and the loss exceeds the size of your trading account, you will get a call from your broker requesting you to replenish your account with more funds immediately to maintain your trading position. This is called a margin call.

Volume

Before you enter into a trade, it is essential to check the volume of the contract. Volume is the number of contracts traded daily. To calculate the volume of a particular day, you have to add only the number of long contracts for that day and not the short contracts. Remember, the futures market is called a net sum zero game.

In other words, for every winning trade, you have a losing trade, and with every trade, you have someone buying and someone selling a contract. Markets with a high volume give you the chance to enter and exit a trade at the levels of your choice. If the volume is too low, no one may be able to take the other side of your trade. This means that you are likely to get poor execution on your orders.

Capital Requirements

The amount of money required to begin trading in futures will vary. Some brokers will require a trader to have about $5,000. However, there are those who would require only $2,000. It is vital for a trader to choose the best broker who is flexible enough to allow them to trade with the little capital they have.

Leverage

Leverage will also vary depending on the type of futures you trade in. The contract value will also have an impact on the amount of leverage that you will have.

Liquidity

Just like leverage, the liquidity aspects of futures will also depend on the futures you are trading. Accordingly, it is important for any trader to regularly check the respective volumes of contracts before trading on them.

Volatility

Futures are volatile. The advantage gained by using high leverage ensures that a trader makes a good profit with little price changes in the market. Keeping the above factors into consideration, futures are a good market to trade. A trader can easily day trade with as little as $2,000. The high leverage ratio will also guarantee that huge profits can be earned.

Open Interest

This is the number of contracts still open at the end of each day. It is also a useful guide for the market's liquidity. Low open interest indicates little trading interest, and potentially bad "fills" are very likely.

Principles of Futures Trading

"What actually happens when you buy futures?" It is actually one of the most frequent questions in relation to futures trading. The answer to this question can be summarized in a sentence that states: when you buy futures, you are actually accepting to buy products or services that the company from which you bought futures has not produced yet. In comparison to stock trading, futures trading is much riskier because you deal with products and services that are not yet produced. With such characteristics, future trading is very popular not only among the producing companies and individuals and customers but also among speculators as well. While stocks or shares are being traded on stock markets, futures are being traded on futures markets. The idea of future markets developed from the needs of agricultural producers in the mid-nineteenth century, where often happened that the demand was much bigger than supply. The difference between the futures markets and futures markets today is that today's futures markets have crossed the borders of agricultural production and entered many other sectors, such as financial. As such, future markets today are used for buying and selling currencies as well as some other financial instruments. What future markets made possible is the opportunity for a farmer to be able to participate in the goods with customers on the other end of the world. One of the biggest and most important future markets is the International Monetary Market (IMM) that was established in 1972. Futures are financial derivatives that obtain their value from the movement in the price of another asset. It means that the price of futures is not dependent on its inherent value but on the price of the asset the futures contract is tracking. One of the advantages of the futures market is that it is centralized and that people from around the world electronically are able to make future contracts. These futures contracts will specify the price of the merchandise and the time of delivery. Besides that, every future contract contains information about the quality and the quantity of the sold goods, specific prices, and the method in which the goods are to be delivered to the buyers. A person who buys or sells a futures contract does not pay for the whole value of the contract. He pays a small upfront fee to trigger an open position. For example, if the value of the futures contract is $350,000 when the S&P 500 is 1400, he only pays $21,875 as its initial margin. The exchange sets this margin and may change anytime.

Which Market to Trade and with Which Broker

There is a huge array of products to trade with on offer, but for scalping, you need products with large volumes exchanged and volatility. I find these in the mini DAX and the e-mini Dow futures. The volatility, i.e., daily range (distance between the low of the day and the high of the day), is wide. In addition, and this point is very important, these products are traded on regulated and centralized markets: Eurex for the DAX futures and CME for the e-mini Dow, as opposed to CFDs, which are OTC products; i.e., your broker is the counterpart of your trade. When you buy, your broker is your seller, and when you sell, your broker is buying from you. On the other hand, on a centralized market, your order is routed and executed when someone else's order matches yours (buyers' and sellers' prices meet). In addition, on the futures markets, you can see the volume of transactions, while on the CFD, your broker may show no volume at all or only the volumes exchanged on their platform.

And more importantly, on the futures markets, you see the prices offered by other market participants, while on CFDs, you only get the prices offered by your broker. To illustrate, this I have just taken below a snapshot of prices offered by two different CFD brokers at the same time.

Which Broker Offers the Right Price?

In case of high volatility, CFDs do not react the same way as futures: the prices may adjust at a different pace, and the spread offered by the broker may increase. A market order may even be repriced if the market is moving very quickly. Stop orders may incur slippage, which means you will lose a few points to your broker as the price you are paid is a few points away from your stop order.

So, I can only recommend that you trade with future or mini futures contracts. However, CFDs can be useful to trade small positions when you make your first steps in trading as you can trade products at only one euro per point instead of 5 euros on a mini futures contract or even 25 euros per point on the DAX future. Note that CFDs are not available in all countries due to local laws and financial regulations.

But if you can and want to trade CFDs, make sure you look at the spreads offered by different brokers before choosing who to trade with. Half a point is not much different, but in scalping, it means a lot. After 20 trades, paying half a point more on each trade at one euro per point will result in an extra 10 euros wasted in commissions; and so on, after 40 trades, you will have wasted 20 euros. Let's say in a month if you perform 600 to 800 trades; you will then have wasted 300 to 400 euros in extra commissions.

How to Choose Your Broker

In order to be able to scalp in good conditions, you need to look out for the following points when choosing your broker:

Tight spreads if you choose to work with CFDs. One euro or dollar per point is the maximum you should pay as you don't want to be working just for your broker; Real-time data flux is essential. The subscription to the Eurex data flux (DAX and mini DAX) will cost you about 20 euros per month and another 25 euros for a subscription to CME CBOT (e-mini Dow) data. Your broker collects the fees for the data supplier; you don't need to pay the supplier directly. If you just want to trade CFDs, you won't have to pay these fees, but you will have only access to the data provided by your broker.

Most of the platforms will let you place simple orders such as buy limit or sell limit orders, with the option to set up an automated take profit and stop-loss orders. But some go even further by letting you set up an automated order for part of the position and another one for the second part of the position and so on if you want to set up 3 different targets.

Be aware that some brokers operate with a first-in-first-out rule, which means that they won't let you have opposite positions on the same product run separately, a.k.a. hedging. A new executed sell order may not open a position but offset or close an already opened buy position. On the other hand, CFD brokers may let you trade, hedge, and operate your positions separately from one another. While short and long positions of equivalent quantities and on the same product offset each other in theory, your broker may still calculate a margin cover for each position separately. So, keep an eye on your margin usage.

If you are starting with a small account, i.e., with less than € 5,000, look for brokers that will let you trade on small quantities, as small as 1/100th of one lot. That way, you can start trading taking minimum risk until you build confidence in your trading.

Being able to trade from a smartphone, an iPad, or similar. I certainly cannot recommend that you use these devices for your scalping, but they shall be used as part of plan B if a problem comes up with your computer while you are trading or if your internet broadband suddenly shuts down or resets itself. Your smartphone connected to a mobile phone network will be your back up device to modify or close some orders if necessary, until your computer and the internet are back up and running. Most brokers offer mobile technology in today's world.

This was plan B. The plan C is that you should be able to call your broker's trading desk as a last resort in case of emergency if your computer and your mobile application don't let you perform an action that needs to be done. Lastly, you absolutely need to work with a minimum of two brokers because if for any reason, there is a technical problem on one of your brokers' platforms, you need to able to act swiftly on your second broker's platform. Let's say you need to close a position, but broker A's platform, for some reason, is not working. Then you can always open an opposite order on the broker's B platform. For instance, you need to close a long position with broker A, but a technical problem doesn't let you do so. Then you should open a short position with broker B until everything is back up and running. Then you can work on closing these positions simultaneously afterward.

Once you are ready to trade with the mini futures, I recommend that you have at least 12,000 euros to be able to scalp with 2 lots when the occasion occurs. For the most accurate information, choose the tick by tick data flux if you can choose a data provider. Some data providers offer market data sent to your computer on a second by second basis while others have their data refreshed on a tick by tick basis, which is every time a transaction occurs on the market, showing you the latest price exchanged.

The choice of broker that you go for is crucial to your trading success. Conduct proper research on the best broker to work with. Some qualities of a good broker include:

- They are regulated by a relevant monetary body.
- They offer all the instruments that you need to trade.
- They are cheap in terms of commissions and other charges.
- They are reputable in all aspects.
- They are accessible any time you need them.
- What are your strengths and weaknesses?

Finally, you must evaluate yourself and see which of your traits make you a better trader and which ones limit your potential. Identifying your strengths will keep you motivated, and you will pay more attention to your stronger side. On the other hand, identifying your weaknesses will allow you to know what needs some improvement. You will become a better trader as you work on more of your limitations.

These are just some of the elements that you can include in your trading plan. You can add more as you please, as long as they add value to your trading career. The most important thing, however, is that you follow the rules in your constitution to the end. If you only compose it and stop at that, it will be as good as seeing a good trade setup and letting it go.

CHAPTER 3

Futures Spread Trading

Many day traders find futures preferable to options because they are sure to always move along with the asset that they are related to. What's more, the futures market can be analyzed directly, which means that you can profit from anticipation on the market without having to take any derivative pricing into account.

Even better, unlike some other markets, there are no artificial restrictions limiting your ability to short trade, making your job as a day trader much easier in the process. Finally, this makes it so that the FINRA's definition of a pattern day trader does not apply. A pattern day trader is required to keep $25,000 on hand at all times, among other things, and being labeled as one will make it more difficult for you to trade as effectively as possible.

- **Always follow the trends:** Odds are, if you are attracted to futures trading, then you are less naturally inclined to follow trends in the market, preferring instead to jump in on opportunities when they are still forming. This is a habit that you are going to need to break if you plan on trading in futures; however, typically, you will find that the practice is much more profitable if you stick with the trends of the major players and deviate from them as little as possible.

- **Don't prioritize trade frequency:** While it is natural for day traders to make more trades than other types of traders, that is no reason to assume that there are always future trades that can be made at the moment. It is important to always keep in mind that it is possible to be a successful day trader while making three trades a day, just as it is to be successful while making 30 trades per day. It is all about choosing your futures targets carefully and with a clear understanding of where all the trades are likely headed. Don't forget, before you finalize any trade, you should always run a full risk/reward analysis to ensure that it is going to be worth your time in the long run.

- **Know what a good futures contract looks like:** Prior to starting any trade, it is important that you take the time to gather as much information as possible in order to ensure you prevent any further surprises from sneaking up unannounced. It is important to keep in mind that futures contracts may have a number of key differences that will need to be considered before moving forward. First, it is important that you know the contract unit in question as each potential futures contract will show the size as well as the units it is trading in. Forex futures will always be specified with a given currency, while those based on stock indices generally include a reference point on the index multiplied by a specific price per share. The specifics of this measurement aren't as important in most instances as they are generally only crucial in the moment to help you understand exactly what you are getting yourself into. Outside of these types of specifics, you will need to keep in mind the quoted price as well as how this quote is likely to change between markets as sometimes, they will be written with dollars and cents while other times they will be written with mathematical equations, possibility points or percentages. The end result will always work out to be the same, but it is important to know exactly what you are working with prior to moving forward.

- **Choosing the right contract:** Prior to choosing the right contracts to follow, it is important to understand the various levels of insecurity that are taking place in the market in question compared to the potential for a serious payout should things go just right. This is vital as there is a great deal more variance in the futures market than in the others as they encompass a far greater variety overall. When it comes to making these types of decisions, it is also important to remember that past performance is not going to be an accurate predictor of future results in this instance. This means that just because a price has remained stable for several days is no indication that it will continue to do so.

- **Look for the right signals:** When day trading futures, it is important to keep in mind that the best results will typically materialize if you use a trio of indicators that aren't specifically corollary to one another. You will need to keep an eye on the sine wave as a means of determining the price when it comes to support and resistance, the momentum to determine the volume in comparison to the supply, and the pro-am as a means of determining the specific trade size to help determine how much interest the market has in the trade at the moment. Generally speaking, you can expect to have the ability to plot the sine wave through the lowest chart pane, which will give you a measure of the current cycle. When levels of support and resistance are both confirmed, you will see the results mapped via dotted lines on the price bars in question.

  You will also find the momentum plotted underneath the bars indicating price, and it will then be represented by waves to show the volume when it comes to buying and selling. You will also find various divergence patterns that can then be directly plotted onto various additional price bars as well. When it comes to tracking the pro-am, you will be able to easily consider what types of active traders are sitting on various price points. If you find a lot of highs, then you can be confident that it means there is lots of position switching taking place at the top of the spectrum. Meanwhile, lots of lows should tell you that the breakout is on its last legs, which means it could likely reverse at any time.

- **Consider the direction the trend is forming:** More so than in more traditional forms of trading, if you manage to find a trend while day trading, then there is a high chance that you will be able to successfully make a profit off of it, assuming it sticks around long enough to let you. When it comes to confirming the direction of a potential trend, you will want to take note of professionals who are trading in the space before confirming that the trend is set to continue on moving forward as well. You will want to keep an eye out for indicators that it has reached a point where its volume is exhausted, as this means it is likely on its last legs.

- **Stick with a single market:** While the futures market tends to have various subsections devoted to various different markets, this doesn't mean that you should bounce between them all as you will have far more success if you stick to those which you see some early success. Once you have mastered a specific subsection of the market, you can then move on to the next, but until that point, you will want to focus on the way you can increase success in the long-term.

Futures Spreads Trading Pricing and Margins
Spreads
It is vital that you keep in mind that if they are part of a spread, then the individual margins on a given contract will be reduced. For example, if the margin on a given wheat contract alone is $2,000, but if you make the decision to go short as well as long on wheat in the same year, then the margin between them could potentially be as little as $200. If you go short and long on one commodity split over different years, then the margin will double to $400. The price differential occurs as the volatility of the spread is less than that of the contract in question. Generally speaking, the futures spread gives you the ability to look at the given market movement in slow motion. Thus, if something major happened in the wheat market, then it would affect both contracts, which would provide enough protection against the increased risk that the singular contract doesn't have.

Price Concerns
The price of a specific futures spread can be easily determined via the perceived difference in two contracts. To properly determine what the spread's pricing is going to be, the easiest way to go about doing so is to simply find the pricing of the spread by just subtracting the month that is being deferred from the price of the front month. If the price of the front-month is the lower of the two, the spread will end up being negative, and if it is higher than the spread, it will end up being positive. The values for the contracts, as well as the spreads, will remain the same. For example, if the price of wheat is $500 in the front month and $510 the next, then the spread can be said to be -$10, and if it instead dropped to $490, then it would be $10.

Market Types
Contango Markets
A market is thought to be contango if the front month is going to clearly have a lower cost than the deferred month. Generally speaking, this means the deferred month is going to cost slightly more than the front month will, thanks to the cost to carry. The cost to carry will take into account the interest rate on the capital that comes along with the operating costs of the location that actually sells the commodity in question, as well as any related storage or insurance costs. This is considered the default state of the market.

Backwardation Markets
A market is said to be in the midst of backwardation if the near months are valued more highly when compared to the months that are the deferred month. Sometimes known as an inverted market, it is the opposite of the standard market condition. This most commonly occurs if the market is in the midst of a bull phase, which tends to be caused by a supply chain issue, often in relation to a substantial increase in demand along with an overall limited supply. This type of price differential typically occurs when the front months feel the full brunt of the change, which is then mitigated as the deferred months start arriving. This is frequently the case if the deferred month ends up in the next crop year after the front month.

Regardless of the state of the market at the moment, it is important that you always factor seasonal concerns into all of your choices as well. Generally speaking, you can count on gasoline prices being higher in the summer while prices of coffee, natural gas, and heating oil will be higher in the winter. Furthermore, it is important that you remember all markets will inevitably experience bearish and bullish periods, but those experienced by commodities tend to be far less consistent overall.

Common Spread Types: Commodity Futures
Inter-commodity Futures
These futures involve contracts that are spread across various markets. As an example, if you believe that the wheat market is going to experience a high demand when compared to the corn market, then you would buy wheat and sell corn. The specific prices for each don't matter as long as wheat prices beat corn prices.

Calendar Intra-commodity
This spread looks at a single commodity between differing months of the year. As an example, if you believe that the wheat market is going to be stronger in November as opposed to June, then you would go long in November and short in June. The specifics of the price don't matter as long as prices are higher in November than they are in June.

Bull Futures
This spread looks at a single commodity under the assumption that the sooner month will boast a higher price than the later month. As an example, if you buy a bullish wheat future in May, then you will want the price to be higher than when you sell it in June. For this type of future, it is important to keep in mind that near future contracts tend to move faster the further you get from the front month, which gives this future its name. A bullish trader would then be one who buys in the front month in hope that it ends up moving at a greater rate than the deferred month.

Bear Futures
This spread occurs if you purchase the same commodity in such a way that you are short in the front month and long on the deferred month. As an example, if you purchase wheat in May and sell it in June, then you are hoping the prices are lower in May than they will be in June. For this type of future, it is important to keep in mind that near future contracts tend to move faster the further you get from the front month, which gives this future its name. If you are confident that prices are at a low point, then this is the type of spread you should consider buying into.

A pattern day trader is required to keep $25,000 on hand at all times, among other things, and being labeled as one will make it more difficult for you to trade as effectively as possible.

CHAPTER 4

How to Make a Profit on the Futures Market

When to Trade and When Not to Trade

The markets go through different phases, and there are times when you will feel like it is difficult to read the market or other times when there are low volumes and high hesitation from market participants making the market evolve in a flat and boring momentum.

DAX future, 5 minutes

For this example, I have used 5-minute candles in order to fit the whole day on one chart. As you can see, the market makes roughly 60 points between its lowest of the day and its highest of the day, which is not too bad. But how did that happen? A rapid 30 points drop in the morning, followed by a return to opening prices by the end of the morning, and then, 6 hours of long awaiting until a little awakening again at 5 pm. Apart from doing mini range trading during these 6 hours, there is not much you can do.

It is difficult to predict how a day is going to be. I am not talking about trends here, but just about price volatility. Is it going to be an active day or a very quiet day? You can't really know in advance. However, there are some hints that you can look for, such as previous day's behaviors and chart patterns.

DAX Future, One Hour

When the market is testing significant levels such as supports and resistances, you can expect some hesitation as no one is willing to buy at the highest and push the market further until an event or something triggers the market to make a breakthrough or consolidate sharply. When reaching significant levels and testing them, expect the market to test that level before breaking it or reversing it.

Another hint to look for market activity can be found in the economic calendars and how the market is reacting to the coming events or news to be announced. The market may enter into a quiet phase, with fewer participants willing to trade, waiting for the news to be released. Some participants will indeed decide to stay on the side, as I will advise you to do next. During this quiet phase, the volumes exchanged could be low, again due to the fact that many day traders don't want to have too many positions opened while facing the risk of high price volatility at the time of the news being released. You should get familiar with the average volume exchanged throughout the day for the product you are trading so that you can assess if the market is being pushed around in low volumes by fewer participants or if indeed there is increased interest. When scalping, you may want to close all your positions before the news is released because the market might get very volatile on and after the news is being released. While volatility normally serves us, at the time of a news release, the market can move erratically in any direction, come back to where it was before the news went out, or set up in a specific direction.

What will happen is that you may have traded in the right direction, but the market went to hit your stop-loss first due to price volatility. Now, you may say, let's not put a stop-loss in this instance or place it further away, but what happens if the market goes against you and then doesn't reverse in your chosen direction? Placing orders just before the news is released, from my point of view, is just gambling.

Don't try to apply logic to the market's reactions to the news either, thinking that if the news is positive, the market will certainly go up or the opposite because it may not happen. The market may already have priced the news with some market participants starting to cash in their profits making the prices go in the opposite direction of where they should logically have gone. When news or a figure is released, you don't have all the information around it. For instance, if crude oil inventories are lower than forecast, is it due to higher oil consumption or lower oil production? What strategies do the market participants have in place?

Many factors and many questions for which we don't have all the answers to be able to analyze the news and predict how the market is going to digest the news. Sometimes, following a news publication, the market reacts strongly by going one way but recovers in the next two hours and resumes its current activity. So, don't try to gamble on the news. With experience, however, you will get to know when important news are likely to have no impact on the market at particular times while they may be strongly scrutinized at other times.

The main macro-economic news that often impacts the markets are interest rates decisions from central banks and their press conferences, crude oil inventories, American employment, inflation figures, GDPs, and home sales. Depending on the context, they may trigger volatility when released. You can find calendars with news release dates and times on many websites. I like to use the economic calendar published on investing.com and apply a filter to show the major news.

Economic Calendar

As the week is finishing, I look at the following week's events and report them to my computer calendar and save reminders and alarms that go off one hour to 30 minutes before the news release. That way, it reminds me not to open any more positions just before a news release and close existing positions while in positive territory.

Below is a list of additional times when I recommend not trading:

The first ten minutes after the stock market opening: I am talking about stock market opening and not futures market. During the first ten minutes, the market can move in different ways, not giving us useful readings. Indeed, some participants may be closing positions they didn't manage to close the previous day or for which they had sufficient margin at that time but no longer. Other participants may open or close positions due to their option hedging work, and so on. Different traders with different agendas. The first ten minutes may create volatility that again may trigger scalpers' stop-losses without giving any opportunity to the scalper.

The triple witching day: this is the name given to the day when, on a monthly basis, index futures contracts, stock index options contracts, and single stock options contracts expire; even quadruple witching day when single stock futures contracts add to this list on a quarterly basis. Triple witching day takes place on the third Friday of the month and quadruple witching day on the third Friday of the month every quarter-end. Volumes become artificially higher due to positions being rolled over to the next contract term. Volatility may also increase as market participants have different agendas, but it may not help the scalper, so I choose to take it easy these days.

The last day of the quarter: Some market participants may be at work to improve their balance sheet and quarterly reporting. However, don't start thinking that it will trigger an uptrend because if rising prices may improve the balance sheet of institutional investors, it may have an adverse impact on those with short positions in their books.

Holidays and festive seasons: during those times, volumes are lower. The market may be in a free-spinning mode or move rapidly in low volumes. If you absolutely want to trade, do it on lower volumes because when institutional investors and big market movers are on holiday, the market may not give you the right opportunities to realize good trades.

Trading after 10 pm: Mini DAX and DAX futures are not tradable after 10 pm, but for the e-mini Dow, CME lets the trader carry on their trading on an OTC system via its GLOBEX platform. So, if you really want to trade e-mini Dow non-stop, you can start at midnight on Monday until 11 pm on Friday (these hours can change slightly during the winter and summertime changes). However, trading after 10 pm is not recommended because the volumes are likely to be very low. Focus your energy instead on the US pre-market opening, which is at 14:30 CET.

Trading the Mini-DAX and DAX Pre-market Opening

Mini DAX and DAX futures markets open at 7:50 am one hour and 10 minutes before the stock market opening. Most of the time, pre-market opening is very quiet with low volume transactions. No need to rush to your screen and start trading at 8 am. However, when the market made a strong move the day before, there may be opportunities arising in the pre-market opening. We know that market participants have different agendas, but when the market reacts strongly in one direction, it can put speculators in difficult positions. For instance, if the market went down by 300 points in one day, some long traders may face margin calls meaning they will have to either put more cash in their account or close some of their positions. This will lead to more sell orders being put on the market. At the same time, some sellers may want to cash in and close winning trades. In the first minutes of pre-market opening, you won't know how the market will evolve, but you can certainly use the Heikin Ashi candles to perform some trades because after a strong move the day before, there is likely to be volatility in the pre-market opening.

DAX, One Minute: 300 points is a strong intraday move for the DAX.

Quiet pre-market opening has prices that move within a ten to twenty-point range. But here, after a strong move on the previous day, we can expect some volatility.

The Most Effective Method to Make Money Trading Futures

Exchanging fates is a type of contributing that can give broadening to a portfolio and assist you with overseeing hazard. Fates contracts apply to agrarian wares, rising and falling as the market interest of things, for example, corn, steel, cotton, and oil change. You can make cash exchanging fates on the off chance that you pursue patterns, cut your misfortunes, and watch your costs.

Follow Trends

Fates markets have patterns, much the same as different protections markets do. Items tend not to have a similar unpredictability as stocks; however, it can likewise be less unsurprising. At the point when you distinguish a pattern through thorough research and testing, it speaks to your most obvious opportunity to benefit. Research includes investigating which components sway the organic market of the item that you're keen on. Testing includes making mimicked interests in prospects that you think you see slants in to see whether a genuine venture would have worked out.

Cut Losses Short

Any individual who puts resources into fates long enough is going to buy gets that lose esteem. On the off chance that a specific agreement begins to move in opposition to your desires, firmly consider undercutting and assuming a little misfortune. The option might be trusting that the agreement will ascend in esteem, just to see it fall further. Since each agreement you purchase is with the desire that it will see gains inside your time skyline, stopping misfortunes by selling will expand the arrival that you return to contribute somewhere else and counterbalance different additions when you ascertain salary venture for your charges.

Margins and Expiration Dates

Financial specialists exchange fates on edge, paying as meager as 10% of the estimation of an agreement to possess it and control the privilege to sell it until it lapses. Edges consider duplicated benefits, yet additionally profit you can't stand to lose. Keep in mind that exchanging on an edge conveys this unique hazard. Select gets that terminate after when you anticipate that costs should arrive at their pinnacle. A March prospects contract is pointless on the off chance that you get it in January yet don't anticipate that the product should arrive at its pinnacle an incentive until April. Regardless of whether April contracts aren't accessible, a May contract is increasingly proper since you can sell it before it lapses yet hold up until after the ware's cost gets an opportunity to rise.

Brokers and Expenses

Financial specialists exchange prospects contracts through conventional representatives just as online agent administrations. Online administrations offer less customized exhortation but, at the same time, are more affordable, offering exchanges for under $1 now and again. Utilize an online specialist and play out your own market investigation to minimize expenses and increment your net addition from exchanging fates. Track all costs, including intermediary charges and memberships to on the web or print productions that help you contribute, to deduct them as speculation costs on your annual expenses.

Most Significant Hints on the Best Way to Profit in the Fates Advertise

Try Not to Attempt the Fates Advertise on the Off Chance That You Have No Cash

Many individuals get the possibility that creation cash on the prospects trade is simple, and they feel free to put enormous sums on that they can't stand to lose. That is a major NO.

Try Not to Attempt Some Trick or Mystery You Read in a Book

The fastest method to lose cash on the fates showcase is to go out and attempt one of the mysteries you got notification from a companion or read in a book. These are simply gossipy tidbits and, for the most part, don't work. In the event that you are going to test a specific methodology, guarantee you do it relaxed and with modest quantities of cash before going hard and fast. Little tests will assist you in seeing reliable results. You won't profit, yet the dangers are little, and you won't lose your whole record on the off chance that things conflict with you.

Think Present Moment and Long Haul

Try not to attempt to make sense of what will occur in the fates showcase in the following 2 hours. Indeed, this can profit; however, there are a ton of effective merchants that are making cash long haul in fates moreover. They couldn't care less about the every day variances or what happens each moment consistently.

Don't Over Investigation

There is such an incredible concept as making a decent attempt on the fates trade. Regularly the great merchants will discover something that works and, afterward, continue attempting to make the framework and procedure work better. Simply acknowledge, there is no sacred goal to exchanging. There is no framework that is going to profit 100% of the time. Acknowledge you will take little misfortunes, and discover a framework that works reliably and stick to it. Keep it near you and use it as your weapon against the market.

Utilize an Expert Exchanging Stage

There are numerous great stages you can use to exchange prospects. In any case, there is a darker side to exchanging prospects, where numerous broking houses offer carriage stages that are more regrettable than inferior. Simply do your schoolwork first and discover what the top dealers are suggesting. These stages ordinarily play out the best and keep customers cheerful. At the point when it is your cash in danger, you need to guarantee you have well-being and dependability on your side. Generally, there can be radical outcomes.

Know What's Going on Out There in the Economy

After the worldwide money related emergency, a few nations are doing ineffectively, and there is, at present, a few monetary standards issues. It may merit your opportunity to discover how the economy is getting along in your general vicinity of the world. In the event that things are not looking great, it is smarter to set aside cash to purchase day by day things before you go gambling everything on the fates advertise.

Utilize a Demonstrated Stop Misfortune the Board Framework

This is the main motivation behind why numerous merchants out there come up short. They toss cash into the fates advertise without pondering what their arrangement is if things conflict with them. Things won't work out as expected 100% of the time. Taking misfortunes are a part of the game and increasingly like a cost of doing business for proficient brokers. Simply acknowledge it and consistently leave a position on the off chance that it conflicts with you. It is difficult to concede you aren't right, yet simply acknowledge it and get out of the exchange. That will guarantee you have cash for the following exchange that presents itself.

Exchanging Knowledge for Success in the Futures Market

Greatness Is a Result of Difficult Work

Appropriate exchanging information is the way to accomplishment in the prospects advertise. You can go right back to the Bible, and it will advise you about the significance regarding shrewdness. Adages reveal to us that shrewdness is the rule thing, and to go get insight and comprehension. The entirety of the incredible brokers and financial specialists from the beginning of time took a stab at securing the information important to get world-class. This is the manner by which they made fortunes exchanging the different markets. There is no easy route to turning into a world-class broker.

Study and Learn as Much as You Can

In the event that you need to make progress in the prospects showcase, you essentially should place in the time and exertion important to secure the best possible exchanging information. Achievement originates from knowing and following demonstrated fixed guidelines. The individuals who need information normally surmise or pursue the counsel of TV characters. This is a sure catastrophe waiting to happen.

Do Not Put Together Your Exchanging Choices with Respect to Feelings

Probably the greatest misstep new brokers, and even experienced ones make, is to be affected by feelings, for example, dread, insatiability, and expectation. One approach to cure this is to execute an effective exchanging plan that accommodates your character. On the off chance that you just pursue flag legitimately from your arrangement, it will assist you with trading just on certainties and not feelings. Try not to belittle the significance of appropriate exchanging brain science. It is a significant piece of your general exchanging information that will prompt achievement in the prospects advertise.

Charts Will Give You Extraordinary Data

On the off chance that you appropriately study the value developments and volume on a diagram, they will reveal to you more about what is happening than any investigator, TV character, or merchant. Diagrams are an incredible wellspring of previous history, with pieces of information to future value developments.

Following an unmistakable pattern is one of the significant keys to making a great deal of cash exchanging the different markets. On the off chance that a market is in an exchanging range, have the tolerance to hold up until it unmistakably breaks obstruction or backing. At that point, float along with the market. Try not to avoid the pattern. Make sure to consistently rehearse sound cash the executives. This can be accomplished by deliberately putting stops following you take a position. When the market goes your direction, actualize trailing stops to ensure benefits. You should rehearse sound judgment through the whole procedure. This originates from appropriate exchanging information and experience. You can turn into a reliable victor in the fates showcase or the financial exchange.

Tips for Intermediate Futures Options Traders

As a futures trader, you should make sure that you understand very clearly what a short position is and a long position is. There are plenty of novice traders who believe that you only make money or are profitable when markets are on an upward trend. However, you need to understand that futures trading constitutes a lot more than just following the upward market trend. You also should know by now that as a futures trader, you can benefit greatly when you focus on asset types that have attained a climax and are close to failure.

As a trader, anytime that you wage your money against an asset, then you will be said to be selling it short. Selling an asset short simply means that you will engage your broker and purchase the rights to access the asset with the hopes of selling it back later once it becomes profitable. Using this analogy, we can purchase apples at the market for $1 each and then selling them back at $2 each, making a profit of $1.

In real life, this $1 can be exponentially multiplied to earn you large sums of money. This is the way futures markets work. You stand to make large sums of money from simple trades.

Long Positions

As a futures trader, you are ready to invest your funds in a particular asset when you take a long position in it. In this situation, you will only benefit from this position when the price of the asset rises. As a futures trader, you need to be able to determine whether and when an asset is likely to rise in price. This determination requires you to learn about the fundamentals of the asset. For instance, how is the supply and demand in the market? Being able to answer such questions with a high level of accuracy will enable you to decide whether to invest in it or not.

Basically, each asset market has its own rules that help interested parties, including traders, to provide intrinsic value as well as the determination of momentum, both negative and positive. The Central Bank is the premier institution when it comes to currency, so currency traders need to take note of the policies and statements released by this institution. In this instance, currency fluctuations sometimes depend on interest rates. If you anticipate a rate hike, then it is advisable to go long on the specific currency. Higher interest rates should provide a suitable incentive to hold long an asset. This way, there will be increasing demand for the currency, and you will be able to eventually sell at a great price and make lots of profits.

When it comes to stocks and other instruments, it is corporations that drive their value. For instance, the earnings report will determine the value of a company's stock in the short and long terms. Earnings reports are often released quarterly. During these events, company executives reveal their earnings for the past three months as well as their forecasts for the future. Therefore, if a company announces a reduction in production, closure of a store or plant, and so on, then you should assume a long position. The reason is that reduced production will very likely result in higher prices within a couple of months.

Short Position

When it comes to short positions, there are plenty of similar factors compared to long positions at play but in reverse. Therefore, factors or elements that cause you to choose a long position will, in reverse, determine a short position. For instance, if you are interested in currency and there are signs of reduced inflation, then you may want to take a short position on the currency.

Basically, when there are signs of declining inflation, central banks may decide to lower interest rates in order to provide a stable financial position in the markets. On the other hand, when interest rates are high, then as a futures trader, you will want to take the path that all other futures traders do. When interest rates are high, products and services are generally expensive for the consumer.

Costly products mean lower sales figures, and this will mean reduced incomes for corporations and so on. As such, it will be appropriate for futures traders to sell short because of the high-interest rates. Some of the instruments that can be sold include shares and stock indices. Commodities markets and their instruments also operate in the same manner. When there are high-interest rates at play, the markets tend to experience low demand. Commodities such as gold and oil will then most likely begin selling short at the markets.

Basically, it is advisable to have a good idea regarding factors that are actually negative and which ones are considered positive, especially with regards to your preferred asset. This way, you can do your research and analysis to determine if you are to sell an asset or buy.

Intermediate Futures Trading

It is often difficult for traders with small accounts to make any significant gains in the futures market. As an intermediate trader, you do not need to be too concerned about this. This is because you can use leverage to overcome your small account size challenges.

Leverage provides an effective pathway that enables you to capitalize effectively on your positions. Leverage also provides a reliable pathway that will enable you to increase your profit potential as you maximize your positions in the trade. This means that you will be able to leverage in a manner that allows you to profit in numerous ways not otherwise possible.

Leverage can help you maximize your gains. However, be extremely cautious because leverage can also compound your losses should you incur any. It is possible that your analysis could travel in the wrong direction. When this happens, you could incur some losses, and these could have an impact on your account. You could, for instance, receive what is known as a margin call. When this happens, you will be required to fund your trading account. Should you not be able to fund your account due to losses, then it will be shut down.

Things That Distinguish Winning and Losing Traders in Options Trading

As an options trader, you need to know how to calculate and find the break-even point. In options trading, there are basically 2 break-even points. With short term options, you need to make use of the commission rates and bid spread to work out the break-even point. This is if you intend to hold on to the options until their expiration date. Now, if you are seeking short term trade without holding on to the options, then find out the difference between the asking price and the bid price. This difference is also known as the spread.

Embrace the Underlying Stock's Trend

As a trader, you should learn to jump successfully on a trend and follow the crowds rather than go to extremes and oppose it. Most amateurs who see an upward trend often think the stock is about to level out. However, the reality is that the momentum is often considered a great thing by seasoned traders. Therefore, do not try and oppose the trend because you will surely lose.

Instead, try and design a strategy that will accommodate the trend. In short, the trend is always your friend, do not resist as momentum is great.

Watch Out for Earnings Release Dates

Call and put options are generally expensive, with the price increases significantly if there is an earnings release announcement looming. The reason is that the anticipation of very good or very bad earnings report will likely affect the stock price. When this is an underlying stock in an options trade, then you should adjust your trades appropriately.

Once an earnings release has been made, then options prices will fall significantly. You need to also watch out very carefully about this. The prices will first go up just before the earnings are released and then fall shortly thereafter. It is also possible for call options prices to dip despite earnings announcements. This may happen if the earnings announced are not as impressive as expected.

As an example, stocks such as Google may rise insanely during the earnings announcement week only to dip significantly shortly thereafter. Consider Apple shares that were trading at $450 at the markets. Call options with Apple as the underlying stock were trading at $460. However, the market had targeted a price of $480 within 3 days, which did not happen. This costs investors' money. Such underlying assets are considered volatile due to the high increase in price, rapid drop shortly thereafter, and a related risk of losing money.

Traps to Avoid on Expiration Day

The ease of the guidelines for participation and the aggressive marketing brings a lively interest of people for the binary options trade. Some greedy brokers take advantage of this desire that touches an audience of new private investors, mostly beginners. The most frequent abuses or frauds found are:

- **The impossibility of withdrawing your money:** Here, the fraudulent binary options broker prevents any withdrawal or does not accept withdrawals until a minimum level is reached in the account.
- **Fraud in the bank card:** Once the bank details are sent (by phone or after a first deposit), withdrawals are made from the client's account without their authorization.

- **An offer of "bonus" is offered to the clients:** The company commits to credit in the customer's account the same amount as this deposit. The client then learns that the bonus is not granted until "bet" at least x times its amount (20 to 30 times in the cases cited).
- **Fraud in managed accounts:** Training offers are proposed, and a "coach" is assigned to the client. Very often, the coach proposes to the debutants to be advised by telephone in their bets. When the first losses occur, the coaches advise the client to place supplementary funds to "redo." When losses accumulate, "the coach becomes unplayable or gives the only explanation that a bad operation is the source of the losses."
- **Conditions of trade impossible to achieve:** The broker demands the investor to make positions more than x days in the month. Maybe even more than the number of days worked in the month.
- **Withdrawal penalty:** The broker applies significant "charges" from 10 to 50% to dissuade the investor from recovering their money. Generally, the merchant has no knowledge of this information until the day he tries to withdraw his funds and has a hard time finding this information before.

On the other hand, if the most serious companies propose access to a market resulting from supply and demand, the majority is happy proposing over the counter products (without going through a stock market). The prices are then decided either by the company itself, which acts as a counterpart for its own account and has an interest in the client losing, 5 either by an affiliated company or friend.

CHAPTER 5

Golden Trading Rules and Mistakes to Avoid

Stock trading is becoming more popular each day. This is basically the most preferred monetary resource by individuals to generate money. Just about every other person or family discusses it. There are a few fundamental principles for successful stock trading that are implemented persistently by successful traders. Of course, if you follow these rules as well, you will probably become successful and make money with stock trading.It is crucial to read through these effective stock trading rules before you decide to get into the stock market, regardless of whether you're a beginner or even an expert.

Trend Is Your Friend

Go long if the stock is bullish and go short if the market is bearish. Never go against the trend. Stick to this vital rule for successful stock trading.

Always Plan Your Trade

Use a proper trading plan to ensure success; that should include a position, the reasons you enter, stop-loss level, profit taking level, along with a sensible money management approach.

Protect Your Capital

Establish a limit for your trading and protect your money. Do not place beyond 10% of your portfolio in one trade. If you do not abide by this stock trading rule, you will likely be out of the market soon.

Don't Extend Losses

In case the trade goes against you, get out of that position and do not hesitate over it. If you hang on for too long, assuming that the price will increase, you will simply end up losing more money. Settle on your stop-loss price level before you actually enter a trade.

Don't Be Greedy; Take a Timely Profit

Once the trade seems to be in profit, book some of that profit. Select how much profit you are prepared to take. Sit back and watch the profit run by adhering to this rule for successful trading. Buy climbing stocks and sell dropping stocks.

Leave Emotions Out of the Trading Ring

Greed and fear are often the two most significant emotions in trading. Do not allow these to have an effect on your trading. Any successful trader is usually emotionally consistent.

Keep Your Trading Record

Whenever you trade a stock, it will help to write down the main reasons why you bought or sold, as well as your emotions during that time.

Evaluate afterward and write down the errors you made, along with the right choices you made. One more successful stock trading rule would be to keep studying and improving.

Don't Listen to Others

Trade only depending on your personal study and analysis. Steer clear of trading based on what your friend or other people are saying. A properly informed trader constantly marches forward.

If in Doubt, Then Do Not Trade

If you are unclear about the trend in the market, keep away. You should not disregard this particular rule for successful stock trading. It can help you achieve a lot by not doing anything.

Overtrading Is the Real Enemy

You must not have more than 3–5 positions at any given time. Several positions could make you lose control and make incorrect sentimental choices. Therefore, never trade just for the enjoyment of trading.It requires plenty of discipline to harvest large profits and guide your journey to the stock trading achievements. So look at the previously mentioned rules for successful trading before you actually get into the stock market, even if you are a profitable stock trader.

Holding Positions Until the Subsequent Day Is Risk

Going long on futures, holding positions long can presumably cause you to lose money. The futures may shut at the tip of the day at one value and open the resulting day at a fully completely different value. Traders who exclude their positions daily do not have to be compelled to worry about losing money once the market opens in the morning. This method could also be an important transaction strategy.

Choose a Liquid Market to Trade

Before you start to trade futures, study the little print of each market. With this, you may build the foremost effective selection. You need to be trained and be careful to attain success in commerce futures. Once new traders begin to be told plenty of and gain some experience, it's simple to form mistakes that can cause problems associated value an excessive quantity of money. A number of those mistakes embody making risky trades and commerce you may afford. You need to be cautious and organized to succeed in the trade.

Settling of Contract

Trading futures contracts do not involve the immediate delivery of assets. Subsiding of contract happens solely on the date that it expires. Traders can even settle before the contract's expiration if they like better to do, therefore.

Don't Stay on the Trend, Follow It

The hardest suggestion for a trader is to follow trends. Traders are independent individuals who do not appear to belong to the group or part of the herd.

Follow a System, Don't Get Into Chaos

Be very clear about the reasons why you need to introduce futures trading techniques if you want to reach the milestones you need to achieve.

Possible futures trading techniques have to do with making clear possible market fluctuations in the coming year. If you're not clear, don't expect to go too far shopping.

Accept Losses, Adjust Gains

Another key is simply to adjust your losses and gains. Learn how to trade from the small side and watch out for divergences in online shopping. Staying out is as important as entering the markets. Patience could be a virtue.

Have a Healthy Business Plan

This includes a clear understanding of entry and exit points, value targets, risk-reward relationships, attitudes, knowledge of historical value levels, seasonal influences, graphical analysis, cost-related markets, and government reporting. Don't expect to make a profit.

The impetus for mercantilism is out

A disciplined system of business selection is important. Being impulsive instead of objective will cost you more than one operation. Swap with inspiration instead of relying on emotions. Find out how to deduct profits, decide the risk of trading on margin, and anywhere to boost market circulation.

Discipline Is Essential

You have a tight schedule for each operation that can change unless thorough knowledge supports it. Disciplined cash management involves smart transaction allocation as well as risk management, and once you create a thriving transaction, don't worry about the success of the successful transaction.

Keep in mind that the future career of commercialism is a kind of chess game. You can only survive if your next move is sweet enough.

Volatility Is Often Explosive

The airline business is a double-edged sword. You cannot simplify it if you decide on difficult decisions an unstable financial process that will form. Keep in mind when calculating the odds/reward ratio before choosing a trade and beware of the risk of keeping it for a long time.

Follow an Idea, Think About the Future

Once a controller is established, and stops are selected, don't choose until the stop or the main reason for changing the controller is reached. Use technical analysis to maintain discipline and not compromise emotional objectivity.

Not Timing the Market Correctly

While everyone is familiar with the old adage buy low and sell high, it doesn't translate particularly well into practical advice. Many investors who attempt to buy low when they think the market has bottomed out or try and sell when the market is at an apparent peak often lose out those to those investors who simply purchase reliable pairs and hang onto them for the long term. What's worse, many of those who attempt to time the market end up losing lots of money, which can be devastating, depending on how heavily they were invested in the scenario.

Making Investments That Are Too Risky

It is important to keep in mind that the further you are from retirement, the riskier of investments you can make as you will have more time to recover if you choose poorly. However, once you are within 5 years of retirement, it is always going to be better to take the safer investment with the lower estimated return than it is to invest in anything even remotely risky. A good rule of thumb when it comes to determining how much of your overall portfolio could be in forex is to take your age and subtract that number from 110. The result is the percentage of your portfolio that should be based around stocks.

Making Investments That Aren't Risky Enough

If you are closer to retirement, then the greater mistake is making investments that are too risky; if you are further away from retirement, then the greater mistake is not taking enough chances. When you have plenty of breathing room between now and your retirement, it is important to take advantage of this fact to the fullest and take greater risks to help maximize your earning potential while you have enough time to mitigate the additional risk. If you are currently in your thirties, then a full 80% of your portfolio could be in the forex market without issue.

Not Knowing Your Limits

It is certainly possible to enter into retirement without having to micromanage your finances. But in order to do so, you are going to need to plan for a less complicated retirement strategy prior to retirement, something that few people take the time to do. This will require meeting with a financial advisor and taking their advice to heart, again, something that not nearly enough people do. You should meet with a financial advisor and then again about five years before you retire, just to ensure you are on the right track. Be sure you have the basics of your retirement investment plan outlined before you go and listen to any of the suggestions they make. After all, you only get to retire once; it is best to make it count.

Being Overconfident

Many people believe that they are smarter than the market as a whole, which means they can be the odds, even if the odds are very, very low. If you don't think this is the case, then consider how many people play the lottery on a regular basis. If you are someone who plays the lottery on a regular basis, it is important to be aware of this propensity and avoid betting more than is rational when it comes to individual trades.

The fact of the matter is that most people are going to be average, at best, when it comes to trading in the forex market. What this means is that you are going to want to do everything in your power in order to mitigate this average performance when it comes to trading.

Never Only Look for Information That Confirms What You Already Believe

If you are dead set on trading in forex pairs that you choose yourself, it is important to do as much research as humanly possible before committing to anything. After all, even if you still have plenty of time before you need to start changing a majority of your holdings away from forex, you never want to throw your money away. As such, when you are doing your research, it is important to look at all of the available data, not just that which conforms to the ideas you have about an existing stock.

Don't Resort to Anchoring

Anchoring is the term given to irrationally being stuck on a specific number for a specific trade without having any real reason for doing so. The same thing can happen to those who hold onto a specific pair for too long and miss a profitable sale point in the process. Or worse, if you are holding onto a currency that you bought at $5, which then drops to $3, an anchoring mindset will cause you to hold onto it despite conventional wisdom saying it is better to cut your losses before it drops even further.

The most efficient way to avoid an anchoring bias is to ensure that you have a firm trading plan in place with buy and sell points determined before you make a commitment. Knowing what you are going to do before you do it is a great way to ensure that your emotions don't get in the way and to prevent you from anchoring without even realizing it.

Accept That Loss Is a Part of the Process

The forex market runs on risk. This is a fact and cannot be changed, no matter how much you wish; this might be the case. Risk drives price and is ultimately responsible for any profits that you make in both the short and the long term. With this fact in mind, it then becomes much easier to deal with loss and respond to it accordingly. While this doesn't mean that you should take unnecessary risks, it also doesn't mean that you should hold onto losing propositions simply because you don't want to accept the loss.

Putting All Your Eggs in One Basket

While there is a difference between investing and trading, traders can learn a few things from our investor brothers (and most people are a little of both anyway). Don't let everything ride on one trade.

If you take all the money you have and invest it in buying options for one stock, you're making a big mistake. Doing that is very risky, and as a beginning trader, you're going to want to mitigate your risk as much as possible. Betting on one stock may pay off sometimes, but more times than not, it's going to lead you into bankruptcy territory.

Investing More Than You Can

It's easy to get excited about options trading. The chances to make fast money and the requirements that you analyze the markets can be very enticing. Oftentimes that leads people into getting more excited than they should. A good rule to follow with investing is to make sure that you're setting aside enough money to cover living expenses every month, with a security fund for emergencies. Don't bet the farm on some sure thing by convincing yourself that you'll be able to make back twice as much money and so cover your expenses. Things don't always work out.

Going All in Before You're Ready

Another mistake is failing to take the time to learn options trading in real-time. Just like getting overly excited can cause people to bet too much money or put all their money on one stock, some people are impatient and don't want to take the time to learn the options markets by selling covered calls. It's best to start with covered calls and then move slowly to small deals buying call options. Leave put options until you've gained some experience.

Failure to Study the Markets

Remember, you need to be truly educated to make good options trades. That means you'll need to know a lot about the companies that you're either trying to profit from or that you're shorting. Options trading isn't possible without some level of guesswork, but make your guesses educated guesses, and don't rely too much on hunches.

Not Getting Enough Time Value

Oftentimes, whether you're trading puts or calls, the time value is important. A stock may need an adequate window of time to beat the stock price, whether it's going above it or plunging below it. When you're starting and don't know the markets as well as a seasoned trader, you should stick to options you can buy that have a longer period before expiring.

Not Having Adequate Liquidity

Sometimes beginning investors overestimate their ability to play the options markets. Remember that if you buy an option, to make it work for you, you're going to need money on hand to buy stocks when the iron is hot. And you're going to need to buy 100 shares for every option contract. Before entering into the contract, make sure that you're going to be able to exercise your option.

Not Having a Grip on Volatility

If you don't understand volatility and its relation to premium pricing, you may end up making bad trades.

Failing to Have a Plan

Trading seems exciting, and when you're trading, you may lose the investor's mentality. However, traders need to have a strategic plan as much as investors do. Before trading, make sure that you have everything in place, including knowing what your goals are for the trades, having pre-planned exit strategies, developing criteria for getting into a trade so that you're not doing it on a whim or based on emotion.

Ignoring Expiration Dates

It sounds crazy, but many beginners don't keep track of the expiration date. Would you hate to see a stock go up in price and then hope it keeps going up, and it does, only to find out that your expiration date passed before you exercised your option?

Over-leveraging

It's easy to spend huge amounts of money in small increments. This is true when it comes to trading options. Since stocks are more expensive, it's possible to get seduced by purchasing low priced options.

Giving in to Panic

Remember that you have the right to buy or sell a stock if you've purchased an option. Some beginners panic and exercise their right far too early. This can happen because of fears that they'll be missing out on an opportunity with a call option or because of fears that a stock won't keep going down on a put.

CHAPTER 6

Proven and Time-Tested Futures Trading Strategies

Fundamental Trading

This is where you have to do research into the markets in which you want to trade, read the daily press reports on weather conditions, study information like supply and demand figures, agricultural reports and economic news, etc.

This takes up an excessive amount of time and money and is mainly used by large institutional investors with the necessary resources to do all the research.

Technical Trading

With this method, you make use of charts to analyze the movement of the markets, also known as Technical Analysis.

It is much more suited for the small trader. It does not require having to make decisions based on a lot of subjective information.

Comparing and Combining Models

The data you are looking for is in Table 19.1, where the strategies that we looked at earlier are listed, as well as the same statistics for the S&P 500 Total Return Index, all covering the backtesting period from the start of 2001 to the end of 2018.

Table 19.1 Futures Strategies Statistics

	Annualized Return	Max Drawdown	Annualized Volatility	Sharpe Ratio	Calmar Ratio	Sortino Ratio
trend_model	12.12%	-25.48%	19.35%	0.69	0.48	0.98
counter_trend	11.00%	-30.09%	18.55%	0.66	0.37	0.92
curve_trading	14.89%	-23.89%	18.62%	0.84	0.62	1.22
time_return	11.78%	-40.31%	21.09%	0.63	0.29	0.9
systematic_momentum	7.84%	-39.83%	16.48%	0.54	0.2	0.76
SPXTR	5.60%	-55.25%	18.92%	0.38	0.1	0.5

Clearly, the curve trading model is the best one, right? And the momentum isn't worth bothering with? Well, conclusions like that are the reason why I did not show these simple statistics earlier. Evaluating trading models is a more complex undertaking than simply looking at a table like this. You need to study the details and study the long-term return profile. And, of course, scalability. At the sharp end of the business, you often look for a specific behavior in the return profile, often relative to other factors. The answer to which model is more promising depends on what you happen to be looking for at the moment and what would fit or complement your current portfolio of models.

All of these models are simple demo models. They are teaching tools, not production-grade models. But they all show potential, and they can be polished up to become production grade models.

You can also see that all of them are orders of magnitudes more attractive than a buy and hold stock market approach. Some readers may be surprised to see just how meager the return of the stock markets is over time. In this period, from 2001 to 2018, the S&P 500 returned less than 6% per year, even with dividends included and even with the last ten years of bull market included. And that was at a peak drawdown of over half.

Another point that may surprise some is the level of the Sharpe ratios. None are over 1. There is an unfortunate misconception that a Sharpe of less than one is poor. That's not necessarily so. In fact, for systematic strategies, it's unusual to see realized Sharpe ratios of over one.

Comparing Futures Models

Shows the long-term development of these five strategies, compared to that of the stock market. On such a long-time scale, the index comparison hardly seems fair. But the fact is that in the shorter run, you will always be compared to it. This is the curse of the business.

Remember that the reason that these backtests start in 2001 is that a current, and hopefully soon addressed the issue in Zipline makes it tricky to use pre-2000 data. The fact that the equity index starts off with a nosedive might make this comparison a little unfair, and for that reason, I will also show you the same graph starting in 2003, the bottom of the bear market. I won't do one from the bottom of the 2008–2009 bear market. That would just be plain silly. Comparing perfect market timing into the longest-lasting bull market of a generation with alternative strategies does not make any sense. Comparison, starting from 2003.

Even if we would have had the foresight of buying the index with impeccable timing at the bottom of the tech crash, the index would still have shown lower return and deeper drawdowns.

Combining the Models

Everyone knows that diversification is beneficial. At least everyone should know that. But most people think of diversification only in terms of holding multiple positions. That's all fine and well, but you can also find added value in diversifying trading styles. Think of a single trading model as a portfolio component.

What you may find is that an overall portfolio of models can perform significantly better than any of the individual strategies that go into it. I will demonstrate this with a simple portfolio consisting of the five trading models we have seen so far.

As we have five models, we will allocate an equal weight of 20% of our capital to each. The rebalance period is monthly, meaning that we would need to adjust all positions accordingly each month, resetting the weight to the target 20%. Such a rebalance frequency on a model level can be both difficult and time consuming for smaller accounts but is perfectly reasonable on a larger scale. Feel free to repeat this experiment with yearly data if you like. Making portfolio calculations like this is an area where Python shines compared to other languages.

Table 19.2 Portfolio of Futures Models

	Annualized Return	Max Drawdown	Annualized Volatility	Sharpe Ratio	Calmar Ratio	Sortino Ratio
trend_model	12.12%	-25.48%	19.35%	0.69	0.48	0.98
counter_trend	11.00%	-30.09%	18.55%	0.66	0.37	0.92
curve_trading	14.89%	-23.89%	18.62%	0.84	0.62	1.22
time_return	11.78%	-40.31%	21.09%	0.63	0.29	0.9
systematic_momentum	7.84%	-39.83%	16.48%	0.54	0.2	0.76
Combined	14.92%	-17.55%	11.81%	1.24	0.85	1.79

Table 19.2 shows a comparison of the performance of each individual model, as well as the overall stock market, to that of the combined portfolio. These numbers should be abundantly clear. The combined portfolio far outperformed each individual strategy, at lower volatility. We got a higher annualized return, a lower maximum drawdown, lower volatility, higher Sharpe, etc.

You may find a model with a low expected return over time, but which also has a low or negative correlation to other models, and thereby can greatly help your overall combined portfolio of trading models.

Portfolio of Trading Models

As the individual models often have their gains and losses at different times from each other, they complement each other well and help smooth out long term volatility. The drawdowns become subdued, resulting in a higher long-term return.

While it was a close call some years, in the end, not a single year of this combined portfolio ended up losing money.

Table 19.3 Holding Period Analysis for Combined Model

Years	1	2	3	4	5	6	7	8	9	10	11	12	13	14	15	16	17	18
2001	8	13	17	18	17	16	18	19	19	20	18	17	17	17	17	16	16	15
2002	18	22	22	20	17	19	21	20	21	20	18	18	18	17	16	16	15	
2003	27	24	21	17	20	21	21	21	20	18	18	18	17	16	16	15		
2004	21	18	14	18	20	20	21	19	17	17	17	17	16	15	14			
2005	15	11	17	20	20	21	19	16	16	17	16	15	15	14				
2006	7	18	21	21	22	19	17	16	17	16	15	15	14					
2007	29	29	26	26	22	18	18	19	17	16	16	14						
2008	29	24	24	20	16	16	17	16	15	14	13							
2009	20	22	17	13	14	15	14	13	13	12								
2010	25	16	11	12	14	13	12	12	11									
2011	8	5	8	12	11	10	10	9										
2012	1	8	13	12	10	11	9											
2013	16	20	16	13	13	11												
2014	24	16	12	12	10													
2015	9	6	8	7														
2016	4	8	6															
2017	13	7																
2018	2																	

Implementing a Portfolio of Models

While a demonstration like this may seem to show a simple solution to all your investment vows, an implementation may not be as easy. Each of these models requires millions to trade. Clearly, trading them all requires even more millions. I recognize that not every reader of this book has a spare hundred million laying around to be traded. But even if you are one of those unfortunate few non-billionaires out there, understanding the power of combining different approaches can be greatly helpful.

As the complexity rises, you lack the simple overview, which is possible with a single model, and you may need more sophisticated software to keep track of positions, signals, risk allocation, etc.

A professional trading organization can build the capability of trading such complex combinations, to monitor the risk and build proper reporting and analysis. For individual traders, this may not be a possibility.

Of course, there is another way to look at it. An understanding of how complex portfolios of models can be constructed and implemented can help you acquire the skillset needed to land a good job in the industry. Working at the sharp end of the industry has the potential to earn you far more money than you could possibly make trading your own portfolio.

Never forget that the interesting money in this business is made from trading another people's money. Whether or not you personally have the money to trade such models is not the important part. Well, it would be nice to have that, of course. But you can still make use of this kind of knowledge, and you can still profit from it. If you land a good job with a hedge fund or similar, you will probably get paid far more by working for them than you could by trading your own money anyhow.

Support and resistance

Understanding support and resistance is crucial to achieving the success you are looking for when it comes to technical analysis. While they may seem complex at first, they will become clearer every time you put the theory around them into practice. At their most basic, resistance can be thought of as the ceiling on the price of a particular currency or currency pair, which means the price is unlikely to move past this point. In contrast, support can be thought of as the price floor, which is unlikely to decrease further.

Understanding the concept of support and resistance is key to the success of your trading. Just about all timing approaches are based on buying near support levels and selling near resistance levels. Support is a certain price level where buying pressure is greater than selling pressure, and resistance is a price level where selling pressure is greater than buying pressure. The 18 and 40-day moving average is a great tool to use to indicate support level on a correction during an uptrend. Prices often find their support level at the 18 and the 40 days moving averages, which means that buying pressure will outweigh selling pressure at such levels and that the prevailing trends are likely to resume again from these levels. The same holds true when the market is in a downtrend when we also will find the resistance at the 18 and 40 days MA levels.

Previous highs and lows can also act as support and resistance levels. Earlier lows tend to slow the declining of the price down because many traders believe that the price previously rallied from these levels and can do so again. Such traders are likely to go long or cover their shorts at these levels. If the price slips below the old low, then the role of this price level is reversed and becomes the new resistance level. The reverse happens when the price reaches old highs.

Moving Averages

Of all the indicators Moving Averages (MA) are probably the most basic and well-known indicators. Moving averages are a way to define a trend mathematically.

 A moving average can be constructed by adding up the closing price of a certain number of days and then dividing the total by that number of days. Then each day, the oldest price in the series is dropped, and the most recent close is added. But you don't have to worry about calculating moving averages because they are available on most charts anyway. What is important is to know how to use them.

The most commonly used is the 4, 9, 18, and 40-day moving averages. The 40-day moving average is a great tool to use to determine the direction of the medium-term trend. A flat or horizontal 40-day moving average line reflects a sideways market or a phase between trend reversals. When the 40MA is sloping upwards, it means the intermediate trend is up, and the reverse is true when the 40MA is sloping downwards. To confirm an uptrend, make sure that the 9-day MA is greater than the 18-day MA and the 18-day MA greater than the 40-day MA. Confirmation of a downtrend means that the 9-day MA is smaller than the 18-day MA and the 18-day MA smaller than the 40-day MA.

Trend Lines

While it is not uncommon for these ceilings and floors to change regularly, being prepared for these changes is what separates the novice traders from the experts. Understanding these movements is done through the use of trend lines. When the market is trending upward, new resistance levels will be formed as that upward price movement begins to slow before starting its trek back down the trendline. This is likely to happen when uncertainty rises with a given stock. This will, in turn, create what is known as a short-term top, which is essentially a temporary price plateau in the overall movement pattern.Shorter trends can be part of trends that are much longer overall, which is why it is important always to double-check and ensure you aren't making a move on something that is only an offshoot of a much larger and much different trend. To decide what's even easier, it is important to always keep an eye on the weekly, daily, and yearly charts if you want to locate any truly long-term trends. If you are looking to get rich quick, you will want to stick to the daily charts instead.

After you have found an especially interesting trend, draw a straight line that correctly illustrates the direction the trend is currently moving in. When it comes to an uptrend, you will want to draw your line in such a way that it connects the dots of all of the lows in such a way that the line is below the relevant data. If you are looking at a reversal trend, you will want to draw the line so that it connects the highs, leaving the data below the trendline.

It is important to start paying extremely close attention to the price of the stock that you are watching when it begins to reach again the point where the trendline begins to broaden as this is likely to be the point where the price is going to cease its downward fall. It is important to note in instances such as this that a trendline can lend support to a given stock for a significant period while changing very little in the interim. Likewise, if the market is in a downward trend overall, then you will want to be on the lookout for a set of peaks at a declining angle and a trendline that connects the point of each peak. As the price gets closer to the trendline, you will want to be on the lookout for indicators that point towards selling, as this is how the price was likely pushed lower previously.

You will also want to keep an eye out for channel lines, a pair of lines to the side of the data you are watching that indicate the levels of resistance and support in play. One trendline connects the highs while the other connects the lows. At the same time, the resulting channel can either go up or down, or even sideways, but the interpretation will always remain constant. The goal should be to establish a long enough channel to show a break from the data that it has been following. This breakout point will mark the best time to get in on the trend you are following to ensure that you have the maximum amount of time to profit from the trend you have discovered.

CHAPTER 7

Technical and Fundamental Analysis

Technical Analysis

Technical analysis is ideal for determining future performance by looking at previous prices without having to dig through mountains of paperwork to find the details you are looking for. While the past will never be able to predict the future 100% of the time truly, technical analysis is useful when combined with a basic understanding of market mentality for generating predictions that are accurate within reason.

You have embarked on a very exciting journey into the profitable world of technical analysis. I will walk you through the core concepts of charting and show you how to time your trades with precision.

When it comes to understanding technical analysis, the most important thing to always keep in mind is that the action that a certain price has taken in the past is likely going to be a reliable way to predict its action in the future. This fact then makes it easy to use what are known as technical tools, things like indicators, charts, and trends to achieve a reliable rate of success that successful traders require. While the ways it can do so can be quite complicated at times, at its heart, technical analysis studies supply and demand in an effort to decide what trend, if any, is likely going to continue moving forward. This is crucial for long term success as the tools that technical analysis provides will increase the reliably of each of your trades nearly every single time.

The goal of technical analysis is not to simply measure the given intrinsic value of a particular asset but rather to use the tools at your disposal to pick out beneficial patterns related to a future activity that others may not yet have noticed.

Who Uses Technical Analysis?

Speculators like us who are looking towards making big profits, Professional fund managers' very livelihood depends upon making other people rich, Hedgers or commercials are the people who actually own the physical commodities. In short, all market participants who demand a professional edge. This tells us only one thing—if the professionals use technical analysis, it must be very important; before we get to really good stuff, it's important to understand why technical analysis works.

Core Assumptions

The goal of technical analysis is not to measure the given intrinsic value of a particular currency but rather to use the tools at your disposal to pick out beneficial patterns related to a future activity that others may not yet have noticed. At its core, technical analysis functions by assuming three things to be true. First, the market will always discount anything; second, prices will always move according to trends; and finally, history will always repeat itself eventually.

The Market Will Always Discount Everything

Detractors say that technical analysis is only concerned with the movement of currency price and little else in reality. Technical analysis assumes that the current price of a currency reflects everything that is going on that could affect that currency, which then makes it an accurate way to assess overall value. This is taken into account along with the broader economic climate as well as the current phase to determine when a valuable opportunity comes along.

The Price Will Always Move According to Trends

If the current value or price of a given currency is said to move according to an established trend, you can determine a trend in past currency performance. You have a much greater chance of seeing that same trend repeat itself when compared to the chances of an entirely new trend or the opposite trend occurring instead. Technical trading strategies tend to assume that this is always the case if they are going to work effectively.

History Will Repeat Itself Eventually

If prices move in trends, then it naturally stands to reason that technical analysis believes that as far as currency prices go, history will always repeat itself. This can be chalked up to the fact that those who participate in the market are likely always to respond the same way to similar market movement. This is often plotted using chart patterns to determine these trends at their start when they can be capitalized on to the fullest. While some of these charts have been in use for over a century, they are still relevant when it comes to how the public reacts to price changes.

Price Charts

A price chart is a core part of technical analysis; essentially, it is a chart with both an x and a y-axis where the price can be seen along the vertical axis. The time can be seen along the horizontal axis.

While there are plenty of different charts to choose from, each with their unique strengths and weaknesses, you will want to keep in mind early on, including the line chart, the candlestick chart, the bar chart, and the point and click the chart.

Line Chart

The line chart is the simplest of all the charts because all it does is showing the closing price of a given stock over a set period. In this case, the lines are formed once the grouping of closing prices has been determined and then connected with the end goal of showing a trend. You won't be able to find details such as what the opening price for the same period was or what the overall results for the day were. However, you will be able to determine if the day over day is positive, which is still quite important, which is why this is one of the first charts that day traders of all skill levels consult when they are looking into the details of new stock.

Candlestick Chart

Another worthwhile technical analysis tool that you want to be familiar with is the candlestick. They provide important data for traders across multiple time frames by creating what is known as price bars. Each day will provide you with details regarding the high, open, close, and low stock points each day. These details can be used to build patterns that make it easier to predict how the price is likely going to move in the future.

The candlesticks that are going to be the most accurate when it comes to plotting the price of stocks are going to fall into two types, continuations, and reversals. Reversal candlestick patterns tend to predict a coming change in the current pricing trends. Meanwhile, continuation patterns predict that the current price action is simply going to continue as is.

A candlestick chart is similar to a bar chart, though the information it provides is much more detailed overall. Like a bar chart, it includes a line to indicate the range for the day. However, when you are looking at a candlestick chart, you will notice a wide bar near the vertical line, which indicates the degree of the difference the price saw throughout the day. If the price that the stock is trading at increases overall for the day, then the candlestick will often be clear, while if the price has decreased, then the candlestick is going to be red.

Point and Figure Chart

While the point and figure chart aren't used as much as it once was, it has been in use for more than 100 years, which means there is still plenty of use left in it. The point and figure chart are useful when you want to know the movement of prices, without worrying about volume or time spent. This makes it a pure pricing indicator without much of the noise that many other charts need to deal with. It is also useful if the other types of charts contain information that skews them in one way or another.When you first see a point and figure chart, you will always be able to tell because it comprises lines of Xs and Os instead of points and lines. In this instance, the Xs will indicate periods of positive trends, while Os will represent downward trends. The numbers and letters along the bottom of the chart indicate months and date estimates. Point and click charts also include a set of reversal criteria set by the trader looking at the chart; these criteria consider the amount the price is going to move for an X to become an O or vice a versa. As the trend changes, it shifts right to indicate this fact.

Bar Chart

A bar chart expounds upon the details provided by a line chart by providing a greater degree of detail regarding the specifics of the day. The top and bottom of the bar represent the high and the low for the day, respectively, while the price at closing is indicated on the ride side of the bar with the help of a handy dash.

The dash on the left side of the bar shows the starting price, while the color of the bar indicates if it experienced an overall increase or decrease by the end of the day.

How to Read the Main Tools and Charts

Each futures contract has a unique one-or two-letter code assigned to it that identifies the contract type. Futures codes or ticker symbols are used by the exchanges to process all trading transactions. For example, the symbol for corn is C, while the mini-sized corn future is YC. It is imperative to use the correct code when you trade; otherwise, you can end up trading the wrong contract. In addition to the contract code, you must also know the month and year code. The month code J represents April and K represents May ETC. So, if you want to trade the May corn futures in 2011, the code would be CK5. See Month Codes Chart below:

It is imperative to understand a contract's value. This is how you will determine the profit and loss as well as the entry and exit price when you trade. Futures contracts have a minimum price increment called a tick. Traders use the word tick to express the contract movement or amount that a market has moved up or down.

Another term you will have to understand is the term "multiplier," which determines the value of a tick. For example, the multiplier for the Canadian dollar is $10. The market moved up by 20 ticks in one day. This means your long contract has gained $200 (20 ticks X $10.00 multiplier = $200).

Contract Codes and Specifications Chart

Full Contracts				
Contract		Delivery	Contract	Minimum
Corn	C	H,K,N,U,Z	5,000 bu.	¼¢/bu = $12.50
Oats	O	H,K,N,U,Z	5,000 bu.	¼¢/bu = $12.50
Soybeans	S	F,H,K,N,Q,U,X	5,000 bu.	¼¢/bu = $12.50
Soybeans Meal	SM	F,H,K,N,Q,U,V,Z	100 tons	10¢/ton=$10.00
Soybeans Oil	SO	F,H,K,N,Q,U,V,Z	60 000 lbs	.01¢/lb = $6.00
US T-Bonds	US	H,M,U,Z	$100,000	1/32 = $31.25
US T-Notes 10yr	TY	H,M,U,Z	$100,000	1/32 = $31.25
US T-Bonds 5yr	FV	H,M,U,Z	$100,000	1/64 = $15.625
Wheat	W	H,K,N,U,Z	5,000 bu.	¼¢/bu = $12.50
Australian Dollar	AD	H,M,U,Z	AD100,000	.01¢/AD=$10.00
Canadian Dollar		H,M,U,Z	CD100,000	.01¢/CD=$10.00
British Pound	BP	H,M,U,Z	BP62,500	.02¢/BP=$12.50
Eurodollar	ED	H,M,U,Z	$1000,000	1pt. = $25.00
Euro	EC	H,M,U,Z	€ 125,000	.01¢/€ = $12.50
Feeder Cattle	FC	F,H,J,K,Q,U,V,X	50,000lbs.	2.5¢/cw=$12.50
Japanese Yen	JY	H,M,U,Z	JY12,500,000	.0001¢/JY=$12.50
Lean Hogs	LH	G,J,M,N,Q,V,Z	40,000 lbs.	2.5¢/cwt = $10.00
Live Cattle	LC	G,J,M,Q,V,Z	40,000 lbs.	2.5¢/cwt = $10.00
Live Hogs	LH	G,J,M,N,Q,V,Z	40,000 lbs.	2.5¢/cwt = $10.00
Mexican Peso	ME	H,M,U,Z	MP500,000	.0025¢/MP=$10.00
S&P 500	SP	H,M,U,Z	$250 x Index	0.05 = $12.50
S&P Mini	ES	H,M,U,Z	$50 x S&P index	0.25= $12.50
Swiss Franc	SF	H,M,U,Z	SF125,000	.01¢/SF=$12.50
US T-Bills	TB	H,M,U,Z	$,1000,000	.01 = $25.00
Cocoa	CC	H,K,N,U,Z	10 metric tons	$1/ton = $10.00
Coffee	KC	H,K,N,U,Z	37,500 lbs.	.05¢/lb =$18.75
Sugar #11	SB	H,K,N,V	112,000 lbs.	.01¢/lb = $12.00
Cotton	CT	H,K,N,U,Z	50,000 lbs.	.01¢/lb =$5.00
Orange Juice	JO	F,H,K,N,U,X	15,000 lbs	.05¢/lb =$7.50
Copper	HG	All Months	25,000 lbs.	.05¢/lb = $12.50
Gold	GC	G,J,M,Q,V,Z	100 troy oz.	10¢/troy oz = $10.00
Silver	SI	H,K,N,U,Z	5,000 troy oz.	.005¢/troy oz = $25.00
Mini Contracts				
Corn	XC	H,K,N,U,Z	1,000 bu.	¼¢/bu = $2.50
Soybeans	XS	F,H,K,N,Q,U,X	1,000 bu.	¼¢/bu = $2.50
US T-Bonds	YH	H,M,U,Z	$50,000	1/32 = $15.625
US T-Notes 10yr	XN	H,M,U,Z	$50,000	1/32 = $7.8125
Wheat	XW	H,K,N,U,Z	1,000 bu.	¼¢/bu = $2.50
Eurodollar	UD	H,M,U,Z	$500,000	.005 = $6.25
Feeder Cattle	FM	F,H,J,K,Q,U,V,X	10,000 lbs	.001 = $10.00
Lean Hogs	HM	G,J,M,N,Q,V,Z	10,000 lbs	.001 = $10.00

Fundamental Analysis

In order to successfully trade in the futures market, one of the most important things you are going to need to learn is how to determine a reliable way to tell a potentially profitable trade from one that is likely to fizzle out or, even worse, cost you money.

Fundamental analysis is used more frequently by new traders, while technical analysis has experienced something of a renaissance in popularity over the past decade or so. While both are useful when it comes to finding the information you are looking for, they go about determining just what that information is in different ways. Fundamental analysis is primarily concerned with looking at the big picture, which often means that it will take longer to perform than its counterpart.

Also, its information comes from external sources, which means you may need to wait for additional information to become available through it will typically end up being easier to digest than the information required to utilize technical analysis effectively.

Broadly, the fundamental analysis makes it easier for you to glimpse the likely future of the futures market based on a wide variety of different variables, including publicized changes to the monetary policy of the countries you are interested in. The end goal is to track down enough information to allow you to find an undervalued currency pair that the market has not adjusted to.

Determine the Baseline

When it comes to considering the fundamental features of a currency pair, you will first want to consider the baseline that these currencies typically return to time after time when compared to the other currency pairs that are commonly traded. This will make it easier to determine when the right time to make a move is likely to be, as you will then be more easily able to pinpoint changes that occur to the pair that make them warrant additional consideration.

In order to determine this baseline, the first thing you will need to consider is any changes to the related macroeconomic policy that affects each based on historical data. In these instances, past behavior is one of the most reliable indicators when it comes to determining likely future events. Once you are aware of the relevant historical context, you will then need to consider the current phase the currency is in and how likely it is to remain in the phase-in question as opposed to moving on to the next.

Each currency regularly goes through 6 distinct phases, the first of which is the boom phase, which can be identified via low volatility and large amounts of liquidity. At the opposite end of the spectrum is the bust phase, which can be identified by the opposite, mainly low amounts of liquidity and high amounts of volatility.

The other phases are post-bust and pre-bust and post-boom and pre-boom, which means that one of the major phases is either on its way in or on its way out. Determining the proper phase is crucial when it comes to ensuring that you are on the right track when it comes to finding a trading pair that is likely to be profitable in the long-term.

In order to determine the current phase, the easiest way to go about doing so is by looking at the current number of defaults along with bank loans as well as the accumulated reserve levels of the related currencies. If the numbers are low, then a boom phase is likely on its way or possibly in full swing already.

If the current numbers have already overstayed their welcome, then you can be confident that a post-boom phase is likely to start at any time. Alternatively, if the numbers in question are higher than the baseline you have already established, then you know that the currency is likely either due for a bust phase or is already underway.

Money can be made regardless of the current phase as long as you can capitalize on it before the market catches up, as it is typically fairly slow-moving. The earlier you can pinpoint the coming phase, the greater the dividends you can expect to see are going to be.

Worldwide Considerations

After you have an understanding of the baseline, the currency pairs you are working with tend to remain at; the next thing you will want to do is to determine is what the related global economic conditions are likely to be and how they are going to affect your trading pair.

In order for this to be effective, you are going to want to look beyond the obvious signals and dig deep to find the indicators that are surely going to make waves after they become public knowledge. One of the best ways to go about doing so is to looking into emerging technologies in the related countries as they can easily turn entire economies on their heads in a relatively short period of time.

Technological indicators are a great way to use a boom phase to its full advantage as by getting in on the ground floor, you can ride the wave for as long as it takes for that technology to become a full-fledged part of the mainstream. After it reaches the saturation point, you are going to want to be on the lookout for the bust phase, as it will likely be right around the corner.

If you feel as though the countries related to the currencies in question will soon be in a post-bust or post-boom phase, then you will want to think twice about moving into speculative markets as the drop off is sure to be coming, and it can be difficult to determine exactly when it will rear its ugly head.

If you feel confident that a phase shift is on the horizon, but you don't know when it will be exactly, then you are going to want to stick with smaller leverage points than you would during the other phases to ensure that they will pay out before the change occurs.

On the other hand, if a phase is just starting, then you will want to go ahead and make riskier trades as the time concerns aren't going to come into play, which means extra caution is less warranted.

Global Implications

While regional concerns are a good place to start, it is also important to take a macro view of the market as a whole, as global currency policies are almost always likely to play a part in the proceedings.

While it might be difficult to determine where you should start, at first, all you really need to do is to apply the same level of analysis that you have performed on the micro-level, just on a larger scale. The best place to start is generally going to be with the interest rates of the major players on the world stage include the Federal Reserve, the European Central Bank, the Bank of England, and the Bank of Japan.

You will also need to be aware of any policy biases of legal mandates that are currently making the rounds in order to ensure that you don't end up getting blindsided from these sources when it comes time for you to make your move.

While this will certainly be time-consuming work, understanding the market from all sides will make it easier to determine new emerging markets when specific areas are fat with supply growth and what the expectations regarding interest rate changes or market volatility are soon going to be.

Understand the past: After you have a clear idea of what the current state of the worldwide economy is looking like, along with the specifics regarding the currency pairs you are interested in trading, then the next thing you will need to do is look to the past so that you can be prepared for history to repeat itself.

This level of understanding will make it easier for you to understand the current strength of your respective currencies while also allowing you to more accurately determine the length of time you can expect the current phase to continue.

In order to capitalize on this knowledge in the most effective way possible, you are going to want to attempt to jump onto trades when one of the currencies is entering a post-bust phase while the other is in the midst of a post-boom phase.

When this occurs, credit channels will not yet be exhausted, and you will be able to take advantage of the greatest amount of risk possible when compared to any other market state.

Be Aware of Volatility

Being aware of the current level of volatility is crucial when it comes to ensuring that the investments you are making are likely to actually payout in your favor. This is relatively easy to do; all you need to do is to pay attention to the stock markets most closely related to the currencies you favor.

This is because the futures market tends to be more stable. The more stable the stock market is, the lower the perceived overall risk is, the lower the amount of perceived risk that can make its way to the futures market.

Remember, the closer to the peak of the boom phase you currently find yourself, the lower interest rates, default rates, and volatility will be, which means it is the best time to increase your level of risk. Alternately, the closer you find yourself to the bust phase, the higher the overall level of volatility, default, and interest rates are going to be.

Decide on the Best Currency Pairs

With a good idea of where the market currently is and how long it is likely to stay there, all that you have left to do is determine the most effective currency pairs to actually sell. To do this, you must first consider any gap between the 2 currencies when it comes to interest rates. You need to have a clear understanding of where each of the pairs is currently and how likely they are going to remain close together and with a proper distribution between them.

To find this information, you are going to want to start by looking at the difference in the output gap as well as related unemployment statistics. When capacity constraints increase, while at the same time, unemployment decreases, this shortage will lead to an inflated economy, which in turn, will cause interest rates will rise until the economy begins to cool. Charting this information will allow you to accurately determine the likely interest rate movement from the pair in question.

Also, you will want to consider the payment balance of the nations related to the currencies in question. The healthier the debt to capital ratio, the stronger the related currency is likely to remain in times of crisis. To determine this amount, you are going to want to consider the capital as well as the current account and the general situation of each.

This will help you to determine if the position the nation in question is holding is due to asset sales or bank deposits or other, long-term potential developments, including things like an accumulation of reserves or foreign investment.

Economic Indicators to Watch

When it comes to major economic indicators, the list is a fairly short one. Unfortunately, if you hope to stay competitive in the futures market, then you are going to need to keep up with far more than just the basics.

This is easier said than done; however, as there are a huge variety of economic surveys and other relevant indicators that can be used to predict numerous types of trends before they happen. While the entire list is too massive to include in its entirety, the options listed below will get you started on the right track.

Beige Book

More formally known as the Summary of Commentary on Current Economic Conditions by Federal Reserve District. This is because, rather than simply present the reader with raw data, it instead uses a tone that is much more conversational as it describes the various regional goings-on of the various members of the United States Federal banking districts.

This allows traders to determine how the Fed comes to various conclusions in various circumstances, which, in turn, can be useful later on when it comes to making bets on how the currency will move in the future. This economic indicator is published prior to each Federal Open Market Committee Meeting, which works out to be 8 times per year.

While the beige book does not typically create that much of a commotion as it doesn't present anything strictly new. Instead, it helps to point knowledgeable traders in the likely direction that things are going to be moving in the future. For example, if the overall tone of a beige book indicates a growing worry about inflation, then you might be able to start making preliminary plans related to a decrease in the current USD interest rate.

Consumer Price Index

A consumer price index is a sort of benchmark for a specific country's economy and its current level of inflation. It utilizes a basket approach as it attempts to compare a steady base of products that don't change much from year to year. These products include many common items, including toiletries and other common groceries, in addition to everyday services like the price of a haircut or an oil change.

These numbers tend to be broken down into a handful of figures, the first of which is broken down into two categories known as the Urban Wage Earners and the Clerical Workers. The second category is known as Urban Consumers. The consumer price index for a given set of urban consumers is often tracked quite closely as it varies dramatically throughout the year.

In the US, the current percentage is shown in comparison to the year 1982, so changes can only be determined based on previous index levels. Numbers are then shown via a run rate of growth to show traders what they can expect from inflation as well.

Meanwhile, the chain-weighted consumer price index often sees a major push when it comes to relevancy. This index provides a numerical visualization of customer purchasing patterns when compared to other indexes. As an example, only the chain-weighted index notes, things like when the public shifts from one brand to another based on things like price increases. In addition to major economic indicators like these, the consumer price index is often viewed by many trades as the final say when it comes to the up to date financial situation of a given country. It is released once per month, and when it is, you can count on serious movement for any related currency pairs.

Durable Goods Report

This report is released monthly and provides valuable updates when it comes to the amount of manufacturing that is being done in a given country when it comes to durable goods. A durable good is any type of capital goods that has an average lifespan of more than three years. Nearly 100 different industries fall under this report's purview, including things like cars, semiconductors, and even wind turbines.

The figures for a given country will be provided in the currency of that company along with a percentage of change for the month over month numbers. Three months of revisions are also included in every report. Data from this report is one of the 10 core components of the US Conference Board Leading Index, which is used to divine futures movement in the global market.

When it comes to reading these reports, it is vital that you always remember that the numbers that are publicly reported often do not include transportation goods or items created by the defense sector as they tend to be volatile enough to skew things dramatically one way or the other. Thus, if you want the full story in a given country, you will need to do your due diligence and sniff these numbers out for yourself. Generally speaking, the durable goods report is an excellent way for savvy traders to get a viable overview of business demand in specific countries. This is the case because these types of capital goods tend to require a larger overall investment, which, in turn, shows that business owners and consumers are both acting with greater confidence than they would be if the economy was not moving in a positive direction.

Based on the results you find, you may also find it especially useful to consider topics like the variation that occurs when it comes to inventory and shipment ratios over a prolonged period of time, in addition to the growth rate of shipments and related inventories.

Taken together, these should provide a much clearer picture of whether or not supply is exceeding demand or vice versa. As these types of goods often take far longer to be created than more transient goods, the durable goods report can also be an excellent way to get an early read on the expected earnings increases for the future month as an influx of orders in one month is a good sign that additional growth will be forthcoming.

Employment Cost Index

The employment cost index is a useful economic indicator that is released four times per year. It focuses on the amount that businesses in a given country pay for each employee, on average, as well as how much that has changed over the preceding quarter.

This report looks at things like employee benefits, hourly wages, bonuses, and any relevant employee premiums for every industry besides government and farm labor, as these would skew the numbers at either end of the spectrum.

This data is then broken down on an industry by industry basis before being split even further based on whether or not the industry is unionized. This information tends to also be broken down industry by industry, which makes it especially useful to traders who are looking for early indicators when it comes to determining potential signs of inflation.

This is due to the fact that the cost for compensating employees is the greatest cost almost any industry faces, and they tend to be presented in terms of the cost to the company in relation to the amount of profit that is generated when it comes to particular goods and services that are being generated.

Based on its overall outlook, the employee cost index can actually be enough to change the direction of a specific currency completely. This will occur if the actual report comes back in such a way that it is dramatically different from what all estimates expected. This is because these types of compensation costs are almost always passed off onto consumers, which leads to further GDP projection reductions when it is left untreated in the long-term.

This is also one of several indicators that is useful when it comes to determining a country's overall assumed level of productivity. If productivity grows at a slower rate than the rate at which compensation costs are increasing, then the valuation of the related currency is going to decrease and vice versa.

Focus on Interest Rates

After you have a clear idea of the market as a whole and major currencies specifically, you are going to want to focus on what many traders in the futures market focus on the most, the difference in interest rates between various currencies.

This is a crucial step if you hope to form an accurate opinion on the strengths of various relevant central banks, which, in turn, factors into an accurate qualitative analysis of the situation as a whole.

To form a clearer picture in this regard, you are going to want to consider the unemployment statistics of both countries as well as the gap in output that each has. If the economy is increasing, while at the same time, available labor is decreasing, then this will eventually lead to inflation and overall higher rates.

This, in turn, will lead to higher rates from the central bank, which will keep them there until the economy starts heading in the other direction. Keeping an eye on these trends will leave you with a clear idea of what your qualitative analysis has revealed.

Take Stock of Each Country's External Position

When it comes to getting the proper feel for a currency or currency pair, it is important to keep in mind how healthy their balance of payments currently is.

If one of the countries in question has a position that is generally considered to be maintained via asset sales and bank deposits, which can dry up or change direction relatively quickly, then that is less reassuring than a country with long-term commitments such as reserve accumulation or foreign direct investment.

CHAPTER 8

The Right Risk and Money Management

Managing Your Money

We cannot stress enough the importance of this part in becoming a successful trader. Anyone's day trading process must have a very strict money management process. First of all, it should be decided how much you are going to risk in your day trading efforts each day, and stick to that amount.

Day trading is in itself a quite painstaking process, and computer-operated algorithmic trades are turning it into a tougher business every day. Most traders who lose big in their trading account do so by day trading or over trading or even irresponsible gambling on short time frames.

It will be beneficial in money management if you know market jargon like bid price, ask price, and how it can impact your trade exit and entry prices. As your experience and expertise grow, you can trade with less loss of money.

Another important step in becoming a successful trader is following the age-old advice of "plan your trade and trade you plan." As these cuts into the chances of having monetary losses, it also increases the chances of maximizing your profits on every trade.

As they say, if you fail to plan, you plan to fail. So, to utilize the maximum potential of trading profits, always first plan your trade and then trade your plan. If you lose confidence in your own capabilities and in your trading plan, especially when you might be holding some market position, then it can result in loss.

One needs to position oneself so as to survive many strings of losses and still be able to maintain a successful day trading method. For this, you must understand how day trading strategies work.

Learning to be a successful trader takes an investment of money and time even if one has the best of tools and trading strategies. Most of the traders mistakenly think that some magic tool or secret will allow them to generate money without any big effort.

Fear, greed, and the egoistical need to prove oneself lead to the road of stock market failure. It would be better to focus on learning which trading strategies and market money management methods work the best for your trading style.

Important Money Management Rules for Traders

Being a trader also means you manage your financial risk and make decisions depending upon your risk-tolerance level. Follow these great money management rules to safeguard your trading capital and maximize your profits, as well as minimize your losses.

Practice Trade Sizing

Never put more than 10% of your stock trading capital in any single trade. As an example, if you have a trading capital of $25,000, any of your single trades should not utilize more than $2,500.

Keep Strict Stop-Losses

For stocks priced over $10, try putting a mental stop-loss of at least 10%, as well as a hard stop-loss of at least 20%. For stocks priced less than $10, keep stop-loss at 20%. A mental stop-loss conveys the meaning of keeping a watch at a 10% loss level in your trade. Suppose at the end of the day you check your portfolio and find that one of your stocks is down by more than 10% from its purchase price. Then you have to watch that stock cautiously and check the related corporate news to see if there have been any significant changes that have caused your stock price to drop.

Hard stop-losses, on the other hand, are real stop orders that are placed with the brokerages. These also work as a safety net in case of any surprise moves in the market direction.

Book Profits

It is always a better practice to take partial profits at the 40% level or more. That means, once the trade has earned a 40% profit, then you should book some profit and leave the rest to continue in the trade. By doing this, you can make sure of getting back your initial investment amount as well as some profits.

Trailing Profits

Whenever you have earned greater than a 15% profit, shift your stop-loss towards the break-even point, and go on to complete it until you get out of the position. This is known as "trailing stop." You need to think about initiating such a technique following the initial 15% profit.

Stay Away from Margin Trading

Make use of margin stock trading sensibly, or you may suffer a loss of more than your original investment. Margins are usually an excellent method of growing your primary stock investment. At the same time, if they are not observed carefully and carried out correctly, this kind of stock investing technique can lead to large losses quickly. A well-known trader stated the whole thing as: "Big positions imply bigger problems."

Small and Steady Wins the Race

Do not attempt to become rich quickly. Begin with little capital and develop your self-confidence as well as your trading account gradually but certainly. Consistency will be the name of the winning game. When you have constant trade returns following a lengthy time-period (more than one year), and including surviving lower periods in the market, you could be able to gradually improve your capital exposure.

Diversify

In a case where you have 20 stocks and one of your options crashes suddenly, you suffer a total loss in that stock. It is uncommon but sometimes happens. Then, you would have lost just 5% of your trading capital. Not too horrible. You will survive, and you may go on trading without substantial harm. On the other hand, if you do not have an effective money management strategy and diversify your trades, putting all your capital in single trades will make your profits continue to take hits, and eventually, you could lose most of your trading capital. You could even get completely wiped out of the markets.

Control Your Risk

If you are a newbie in trading, it is recommended that you begin with a paper trading practice system. Maintain a written record of all your stock trading and record all feelings and errors you go through while trading. After you complete roughly a month, begin a little trading with real cash. Yes, little! Remember: Large positions mean large problems. Use Limit Orders to get in and get out of a position. Market orders may assure you a fill, but not at the price you wanted. A limit order placed a bit below the last close usually gets fulfilled, most of the time. Simply because a stock generally does a retracement after the initial part of the session.

In case you cannot check the market all through the day—and several of us can not—then the market order would get the job done. Remember that the price you may pay whenever your order is carried out could be a lot higher (or lower) compared to what you anticipated.

The greatest error investors commit when practicing a trading method is to follow it blindly. The method works exactly how it is, but there are always a number of variables that you need to take into consideration.

Keep an Eye on Brokerage

Maybe you do not realize, but this is the biggest money eater when you enter the trading ring. There are hidden charges that eat into your profits or compound your losses. Most of the time, your broker will hide less expensive brokerage schemes and try to sell you some scheme that is beneficial for his business, not yours. So check all brokerage offers carefully. Always check your trading statement to see if you are being charged unnecessarily.

Money Management Skills

Do you know your income expenditure? Do you know your shopping, clothing, and entertainment expenses? Money Management is a life skill that is not taught in the school curriculum. Most people learn it from our parents how to handle money.

Since most people didn't learn about financial skills in school, you can still learn them now. Here are some of the Money management aids you can follow to improve your skills.

Set a Budget

Track how you spend your money. Do you spend on food, movies, entertainment, and clothes? Do you frequently have an overdraw of your bank account? If this is true, then set a budget. Check your bank statements and note down how much is your expenditure categorically. You will find out how much wastage of money you are not aware of.

Spend Wisely

Have a shopping list when you go to the grocery store? Do you first check the price of an item before putting the item in your basket? Use coupons if available. Use online resources and mobile apps to stay focused on your expenditures.

Monitor your spending! By not being attentive to these small tips, you will keep on losing money. It takes time to get coupons, and It takes some effort to find coupons and writing a shopping list and checking the price of an item before buying. It will all be worth it in the long run.

Balance Your Books

Most people rely on going online to look at their bank balance. By doing this, you won't be able to know how much you are spending at the moment. The best advice is to be accountable by recording all your expenses; you will have avoided overspending.

Set a Plan

You must have a plan for you to accomplish anything. For you to go from location A to B, it won't be possible without a GPS to show the routes. You will end up driving aimlessly going nowhere.

This is similar to not having a financial plan. You will always be broke and not knowing where your money is spent on. "Where did that money go?" With a great plan, you will be able to track your money and expenditures.

Think Like an Investor

The education system does not teach about handling money, mainly how to invest in growing your wealth. The rich people did not just save $500 a month; they learned how to grow their savings and invest. Turning that $500 into $1,000, then into $10,000 and eventually into $100,000 and more.

By investing and growing your money, you will have secured a stable financial future. Think like an investor, and see your money grow.

Have the Same Financial Goals As Your Partner/Spouse

If you're married and you have a joint bank account, then learn to work together. You must both agree with the financial goals. Make a budget and also see a financial adviser to learn how to invest your money. You must ensure that you have the same financial goals and stay focused.

Save Money

Have a strong commitment to saving your money and securing your future. You can improve your financial situation and make it better! But you need to start with the decision to do so. Make a decision to start saving your money and improving your management skills.

Importance of Money Management

Sticking to a budget and living within your means—is proper money management. Look for great price bargains and avoiding bad deals when purchasing. When you start earning more money, understanding how to invest will become an essential way of reaching your goals, like having a down payment for a home. Understanding the importance of excellent money management will help you achieve your plans and future goals. Some of the importance of Money Management are:

Better Financial Security

Being cautious of your expenditures and saving, you will be able to save enough for the future. Saving will give you financial security to deal with any unexpected expenses or emergencies like loss of employment, your car breaking down, or even saving for a holiday. Having savings, you will not have to use a credit card to settle crises. Saving is a crucial part of money employment as it helps you build your financial security for a secure future.

Take Advantage of Opportunities

You may encounter opportunities to invest in a business to make more money or an exciting experience like a good deal on a holiday vacation. A friend may inform you of a great investment opportunity or get a great once-in-a-lifetime dream holiday vacation. It can be frustrating not having the money to jump right into these opportunities.

Pay Lower Interest Rates

With excellent money management skills, you can determine your credit score. The highest score means you pay your bills on time and with low-level total debt. Having a higher credit score, you can save more of what you have and have a lower interest rate for car loans, mortgages, credit cards, and even car insurance. And there is the chance to brag to your friends about your high credit score at the parties.

Reduce Stress and Conflict

Paying your bills on time can have a relieving feeling. But on the other hand, being late in paying your bills cause stress and have a negative impact like a shutdown in your gas and water supply. Always being broke before your next paycheck can bring conflict and a significant amount of stress for, couple. And, as we all know, stress brings health problems, experts say, like hypertension, insomnia, and migraines. Being aware of how you can manage your finances so you have extra cash and savings can put your mind at ease. You will enjoy a stress-free life.

Earn More Money

With your income growing, your financial planning will not only include budgeting for monthly expenses but also figuring out where to invest the extra cash that has accumulated. Knowing different kinds of investments, for example, stocks and mutual funds, you can earn more money from the investments than what you could have made by leaving the money in your savings account in your bank.

But be aware not all investments are recognized as a good investment idea, for example, offshore casinos. One of the best benefits of having investments, you can be at work earning monthly income, and your investments, on the other hand, are making more money for you.

More Saving and Time

Excellent money management can assist in avoiding your finances from spiraling out of control. It is easy to be in debt if you are unaware of how all your income it's spent monthly. Effective money management means better use of your spare time. You can spend time with your family and friends; by having a clear budget, you will be able to plan for fun days out as you will have available cash to do so.

Peace of Mind

Excellent money management gives you some level of calm and peace of mind. With your income and savings, you can handle any financial demands with the confidence that you have the resources to handle any need that will arise.

Managing Your Money

Investing can seem daunting. You may feel timid when you begin to invest. There are also options to choose thousands of shares and at least that amount of money. And then you still need to determine when it's time to buy and sell. For beginners, the stock market can seem incredibly profitable, dangerous, and confusing. Some basic lessons from the stock market can already save you from the most common mistakes and difficulties. That way, you will stay motivated to learn more about investing.

Start with a Diversified Basis

Leonardo DiCaprio stated in the famed "Wolf of Wall Street" movie: "Simplicity is the ultimate sophistication." A good portfolio excels in a good diversification strategy. A portfolio does not have to contain 30 items, but a correctly balanced mix that keeps risk and returns in balance. Or, as John Templeton said: "Diversify. In stocks and bonds, as in much else, there is safety in numbers." There are plenty of options: from gold, over ETFs, to real estate, currencies, index funds, or shares. Create a clear portfolio where you, as an investor, know how to deal with the risk.

Build in a Buffer for Yourself

Investing is never without risk. The risk-free investment does not pay off; it only costs money. To avoid jeopardizing your healthy financial situation, put some money aside in advance. We usually assume that six months of fixed costs is enough to bridge worse times. If there are indispensable opportunities in the financial markets, you can still use part of this capital to participate. Do estimate whether these opportunities are worth your buffer.

Search for the Adventure and Discover

If there is still some financial breathing room, you can always look for the adventure. A more aggressive investment means more risk but also a potentially higher return. Again, you can limit the danger here by diversifying. As they say about the channel: "Don't put all your eggs in one basket."

Limit Losses and Cash Your Winnings

Every investor experience it sometimes. You have a fantastic share in your portfolio, and week after week, it performs better. And suddenly, there is a turning point, you have hope for recovery, but the decline continues. Until it gets to a phase where you get to make decisions. If you are not prepared to undergo such a rollercoaster, then be wise. Is your investment doubling? Then sell half and secure your investment. When you purchase a share, you can work with a stop-loss order. A percentage of 20% is common.

View the Whole Financial Picture

Making a profit on an investment is quite a pleasant feeling. But investments are not alone, not on an island, or floating in a vacuum. Investments are part of your total financial life. Many asset managers give their clients wise advice: you have to manage your accounting as a business.

Feel Comfortable with Your Investment

Many people who invest and invest today grew up in a different spirit of the times. Thirty years ago, it was fashionable to get as much return as possible. Thanks to the internet, the declining pensions, and changes in the banking landscape, a lot has changed over time. Modern investing and investing are mainly focused on risk and no longer on returns. Most people who invest because of a supplementary pension are focused on avoiding losses instead of making big profits. So, their hope is not to become rich or richer per se, but to have enough capital in their old age to survive.

Investing Is Not a Hobby

Don't get us wrong: investing can be incredibly fun, but you cannot view it as a non-binding hobby. Of course, big banks see investing as a very competitive business. That's why it's best to look at your portfolio through the eyes of a professional. It is important to understand your portfolio well, understand where your profit but also loss comes from.

You must also be able to understand the companies in which you invest. Once you have completed this entire process, everything becomes so much easier. "Will this investment or investment earn me money, or will I tear it off?" An obvious question is not always asked.

How to Manage Risk

Risk management will help shield a dealer's record from losing the entirety of their cash. The hazard happens when the dealer endures a misfortune. On the off chance that it tends to be overseen, the dealer can open oneself up to profiting in the market. It is a basic yet regularly ignored essential to effective dynamic exchanging. All things considered, a merchant who has produced significant benefits can lose it all in only a couple of awful exchanges without an appropriate hazard the executive's methodology.

Consider the One-Percent Rule

A great deal of informal investors pursues what's known as the one-percent rule. Fundamentally, this dependable guideline proposes that you should never put over 1% of your capital or your exchanging account into a solitary exchange. If you have $10,000 in your exchanging account, your situation in some random instrument shouldn't be more than $100.

This technique is normal for brokers who have records of under $100,000—some even go as high as 2% if they can manage the cost of it. Numerous merchants whose records have higher adjustments may decide to go with a lower rate. That is because as the size of your record increments, so too does the position.

The most ideal approach to hold your misfortunes within proper limits is to keep the standard underneath 2%—and you'd hazard a considerable measure of your exchanging account.

Setting Stop-Loss and Take-Profit Points

A stop-misfortune point is a cost at which a broker will sell a stock and write off the exchange. This frequently happens when the exchange doesn't work out how a dealer trusted. The focuses are intended to avert the "it will return" mindset and point of confinement misfortunes before they heighten. For instance, if a stock breaks underneath a key help level, merchants regularly sell as quickly as time permits. For instance, if a stock is moving toward a key opposition level after a huge move upward, dealers might need to sell before the time of union happens.

Instructions to More Effectively Set Stop-Loss Points

The setting of stop-misfortune and take-benefit focuses is frequently done utilizing specialized examination; however, a crucial investigation can likewise assume a key job in timing. For instance, if a broker is holding a stock in front of income as fervor constructs, the person might need to sell before the news hits the market if desires have gotten excessively high, paying little heed to whether the take-benefit cost has been hit. Moving midpoints speak to the most mainstream approach to set these focuses, as they are anything but difficult to compute and broadly followed by the market. Key moving midpoints incorporate the 5-, 9-, 20-, 50-, 100-and 200-day midpoints. These are best set by applying them to a stock's graph and deciding if the stock cost has responded to them in the past as either a help or opposition level. Another incredible method to put stop-misfortune or take-benefit levels is on help or opposition pattern lines. These can be drawn by associating past highs or lows that happened on huge, better than expected volume. Like with moving midpoints, the key is deciding levels at which the value responds to the pattern lines and, obviously, on high volume.

When Setting These Focuses, Here Are Some Key Contemplations

Utilize longer-term moving midpoints for progressively unstable stocks to lessen the opportunity that a good for nothing value swing will trigger a stop-misfortune request to be executed.

Stop misfortunes ought not to be nearer than 1.5-times the present high-to-low range (instability), as it is too liable to even think about getting executed without reason. Modify the stop misfortune as indicated by the market's unpredictability. On the off chance that the stock cost isn't moving excessively, at that point can be fixed. Utilize referred to central occasions, for example, income discharges, as key timespan to be in or out of the exchange as unpredictability and vulnerability can arise.

Calculating Expected Return

Setting stop-misfortune and take-benefit indicators are likewise vital to figure the normal return. The significance of this count can't be exaggerated or exchanged. It also gives them an efficient method to analyze different exchanges and select just the most gainful ones.

This can be determined utilizing the accompanying recipe:

[(Probability of Gain) x (Take Profit % Gain)] + [(Probability of Loss) x (Stop-Loss % Loss)] The aftereffect of this estimation is a normal return for the dynamic merchant, who will, at that point, measure it against different chances to figure out which stocks to exchange. The likelihood of addition or misfortune can be determined by utilizing authentic breakouts and breakdowns from the help or opposition levels—or for experienced brokers, by making an informed conjecture.

Diversify and Hedge

Ensuring you benefit as much as possible from your exchanging implies never placing your eggs in a single crate. In case you put all your cash in one stock or one instrument, you're setting yourself up for a major misfortune. So, make sure to broaden your ventures—crosswise over both industry areas just as market capitalization and geographic district. In addition to the fact that this helps you deal with your hazard; however, it additionally opens you up to more chances.

You may likewise get yourself when you have to fence your position. Consider a stock position when the outcomes are expected. You may think about taking the contrary situation through choices, which can help ensure your position. When exchanging action dies down, you would then be able to loosen up the fence.

Capital Management
Characterize a thorough capital administration approach and tail it. Keep theoretical capital separate from speculation capital and downplay it of the general portfolio esteem. Also, ensure you are appropriately promoted consistently. If you don't have at any rate, for example, £10,000 that you can focus on a theoretical view, at that point, you will wind up in a default position. Submitting reserve funds, retirement cash, lease cash, youngsters school investment funds, and so on into theoretical capital ought to be viewed as restrictive for any financial specialist or merchant.

Exchanging Limits
To guarantee that you don't lose your theoretical capital, build up, and pursue exchanging limits for any Futures exchange. For instance, limit your drawback to close to 10% of your capital for sums under £100,000; for sums somewhere in the range of £100,000 and £500,000, this rate ought to be decreased 1% for each extra £100,000 down to 6% for £500,000; for accounts £1,000,000 + 5% or less per exchange ought to be gambled.

Expand Your Portfolio
This is a typical dependable guideline for financial specialists exchanging crosswise over various resource classes; for example—don't place all eggs in a similar container. Enhance your hazard among in any event at least three not legitimately related markets. The more markets your exchanges are broadened over, the less unstable your portfolio will be, decreasing the danger of acquiring in all-out misfortunes.

Influence
Never utilize most extreme influence as it may be important to cover inert assets in your prospects record, money and reciprocals held in different records, and so on. It is constantly a decent rule to keep an enormous enough cushion to cover intraday instability and point of confinement moves. The size of the support will rely upon the specific markets you exchange and your hazard the board methodology.

Making Sure You Can Handle the Stress
And finally, to manage your risk, you need to make sure that you are actually able to handle the stress that comes from day trading. This is a stressful job. You are not able to just place your money on the market and then walk away from it, checking in on occasion. Rather, you need to be watching your stock the whole day. All those little fluctuations up and down can have a big impact on your potential earnings, and this can add a lot of stress to your day.

If you do not have the time to devote to this, at least on the days that you decide to trade, then this is not the right investment option for you. If you have trouble dealing with stress or you already have enough stress in your life, then day trading is not right for you. If you are not good at making decisions at the last minute and you let your emotions take over, then day trading is not for you.

Day trading can be a great investment option for you to work with, but you need to make sure that you are managing your risks and keeping them as small as possible. With the right strategy and risk management plan in place, even when you lose a little bit of money on an occasional bad trade, you will still be able to make a lot of money with day trading.

Make the Trend a Companion
One may have decided to hold a position for an extended time. However, every trader should recognize that no matter the position they take, there is no fighting against the market trends and movements. Accommodate the changes and make sure that the trading strategies reflect the new aspects; this will help one to reduce risk.

Keep Learning
There is always new information coming up in the market every day. As the world changes, so do the economy and the market. A trader should know how the market functions currently, how it evolved, and where it might be heading.

Use Tools and Software Programs
The use of tools and programs can help one select a good choice and avoid risk. However, it is important to note that these systems are man-made; therefore, aren't entirely perfect. It is best to use them as a tool of advice rather than a complete basis of trading decisions.

Use Limited Leverage

Leveraging is very attractive because it gives a trader the opportunity to make bigger profits. However, leverage also increases the chances of losing capital; therefore, one should avoid taking massive leverage. One wrong move with leverage and the entire account is wiped out.

The Three-Step Risk Management Plan

Step 1: The First Step That You Should Take Is to Determine the Absolute Maximum Dollar Risk That You Will Take for the Trade You Are Planning

It is recommended that as a beginner, you should never risk more than 2% of the equity in your account, but you can choose to go up and down from this number based on how much money you have and how much you are willing to risk. You need to have this amount calculated before you even start trading for the day.

Step 2: The Second Step Is to Estimate the Maximum Risk Per Contract That You Will Take, the Strategy Stop-Loss, from Your Entry

We will learn more about how to do this later because you will have a different stop-loss based on the strategy that you choose.

Step 3: Take the Number from Step 1 and the Number You Got from Step 2 so You Can Calculate the Max. Number of Contracts You Can Use

This will give you the maximum number of contracts that you can trade each time. Do not go about this level, or you are increasing your risk too much. Let's take a look at how this would work. Let's say that you will get some futures contract, and you have $40,000 in your account. If you stick with the rule of only using 2 percent, then you would limit your risk to $800. We will be conservative for this trade as beginners and only risk 1 percent of the account, or $400. Now we have finished step one.

As you are monitoring the futures contract, you decide to sell the short it when it reaches $50, and you want to cover them at $48, with a stop-loss at $51. This means that you will be risking about $1 per contract. Now let's say that the futures contract has a value of 400$ per 1$ move. This will be step 2. Now we are moving on to step three. We will calculate our size by dividing the numbers in step 1 and step 2, so we can find the maximum size that we can trade. For this example, we would be able to purchase a maximum of 1 contract.

CHAPTER 9

The Correct Trading Psychology

Why Trading Psychology Is Important

Most people fail in day trading because they start at the wrong end. They start by learning trading skills first, then move on to money and risk management techniques, and the last stop is to learn, superficially, about trading psychology.

In fact, the right sequence of learning day trading should be learning the trading psychology first, then money and risk management techniques, and the last part should constitute learning the trading skills.

It is very easy to learn technical analysis and how to use technical indicators. But it is very difficult to control one's emotions like fear and greed while trading or astutely manage money while day trading.

If you look at people in different fields, you will find the mindset is the main difference between those who reach the pinnacle of their chosen career and those who remain mediocre. Be it business, science, technology, sports, or any other creative pursuit; people who train their minds for success are the ones who win the race.

In intraday trading also, hundreds and thousands of day traders use the same methods of technical analysis; however, only a few of them succeed in making profitable trade, and others go home with losses. It is the trading psychology that makes the difference between successful traders and those who failed.

Every trader, who tries to learn day trading, knows that there are certain rules to be followed, and still, the majority of them fail to do so find; therefore, if you want to succeed in day trading, you must pay attention to how you react to markets. Stock trading is nothing but watching the price rise and fall and trading off with the trend. But still, traders fail to follow this simple method of trading.

Day trading happens 90% in the mind of a day trader, and only 10% in what happens in markets. A day trader takes decisions based on what he or she thinks is going to happen in stock markets and not on what is happening. This is the biggest mistake day traders make, and the reason is their emotions.

To overcome this psychological hurdle, day traders must learn how to manage their trades without emotions. They can do so only with the help of technology and self-discipline. If they do not have self-control or do not follow a disciplined trading plan, they cannot make profits in stock markets.

At a fundamental level, traders' emotions usually drive markets across the globe.

There are essentially two sentiments and states of mind that determine failure or success in stock trading: greed and fear. A trader's emotional nature largely establishes if he/she is going to be successful in stock trading. In establishing trading success, any trader's trading psychology can be as crucial as some other qualities, like knowledge, skill, and experience. Self-discipline, as well as risk-taking, are two extremely crucial parts of trading psychology. For the success of one's trading plan, following these factors is very important. Although fear and greed are definitely the two common emotions related to trading psychology, some other emotions also generate trading habits, such as hope and regret.

To have an understanding of trading psychology, just think about a few examples of the emotions connected with it.

Greed is usually an extreme wish for riches. Greed frequently motivates traders to remain in a profitable trade more than is sensible, in an attempt to get more profits from that trade, or even undertake big risky positions. Greed can be most evident in the last stage of bull markets, where speculation operates on a wider level, and traders and investors become careless.

On the other hand, fear makes traders exit positions too early or even stay away from tasking risk due to anxiety about big losses. Fear can be prevalent in the times of bear markets, which, as a powerful emotion, can induce traders and investors to do something irrational in their rush to close the trade. Fear usually turns into panic, which usually provokes markets to fall at a considerably faster pace compared to their upward trend.

Regret is another emotion that could cause a trader to enter a trade after originally missing it, as the stock changes too quickly. It is against trading wisdom and quite often leads to the trader entering way too late in the trade. Successful traders follow some common psychological rules that add to their success. These include:

- They do not over trade. They know their limits.
- They preserve their trading capital through risk management to gain trading success.
- They maintain their trading discipline at all times.
- They know the difference between not going against the trend and following the herd.

Psychologically Approach Toward Success

It may not seem to be a significant factor on the surface. However, psychology plays a huge role in the way investors conduct their trades. Psychology is arguable the most important aspect when investing. The fact of the matter is that for all of the analysis and research that you can conduct, you may find yourself falling victim to some of the most common issues that occur traders. When an investor can control their emotional responses to the way trades are conducted, there is a greater possibility of success.

The most important factor you can put into practice when it comes to devising your investment approach is realistic expectations. This means that you are aware of the fact that investing takes time and effort. Of course, you're not expecting to take years before making a profit. However, you should keep in mind that starting small can ultimately pay off in droves later on. When you start small, you can build momentum. When you build momentum, there is a snowball effect that makes you make more money. Sure, it's tempting to think that you could make a year's salary when in a single trade. Still, then again, you will eventually reach that level after gaining the experience that top traders have gained. It's like pilots; as they accumulate flight hours, they can fly without instrumentation, relying on their experience and better judgment. Now, that doesn't mean that the pilot no longer needs the plane's instrumentation. It just means that they can use their judgment, especially when unexpected circumstances arise.Also, having realistic expectations is vital to ensure that greed doesn't get the better of you. You see, greed is a very powerful force, particularly when you are good at investing. There is a temptation to take greater and greater risks. Eventually, though, you make one mistake that can derail a long time's worth of success. So, having realistic expectations is a great way of curbing the temptation to take unnecessary risks.

Fear

Fear can be one of the most very dangerous weapons that we use against ourselves. It holds us back from the things we want and makes us push away the things that we need. If you let fear control your life, you'll never really be in charge of any of your thoughts or emotions. Fear can make us nervous, grumpy, and even sick. Almost as bad as this, it can make us lose a ton of money. Those going into options trading need to make sure that they don't allow fear to hold them back. Though you have to be cautious, you should understand that you can't be too afraid of making a move you might trust. Know the difference between being smart and safe and blinded by worry.

Looking at the Analysis

It's important to understand how to perform a proper technical analysis not just to determine the value of a certain option but also to make sure you don't scare yourself away with any certain number. You might see a dip in a chart, or a price projection lower than you hoped, immediately becoming fearful and avoiding a certain option. Remember not to let yourself get too afraid of all the things you might come across on any given trading chart. You might see scary projections that show a particular stock crashing, or maybe you see that it's projected to decrease by half.

Make sure before you trust a certain trading chart that you understand how it was developed. Someone that wasn't sure what they were doing might have created the display, or there's a chance that it was even dramatized as a method of convincing others not to invest. Always check sources, and if something is particularly concerning or confusing, don't be afraid to run your own analysis as well.

Hearing Rumors

If you are someone that hangs around with other traders, maybe even going to the New York Stock Exchange daily, there's a good chance you are talking stocks with others. Make sure that any "tips" or "predictions" you hear are all taken with a grain of salt. Tricking others into believing a certain thing is true about different stocks and options can sometimes dapple into an area of legal morality, but it's important to make still sure you don't get caught up with some facts or rumors that have been twisted. You should only base your purchases on solid facts, never just something you heard from your friend's boyfriend's sister's ex-broker. While they might have the legitimate inside scoop, they could also be completely misunderstanding something that they heard. Before you go fearfully selling all your investments from the whisper of a stranger, make sure you do your research and make an educated guess.

Accepting Change

As animals, we humans are constantly looking for a constant. We appreciate the steadiness that comes along with some aspects of life because it's insurance that things will remain the same. Sometimes, we might avoid doing something we know is right just because we are too afraid to get out of our comfort zone. Make sure that you never allow your fear of change hold you back. Sometimes, you might just have to sell an old stock that has been gradually plummeting. Maybe you have to accept that an option is no longer worth anything, even though it's been your constant for years. Ask yourself if you are afraid of losing the money or just dealing with the fear.

Greed

Greed can be one of the biggest issues that certain traders run into. The reason we're doing this in the first place is for money, and some people think that's greedy enough. While we do need money to feed our family, pay off debt, and just have some cash to live from day-to-day, there are other sources of income than stocks. Still, you get the opportunity to make big money just from the money that you already have. If you are good enough at trading, you can even make it your full-time job. To ensure that you are trading for the right reasons, always ask yourself questions. Why do you need to take such a big risk? Is it worth sacrificing money that could go towards a vacation? Are you making these decisions to feed your family, or are you doing it so that you can go on a self-indulgent shopping spree? We indeed deserve to have some "me time," and we all should spoil ourselves every once in a while, as we can't depend on other people to always do that for us. However, greed can be a downfall if we're not careful.

Know When to Stop

For you to know when to stop can be the most challenging part of life. It's so hard to say no to another episode when your streaming service starts playing the next one. How are we supposed to say no to another chip when there are so many in the bag? Sometimes, if you see your price rising, you might just want to stay in it as long as you can. In reality, you have to make sure that you know when it's time just to pull out and say no.

If you wait too long, you could end up losing twice as much money as you were expecting to make. This is when the gambling part comes in, and things can get tricky. Make sure you are well-versed in your limits and that you are not putting yourself in a dangerous position if you don't trust your own self-control.

Accept Responsibility

Sometimes, we don't want to have to admit that we're wrong, so we'll end up putting ourselves in a bad position just to try to prove it to someone, even just ourselves, that we were right. For example, maybe you told everyone about this great investment you were going to make, sharing tips and secrets with other trader friends about a price you were expecting to rise.

Then, maybe that price never rises, and you are left with just the same amount that you originally invested. You were wrong, but you are not ready to give up yet. Then, the price starts rapidly dropping, but you are still not ready to admit you are wrong, so you don't sell even though you start losing money. You have to know when just to accept responsibility and admit that you might have been wrong about a certain decision.

Discipline

Having a good knowledge and understanding of different stocks and options is important, but discipline might be the most crucial quality for a trader to have. Not only do you have to avoid fear and greed, but you have to make sure to stay disciplined in every other area. On one level, this means keeping up with stocks and staying organized. You don't want just to check things every few days. Even if you plan on implementing a longer strategy for your returns, you should still keep up with what's happening in the market daily to make sure that nothing is overlooked.

On a different level, you have to stay disciplined with your strategy. Decide where personal rules might bend and how willing you are to go outside your comfort zone. While you have to plan for risk management, you should also plan that things might go well. If the price moves higher than you expected, are you going to hold out, or are you going to stay strict with your strategy?

Stick to Your Plan

If you don't stick to the right plan, you might end up derailing the entire thing. You can remember this element in other areas of your life. You can be a little loose with the plan, but if you go off track too much, what's the point of having it in the first place? If you are too rigid, you could potentially lose out on some great opportunities, but too loose can make everything fall apart.

Prepare for Risk Management

Aside from just knowing when to pull out to avoid being greedy, you also need to make sure that you are doing it so you don't end up losing money. Have plans in place for risk management, and make sure that you stick to these to ensure you won't be losing money in the end.

Determine What Works Best

The most important aspect of a trading mindset is remembering that everyone is different. What works best for you could be someone else's downfall and vice versa. Practice different methods, and if something works for you, don't be afraid to stick to that. Allow variety into your strategies, but be knowledgeable and strict with what you cut out and what you let in. Identify your strengths and weaknesses so that you can continually grow your strategies and always determine how you can improve and how you can cut out unnecessary losses.

Exercise Patience

In the world of investing, patience is the greatest virtue you can exercise. Most folks who venture into the world of investing in financial markets are hopeful they can make a good amount of money quickly. However, like anything in life, it takes time before you can become good at it.

This is why professional investors always preach patience.

If you go to your local bank right now and talk to an investment advisor, they will tell you to be patient, especially if it is going through a rough patch. They will tell you that you can make good returns, but you need to stay in the market long enough to see the results. They may even show you calculations of how your money compounds over time, thus giving you fabulous returns after 10 or 20 years. Now, you surely don't have 20 years to make money at the moment. Well, it might be a good secondary investment, but certainly not something that you'd be betting on. Nevertheless, being patient is essential to making money in any type of investment. You are only risking a small portion of your overall investment. This means that you can start small, but due to the power of compounding, you can make a serious amount of money. This strategy has been successful for plenty of investors. But it takes time and study before you can make this strategy work. You need to keep in mind that rolling over money like this requires you to go on a winning streak. Therefore, you must have the right tools and information before making it big.

Implementing an Organized Approach

Your trading approach needs to be systematic. Otherwise, you'll end up placing trades haphazardly. This will only cause you to make mistakes and lose out on potentially big gains. This is why becoming familiar with technical analysis and fundamental analysis is essential. It's important to note that you need to keep a level head as much as possible. This will enable you to make trades so that you won't waste your time and effort.

But being organized implies so much more. For instance, you need to stick to a proper schedule and adhere to the guidelines we have set up in money management. As you create discipline in your investing, you can give yourself the structure you need to be successful. Otherwise, you'll only find yourself guessing at what might happen.

Another integral part of an organized approach lies in getting to know the patterns of markets. This is important insofar as having a clear understanding of how markets can allow you to make the most of the current economic, political, and social situations.

Consider this situation.

A major oil-producing country has taken a serious hit to their economy as oil prices have plunged on the international market. This means that their currency is set to dive. You could potentially take advantage of that dive by buying up some of the currency at a low price. Then, when it rebounds, you can sell it for a profit. Often, shifts in the marketplace happen very quickly. Such fluctuations can lead you to make pennies on an individual deal. But when you compound them, they can make a significant profit.

This example requires you to be methodical in your study of economics and politics. After all, it's hard to get the full picture without having all of the relevant information at your disposal. Moreover, if you don't pay attention to the way events are unfolding in the world around you, you can miss the boat on significant trading opportunities.

Lastly, an organized trading approach will allow you to keep your emotions in check. Once again, this is a fundamental issue to keep in mind. If you cannot keep your emotions in check, they will eventually get the better of you. And while we have touched on greed and anger, it's also important to learn how to manage fear. When there are negative economic conditions, investors tend to panic. When everyone around you is panicking, it is the time when you can keep your cool and make some serious money. By being able to see opportunities where others are panicking, you can seriously make money. But the only way you can seize an opportunity of this nature is to be systematic and organized in the way you approach investing. Otherwise, you, too, will become prey to the fear and panic of other investors.

Defining Your Trading Edge

Just like any business or company, you need to define what your edge is. This edge could be a keen understanding of a particular region of the world. In such cases, you might have a slight edge since you understand the dynamics of a particular currency. This can help you better understand how you can place a trade taking into account factors that other investors may not necessarily be aware of.

When you go about defining your trading edge, it's all about what makes you a successful investor. As mentioned earlier, it could be that you have specific knowledge about a country or region that provides you with incredible insight into the movements of that currency. Also, you might have the opportunity to dedicate time to research. In such cases, you can become highly successful as you can put in the hours needed to conduct the research needed to gain a foothold on your investment strategy. This is important to note as not all investors have abundant time at their disposal. You might have a financial brain that can help you figure out the numerical side of investing. For other investors, their experience is a great boost. This experience may be focused on banking, economics, history, or a genuine interest in financial matters. This can be a great advantage to you as you won't have to spend as much time figuring out how markets work. Of course, you may still need to do some legwork though it won't be nearly as much.

That shouldn't hold you back. If anything, your advantage can be a diligent and careful study of markets. It could be patience or even a level head. Your biggest edge might be that you are willing to risk entering markets when things are rough.

Ultimately, your trading edge will emerge as you begin to study the market and see what it's all about. Many times, you won't define your identity until you have gotten some flight hours under your belt. It could be that you gain a better understanding of Asian markets. Perhaps you feel more comfortable with Latin American currencies. Or, you might decide to specialize in only two or three currency pairs. What you choose to do will be reflected in the way you approach your investments.

For most investors, they try various types of deals early on. Then, as they gain a deeper understanding and knowledge of markets, will gradually specialize in a certain type of currency or currency pairs. Some investors make a living out of a single currency pair.

This could be you. But you need to start somewhere. You can't expect to make lots of money without having to define what your approach will be. It doesn't take a Ph.D. or 20 years of experience in financial markets. It takes a careful understanding of the conditions in the market and how you can make the most of those conditions to your advantage. Often, investors are surprised to find they can understand the dynamics of some markets better than others.

Still, developing that intuitive feel comes when you are willing to keep an open mind. This is one of the best traits to assume. Having an open mind will always keep you receptive to the opportunities that the markets have for you.

View Trading as a Long-term Venture

As with most things in life, trading is a venture that takes time and effort to master and be successful. As simple as this concept sounds, this is not the first thing most new traders keep in mind when they first hear and become excited about this business.

To understand this better, let me lay it out for you.

As you browse through the internet, you come across an ad on social media that reads, "Emerson makes $100 a day day-trading from his home. Find out how." Then you think to yourself, "What if I could make $100 a day from home?" "Perhaps I could quit my job." "I've heard of many people who make money from home. Maybe I should try it."

So, you answer the ad.

Then the landing page contains a video describing a trading system in which you could invest as little as $100 and make twice perhaps thrice the same amount every time it gives you a signal.

Then you find endless testimonials from customers who say that it's working and has even made their lives better. Most of them describe the financial problems that they had before they began using the system, which is now gone. Then you start thinking, "Maybe this thing is real." And the system sells for only $300! You say, "I could afford that. I have my credit card."

As you pull out the card to make the purchase, you start imagining the thousands of dollars you are going to get out of this system. How you will suddenly start going on vacation in a few days. How you could get a new car, perhaps a new house. Or even pay your mortgage in full.

Sounds familiar?

Long story cut short, a month after getting this system, you are nowhere near where this system promised it would put you. As a matter of fact, you are $5,000 in debt and no longer trust ads from the internet anymore.

This has happened to countless people the world over and is probably going on now.

Don't get suckered in by the prospect of quick and easy money. Trading is a business just like any other in which you need to put in a lot of hard work, time, money, hope, the risk, among other things, before you can start enjoying its fruits.

Think of it this way. Could you imagine how many years it takes to stay in school in order to emerge as an undergraduate doctor? In case you didn't know, it takes seven. Majoring in other disciplines in medicine takes even longer.

At the same time, think about the years of sleepless nights that a lawyer spends in school studying, trying to master the discipline so that he or she can emerge as a top lawyer. Think of the years it took a businessman to build up a business empire. Think about the deals that went bad, the stiff competition, lack of money to pay workers, among other business headaches.

Why should it be any easier for you? Why do you think that you should strike 1,000%+ return every year just after spending a few weeks learning how to trade?

The point I am trying to make here is this. Dump the get rich quick mindset as fast as you can. If you do, you will have saved yourself a lot of wasted energy and money.

Trading can end up being one of the most rewarding ventures you can find in this world, but in order to succeed in it, you need to develop a long-term view of it and be willing to put in the hard work that is required.

For instance, you need to study books like this one for as long as is necessary. You need to invest your own money in this business. You need to be willing to delay gratification. You need to take risks. You need to network with other people in the business. You need to fight to stay on top of your game.

In the end, if you work at it, you will attain success in it just like any other professional.

Start Viewing Losses As Part of the Game

If you are one of those people who seems to believe that there is a magical crystal ball, the holy grail, that little truthful piece of information that makes a trader win every time, then you had better change your point of view.

In the trading business, there is no guarantee of succeeding every time. All we are trying to do as traders is beat the odds. We have to accept that losses are going to be part of that process no matter what.

This is one of the reasons why the subject of risk management is so important in this business

It comes down to making more money than you lose.

Winning 100% of the time is statistically impossible. Losses come by even to the best in this business. There is a kind of myth going around that the professionals in Wall Street know something that we don't, something that gives them some kind of inside edge. That is simply wrong.

The best in this business have learned the hard way. They have learned that you cannot eliminate losses in this business. They learned a long time that the only secret is to manage than in a way that makes you win in the long run. That is what they strive to do every day. You must do the same if you want to succeed.

This brings me to another point; you need to adopt a system, a strategy if you will, that you prefer and that you prefer to work with above anything else. Then you test it with a demo to see how well it performs in the long run. Get a feel of the winners and losers your system gives out. As you do this, you will begin to understand that losers are just a part of this game as is winning and that if you manage them well, then you have little to worry about.

As you do this, you will start developing confidence in your system. One of the worst challenges you will ultimately run into in this business is that of hitting a losing period (also popularly known as a losing streak). This is a period during which your system seems to be performing poorly with every signal that comes out of it.

If you aren't experienced or well versed in the knowledge that at times this happens in trading, then you are likely to throw in the towel. If, however, you took the time to learn about the challenges that occur in this business, you will learn that perhaps if you took a break from trading, then you could go back again later when conditions get better.

So, starting today, realize that losses are trading will always happen and are part of the game. If they are well managed, there is less reason to worry about them. Stick to the 2% rule of money management, and you will be okay. Realize that you could be right even 50% of the time and still make plenty just like the professionals do.

Keep Trading As a Part-time Activity

Another successful trick that can help you turning trading into a successful venture is that of keeping it as a part-time activity.

It is very difficult to trade successfully if you are in a position of trying to make a living out of it. Sure, there are professional traders who trade for a living, but most of them are getting a regular paycheck from the firm that employs them. The proceeds from their trading only get paid in the form of bonuses. This is how Wall Street works for the most part.

Big time professionals in trading are the hedge fund managers and other professional money managers. These people charge professional management fees from the people who invest with them, whether or not their performance is at its peak.

If you look at the big picture, these professionals are not depending on the money they are making from their trading, even if they are earning it. This is perhaps why they are so good at the game.

The reason is simple. The best trading decisions are made when you are in a position where you do not need the money.

When you are constantly under pressure of things such as, "How will I pay my rent this month?" or "How will I pay my daughter's school fees?" you are likely to make some very bad trading decisions. You are more likely to take action, such as trading excessively or placing trades when action is not warranted, all in a desperate attempt to make some money.

So how do you deal with that?

Get a day job. Find something else you can always do on the side that will help keep things in order financially and then trade part-time. As we discussed before, you can use swing trading strategies even if you are currently employed. The analysis only takes a few minutes per day, and this is something most of us can deal with.

You can even decide to trade when you get out of work. Markets such as the Forex market trade 24 hours a day, and this guarantees every person in the world that each person can at least find some time to trade that market. You can use this feature to your advantage.

Getting a day job and trading part-time helps in a number of ways. Firstly, it helps you take care of your bills and other financial responsibilities without putting a strain on your trading.

Secondly, it helps grow your account financially. This is especially true if you intend to use trading as a way of investing in order to grow rich. You can always put aside some money every month, so your account grows, and you can trade more.

Thirdly, it takes away the stress from trading. Let's face it, trading can be very challenging. When you are dealing with losing and making money, then stress can build up very quickly. It gets worse if you are thinking of using the money to maintain a decent living.

When you have something taking care of your financial responsibilities, then you are able to relax. When this happens, then you will be to think clearly. You will be patient enough to wait for the right opportunities to trade. If you make decisions from a position like this, then over time, your account only will soar.

Cultivate a Habit of Discipline

Discipline is another habit that trading as an activity demands a lot. If you aren't disciplined, then you will find it very hard to succeed in this business.

So, what is discipline exactly, and how do you cultivate it?

In simple terms, discipline is simply the ability to stick to a certain set of rules or code of conduct. In other words, it is the ability to exercise self-restraint and deny your indulgent behavior in a given situation.

Lack of discipline is a problem that plagues many traders who fail to get consistent results in the markets. In many instances, it is not the lack of knowledge of what to do that is the problem. It is the failure to implement what you know that is often the enemy. For instance, you are probably aware that you should study instead of going out clubbing because your grades are dependent on it. You are also aware that exercising is good if you want to keep physically fit.

Additionally, you may also be fully aware you are supposed to avoid certain types of meals because they are harmful to your health. But somehow, you still keep doing the wrong things.

That is the same case when it comes to trading. You are aware that you should have a stop-loss order in place and stick to it. But somehow, you keep moving it around because you believe that the market will always come back. Over time, your loss grows to unmanageable levels. Likewise, you may already be fully aware that you should stick to one trading system that fits you. Yet, for some reason, you keep hunting for the latest system, the Holy Grail. It is clear what is wrong here. Simply knowing what to or what not to do isn't enough. You need a set of actions that you need to take in order to keep your discipline intact. Those actions include:

Plan Every Trade Ahead of Time

You need to plan every trade and trade the plan.

By this, I mean to say that you should sit down and invest time in coming up with a set of rules that you should always follow. Your plan should contain the following;

1) The market setup that you are waiting for.
2) The rules governing the entry price.
3) The rules governing where you should place your stop-loss order.
4) The rules governing where you should place your take profit order.

If your plan contains the parts above, then you are all set.

Make sure that you have written them down. Do not plan things in your mind and imagine that all is well. A plan is better written down instead of in your mind. You also need to vow to always stick to your plan no matter what. Go over your plan at the beginning of every day and before you place any trade. It will improve your discipline over time.

Keep a Trading Journal

A trading journal is another vital tool to have.

In the same way, a personal journal records the events of your life on a certain day. A trading journal is meant to record the events that took place on a typical trading day.

In it, you record everything that happened right before and after you took the trade. Did you follow the plan that you had? Did you stick to the 2% risk management rule? Did you wait for the right set up to form before you acted? Were you tempted to move your stop-loss order or to close out the trade prematurely?

Record Everything. Then Review It Later

A trading journal helps serve two important purposes. First, it provides a record that you can always revisit and see what you did right at a given point. At the same time, you will be able to know what you did wrong at a certain point and stay away from it in the future. Secondly, it keeps you in check-in that if you remember that you are going to have to record your trading in your journal, you will try your best and avoid deviating from your plan and making a mistake. It is another tool that helps you develop your discipline.

Keep a Physical Reminder

A physical reminder, in this case, means a simple note that you write down.

In all likelihood, there are those times when for some reason, you simply deviated from your plan and made a huge mistake that cost you dearly. We all have had such times, and it has probably happened to you in the past. Maybe you overtraded, maybe you raised your stop-loss, maybe you acted prematurely, and maybe you traded a different setup from the one you vowed to stick to, which resulted in a significant loss to your account. Instead of just letting it go, which increases the likelihood of you repeating that mistake, simply write it down and stick it somewhere. You could stick it on the wall of your home office or at your trading desk, somewhere where you will always see it.

Doing so will always keep you aware of your past actions and will likely curb your habit of repeating mistakes in the future. In conclusion, discipline is a must-have for any trader. It doesn't matter how intelligent you think you are right now or how good a track record you have kept in the past. If you do not make an effort of becoming disciplined, then it will only be a matter of time before you learn otherwise. The tools we have looked at will help you figure that out.

Let's now look at the last point in our discussion of trading psychology.

View Trading As a Game and Not a Way of Making Money

Trading in general needs to be an activity that is fun, exciting, and financially rewarding.

Yet, for some reason, we tend to overcomplicate it and take the fun away from it. This is probably one of the reasons why many fail so terribly at it. One solution to this problem is to change your view of the whole activity and begin looking at it as a game of sorts.

When you think of a game, what comes to mind?

Mostly, we associate games with a lot of fun. We also view games as a way to challenge ourselves mentally. In addition to that, we view games as activities we engage in that have no real consequences in the case of failure. You can apply the same view in trading.

Pretend that trading is simply a game of points. The points are the money that you invest in it. Your goal in this game is to play and accumulate as many points as you can over time. The nature of the game is you are going to lose your points some of the time and also win likewise.

At some point, when you play and accumulate so many points, you can increase the size of your operations. You can even redeem some of the points into your bank account for use in real life, but that isn't the point. What matters is that you are simply playing a game that you are enjoying and having fun beating the game as it challenges you to get better. And you will keep playing for as long as you possibly can. Notice how you feel, aren't you now feeling better? If you have traded before, can you now see how it seems to take away almost all the stress out of trading? Can you now see how it can potentially open up an entirely new world for you? What if you chose to live your life as a trader bearing this perspective?

Now, compare it to this. You are trading a $100,000 account, and you were up 20% this month. And you are thinking to yourself, "Wow, I have made so much money I could buy a car with it!" Then, all of a sudden, you hit a losing streak, and you lose 10%. Then you start lamenting, "I just lost money that I could spend on a holiday vacation." Or you start telling yourself, "Oh my God, that money is equal to my two monthly paychecks! How could I have done that?"

Can you see the difference between these two points of view? One allows you to have fun and the other one puts you on an emotional rollercoaster ride. Which one do you think helps you last longer and succeed as a trader? If you want to enjoy success as a trader, you have to change the traditional view of money that the rest of the world holds. You have to view trading not as a way of making money but simply as a game of points that you are playing and having fun with it. If you do so, you will enjoy immense success in this business for years to come, all while managing to stay happy and keeping a level head.

Conclusion

Now that you have made it to the end of this book, you hopefully have an understanding of how to get started trading futures, as well as a strategy or two, or three, that you are anxious to try for the first time. Before you go ahead and start giving it your all; however, it is important that you have realistic expectations as to the level of success you should expect in the near future.

Trading successfully demands time, practical knowledge, and market comprehension. Usually, day trading means holding the stock for just the day and exiting the trade by the end of that session. Day trading does not imply trading EVERY day. Day trading is meant for benefiting from price actions in stocks within a single trading session.

Day trade for just days in any week and you might become a sharper trader in real-time than if you trade every day. Day trading can be quite risky, which means you should mainly trade with money which you can afford to lose. Online trading is fast and simple, but generating money through day trading and online investing demands a lot of time and hard work. There are many types of instruments to trade; stocks, bonds, options, forex, etc. Also, there are various methods of trading, such as day trading, swing trading, long positions, short positions, long-term value investing, etc. It all depends on what you choose to trade and in which manner. In case you don't have much time to trade, then you should think of swing trading rather than day trading. Think about every single trade as the largest winner of your trading profession and trade it with that importance.

The next step is to stop reading already and to get ready to get started taking advantage of the benefits that are unique to the futures market. While it may not be exciting, what this means in practical terms is that it is time for you to get down to business and start doing your homework. While you might want to avoid all of that and jump right in, as previously mentioned, all this is likely to do is to nip your options trading career in the bud before it even begins. You will need to start by considering which type of underlying asset you are going to want to pursue if stock market options don't sound that appealing to you.

With this out of the way, you will then need to consider the current state of the market in question and how you can craft a plan to take advantage of those specifics. Remember, haste makes waste, and in this case, waste is going to be all of the money you are throwing away by not taking the time to go through to reach the success that is otherwise almost in reach. Take things slow, and you are far more likely to find the success you seek. To become a smart trader, you have to avoid entering any trade at market price. Being aware of market jargon, bid price, and ask price is likely to make your trading functions less difficult. And then, when any trader's experience and abilities develop, they are able to trade without taking a loss. These activities can help you plan your trade and develop it so that you increase the profit from each and every single trade.Therefore, you must always plan your trade, and always trade that plan in order to achieve its optimum possibilities. Losing self-confidence as well as faith in your trading plan, even while holding a market position, usually leads to losses. A person's day trading strategy should have a stringent money management process. One must realize exactly how day trading strategies function.

As you become a more skilled trader, you can start to create particular trading methods, which perform in the best way in any particular market time. A successful trader would need to build trust in his personal capability to evaluate the market and select possible trades. While trading, constantly observe your trades throughout every single minute during the trading session. Equally important is taking a break from trading, which can assist you with noticing patterns, strategies, and the overall market trend with a new, different viewpoint.

It is very important for traders to obtain information regarding the market before they start their trading activity for the day. Appropriate market research is essential for successful trading. It is important for beginners to obtain insight into market conditions and the trading platform before putting a foot in the trading rings.

Do not let your emotions influence your day trading. Usually, emotions turn intense and can be overpowering in trading. For that reason, you should always trade your plan. Changing or modifying your trading plan during any open trade could be disastrous.

Remember, markets are not our friends or foe; we are. Apply these trading money management and emotion-management rules, and you can surely become a successful trader!

Good luck.

OPTIONS TRADING FOR BEGINNERS

*The Ultimate, Simple & Practical Options Trading Guide
to Start Investing Consciously. Become an Intelligent Investor
to Buy Options After Adequate Technical Analysis*

Alexander Taylor

Introduction

Before we get into some of the strategies that come with options trading, let us look at the basics of stock options. You probably have a good idea of what a share or stock of a company is. In the stock exchange, a lot of things can go on. You will notice that there are going to be many high profiles shares that trade in huge volumes. These also may have some derivatives that are associated with them. A derivative is a contract that can occur between at least two parties, and sometimes more, in which the contract will derive its value from an underlying security, such as an index or a stock.

The most traded derivatives that you can find on the stock market will be options and futures. We will not spend a lot of time on futures in this guidebook, but they are often easier to understand compared to options, but they often have less flexibility and will carry more risk with them.

An option, on the other hand, is going to be a type of contract, one that is sold by one party to another that will give the buyer the right, but not the obligation, to either sell or purchase an underlying stock at a pre-determined price. There is usually an expiration date or time that comes with these options and the buyer must decide what to do with it in that time frame. They can also choose to work with the underlying asset at any time before the expiration date occurs.

These options cannot exist indefinitely and each of them has this expiry date. The option buyer will have the right to exercise their buyer at the time of the expiry, or they can use it before the expiry point. So, when would you want to use an option rather than relying on stocks?

One option is when you know that the price of the underlying option may go up in the future. You can purchase the option now, and then when the price does go up, you can exercise your right to purchase that stock at the lower price, and then sell it to make a profit.

A good example of this is when a land developer is waiting to hear if there will be some new regulations put in place on land. If the regulations or zoning rules do go into effect, the price of that land will go up. The land developer may enter an options contract with the owner of the land. This gives them the right, but not the requirement, to purchase the land by the end of the expiry date that the two parties agreed upon. The land developer will have to put some money down as an incentive to the landowner to do the contract.

If the regulations do go through, then the land developer will agree to purchase the land at the reduced price. Their down payment will go towards the amount that they now owe. They never pay more than what the contract stated, no matter how much the land may be worth at the time of purchase. The land developer can now make homes in that area and sell them for a good profit because they got such a good deal. There is some risk involved in this, though. In the example above, if the regulations do not go through, the land developer may decide not to purchase the land. They do not have to go through and make the purchase, but they will have to forfeit the down payment that they made earlier, so there is some monetary loss in the situation.

Types of Options

When it comes to options, there are going to be two different types of options that you can work with. There will be the call options. These will give the buyer the right to purchase the underlying security of the contract at a fixed price. This would be like the example that we talked about above. There is also the put options, which includes options that give the buyer the right to sell the underlying security at a fixed price.

The biggest thing to remember here is that when working with the call option, the buyer of this option can only start to profit from that option if the value of the underlying stock or underlying index goes up. But in the other case with the put option, the buyer of the option can only start to profit when the value of the underlying stock or index goes down.

The Benefits and the Negatives of Working with Options

We have spent a bit of time looking at options and what they are all about. There will also be a ton of strategies that you are able to use when you decide to get into this kind of market, and we will talk about them more as we go. But at this point, you may be wondering why a trader would be willing to start in the options market at all. It often seems more complicated than other forms of investing, and a new options trading investor may wonder if the risk is worth the profits in the long run?

There are several reasons why people would choose to work in the options market as their investment choice. First, an investor can profit on changes that occur in an assets price on the market, without ever having to put money up to purchase that equity. They do have to pay a premium on that, but they do not have to pay the full price of the asset in order to enter the market. The premium that needs to be paid is going to come in at a fraction of the cost of what the investor would pay if they bought that asset outright. This can help them to leverage their account more to get into a bigger trade, without having a lot of capital to start with.

CHAPTER 1

What Is Options Trading

There are two significant ways you can trade options. The first involves buying the option itself and speculating on the price of the premium. The price of the premium is going to fluctuate based on how the underlying stock moves so you can profit from these movements. For example, if you think a stock is going to go up, you can buy an in the money call, and as the stock rises, the intrinsic value increases as well.

Thus, you benefit from the rise in the overall premium value. With a put, as the stock falls, the intrinsic value of the put rises, and so does its premium. Remember, you're buying a put to benefit from the price drop (you're not selling a put). The second method of speculating in options is not to pay as much attention to the premium but to the underlying.

What I mean is that you're not concerned with the price rise in the underlying, you're far more concerned with exercising the option. This involves an additional step, but if you aim to own the stock, then this could be a better method for you to deploy. Generally speaking, a lot of options traders don't bother exercising the contract since the premium tends to capture the intrinsic value change pretty well.

Pretty straightforward so far, isn't it? You can swing or day trade options like common stock, but these methods will need you to develop a directional bias in the markets. As we've seen, this increases your risk and is no different from usual trading activity. The point is, you don't need options to trade this way. So how does one trade options intelligently?

Well, the best method to do this is to use the structure of the contracts themselves to isolate yourself from major market risk factors such as volatility. Often when swing or day trading, traders will use what is called a stop-loss order to limit their downside. This is a safety net only on paper since the market is liable to simply jump the stop loss level during times of high volatility.

So, the trader is faced with larger than expected losses, and in some cases, such volatility might wipe out their entire account as well. Options avoid all this drama since you will only pay the premium upfront, thereby limiting your initial investment greatly. Then, you will be using ironclad contracts to protect your downside, and therefore, there is no possibility of the market jumping the price. Even if it does, your contract specifies the price, so you will always receive the price as stated on it.

The Risks of Options Trading

Thus far, I've only been mentioning the trading of options concerning the underlying stock's movements. If you think it's going to rise, you buy a call. If you think it's going to fall, buy a put. Well, can you short call or a put? Yes, you can, and this is precisely where the risks inherent to options trading enter the picture.

When you buy an options contract, your risk is limited to the terms of the contract. The person who sold you the contract receives the premium in exchange for selling it to you. They keep this premium no matter what. The seller of the option is generally called the writer.

Option writing has its advantages. For one, the majority of options traded tend to expire out of the money. Hence, the writer keeps the premium on the option and usually doesn't have to worry about the contract being exercised. If the contract does get exercised, this leads to a whole world of trouble. Think about this scenario: if you've written a call (that is, sold it), and if it moves into the money, your downside is unlimited.

Remember that when you're writing a call, you're betting that the underlying stock will not rise. Well, if it does arise, it can rise to infinite levels. What if your call's strike price is at $10 and before the expiry date, the stock rises to $10,000? Unlikely, I know, but theoretically possible. The loss will easily exceed your account's equity.

Writing a put doesn't have an unlimited downside, but it does have a large one, nonetheless. If the strike price of the put you wrote is at $50, your downside is a total of $50 per share (since the stock can decline only till 0). This is why writing options needs to be carried out carefully.

So, if the risks are this huge, why do people write options in the first place? Well, aside from the fact that option writing usually results in a profit (via earning the premium), most option writers cover their downside by covering their option positions. So, if someone writes a call, they buy the underlying stock first. Another option is to buy a put at a lower strike price since this covers their downside.

You must understand the differences between writing options naked and writing them when covered. Naked option writing is the riskiest thing that you can do, and in fact, your broker will not allow you to do this. Covered writing is perfectly fine, and no broker is going to stop you from doing this.

In case you're wondering, once you write an option, you can buy it back at a lower price before the expiry date. In other words, you can short an option like you would a stock. Generally, with the strategies, you won't need to do this unless you adjust your trades.

Options have leverage inherent in them, and you should be aware of this fact. Every contract represents control over 100 shares of the underlying stock, so everything that happens is magnified by a 100x multiple. This makes it even more crucial that you execute your strategies perfectly.

Other than this, options don't present any risks. They reduce your risk of trading in the market thanks to minimizing the effects of volatility. Volatility is both a blessing and a curse for directional traders. On the one hand, it makes them money via massive swings. However, it's not so much fun when the swings go the other way and wipe them out.

Options Trading Accounts

To trade options, you will need to open a brokerage account. At this point, you have a choice. You can either go with a full-service broker or a discount broker. A full-service broker is an institution that is like a financial supermarket. They have financial advisors on their payroll and can help you with stuff like retirement planning, tax planning, and so on.

A full-service house will also have its line of ETFs and mutual funds, which you can invest in. People generally open their retirement accounts with full-service brokers since it gives them a feeling of greater security. However, this is a false impression. The markets in the United States are extremely well regulated, no matter what the doomsday experts tell you. You don't face lesser risks with a full-service broker than you would anywhere else. Full-service brokers charge higher commissions, and the only advantage of such an institution is that connecting your various accounts becomes easier. If someone has a retirement account with one firm, inertia leads them to open another with the same institution, much like how people usually stick to the same bank for their entire lives (Pritchard, 2019).

A mistake that people make when choosing full-service brokers is to think that they'll receive trading advice. Get this clear: your broker has zero obligation to provide you with advice. Their fiduciary duty extends only as far as executing your trades as best as possible. Your broker isn't there to tell you which stock is going to go up or which is the best stock for your retirement account.

Sure, they might have an army of CFAs in house, but these employees are not allowed to recommend outside ETFs and products to their clients. The in house funds always have a higher fee attached to them. So, there's a huge conflict of interest there. My point is, don't blindly trust your broker, especially if they have CFAs on their payroll. They don't provide unbiased investment advice, so why would they ever give you trading advice?

Generally speaking, remember that your broker is not your friend. This is not to say they're your enemy, but they have a certain function in the market, and their job is to execute that. It isn't to do anything else. It's a bit like going to the florist and asking for bread. The fault isn't with them; it's with those who expect the wrong things from their broker.

This brings me to discount brokers. Discount brokerage houses are all about trimming the fat and will offer you one thing only: execution. As a result, you'll pay far lower commissions. Transaction costs are extremely important when it comes to trading. Traders usually think that buying and selling in the market is a zero-sum game.

If someone wins an amount, someone else loses that same amount. This is not true. The broker makes money no matter what happens in the market. Your transaction costs form a hurdle that you must jump to profit. Consider this example: let's say your broker charges you 0.1% per trade. So, when you buy, you pay 0.1%, and when you sell, you pay 0.1%. Remember, this is whether you win or lose.

So, every trade needs to make at least 0.21% to profit. It doesn't sound like much. However, if you place 100 trades per year, this means you need to make 20% just to breakeven (0.2*100). Most days, traders place 100 trades per month! So over time, you can see how this hurdle rate adds up massively.

This is why you should include your commissions in all your profit and loss calculations. If you choose to risk a certain percentage of your account on a trade, you need to factor in the commission costs on the gain or loss amount.

Both directional and options traders need to follow this advice, although the impact is reduced quite a bit for options traders.

Discount brokers' fees will vary depending on the type of trader they're geared towards. Platforms that are beginner appropriate will have fees per leg or a fixed fee, which is on a per-share basis plus an additional fee since it involves an option transaction. Make sure you differentiate between the per share fees and the fees for a contract.

Some brokers quote prices for a contract while some quote it per leg and so on. There's no standardized method here. Simply go for the lowest price and the best platform. This invariably happens to result in traders choosing Interactive Brokers. Light speed is another great platform, but this is aimed at more advanced and very active options traders so that I wouldn't recommend this for beginners.

CHAPTER 2

How Day Trading works

Always keep the primary rule of day trading in mind: never hold on to a position overnight, even if it means taking a loss on trades. But why do you have to stick to this rule even if it means suffering trading losses? After all, isn't making money the point of day trading? Yes, making money is the point of day trading. But given that the ideal securities to day trade are volatile ones, holding on to them overnight can put you at high risk for more significant losses the next day. It's okay to take small losses on day trades than large ones when you try to hold on to day trading securities overnight in the hopes that prices will recover significantly the next day.

By closing your position at the end of the day, even at a loss, you get to minimize day trading losses. And if you close positions at a profit, awesome! Don't feel like you could earn more by waiting until tomorrow. Remember, a bird in the hand's better than three in the bush.

You'll also need to remember that trading is a lot different than regular investing. While trading is a form of investing, regular investing usually refers to a more passive, buying-and-holding strategy that waits for months and years before taking profits. Trading has a much shorter time frame, which is only several hours for day trading and a couple of months at most for swing trading.

Buying Long and Selling Short

When you buy a financial security, you take a long position on that security. When you hear a trader say that he or she's long 100 shares of Intel stocks, it means that the trader bought and is currently holding a hundred shares of Intel's stocks.

The point of taking a long position on a financial security is selling them later on at higher prices. To close a long position, you sell the securities you're holding.

When you sell securities that you don't own yet, you take a short position on that security. When you hear a trader say he or she shorted or sold short 100 shares of Intel stocks, it means that the trader sold 100 shares of Intel stocks, hoping that its price will continue dropping so he or she can repurchase it at a much lower price. It's the same principle as buying low and selling high, except that the "selling high" part comes before the "buying low" part.

How can you sell something you don't have and more importantly, why would you even do that?

First, let's answer why you should do that? And the answer is: to make money when prices of securities are dropping. As mentioned earlier, it's just a reversal of the general trading strategy of buying securities at low prices and selling them at higher ones. By selling securities while their prices are high and buying them later on at lower prices, you can trade profitably even during market downturns.

Now, how can you do it? Depending on your broker and whether you're qualified, you can borrow the securities from your broker, sell them, repurchase them when prices drop, and return the securities you acquired from your broker. In the process, you profit from the short sell.

Keep in mind, however, that just like taking long positions, short selling also has its risks, which include that prices may actually go up instead of continuing to go down. In that case, you may also suffer trading losses.

You may be wondering, why would brokers or exchanges lend securities to their clients for short selling instead of selling the securities themselves? That's an excellent question. And the answer is: brokers usually want to take long term positions on securities. Why?

Why take risks with short-term trades on a downward trending market when they can make money with much lower risks by merely lending it to customers who want to short sell for a fee. This way, everybody wins. The long-term investors get to keep their securities and profit, even during bear markets, while those who don't own securities can have opportunities to make profitable trades via short-selling.

Retail Vs Institutional Traders

Retail traders are individuals who can be either part-time or full traders but don't work for a firm, and are not managing funds from other people. These traders hold a small percentage of the volume in the trade market.

On the other hand, institutional traders are composed of hedge funds, mutual funds, and investment banks which are often armed with advanced software, and are usually engaged in high-frequency trading.

Nowadays, human involvement is quite minimal in the operations of investment firms. Backed up by professional analysts and huge investments, institutional investors can be quite aggressive.

So, at this point, you might be wondering how a beginner like you can compete against the big players?

Our advantage is the freedom and flexibility we enjoy. Institutional traders have the legal obligation to trade. Meanwhile, individual traders are free to trade or to take a break from trading if the market is currently unstable. Institutional traders should be active in the market and trade huge volumes of stocks regardless of the stock price. Individual traders are free to sit out and trade if there are possible opportunities in the market. But sadly, most retail traders do not possess the know-how in identifying the right time to be active and the best time to wait. If you want to be profitable in day trading, you need to eliminate greed and develop patience.

The biggest problem of losers in day trading is not the size of their accounts or the lack of access to technology, but their sheer lack of discipline. Many are prone to bad money management and over-trading.

Some retail traders are successful by following the guerilla strategy, which refers to the unconventional approach to trading derived from guerilla warfare. Guerilla combatants are skilled in using hit-and-run tactics like raids, sabotage, and ambushes to manipulate a more prominent and less-mobile conventional opponent.

Remember, your mission is not to defeat institutional traders. Instead, you should focus on waiting for the right opportunity to earn your target income.

As a retail trader, you can make profits from market volatility. It can be impossible to make money if the markets are flat. Only institutional traders have the tools, expertise, and money to gamble in such circumstances.

You must learn how to choose stocks that can help you make fast decisions to the downside or upside in a predictable approach. On the other hand, institutional traders follow high-frequency trading, which allows them to profit from minimal price movements.

But for a brief overview, Alpha Predators are what retail traders are hunting for. These stocks usually tank when the markets are running, and they run when the markets are tanking.

It is generally okay if the market is running, and the stocks are running as well. Just be sure that you are trading stocks that are moving because they have a valid reason to move, and are not just moving with the general market conditions. Probably, you are wondering what the necessary catalyst for stocks is to make them ideal for day trading. Here are some catalysts:

- Debt offerings
- Buybacks
- Stock splits
- Management changes
- Layoffs
- Restructuring
- Significant contract wins/losses
- Partnerships/alliances
- Major product releases
- Mergers and/or acquisitions
- FDA approval/disapproval
- Earnings surprises
- Earnings reports

Retail traders who are engaged in reversal trades usually choose stocks that are selling off because there has been some bad press about the company. Whenever there's a fast sell-off because of bad press, many traders will notice and begin monitoring the stock for what is called a bottom reversal.

How can you identify the stocks that are alluring retail traders? There are some proven ways to do this. First, you can use day trading stock scanners. Basically, the stocks that are significantly moving up or down are the stocks that are being monitored by retail traders.

Second, find online community groups or social media groups where retail traders hang out. Twitter and Stock Twits are often good places to learn what is currently trending. If you regularly follow successful traders, then you may see for yourself what everyone is following. There's a significant advantage to being part of a community of day traders.

Securities in Play

There's a reason why many investors, traders and analysts focus on market movements or indices. It's because they know that for the most part, most financial securities follow the overall trend of their respective markets unless they have an excellent reason not to. For example, the prices of most stocks in the NYSE tend to go up when the Dow Jones is trending upwards and vice versa.

However, there will always be outliers that will—for one reason or another—go against the general trend for some specific purpose. When their general markets are tanking, they're picking up. When their general markets are picking up, they're tanking.

These securities are called securities in play (SIP). As a retail or individual day trader, these are the securities you should focus on within your chosen day trading market. If you want to day trade stocks, these are stocks that buck the general trend of the NYSE or the NASDAQ. If futures contract, these will be futures contracts that go against the general direction of most other similar agreements.

You get the drift, right? Right!

What are some of the reasons that may account for the contrarian behavior of SIPs? These may include:

- Unexpected results of earnings;
- Surprise company or economic developments; and Major policy changes by the governing authorities.

So, just because a particular security bucks its general market trend doesn't mean you can consider it a SIP. There should be an underlying reason for the contrarian movement. If none, it's probably not a SIP.

Always remember another important day trading rule, particularly for choosing SIPs to day trade: Find out if a particular security's movement is due to general market sentiment or is it due to some unique fundamental reason? For this, you'll need to do your homework. As a beginner day trader, you may have to do a bit more research than what you're accustomed to. But as you become a more experienced day trader, you'll be able to easily distinguish when a particular security is just going with the general market flow or when it's trending based on a unique and specific reason.

Professional day traders are those who do this type of trading for a living. While other forms of trading can sometimes be done as a hobby or a gambling high, day trading is often not included here. If you don't have a good understanding of the market and its fundamentals, you will most likely lose money.

CHAPTER 3

Basic Options Strategies

To quick start your trading in options, you need to understand the basic options strategies. Sometimes options trading can sound complicated to the point that you might not even know when to enter and exit the market. But this is simply because you don't have a good understanding of the basic strategies to use in the options trading.

After you understand the fundamentals of how options work, the trends, the moods and the emotions of the market, you need to clarify your strategies. For beginners, starting with basic strategies is good. You want to make sure you are brilliant with the basics before proceeding with more complex, advanced and sophisticated trading strategies.

Even though you might have gotten the fundamentals of options, you want to review them until you are clear about them. Generally, options trading is a two-way game. One party is selling, and the other party is buying. What is sold here is not stocks or any other financial instruments. The seller is selling the right to buy or sell an asset that he or she owns at a given price before a set period of time.

Options trading goes beyond stocks even though most people associate options trading with stocks. There are other financial instruments that are traded in the financial market through options. Some of these include stocks, bonds, indexes, EFTs, commodities, currencies, futures, and other derivatives. The securities or derivatives may vary, by the same trading principles that are used in all cases.

Bearish, Bullish and Neutral Trading Strategies

The stock market is always in motion. To make money in the market, a trader needs to analyze the moods and the trends of the market to know when the market will be moving upward or downward. Based on these decisions, various options strategies can be used. Success in the stock market requires understanding market trends and stock movements and leverage that insight to tell when to make a strike. Instead of just getting into the stock market and then buy a stock outright which can cause you to lose if the stock price goes down, you can use bearish and bullish options strategies to get make profits will still managing your risk and trading capital.

Bullish Trading Strategies

If based on your fundamental and technical analysis, you realize that the value of a security will be going upward, then a bullish trading strategy will be adapted. The underlying security can be a stock/index or any other security. The way to make profits with bullish trading strategies is to trade in options with the prediction that a stock price (the underlying security) will go up in value. When your predictions come true, then you will stand the chance of making money from that analysis.

Sometimes it might not even be a prediction in the movement of the stock price, it could be that you realized that the market is likely to move upward at a particular point in time and then use an options trading strategy to capitalize on that analysis. Generally speaking, the best bullish trading strategy is buying a call option.

When you buy a call option, you make money when the stock price moves beyond the strike price, at the specified period of time in the contract. In this case, your options trading makes a profit. It is important to note that your profit is made if, at the time of the contract, the call option comes "in the money." This ensures that you generate a decent profit due to the increase of security beyond the strike price of the options contract. The call option will incur a loss if your prediction does not come through at the time of the call options contract.

Buying a Protective Put

Another way to profit from a bullish options trading strategy is to adopt a protective put. Volatility and uncertainty in the market can cause an owner of a share to consider protecting and hedging the shares of stock through a put. A put option allows the stockholder to be able to protect the stock against price declines so that he can maintain the long term position of the stock.

The owner of that stock has "insured" the stock from incurring losses, but this comes through a price called "put premium." If the stock price declines rather than go up value, the owner of the put option may create a profit on the transaction. But if the stock increases in value slightly above the strike price the trader may lose on the put trade since the put option might even be necessary.

Bearish Trading Strategies

Are you expecting the price of an underlying security to fall? If you are betting on the market based on this analysis then, the best approach to use is a bearish options trading strategies. With this strategy, you are looking to make a profit when the stock price falls below the strike price of your options contract within or before the expiration date. When this happens, you stand the chance of making a profit. There are a lot of strategies to use if your analysis proves that the market will be experiencing a falling in an underlying security. Some of these strategies include the following: Long Put and Put Back spread strategies. For those expecting the market to fall just moderately beyond the current level, the best approach to use are Bear Put Spread and Covered Put. While Naked Calls are also good, the risk associated with this trading method can be very severe if you are not well experienced in the options trading market. It is very important that you understand that sometimes the market can go above or beyond your prediction. When the market goes up rather than falling, you might stand the chance of losing on your stock options trading. It is, therefore, important that you consider all other factors before making your trading analysis and decisions.

A Put Option in a bearish trading strategy is slightly different from what is being used when the market is forecasted to be bullish. In a protection put option, you actually own the underlying stock, but you are rather trying to hedge the stock against loses due to uncertainty in market conditions. A put-call, on the other hand, means that you do not own the underlying stock at the time of put options contract. In this case, you are opening the market by writing the option.

Neutral Option Strategies

A neutral trading strategy is employed when you are looking to predict that there will no significant changes in the stock market. For example, you did your technical analysis and also considered the central fundamental events considering an underlying stock, and then you realize the company's stock will remain stable. If a company's stock is going to remain stable due to market conditions, the best strategy to adopt is a neutral options strategy.

In a neutral market analysis, there is reduced volatility, and therefore, the movement of the stock price in the financial market remains stagnant. Some of the techniques to use in the case of these events are Ratio spreads, Strangles, Straddles, and Condors.

CHAPTER 4

Variety of Options and Their Styles

No matter what style or strategy an options day trader chooses to use, he or she needs to factor in three important components every single time. These elements are:

- **Liquidity**: This factor describes how quickly an option or other asset can be bought and sold without the current market price being affected. Liquid options are more desirable to an options day trader because they trade easier. Illiquid options create more resistance in the ease at which a trader can open or close his or her position. This extends the time needed to complete the transactions involved and thus can lead to a loss for the options day trader.
- **Volatility**: This describes how sensitive the assets attached to the options, is to price changes due to external factors. Some assets are more volatile than others. Stocks and Cryptocurrencies are volatile assets. Volatility has a great impact on an options day trader's profit margin.
- **Volume**: This describes the number of options being traded at a specific time interval. Volume is an indication of the associated asset price movement on the market because it is a gage of the asset's interest in the market. The higher the volume, the more desirable traders typically are in pursuing an option. Volume is one of the factors that make up open interest, which is the total number of active options. Active options have not been liquidated, exercised or assigned. If an options trader ignores taking action on options for too long, this can make circumstances unfavorable, which can lead to unnecessary losses. An options trader needs to always be on the ball about closing options positions at the appropriate time.

To take advantage of the options day trading choices listed below, the day trader needs to be very familiar with these factors and how he or she can use them to his or her advantage.

Breakout Options Day Trading

Breakout describes the process of entering the market when prices move out of their typical price range. For this style of trading to be successful, there needs to be an accompanying increase in volume. There is more than one type of breakout, but we will discuss one of the most popular, which is called support and resistance breakouts.

The support and resistance method describes the point at which the associated asset price stops decreasing (support) and the point at which the associated asset price stops increasing (resistance). The day trader will enter a long position if the associated asset price breaks above resistance. On the other hand, the options day trader will enter a short position if the associated asset breaks below the supported price. As you can see, the position that the trader takes depends on if the asset is supported or resisted at that new price level. As the asset transcends the normal price barrier, volatility typically increases. This usually results in the price of the associated asset moving in the direction of the breakout.

When contemplating this trading style, the options day trader needs to carefully deliberate his or her entry points and exit strategies. The typical entry strategy depends on whether or not the prices are set to close above the resistance level or below the support level. The day trader will take on a bearish position if this price is said to be above the resistance level. A bullish approach is a typical maneuver if prices are set to close below the support. Exit strategies require a more sophisticated approach. The options day trader needs to consider past performance and use chart patterns to determine a price target to close his or her position. Once the target has been reached, the day trader can exit the trade and enjoy the profit earned.

Momentum Options Day Trading

This options day trading style describes the process of options day trading relying on price volatility and the rate of change of volume. It is so-called because the main idea behind the strategy is that the force behind the price movement of the associated asset is enough to sustain it in the same direction. This is because when an asset increases in price, it typically attracts investors, which drives the price even higher. Options day traders who use this style ride that momentum and make a profit of the expected price movement.

This style is based on using technical analysis to track the price movement of the associated asset. This analysis gives the day trader an overall picture that includes momentum indicators like:

- The Momentum Indicator, which makes use of the most recent closing price of the associated asset to determine the strength of the price movement as a trend.
- The Relative Strength Index (RSI), which is a comparison of profits and losses over a set period of time.
- Moving Averages, which allows the day trader to see passed fluctuations to analyze the trends in the market.
- The Stochastic Oscillator, which is a comparison of the most recent closing prices of the associated asset over a specified period of time.

Momentum options day trading is highly effective and simple as long as it is done right. The day trader needs to keep abreast of the news and earnings reports to make informed decisions using this trading style.

Reversal Options Day Trading

This style relies on trading against the trend and is, in essence, the opposite of momentum options day trading. Also called trend trading or pull back trending, it is performed when an options day trader is able to identify pullbacks against the current price movement trends. Clearly, this is a risky move, but it can be quite profitable when the trade goes according to plan. Because of the depth of market knowledge and trading experience that is needed to perform this style effectively, it is not one that is recommended for beginners to practice. This is a bullish approach to options trading and entails buying an out of the money call option as well as selling an out of the money put option. Both profit and loss are potentially unlimited.

Scalping Options Day Trading

This options day trading style refers to the process of buying and selling the same associated asset several times in the same day. This is profitable when there is extreme volatility on the market. The options day trader makes his profit by buying an options position at a lower price, then selling it for a higher price or selling an options position at a higher price and buying it at a lower price depending on whether or not this is a call or a put option. This style of options trading is extremely reliant on liquidity. Illiquid options should not be used with this style because the options day trader needs to be able to open and close these types of trades several times during the space of one day. Trading liquid options allow the day trader to gain maximum profitability when entering and to exit trades.

The typical strategy is to trade several small options during the course of the day to accumulate profit rather than trying to trade big infrequently. Trading big with this particular style can lead to huge losses in the space of only a few hours. This is why this style is only recommended for disciplined options day traders who are content with seeking small, repeated profits even though it is a less risky method compared to the others.

Due to the nature of this style, it is the shortest form of options day trading because it does not even last the whole day—only a few hours. Day traders who practice this style are known as scalpers. Technical analysis is required to assess the best bets with the price movement of the associated assets.

Scalping is an umbrella term that encompasses several different methods of scalping. There is time and sales scalping, whereby the day trader uses passed records of bought, sold and cancelled transactions to determine the best options to trade and when the best times for these transactions are. Other types of scalping involve the use of bars and charts for analysis of the way forward.

Using Pivot Points for Options Day Trading

This options day trading style is particularly useful in the Forex Market. It describes the act of pivoting or reserving after a support or resistance level has been reached at the market price. It works in the same way that it does with support and resistance breakouts.

The typical strategies with this particular options day trading style are:

- To buy the position if the support level is being approached, then placing a stop just below that level.
- To sell the position if the resistance level is being approached, then placing a stop just below that level.
- To determine the point of the pivot, the day trader will analyze the highs and lows of the previous day's trading and the closing prices of the previous day. This is calculated with this formula:
- (High + Low + Close)/3=Pivot Point

Using the pivot point, the support and resistance levels can be calculated as well. The formulas for the first support and resistance levels are as follows:

- (2 x Pivot Point)–High=First Support Level
- (2 x Pivot Point)–Low= First Resistance Level

The second support and resistance levels are calculated with the following formulas:

- Pivot Point–(First Resistance Level – First Support Level) = Second Support Level
- Pivot Point+ (First Resistance Level – First Support Level) = Second Resistance Level

The options trading range that is most profitable lies when the pivot point is between the first support and resistance levels.

The options day trader is vulnerable to sudden price movements with his style of trading. This can result in serious losses if it is not managed. To limit losses with this strategy, the options day trader can implement stops to marginalize losses. This is typically placed just above the recent high price close when the day trader has taken on a short position. This is placed just below a recent low when the day trader had taken on a long position. To be doubly safe, the options day trader can also place two stops, such as placing a physical stop at the most capital that he or she can afford to part with and another where an exit strategy is implemented.

CHAPTER 5

Pitfalls to Avoid

All successful options traders go through a learning curve before they start profiting consistently. Some of them put in an all-out effort to learn by spending countless hours reading on the topic or by watching video tutorials. Others learn at a more leisurely pace, and once they get a grip of the basics, they lean more towards learning from their own experience. Irrespective of the type of learner you are, one way to cut short that learning curve is by learning from the mistakes of others.

This section lists out six of the most common mistakes made by inexperienced traders that can be easily avoided.

Buying Naked Options without Hedging

This is one of the most fundamental mistakes made by amateur options traders and is also one of the costliest ones that could make them go broke in no time.

Buying naked options means buying options without any protective trades to cover your investment if the underlying security moves against your expectations and hurts your trade.

Here Is a Typical Example

A trader strongly feels a particular stock will go up in the short term and assumes he can make a huge profit by buying a few call options and therefore goes ahead with the purchase. The trader knows if the underlying stock's price were to rise as expected, the potential upside on the profits would be unlimited, whereas, if it were to go down, the maximum loss would be curtailed to just the amount invested for purchasing the call options.

In theory, the trader's assumption is right, and it may so happen that this one particular trade may pay off. However, in reality, it is equally possible the stock would not move as per expectations, or may even fall. If the latter happens, the call options' prices would start falling rapidly and may never recover, thereby causing major losses to that trader.

It is almost impossible to predict the short-term movement of a stock accurately every time, and the trader who consistently keeps buying naked options hoping to get lucky is far more likely to lose much more than what he/she gains in the long term.

For a person to make a profit after buying a naked option, the following things should fall in place:

- The trader should predict the direction of the underlying stock's movement correctly.
- The directional movement of the stock price should be quick enough so that the position can be closed before its gains get overrun by time-decay.
- The rise in the option's premium price should also compensate for any potential drop in implied volatility from the time the option was purchased.
- The trader should exit the trade at the right time before a reversal of the stock movement happens.

Needless to say, it is impractical to expect everything to fall in place simultaneously always and that is why naked-options traders often end up losing money even when they correctly guess the direction of the underlying stock's movement. Having said all this, many such traders often think they would fare better the ensuing time after a botched trade and rinse and repeat their actions till they reach a point where they would have lost most of their capital and are forced to quit trading altogether. My advice to you—never buy naked options (unless it is part of a larger strategy to hedge some position) because it's simply not worth the risk.

Note: While buying naked-options has only finite risk limited to the price of the premium paid, selling of naked-options has unlimited risk and has to be avoided too unless hedged properly.

Underestimating Time-Decay

A second major mistake of inexperienced traders is underestimating time-decay.

Time-decay is your worst enemy if you are the buyer of an option and you don't get a chance to exit your trade quickly enough.

If you are a call options buyer, you will notice that sometimes even when your underlying stock's price is increasing every day, your call option's price still doesn't rise or even falls. Alternately, if you are a put options buyer, you sometimes notice that your put option's price doesn't increase despite a fall in the price of the underlying stock. Both these situations can be confusing to somebody new to options trading.

The above problems occur when the rate of increase/decrease in the underlying stock's price is just not enough to outstrip the rate at which the option's time-value is eroding every day.

Therefore, any trading strategy deployed by an options trader should ideally have a method of countering/minimizing the effect of time-decay, or should make time-decay work in its favor, to ensure a profitable trade.

Buying Options with High Implied Volatility

Buying options in times of high volatility is yet another common mistake.

During times of high volatility, option premiums can get ridiculously overpriced and at such times, if an options trader buys options, even if the stock moves sharply in line with the trader's expectation, a large drop in the implied volatility would result in the option prices falling by a fair amount, resulting in losses to the buyer.

A particular situation I remember happened the day the results of the 'Brexit' referendum came through. The Nifty index reacting to the result (like most other global indices such as the Nasdaq 100) fell very sharply, and the volatility index (VIX) jumped up by over 30%. The options premium for all Nifty options had become ludicrously high that day. However, this rise in volatility was only because of the market's knee-jerk reaction to an unexpected result and just a couple of days earlier, the market stabilized and started rising again; the VIX fell sharply and also brought down option premium prices accordingly.

Options traders who bought options at the time VIX was high would have realized their mistake a day or two earlier when the option prices came down, causing them substantial losses because the volatility started to get back to normal figures.

Not Cutting Losses on Time

There is a famous saying among the folks on Wall Street – "Cut your losses short and let your winners run."

Even the most experienced options traders will make a bad trade once in a while. However, what differentiates them from a novice is that they know when to concede defeat and cut their losses. Amateurs hold on to losing trades in the hope they'll bounce back and eventually end up losing a larger chunk of their capital. The experienced traders, who know when to concede defeat, pull out early and re-invest the capital elsewhere.

Cutting losses in time is crucial, especially when you trade a directional strategy and make a wrong call. The practical thing to do is to exit a losing position if it moves against expectation and erodes more than 2-3% of your total capital.

If you are a trader who strictly uses spread-based strategies, your losses will always be far more limited whenever you make a wrong call. Nevertheless, irrespective of the strategy used, when it becomes evident that the probability of profiting from trade is too less for whatsoever reason, it is prudent to cut losses and reinvest in a different position that has a greater chance of success rather than simply crossing your fingers or appealing to a higher power.

Keeping Too Many Eggs in the Same Basket

The experienced hands always know that once in a while, they will lose a trade. They also know that they should never bet too much on a single trade, which could considerably erode their capital were it to go wrong.

Professionals spread their risk across different trades and keep a maximum exposure of not more than 4-5% of their total available capital in a single trade for this very reason.

Therefore, if you have a total capital of $10,000, do not enter any single trade that has a risk of losing more than $500 in the worst-case scenario. Following such a practice will ensure the occasional loss is something you can absorb without seriously eroding your cash reserve. Fail to follow this rule, and you may have the misfortune of seeing many months of profits wiped out by one losing trade.

Using Brokers Who Charge High Brokerages

A penny saved is a penny earned!

When I first entered the stock market many years ago, I didn't pay much attention to the brokerage I was paying. After all, the trading services I received were from one of the largest and most reputed banks in the country, and the brokerage charged by my provider wasn't very different from that of other banks that provided similar services.

Over the years, many discount brokerage firms started flourishing that charge considerably less, but I had not bothered changing my broker since I was used to the old one. It was only when I quantified the differences that I realized having a low-cost broker made a huge difference.

If you are somebody who trades in the Indian Stock markets, check the table below for a quantified break-up of how brokerage charges can eat into your earnings over a year if you choose the wrong broker. The regular broker in the table below is the bank whose trading services I had been hitherto using, and the discount broker is the one I use now. For the record, the former is also India's third-largest bank in the private sector, and the latter is the most respected discount broker house in the country. It is obvious from the table above that using a low-cost broker makes a huge difference, especially when trading a strategy such as the Iron Condor (a relatively low-yield but high-probability strategy).

Also, it is not just the brokerage that burns a hole in your pocket; the annual maintenance fee is also higher for a regular broker, and all these costs will make a huge difference in the long run. Irrespective of which part of the world you trade from, always opt for a broker that provides the lowest possible brokerage because this will make a difference in the long term. Do a quantitative comparison using a table (something similar to the one I used above), and that would make it easier to decide who you should go with.

Note for India-based Traders: If you are a trader based in India or if you trade in the Indian Stock markets, I would strongly suggest using Zerodha, which has been consistently rated the best discount broker in the country. I have been using their services for the past couple of years and have found them to be particularly good. Their brokerage rates are among the best in the country, and on top of that, they provide excellent support when needed, and also maintain an exhaustive knowledge-base of articles. Lastly, their trading portal is very user friendly, and therefore, placing an order is quick and hassle-free.

CHAPTER 6

Understanding of Options

The big question is: how do you apply your skills to make money on the stock market? You need to see the patterns and setups as they appear. This is followed by a possible application method. Rules are created. Charts show patterns and the locations where the rules for determining entry and exit points should be applied.

Determine whether the congestion is a re-accumulation or re-distribution based on the last increase or break. Assume this until the congestion pattern tells you otherwise.

The Stop

We propose two steps: an average spread below the last reaction low or the span of the entry bar below the entry bar. Once we have some freedom of movement, the stop will be tightened. Close the position if the price does not behave within three bars. Then do not wait until the stop is triggered.

Trade or Not?

You do not risk your capital if you are not invested in the market. This trading style limits exposure to approximately 10% to 15% of the total observation period. Between 85% and 90% of the time, you are not in the market. During an accumulation or distribution phase, a position can be held. Although there is nothing wrong with this approach, it involves the risk of losing significant portions of the profits. The pattern may be distribution rather than accumulation. You need to study many charts until you find that this approach is workable and fits your trading style. This approach requires a lot of judgment. They should try to automate as many rules as possible to minimize uncertainty.

Trade High-Value Assets

Active trading is best suited for the stocks and/or futures that are moving or in trend phases, and not the boring ones like the securities that are constantly going sideways. The definition of a value that moves is quite subjective. Many sources cite lists of securities that outperform and outperform others, and one of the best is Investor's Business Daily.

Moving securities may have the following characteristics:

- Increased volatility
- Reaching a new four-week high
- Securities in the rising phase
- Significantly upwards or downwards inclined sliding average of the last 20 days
- The leading values in a specific market segment

Brief Summary

Remember, the goal of this game is to win, not that you're in 90% of all price moves. Open your positions when certain patterns occur and realize your profits when the target price is reached or at the first sign that the offer exceeds demand.

These basic principles apply to every time horizon, including day trading. If you are long-term oriented, use weekly charts. This will lead to many false signals, but there are indeed the stops. You will only earn money by studying countless charts and drawing your entry points, exit points, and stop loss. Thereby you internalize these approaches and make them suitable. After that, you could succeed in trading. One of the hardest things in trading is closing a position towards the end of an outbreak or during a buying spike. Just tell yourself that you are a nice person: everyone wants to have the stock, and you give yours.

The General Motors study might be one example of how you can create a supply-demand based trade system. Create two charts: one shows what you should have done and the other what you did. Learn by comparison. Recognize the forces that act at important turning points.

Practical Application of the Elliott Wave Theory

The Elliott Wave Theory confuses many traders. We do not want to discuss the ambiguity of this theory, but we apply it to a trading plan that should develop into a successful approach. This theory is one of the best theories of the Cycle because it allows non-harmonic movements.

There are many different approaches to securities trading. These are roughly divided into fundamental and technical approaches. Some technicians like to mix both methods for an optimal market approach. The fundamental access includes bushels, hectares, consumption units, revenues, book values, and so on. Technical analysis examines past price movements and predicts future ones. In 1939, Elliott published a series of articles describing the principle of Elliott waves.

The Elliott Wave Theory is one of the best technical methods for market analysis, and the serious interest should certainly include it in his studies. Is it possible to predict price trends using the Elliott Wave Theory and use this information profitably? The answer to that is a cautious yes if you do not make the theory an exact science.

The Elliott Wave Theory allows harmonic and non-harmonic course movements. Most cycle theories use principles based on harmonic movements. As soon as nonharmonic movements occur, it becomes difficult. The following summary of the Elliott Wave Theory reduces the ideas to a useful size:

Ascending moves consist of five waves, two of which are corrections. Falling movements are counterproductive. The odd waves run in the direction of the main motion. Straight waves run against the main direction. Shaft 2 corrects shaft 1. Shaft 5 corrects shaft 4. Sometimes there are nine or more waves. Elliott solves this problem by calling these movement extensions.

The endpoint of shaft 4 is higher than the height of shaft 1. Elliott specifies lengths proportions exactly, such as that the shaft 4 should be shorter than the waves 3 and 5. However, it has been found that this is not necessarily true.

The movements are divided into waves that are one degree smaller. What does "one degree smaller" mean? This question is difficult to answer, and that is one of the reasons why applying the theory is so difficult. One suggestion is to look for it in the next shorter timeframe. If you have a daily chart, look for the smaller grade on a 30-minute chart. The next smaller degree also needs five waves to complete the higher-order wave 1 and is therefore identical to the daily chart.

Triangular Corrections

Triangular corrections consist of a five-point pattern (ABCDE) after a thrust. The type and position of such a pattern often allow conclusions to be drawn as to whether a turnaround is pending or not.

A-Shaped Corrections

The length and duration of the first correction wave or A-shaped correction of the thrust are of utmost importance for determining the further course of the total correction and the probability of a turnaround.

Look for the application of the A-wave (the first correction wave to increase) to determine the type of correction and the probable direction of the price after the correction has been completed. Then, you can see four possible price movements. If the extent of the A correction wave is the same, the following should be deduced:

- 25% - 35%: Indicates a single correction wave.
- 35% - 50%: Indicates a three-wave correction.
- 50% - 75%: Indicates a five-wave correction.
- Over 75%: mostly a possible trend reversal.

Prediction of the Corrections

This type of price development can lead to a turnaround. Here are the forces of supply and demand at work. A reaction at a distance of 75% from the starting point makes a clearer statement than a low-25% reaction.

Understanding Options Terminology

For logical reasons, the option's duration is a factor. If you'll like an asset to be controlled for five years rather than one year, normally, having it controlled for a longer period would cost more. Alternately, it would not cost as much, if you need the asset controlled for just one day.

This is because the more the asset is being controlled, the more likely it is that something can happen (there's that word again) to affect its price. If for example, the property was controlled for just one day, it isn't too likely that a major real estate bargain involving your property will be reported that day.

CHAPTER 7

Stock Picking

Stay Away from Penny Stocks

Many people like to trade in penny stocks as they are cheap, and they can give great momentum. These two qualities that make them a darling of most small budget traders. However, these are the very qualities due to which every trader must stay away from penny stocks. It's very hard to tell which way the stock would move, and most of the companies that penny stocks trading in are shady.

As a beginner, your focus should remain to trade in solid stocks that have a proven track record of performance. Therefore, whosoever may push them to you, stay away from the penny stocks.

Qualities to Look for

Liquidity

Many things in the market can make the life of a trader difficult, and poor liquidity would easily top the list among them. Liquidity in the stocks means the volume or the number of shares getting traded in a day. If a stock has poor liquidity, then selling the stocks or squaring off your position in that stock would become difficult. Stocks with poor liquidity are also easy to manipulate. Even a limited number of big traders can create fake momentum in such stocks, and you might fall into that trap. Another big issue with low liquidity stocks is a wider spread. The difference between the bid price and the asking price is so high that most traders are not able to close their positions profitably.

In the beginning, you must only choose stocks with good liquidity.

Mind the Volatility

Volatility in the stock market isn't a bad thing. A certain level of volatility is desirable in good stocks so that you can make money trading them in a round-trip within one session. However, if the whole market is highly volatile, or a certain stock has become very volatile due to certain news, result declaration, litigation, or any other positive or negative information, you must avoid trading in such a stock. Certain strategies can help you in making money through options trade, but when a stock is highly volatile, trading can be really risky.

Most of the action in a highly volatile stock is within a few minutes, and by the time most day traders enter into that stock, it starts to move in the opposite direction. Therefore, it is better to avoid such mayhem and let the market settle down a bit before you place your trade. As a beginner, your focus must remain on making normal trades in a normal market.

Good Correlation Stocks

Although the stock market runs on uncertainty, yet every trader likes to lean on dependable stocks. Stocks that don't perform erratically always have a better scope for a day trader, as mapping them becomes easier. These are called Correlative Stocks because they have a very strong correlation with the movement of specific sectors, indices, and segments. As a new trader, your focus should also be on such stocks that are not very unpredictable. You may not see very sudden or erratic moves in them, but that would also save you from several unpleasant surprises.

Stocks That Follow the Market Trend

We have always been taught to be different and swim against the tide. We have been told that the winners don't follow the league they create one of their own. Well, when it comes to the stock market, you wouldn't want to bet on such winners to start with. Such stocks can give you an excellent start, but there is no way in the world that you will be able to predict them. They are rocky and risky. It is always better to find the stocks which follow the market trend. This simply means that look for those stocks that run as the market runs. If the markets are bullish, these stocks will rise with the market. If the market sentiment is bearish, they will show a negative trend. Such stocks will give you a chance to earn money both in the bull runs as well as bear runs.

Most of the stable stocks show such movements. You can rely on them, and taking a position and getting out of it on the same day in such stocks is comparatively easy. You wouldn't want to get into a stock that's rising when the market is falling, and as soon as you put your money in it, the movement stops or takes an opposite turn. Such stocks are very dangerous, and there are plenty of them out there. Sticking with the big and reliable ones can help you in preventing such issues.

Good Fundamentals

Although many experts would say that fundamental analysis doesn't play an important role in day trading, don't get sold on that completely. When the mood of the market is bad, only these kinds of stocks survive. The reason is simple when the tide is over, and the traders like to go with safer options.

Stocks with good fundamentals will always be more reliable and dependable. The market trusts them. Even small news about their profits and expansion can bring big moves in such stocks. You may not find such movement in smaller stocks even with big news because most traders don't trust them. Initially, only trade with stocks that have good fundamentals. They will help you understand the way market functions, and once you feel you are ready, you can also start trying others.

Ownership Pattern

This is another very important point that usually gets ignored. Stocks are held by retail investors and traders like me and you and also by institutional investors. Both types of investors have different buying and selling patterns. A retail investor can dump all the held shares with the drop of a hat. As soon as a piece of bad news comes, the retail investors are the first to exit. However, institutional investors can't do that. They maintain very large portfolios, and their decision-makers need to have approval at several levels. This means a stock in which institutional investors also have a good stake will be more reliable as they'll have a lot of volatility even after a major news event. The slow response of the institutional investors also ensures that there is no panic or crisis like situation all of a sudden because a lot of stocks are locked with them. Looking at the ownership pattern of stocks can help you in understanding the risk involved with the stock. If a stock is primarily held by retail investors, there can be no definite knowledge about the people who hold them. It can be just a group of certain individuals who can start creating momentum in the stock artificially. They can also dump all the shares all of a sudden. Institutional investors simply can't do that. As a new trader, trade in the stocks in which institutional investors like mutual funds, hedge funds, etc. have a good stake. Such trading will keep your risk contained.

Understandable Chart Patterns

Once you start reading the technical charts, you'll find that some stocks make real sense on the charts. They follow patterns. Their movements are somewhat predictable. They aren't very jumpy or choppy. While doing this, you'll also come across stocks that don't follow any pattern. They don't correlate to the indices or segments. They are vagabonds. Such stocks are risky for day trading. One thing that every day trader must engrave on to their minds is you don't want to get stuck with a stock forever. No matter how good or bad that stock is. You want a quick in and out of that stock. The stocks that don't follow an understandable pattern can get stuck with you. Once you buy them, understanding or predicting their movement will become difficult, and you won't find a way out.

The best way out is to look for stocks that have an understandable chart pattern. The stocks that are moving in a definite pattern are always a better bet.

Sensibility to the New Flow

Last but not least, sensibility to the news flow can be a big asset for an intraday stock. Some stocks react great to news events and give a good trading opportunity. However, some stocks would remain dormant, no matter what kind of news pours in. They are thick-skinned and become unpredictable as far as trading is concerned. You should avoid such stocks.

Look for stocks that show a great movement and sensibility to news events and give you trading opportunities.

High Volume

No matter how good the stock looks, if it does not have the volume, it is not fit for intraday trading. Don't fall for such stocks as the risk of getting caught in them will be very high. This is the first and foremost quality you must look for while picking your stock of the day for trading.

Testing Support and Resistance Levels

Look for stocks that are testing their support or resistance levels. These stocks can give a breakout, and you will have a great opportunity to earn from such stocks. Examine their levels carefully and study their historical patterns. If they have done that even in the past, it can be a great sign.

Near 52 Weeks Low or High

Stocks that are near their 52 weeks low or high can also give you a good opportunity to trade. Such traders can make a breakout and set new targets, and hence if you can correlate that with the fundamentals of these stocks, you can build an opportunity to trade.

Gainers or Losers of the Week

These stocks will be in the news and, therefore, trading in these stocks can be a good idea. However, you'll have to remain cautious as a stock that has been continuously gaining for some time can't continue to do so. You'll have to study whether the stock is already overbought or under bought as consolidation and profit booking can take place. While you look at these factors, you would also like to consider the fact whether the stock is undervalued or overvalued as that would also have an impact on its escalation and fall.

Stocks with High Market Anticipation

These stocks are the newsmakers, and they would be riding a wave. Their movements are hard to predict as more than the fundamentals and technical aspects; they are running on the market sentiments. Anyway, these stocks can also give you short trading opportunities. However, you must keep in mind that quick in and out of such stocks is always the best. Do not try to hold your position for too long as they can take a serious turn on any side, and you can get locked in them.

From Your Niche

Finally, pick the stocks from your niche. As a new trader, it always feels better to have an open field. However, as you grow in the stock market, you'll realize that having a niche is always a better and more reliable option. Look for all these qualities in the stocks from your field, and you will have very few things to worry about.

CHAPTER 8

How Prices Are Determined

Right before you start venturing into the world of options trading, as an investor, you need to have a proper understanding of the several factors that determine the value of options. The factors include the intrinsic value, the current price of the stock, expiration time, rates of interest, volatility, and paid cash dividends. You might come across various models of options pricing that uses up all of these parameters for determining the option fair value of the market. In several ways, options trading is more or less like any other branch of investment, all that you need is to understand all those factors that are used for pricing them.

For starting, let's begin with the most important drivers of options price: the current price of the stock, intrinsic value, volatility, and expiration time. The current price of the stock is somewhat very obvious. The movement of the stock price up or down comes with a direct, but not equal, effect on the option price. When the price of the stock rises, the price of a call option is most likely to rise as well, and the price of the put option will fall down. When the price of the stock tends to fall, the reverse takes place for the prices of puts and calls.

Intrinsic Value

It is the value that any option would have if the option is exercised today. In simple terms, intrinsic value is the overall amount by which option strike price is within the money. It is also that portion of the price of an option that is no lost when time seems to exceed the expiration time or when it is near the expiration time. Calculation of the intrinsic value of any call or put option is quite easy and can be done in this way:

Intrinsic value of call option = USC – CS, in which USC stands for underlying stock's current price, and CS stands for call strike price.

The intrinsic option value can directly reflect the effective nature of financial advantage that can result if the concerned option is exercised immediately. In simple terms, it can also be regarded as the minimum value of an option. Options trading out of the money or at the money do not come with any form of intrinsic value.

Intrinsic value of put option = PS – USC, in which PS stands for put strike price, and USC stands for underlying stock's current price.

For instance, say the stock of Elegant Electric (EE) is selling out at $35. The EE 20 call option would have the intrinsic value of $15 ($35-$20 = $15) as the holder of the option can easily exercise the option for buying shares of EE at $20, turn around, and then automatically sell them out in the market for $35 and have a profit of $15.

Time Value

The time value, often known as the extrinsic value, is the total amount by which the option price exceeds the intrinsic option value. It is directly linked to the total amount of time that any option has in hand until the date of expiry. The formula for the time value of options is quite easy:

Time value = Price of option – Intrinsic value

The more time that any option has in its hand until the date of expiry, the more are the chances of it ending up in the money. The component of time of any option tends to decay exponentially. The actual derivative of the option time value is actually a complex equation. As the general rule, an option will be losing its one-third value right during the first half of the life of the option and will lose two-thirds in the second half. This is a very important aspect for the security investors as the closer is the expiration time, the more movement will be needed at the price of the underlying assets for impacting the option price. The time value of an option is also dependent on market volatility. For the stocks that are not expected to have much movement, the time value of the option will tend to be very low. For all those stocks that are not expected to have much movement, the time value of the option will tend to be low. The opposite is also true for the more volatile stocks.

Volatility

The overall effect of volatility is, most of the time, difficult and subjective for quantifying. There are various types of calculators available today for calculating the estimated volatility. There are several types of volatility that you are most likely to come across while dealing with options trading. HV or historical volatility helps in determining the most possible magnitude of the future moves of any underlying stocks. Two-thirds of all possible occurrences of the price of a stock will take place within minus or plus of the stock's one single standard deviation move over a fixed period of time. HV is used for showing the volatile nature of any market.

Implied volatility is implied by using the current prices of the market and is often used up with the theoretical models. It helps a lot in setting up the current price of any existing option. It also helps the players of options to assess the trade potential properly. Implied volatility is used for measuring the expected upcoming volatility for an options trader. In simple terms, it can indicate the present sentiment of the options market. This very sentiment will then be reflected directly in the options price and thus helping the traders in assessing the future option volatility and also of the stock-based only on the current prices of the option.

Any investor of stocks who is really interested in using up options for capturing the potential nature of moving in a particular stock needs to understand the overall process of how options are being priced. Having proper knowledge of the current and also the expected volatility in the options price is also essential for any type of investor who is willing to take full advantage of the stock price movement, up or down.

CHAPTER 9

Volatility in the Markets

While the stock market has long-term trends that investors rely on reasonably well as the years and decades go by, over the short-term, the stock market is highly volatile. By that, we mean that prices are fluctuating up and down and doing so over short time periods. Volatility is something that long-term investors ignore. It's why you will hear people that promote conservative investment strategies suggesting that buyers use dollar-cost averaging. What this does is it averages out the volatility in the market. That way, you don't risk making the mistake of buying stocks when the price is a bit higher than it should be, because you'll average that out by buying shares when it's a bit lower than it should be.

In a sense, over the short term, the stock market can be considered as a chaotic system. So from one day to the next, unless there is something specific on offer, like Apple introducing a new gadget that investors are going to think will be a significant hit, you can't be sure what the stock price is going to be tomorrow or the day after that. An increase in one day doesn't mean more increases are coming; it might be followed by a significant dip the following day.

For example, at the time of writing, checking Apple's stock price, on the previous Friday, it bottomed out at $196. Over the following days, it went up and down several times, and on the most recent close, it was $203. The movements over a short-term period appear random, and to a certain extent, they are. It's only over the long term that we see the actual direction that Apple is heading.

Of course, Apple is at the end of a ten-year run that began with the introduction of the iPhone and iPad. It's a reasonable bet that while it's a solid long-term investment, the stock probably isn't going to be moving enough for the purposes of making good profits over the short term from trades on call options (not to mention the per-share price is relatively high).

The truth is volatility is actually a friend of the trader who buys call options. But it's a friend you have to be wary of because you can benefit from volatility while also getting in big trouble from it.

The reason stocks with more volatility are the friend of the options trader is that in part, the options trader is playing a probability game. In other words, you're looking for stocks that have a chance of beating the strike price you need in order to make profits. A volatile stock that has large movements has a higher probability of not only passing your strike price but doing so in such a fashion that it far exceeds your strike price enabling you to make a substantial profit.

Of course, the alternative problem exists—that the stock price will suddenly drop. That is why care needs to be a part of your trader's toolkit. A stock with a high level of volatility is just as likely to suddenly drop in price as it is to skip right past your strike price.

Moreover, while you're a beginner and might get caught with your pants down, volatile stocks are going to attract experienced options traders. That means that the stock will be in high demand when it comes to options contracts. What happens when there is a high demand for something? The price shoots up. In the case of call options, that means the stock will come with a higher premium. You will need to take the higher premium into account when being able to exercise your options at the right time and make sure the price is high enough above your strike price that you don't end up losing money.

Traders take some time to examine the volatility of a given stock over the recent past, but they also look into what's known as implied volatility. This is a kind of weather forecast for stocks. It's an estimate of the future price movements of a stock, and it has a significant influence on the pricing of options. Implied volatility is denoted by the Greek symbol σ, implied volatility increases in bear markets, and it actually decreases when investors are bullish. Implied volatility is a tool that can provide insight into the options' future value.

For options traders, more volatility is a good thing. A stock that doesn't have much volatility is going to be a stable stock whose price isn't going to change very much over the lifetime of a contract. So while you may want to sell a covered call for a stock with low volatility, you're probably not going to want to buy one if you're buying call options because that means there will be a lower probability that the stock will change enough to exceed the strike price so you can earn a profit on a trade. Remember too, that stocks that are very volatile will attract a lot of interest from options traders and command higher premiums. You will have to do some balancing in picking stocks that are of interest.

Being able to pick stocks that will have the right amount of volatility so that you can be sure of getting one that will earn profits on short term trades is something you're only going to get from experience. You should spend some time practicing before actually investing large amounts of money. That is, pick stocks you are interested in and make your bets but don't actually make the trades. Then follow them over the time period of the contract and see what happens. In the meantime, you can purchase safer call options, and so using this two-pronged approach, gain experience that will lead to more surefire success down the road.

One thing that volatility means for everyone is that predicting the future is an impossible exercise. You're going to have some misses, no matter how much knowledge and experience you gain. The only thing to aim for is to beat the market more often than you lose. The biggest mistake you can make is putting your life savings into a single stock that you think is a sure thing and then losing it all.

Options to Pursue If Your Options Aren't Working

At this point, you may think that if the underlying stock for your option doesn't go anywhere or it tanks that you have no choice but to wait out the expiration date and count the money you spend on your premiums as a loss. That really isn't the case. The truth is, you can sell a call option you've purchased to other traders in the event it's not working for you. Of course, you're not going to make a profit taking this approach in the vast majority of cases. But it will give you a chance to recoup some of your losses. If you have invested in a large number of call options for a specific stock and it's causing you problems, you need to recoup at least some of your losses may be more acute. Of course, the right course of action in these cases is rarely specific, especially if the expiration date for the contract is relatively far off in the future, which could mean that the stock has many chances to turn around and beat your strike price. Remember, in all bad scenarios, actually buying the shares of stock is an option—you're not required to do it. In all cases, the most significant loss you're facing is losing the entire premium. You'll also want to keep the following rule of thumb in mind at all times—the more time value an option has, the higher the price you can sell the option for. If there isn't much time value left, then you're probably going to have to sell the option at a discount. If there is a lot of time value, you may be able to recoup most of your losses on the premium.

Let's Look at Some Specific Scenarios

The stock is languishing. If the stock is losing time value (that is getting closer to the expiration date) and doesn't seem to be going anywhere, you can consider selling the call option in order to recoup some of your losses related to the premium. The more time value, the less likely it is that selling the option is a good idea. Of course, the less time value, the harder it's going to be actually to sell your option. Or put another way, in order to actually sell it, you're going to have to take a lower price.

There are two risks here. The first risk is that you're too anxious to sell, and so do it at the first opportunity. That really isn't a huge downside; you're going to make some profits in that case. On the other hand, it's going to be disconcerting when you sit back and watch the stock continuing to rise. That said, this is better than some of the alternatives.

One of the alternatives is waiting too long to buy and sell the shares. You might expect and see the stock apparently reaching a peak, and then get a little greedy, hoping that it's going to keep increasing so you can make even more profits. But then you keep waiting, and suddenly the stock starts dropping. Maybe you wait a little more, hoping it's going to begin rebounding and going up again, but it doesn't, and you're forced to buy and sell at a lower price than you could have gotten. Maybe it's even dropping enough so that you lose your opportunity altogether. A really volatile stock might suddenly crash, leaving you with a missed opportunity. The reality is that like everything else involved in options trading, since none of us can see the future, it's going to be flat out impossible to know if you are making the right call every single time. Keep in mind that your goal is to make a profit on your trades. Don't get greedy about it, hoping for more riches than you actually see on the screen. In other words, the goal isn't to sell at maximum possible profits. Nobody knows what those are because it's going to be virtually impossible to predict what price the stock will peak at before the contract expires. Instead, you're going to want to focus on making an acceptable profit. Before you even buy your call options, you should sit down and figure out a reasonable range of values that define ahead of time what that acceptable profit level is. Then when the stock price hits your target range, you exercise your options and sell the shares. You take your profit and move on, going to the next trades. That is not a guarantee that you're going to make money on every trade, but it's a more rules-based system that gets you into the mindset of trading based on objective facts rather than relying on unbridled emotions.

Also, remember that you can exercise the option to buy the shares, and then hold them until you think you've reached the right moment to sell. At other times, you may want to exercise the option to buy shares and stay in your portfolio as a long-term investment.

CHAPTER 10

Candlesticks

Candle outlines are a specific gadget that packs data for different periods into single worth bars. This makes them more important than traditional open-high, low-close bars (OHLC) or fundamental lines that make a conspicuous inference of closing expenses. Candles gather plans that foresee esteem heading once wrapped up.

Value Action

Value activity delineates the characteristics of securities worth turns of events. This improvement is consistently inspected in regards to esteem changes in the progressing past. In fundamental terms, esteem action is a trading technique that empowers a vendor to scrutinize the market and choose enthusiastic trading decisions reliant on the continuous and genuine worth turns of events, instead of relying totally upon particular pointers.

Since it disregards the foremost examination factors and focuses more on later and past worth turn of events, the worth movement trading method is liable to particular assessment gadgets.

A candle comprises of a body, and upper or lower shadows.

Gadgets Used for Price Action Trading

Since esteem action trading relates to later chronicled data and past worth turns of events, all particular examination instruments like diagrams, design lines, esteem gatherings, high and low swings, specific degrees (of help, restriction, and blend, etc.) are considered by the intermediary's choice and procedure fit.

The instruments and models seen by the merchant can be clear worth bars, esteem gatherings, break-outs, design lines, or complex blends, including candles, unsteadiness, channels, etc.

Mental and lead interpretations and resulting exercises, as picked by the seller, moreover make up a noteworthy piece of significant worth movement trades. For e.g., paying little mind to what happens, if a stock gliding at 580 crosses the before long the set mental level of 600, by then the specialist may acknowledge a further upward move to take a long position. Various shippers may have an opposite view—when 600 is hit, the person being referred to concurs with a worth reversal and hence takes a short position.

No two merchants will disentangle a particular worth movement; likewise, as each will have their own interpretation, described guidelines, and unmistakable social cognizance of it. On the other hand, a specific assessment circumstance (like 15 DMA navigate 50 DMA) will yield practically identical lead and action (long situation) from various traders.

Essentially, esteem movement trading is a conscious trading practice, bolstered by particular examination instruments and late worth history, where vendors are permitted to take their own one of a kind decisions inside an offered circumstance to take trading positions, as indicated by their theoretical, lead, and mental state.

Who Uses Price Action Trading?

Since esteem action trading is an approach to manage esteem desires and speculation, it is used by retail handles, scholars, arbitrageurs, and despite trading firms who use shippers. It will, in general, be used on a wide extent of assurances, including values, bonds, forex, items, subordinates, etc.

Worth Action Trading Steps

Most experienced traders following worth movement trading save various decisions for seeing trading models, entry and leave levels, stop-hardships, and related recognitions. Having just a single framework on one (or unique) stocks may not offer satisfactory trading openings.

Most circumstances incorporate a two-advance strategy:

- Identifying a circumstance: Like a stock expense getting into a bull/bear stage, the channel goes, breakout, etc.
- Within the circumstance, perceiving trading openings: Like once stock is in the Bull Run, is it inclined to overshoot or a retreat. This is an absolutely enthusiastic choice and can vacillate, starting with one shipper then onto the next, even given the identical undefined circumstance.

The Popularity of Price Action Trading

Worth movement trading is progressively equipped for short-to-medium term obliged advantage trades, instead of long stretch theories.

Most vendors acknowledge that the market seeks after a sporadic model, and there is no exact sensible way to deal with describe a framework that will reliably work. By joining the particular assessment instruments with the continuous worth history to perceive trade openings reliant on the vendor's own special comprehension, esteem action trading has a huge amount of help in the trading system. Focal points join self-described approaches offering flexibility to vendors, real nature to different asset classes, basic use with any trading programming, applications, and trading passages, and the probability of straightforward backtesting of any perceived system on past data. Most importantly, the specialists feel in-charge, as the framework empowers them to pick their exercises, as opposed to erratically following a ton of standards. At long last, a great deal of theories and frameworks are available on esteem action trading, ensuring high accomplishment rates. However, shippers should think about survivorship tendency, as only instances of defeating misfortune make the news. Trading can possibly make alluring advantages. It is needy upon the individual vendor to clearly get, test, select, pick, and follow up on what meets his requirements for the best advantage openings.

Candle Patterns

Diagram designs structure a key bit of day trading. Flame and various charts produce an ordinary banner that cuts through worth action "disturbance." The best models will be those that can shape the establishment of a gainful day trading strategy, on account of trading stocks, the advanced cash of forex sets.

A candle diagram for Tesla, indicating value activity on an everyday premise.

Reliably you have to pick between many trading openings. This is an outcome of a wide extent of segments affecting the market. Day trading models enable you to decipher countless decisions and motivations—from any craving for expansion and fear of setback to short-covering, stop-incident triggers, supporting, charge results, and abundance more.

Light models help by painting a sensible picture and hailing up trading signs and signs of future worth turns of events. While it's said you'll need to use particular assessment to succeed day trading with a light and various models, it's basic to note utilizing them to promote your potential advantage is a more prominent measure of a gem than an inflexible science.

You will get comfortable with the power of outline plans and the theory that directs them. This page will, by then, reveal to you the ideal approach to profit by likely the most notable day trading plans, including breakouts and reversals. Your conclusive task will be to recognize the best guides to improve your trading style and systems.

Use in Day Trading

Used precisely, trading models can add a helpful advantage for your weapons store. This is on the grounds that history has an affinity for reiterating itself, and the budgetary markets are no extraordinary case. This emphasis can empower you to perceive openings and imagine likely entrapments. RSI, volume, likewise, to aiding and impediment levels all partner your particular examination when you're trading. Regardless, stock graph models accept a basic activity in recognizing breakouts and example reversals. Acing the art of examining these models will empower you to make progressively shrewd trades and fortify your advantages, as included in the extraordinarily regarded, 'stock models for day trading,' by Barry Rudd.

Breakouts and Reversals

In the models and layouts underneath, you'll see two rehashing subjects, breakouts, and reversals.

- Breakout – A breakout is basically when the worth clears a foreordained essential level on your chart. This level could be any number of things, from a Fibonacci level to support, check, or example lines.
- Reversal – A reversal is only a modification throughout a worth example. That change could be either positive or negative against the prevalent example. You may moreover hear it called a 'rally,' 'reviewm,' or 'example reversal.'

A pattern inversion. Note the huge bullish flame toward the finish of the downtrend.

On this page, you will see how both affect different frameworks and models. You can, in like manner, find express reversal and breakout methods.

A portion of the examples include:

Bull Banner

Bullish banner improvements are found in stocks with strong upswings. They are called bull flags in light of the fact that the model takes after a standard on a post. The pole is the delayed consequence of a vertical climb in stock, and the flag results from the hour of cementing. The pennant can be a level square shape, however, then again, it's as often as possible determined down away from the larger example. Another variety is known as a bullish banner, in which the association shows up as a balanced triangle. The condition of the flag isn't as noteworthy as the concealed mind science behind the model. Basically, paying little heed to a strong vertical assembly, the stock won't drop clearly, as bulls gobble up any offers they can get. The breakout from a standard much of the time achieves a stunning move higher, evaluating the length of the previous flag shaft. Note that these models work comparable in modify and are known as bear pennants and banners. Bull standards have been exceptional throughout the latest couple of significant stretches of 2008, anyway they have been beginning to surface identified with the progressing industry area rally.

Bull Banner Development

The mind research behind pennant models is huge. There is an arrangement of purposes behind the cementing time span.

CHAPTER 11

Market Trends

Y ou need to know your way around the options market to leverage your daily investments. Many day traders begin with the stock market simply because there are many similar nuances between options and stocks. In fact, trading stocks is what most people immediately think of when they hear day trading. Therefore, it is in every option day trader to become familiar with the stock market as well, even though the trader should never confuse the two entities. This chapter is dedicated to giving you information on the market influences that affect your success.

Deciding What Market to Trade in

Before you jump into the market looking for options to trade, you need to decide what types of assets are good for day trading options. Not doing so will only leave you feeling dazed and confused because the market can seem endless. Yes, stocks are the easy, popular choice, but they are not the only choice, and they might not be the right choice for you. Futures, Forex, Cryptocurrencies, and even Corn are also good options for day trading options. Stock trading is facilitated by the buying and selling of shares in a company's portfolio, and day trading stock options means that all positions must be opened by 9:30 AM EST and closed by 4 PM EST on the American stock market. The future market is one where the contract is created between the seller and the trader to buy or sell a predetermined value of the associated asset at a future date. An options day trader can profit due to the price fluctuations that can happen in the space of a day. The day trader needs to be cautious with the futures market working hours because they can vary. As such, the trader needs to be aware of the time his or her position needs to close. The forex market is accessible at any time of day and is the biggest financial market in the world. This market allows for the exchange of different currencies. There are many more markets to choose from when starting your options day trading career, but it all boils down to your circumstances and the resources you have available to you. For example, the startup fund can be an issue. This is particularly prevalent in the stock market. On the stock market, a trader needs to have an excess of $20,000 on his or her trading account to participate, while the forex market allows trades that are as low as a few hundred dollars. Therefore, you can only pursue options in the stock and futures market if you have the capital to back you.

Time is another consideration. Remember that some markets like the stock market only function at certain times of the day, some fluctuate in time operation, and others operate 24 hours a day. The strategy is also a factor. We will speak on this in a later chapter, but some strategies work best in a certain market at certain times of the day. Therefore, if there is a particular strategy that a day trader is great at, then he or she might have better results in certain markets.

How to Find the Best Options to Day Trade

After you have set your sights on a particular market, then you can move on to determine which particular assets you will pursue options in. You need to be able to pinpoint niches that work, and luckily, there are systems in place that can help you do that. Such tools include:

Technical Analysis

This is the first tool that we will discuss. It allows day traders to examine market sectors to identify strengths and weaknesses. By identifying those strengths and weaknesses, the options day trader can narrow down the options niches he or she would like to pursue within a given market.

There are several types of tools for performing technical analysis, and they include:

- Bollinger Band, which is a measure of market volatility.
- Intraday Momentum Index (IMI), which is an indicator of how options will play out within 1 day.
- Open Interest (OI), which indicates the number of open options, contracts to determine trends in options.

- Money Flow Index (MFI), which indicates the flow of money into assets over a specific amount of time.
- Relative Strength Index (RSI), which allows the trader to compare profits and losses over a set period of time.
- Put-Call Ratio (PCR), which indicates the volume of the put options relative to call options.

Price Charts

These tools give a visual representation of price and volume information so that market trends can be determined. More precisely known as price charts because they show price movement over a specific amount of time, charts come in different types. Common types include:

Line Charts

These easy-to-interpret charts document price movement over a specific period of time, such as months or years. Each price data point is connected using a single line. While the biggest advantage of this type of chart is the simplicity, this also causes a disadvantage to day traders as they provide no information about the strength of trading during the day. The line chart also does not provide price gap information. A price gap is defined as the interval between one trading period that is completely above or below a previous trading period. This price cap information is critical for options day traders to make effective decisions.

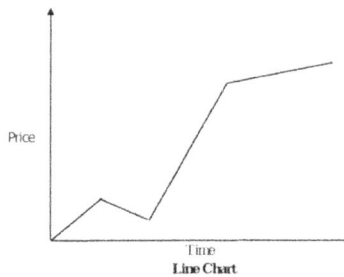

Line Chart

Open-High-Low-Close Bar Chart

This type of chart illustrates price movement from highest to lowest as specific amounts of time, such as 1 hour or one day. It is so named because it shows open, high, low, and close prices for the time period specified. The low to the high trading range is displayed with a vertical line while the opening and closing prices are displayed on a horizontal tab. All four elements make up one bar on the chart, and a series of these bars show movement over an extended period of time.

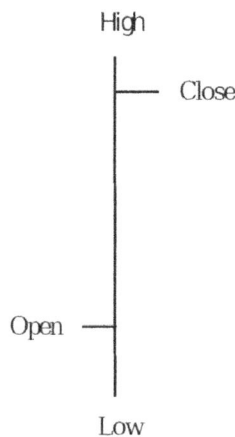

Example of Single Bar on
Open-High-Low-Close Bar Chart

This type of bar chart is advantageous as an options day trading tool because it provides information over 1-day trading periods as well as price gap knowledge.

Candlestick Chart

This is the kind of chart that is used by professional options day traders. It is similar to the open-high-low-close bar chart and is represented by price on the vertical axis and time on the horizontal axis. As such, it depicts price movement over time.

The structure of the candlestick chart has individual components. They are called candlesticks, hence the name of the chart. Every candlestick has 3 parts. They are called:

- The Body: This depicts the open-to-close range.
- The Wick: This represents the daily highs and lows. It is also called the shadow.
- The Color: This depicts the direction of price movement. White or green indicates an upward price movement. Red or black indicates a price decline.

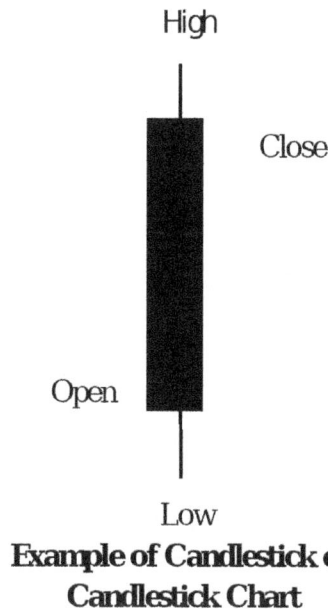

Example of Candlestick on Candlestick Chart

Using the candlestick chart allows day traders to see patterns on the market. There are several types of candlestick charts.

Factors That Affect the Options Market

After you have analyzed the options market and decided on the options that you will pursue, it is time to navigate the market and make a bet on the options you have decided on.

The first thing you need to do is execute a trade. If you are using an online broker as most options day traders do these days, you will make an order through the broker's digital system. When this is done, the options day trader needs to identify whether or not, he or she will be opening a new position or closing an existing position.

After this has successfully been executed, the trade details will be sent to the options day trader electronically. Factors that affect how the option will play out include interest rates, economic trends, and market volatility.

Chapter Summary

An options day trader needs to know his or her way around the options market to be effective in this career. The first thing the day trader needs to do is decide on the particular market that he or she will trade options in. The stock market is a popular choice, but it requires a high initial investment and has set hours for options trading.

The Futures and Forex Market are also popular options trading markets with different operating times and lower initial investment amount requirements. These might work better for some options day traders.

After the options day trader has figured out the particular market that he or she will trade options in, he or she has to pick a particular niche within that market to trade options in. Using technical analysis and price charts like the line chart, open-high-low-close bar chart, and candlestick chart help options day traders decide on the best options to pursue.

After this decision has been made, the day trader will execute the options trade via the brokerage firm he or she works with. This is typically done online as most options day traders turn to digital means in this age of technology. The success of how this options trade will play out is affected by factors like interest rates, economic trends, and market volatility.

CHAPTER 12

Day Trading Options Strategies

I f you set up with a dealer, and you've got your very own trading room ready to go, a successful plan would be needed. Day-trading techniques come in all shapes and sizes, some simple and others complex. Before we look at an example, there are a few critical components that will involve most techniques. When you transact using the internet, you can typically use charts and trends to forecast potential changes in prices. They are based on the fundamental theory that history is repeating itself, and you will find many a wealthy trader who wholeheartedly agrees with that assertion.

Your map will claim the latest selling options indicators. These vary from strategy to strategy, which includes the Put-Call Ratio Tracker, Capital Flow Index, Open Interest, Relative Strength Index, Bollinger Bands. You'll find that it takes hard work and experience to exchange trends for options. You would need to smooth out any creases and try several different charts before you find one with numbers that paints a good picture.

Covered Call Options

A call option is a contract option in which the holder (buyer) has the right (but not the obligation) to purchase a defined volume of a commodity at a predetermined date (strike price) within a given time (until its expiry).

This constitutes a duty for the writer (seller) of a call option to sell the underlying security at a strike price if the option is exercised. A prime is paid to the call choice writer for taking on the risk involved with the responsibility. Each deal includes 100 shares, with stock options. The short call is protected if the writer of the call option owns the required amount of the security underlying it. The covered call is a common option technique that helps the stockholder to produce additional income from their stock holdings by periodic call options sales. For more info, please see our covered call strategy post. Someone should buy a bull call spread as an alternative to writing covered calls with a comparable benefit opportunity but with considerably less capital need. Instead of buying the underlying shares of the covered call strategy, the preferred bull call spread approach requires only that the trader purchase deep-in-the-money call options.

Because the aim of writing protected calls is to collect premiums, it makes sense to sell near-month options when time decay on those options is at its highest.

Hence, the two tactics we equate would include selling marginally out-of-the-money call options in the near-month timeframe.

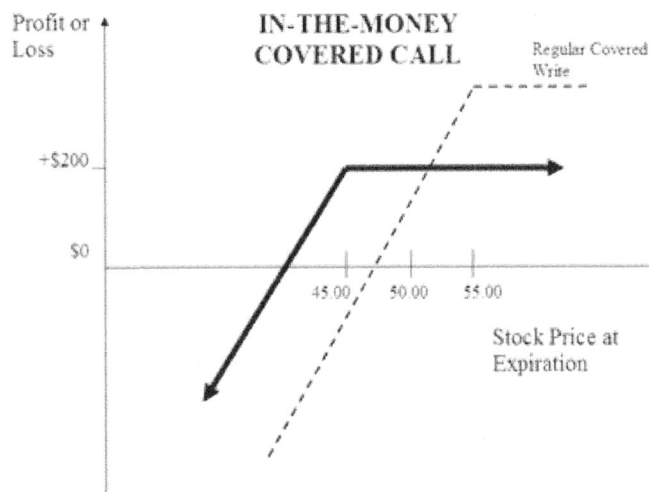

Married Put Options

Both married put and long call have the same infinite benefit potential with no cap onto the underlying stock price appreciation. However, benefit is often lower than just owning the stock, lowered by the cost or premium of the purchased option. Reaching break-even for strategy happens when the underlying stock increases by the amount of premium options received. Anything beyond that is income. The advantage of a married put is that the stock now has a floor minimizing downside risk. The floor is the difference between the underlying stock price, when the put was bought, and the put strike price. Simply put, when the option was acquired, if the underlying stock sold precisely at the strike price, the strategy loss is capped at exactly the price paid for the opportunity. A married put is also called a long synthetic call, as it has the same profile. The strategy resembles purchasing a standard call option (without the underlying stock) because, for both, the same dynamic is real: limited risk, infinite profit potential. The difference between these approaches is clearly how much less money a long call takes.

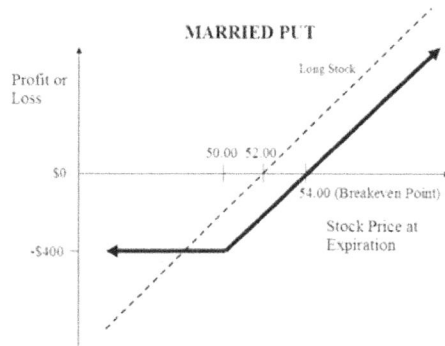

Bull Call Spread Options

One may buy a bull call spread as an alternative to writing covered calls with a comparable benefit opportunity but with considerably less capital need. Because of purchasing the underlying stock of the covered call strategy, the preferred bull call spread approach requires only that the trader buy deep-in-the-money call options. If the aim of writing protected calls is to collect premiums, it makes sense to sell near-month options when time decay for those options is at its highest. Hence, the two tactics we equate would include selling marginally out-of-the-money call options in the near-month period. The distribution of the bull call reduces the call option's risk, but it comes at a trade-off. The stock market returns are also capped, thereby having a small spectrum where the buyer will make a return. Traders will use the spread of the bull call as they expect the valuation of a commodity should increase moderately. Quite likely, they'll use this technique at periods of high uncertainty. The distribution of the bull call consists of steps which require two call options. Pick the investments that you believe would grow over a given span of days, weeks, or months. Buy a call option on a particular closing date at a strike price above the selling rate, and pay the premium. With this alternative, another name is a long call. Around the same time, sell a call option at a higher strike price and has the same expiry date as the first call option. Another term for a quick call for this alternative is.

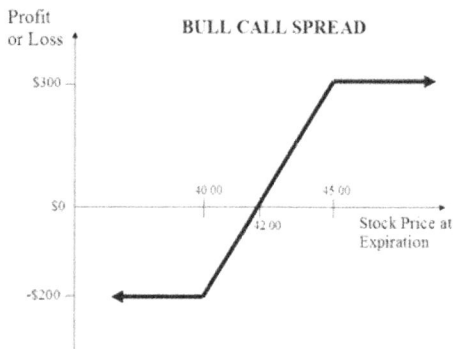

Bear Put Spread Options

A bear put spread is a form of options strategy where an investor or trader expects a moderate downturn in security or asset prices. Bear put propagation is accomplished by purchasing put options when selling the same number of puts on the same security at the same expiry date at a lower strike price. With this method, the potential profit is the difference between the two strike costs, minus the options' net value.

For a note, an option is a right to sell a given quantity of underlying security at a defined strike price.

Often known as a debit put spread or a long put spread. A bear put spread is an options technique executed by a bearish trader who aims to increase income while reducing profits.

A bear put spread approach entails purchasing and selling puts on the same underlying asset at the same expiry date but at different strike rates. A bear puts spread net profit as the price of the underlying security decreases. Therefore, net capital outlay is smaller than buying a single put outright. It also carries much less risk than shortening stock or protection, as the risk is limited to bear put spread net expense. Theoretically, selling a stock short has an infinite chance if the price goes higher. Unless the investor assumes the underlying stock or asset would decline by a small sum between the day of settlement and the expiry date, a bear put spread may be a perfect strategy. But, if the underlying stock or security declines by more than the dealer gives up the right to demand the extra Benefit. The trade-off between risk and future gain draws many traders.

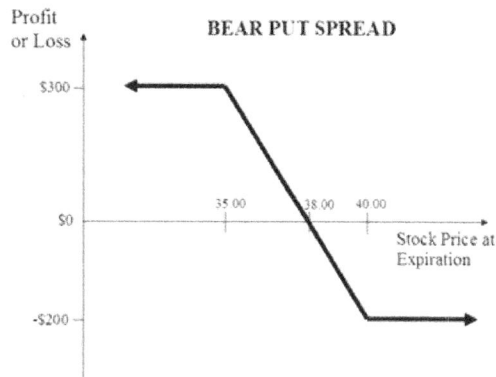

Protective Collar Options

The protective collar technique is where you purchase some protection options, sell a short call option, and purchase a long-placed option to reduce downside risk. This technique defends stocks from low market values. It uses cash-on-call options when sold and a Put option when purchased.

Everyone else holds short securities, and the lender must pay the responsibility. Long Put Option is purchasing shares, assuming the stock price should be smaller than the expiry strike price. The investor holds the shares.

Fast call option—selling the current call option until the investor feels market price would sink below the call strike point. The holder will benefit. Although the buyer will not own these shares, they must purchase them again later as the price falls and pay the owner.

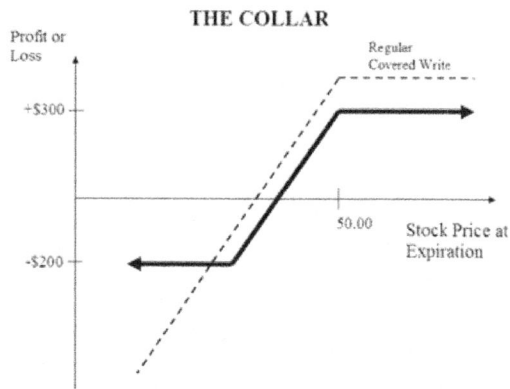

Long and Short Strangle Options

The endless options strangle a tremendous benefit, minimal risk approach that is taken while the dealer of the options considers the underlying stock and expiry date. Significant returns are obtained with the long strangle option strategy when the underlying stock price takes a very considerable step either upward or downward at expiry. The formula for estimating profit is given below:

Maximum Benefit = Unlimited Benefit Gained When Underlying Price > Long Call Strike Price + Net Premium Paid OR Underlying Price < Long Put Strike Price — Net Premium Paid Income = Underlying Price — Long Call Strike Price — Net Premium Paid OR Long Put Strike Price — Underlying Price — Net Premium Paid

A medium strangles one quick call with a higher trigger price and one low shot. All options have the same underlying supply and expiry date but different strike rates. If the underlying stock trades in a narrow range below the break-even points, a short strangle is formed for a net credit (or net receipt). Benefit opportunity is limited to cumulative contributions earning fewer commissions. Potential liability is infinite if stock demand increases, and asset selling declines significantly. Full benefit efficiency is limited to overall fewer commissions earned. Total Benefit is gained if the short strangle expires, the stock price trades at or below strike rates, and all options expire worthlessly. The maximum probability of profit loss is infinite because the stock price can grow forever.

The potential risk is significant on the downside when the stock price can fall to zero.

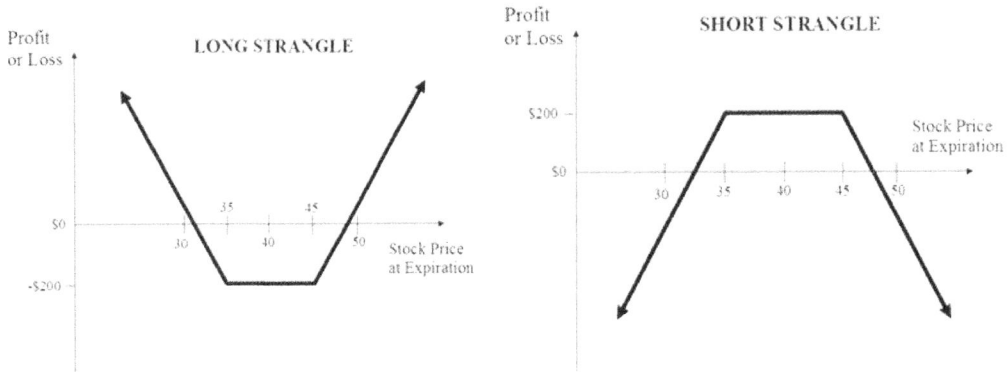

CHAPTER 13

What Are Financial Leverages

Leverage is a term that is, in most cases, made use in financial management. It comes up from borrowing capital as a way of funding as well as expanding an investment. It will then generate some returns on the risk capital. It is a strategy to invest in using money that is borrowed. It increases the profits of the investment made. Leverage can as well be the debt amount that a company puts in use to finance its assets. When the leverage is high, that means that the investor has more debt that has accumulated than equity. Leverage is known to boost the returns and hence, an increase in the profit.

It multiplies the potential returns from a particular investment. It will bring down the is likely to come up in case the investment you have made does not turn out as you had expected. The idea of leverage is put I use by investors as well as firms. An investor will use to make sure that there is an increase in returns on the investment. The investment will be levered using specific instruments, including margin accounts, options as well as futures. Companies will use leverage to finance their assets. Instead of issuing stock so that they can raise capital, they decide to use the debt to finance, aiming to increase the shareholder value.

Investors do not prefer to use leverage immediately. They have their means to access it indirectly. They opt to invest in a company that they know uses force to fund as well as expand their investments. The company does not have to increase the outlay necessarily. Leverage is an excellent approach anyone can put in use to multiply the buying power in the trade out there. However, you can decide to use margin as a way of creating leverage.

Types of Leverages

There are several types of leverage, but they do not need to be combined with being productive. They instead form the entire process even though they are independent. They include;

Operating Leverage

Operating leverage is just concerned with the investment activities of an individual firm. It is about the incurrence of the fixed cost of operation in a company's income stream. The operating price can either be fixed, semi-fixed, variable as well as semi-variable. The fixed fee is contractual, and it is subject to time. It does not necessarily have to change when the sales change, and it is supposed to be paid despite the number of sales. Variable cost has a direct variation with the level of sales revenue. There will be no variable cost if there will be no any sales that are made in a certain period. Semi-variable, as well as semi-fixed, will vary partly with the number of purchases made, and it will remain partially fixed. The fixed operating cost can be subject to be put in a lever, and hence the decisions of investment will go in favor of using assets that have a fixed price. When a firm decides to use the fixed cost, it will increase the effect that a change will have on the sales when EBIT changes. The ability that a firm will have to put the fixed operating cost in use to increase its earnings before the interest, as well as the taxes, is what is known as operating leverage. The leverage will be concerning the variation of the sales as well as profit. When the percentage of the operating cost is high, and then there will be a rise in the level of operating cost.

Financial Leverage

When there are financial charges in existence, the financial leverage will as well exist. The business costs should not depend on the operating profits in any way. The sources which the funds that help to boost an investment come from can be put in categories. The funds can either be having a fixed charge, and some may not be having the fixed financial cost. Debentures, preference shares, bonds as well as long- term loans have a fixed financial burden. Equity shares are known to have no fixed charge at all.

The fixed financial charge is used as a lever, and hence, the business decisions will go in favor when you employ such funds. When there are fixed charges in a company's income stream, financial leverage will be an outcome. It is an excellent idea to make sure that the change that will be made in EBIT to affect EPS will be significant. The higher the level of fixed charges, the higher the probability that the degree of financial leverage will go up. When the fixed costs go down, the economic advantage will go down as well.

Combined Leverage

If you bring both the operating leverage and the financial leverage together, they will come up with the combined force. It is concerning the risk of one not being able to cover up for the total amount of the fixed charges when a firm can cover fully on the operating as well as the financial burdens, that is when the term combined leverage comes in. The higher the fixed operating cost as well as the financial charges, the higher the level of the combined force.

Working Capital Leverage

When there is a decrease in the investment of a particular asset, there will be an increase in profit. That means that risks, as well as returns, have direct relations. When the probability of risk goes up, there is a likely hood that the profit will increase as well. The ability of an individual firm to increase the effect of the change in the current stock on the firm's returns is working capital leverage. It is so when there is an assumption that the liabilities are constant.

CHAPTER 14

Technical Analysis

No matter the kind of vehicle you choose for your actions, there are some basics that you have to be familiar with. This fundamental knowledge is mostly connected to the behavior of the markets. If you learn how to recognize the way they behave, you will be able to anticipate the movement of the prices more accurately, thus make smarter decisions while trading. It can be interesting to note that regardless of the value that is traded on the market, some concepts can always apply to the prices and their way of performance on the market.

This can be explained by independent traders and investors being responsible for short-term price fluctuations. We can say that the price depends on the actions of the people who invest or trade values on the market, and those prices react in a similar way when they are given similar input or stimuli. The study that is dedicated to researching the ways of price behavior is called technical analysis, and understanding its basic is one of the most essential education points that you will need to be able to make correct financial decisions on the market.

The Basics of Technical Analysis

Technical analysis represents a huge topic. If you decide to enter the market and become an investor, there is a high possibility that you will catch yourself coming back to studying and learning something new many times for as long as you intend to work as a trader. That is why every person knowledgeable in options trading would advise that a basic understanding of technical analysis is a very important step for every person involved in the market. However, you don't need to know everything about it right away. Since it is a large area of research, it is ok if, for some aspects of your business, you just research parts of the technical analysis that you are particularly interested in for that concrete project. For instance, the technical analysis offers more than a hundred indicators for analyzing the market. In reality, traders usually use three or four, mostly the most popular ones or just those that they were familiar with in the first place. If you don't limit yourself only to option trading, but you do trading in general, you will realize that technical analysis can be applied to any financial instruments such as futures or stocks, for example. We can say that their basis is in psychology and human nature in general and how they behave in practice. For better understanding, we will overview some of the main topics in technical analysis. These topics will be: Technical analysis' foundation; how to chart principles and trends; patterns in technical analysis; technical analysis through the movement of the averages, and Indicators in technical analysis.

Technical Analysis' Foundation

The main basis of the technical analysis is found in the term known as "market action." Market action represents a whole personal knowledge about the trading market, and it doesn't include information that you might obtain from an insider. It can be simply defined as a study that determines: "the way that the price moves over time." If possible, it also examines its volumes and how they change over time too.

Still, the fundamental concept of technical analysis is based on the premise that the behavior of the market is a reflection of everything that happened and will happen with the price at a certain moment. Many things can have an impact on the price, and the amount of the impact depends on the market in which the trade is made. That's where technical analysis comes in, it cuts across all of those possibilities and states that all the things that can be known about the price are basically already included in the price that we see at the moment we want to trade.

This means that you shouldn't worry too much about the things that influence the price, as according to this, it is enough to follow how the price changes over time, and you will get all your answers. At first, many people wondered if this kind of principle can work because it sounded rather easy. If you had any doubts, the answer was already proven, and it says that yes, technical analysis is successful, although this kind of definition doesn't seem that complicated.

However, there is one very important point coming out from all of this. Technical analysis doesn't guarantee the behavior of the price. It can tell you that the price will increase or decrease for a certain period, but that doesn't necessarily happen. It may or it may not. The reason for this is that regardless of the calculation that the market has to do something, it is impossible to be 100 percent sure that it will. The market has its own ways and eventually does what it wants. So what technical analysis does is that it gives you the indication that shows what will be the most probable outcome, which means that the only certainty that you get is to know if the law of probability is on your side or not.

You can do a large number of average trades and hopefully make some profit, but you should never invest an amount of money or some valuable goods such as your house or your car if you can't afford to lose it. It is not recommended, especially if one successful trade makes you confident that just one is enough to be a good technical indicator for certain gain. This is one of the reasons why the first task of technical analysis is to improve your chance for success by analyzing the prices and the way they behave on the market.

The second reason for the analysis is the fact that prices almost always change using certain trends. For instance, if the price increases, its trend will be to rise until there is something that disables it from further growth. In comparison, we can say that prices act like Newton's motion law, which says that: "a body in motion will stay in motion unless acted upon by an external force." Of course, to prove this to be true, it has to happen over time. If this weren't the case, the price charts represented in many analyses wouldn't be the way they are. They would be illustrated as a random movement of the prices. The third reason is that technical analysis supposes that history will, as always, repeat itself. If certain situations happened in the past, and you see them happening once again in the present, then it is highly expected that the same thing will happen in the future too. Since people are not expected to change in this equation, the second logical conclusion would be that their results will be the same too. In a nutshell—this was the very foundation of technical analysis. Don't forget that one of the most efficient ways to become good in trading and to increase your chance to become a successful investor is to be able to use most of the things that this analysis can give you.

There are a few arguments that you can hear against the use of technical analysis. Still, the only proof that you really need is the fact that this analysis works and that at least it can improve your chances to get more percentages while trading. However, we will point out some of the attitudes toward technical analysis:

One of the traders said: "Charts only show what has happened in the past, how can they reveal what hasn't happened yet?" The answer to this is quite simple, there is evidence from earlier trades, and those pieces of evidence are used in technical analysis with the premise that history will repeat itself. This way, you can anticipate at least with some fair certainty what is the next thing that will happen with the price on the market. In comparison, it works in a similar way as the weather forecast, if they say that it will rain on the TV, you know that it might not rain even though they said it would, but you take your umbrella with you anyway. The same principle applies to the technical analysis, and that is how you can predict the future by using past events.

Another trader noted: "If the prices already incorporate everything there is to know, then any change in price can only come from new information that we don't know yet." This kind of idea doesn't only appear in trading options; it is present in all financial markets. It surfaces in many areas, and even academics are still discussing it. Differently, from the opinion that is popular between the traders, this concept doesn't actually say that the price that is currently on the market is the correct one. It just states that it isn't possible to establish if that current price is too low or too high. That is why the smartest choice to deal with this concept is to prove in which way technical analysis really works. In the end, if everyone supported this kind of idea, then we would have zero analysis, and the price would always be the same. We can imply that technical analysis has self-fulfilling characteristics.

This means that if the majority of traders do the analysis and estimate that the price has to increase, all of them would become buyers on the market, which would mean an increase in demand, thus price that went up. The same principle applies to the price that is supposed to go down. This is one more example in which technical analysis showed that it works. Of course, there can always be some doubts, but does it really matter to prove why the price went in the direction that you thought it would? Additionally, if a large number of traders who are not well educated and they just want to make quick profit fail, it can be seen as a sort of evidence that the idea of having a massive amount of traders regardless of their knowledge and dedication is somehow wrong from the beginning.

How to Chart Principles and Trends

After we have seen what the basic principles of the technical analysis are, it is time to see how the prices are charted or graphed and what those graphs mean. There is no way of escaping this, even though some might find it unnecessary. You will be forced to see this kind of chart during your whole trading career. It is easier to understand these principles if you go slowly, step by step, and try to remember how these principles work. There are few diverse types of the chart, but all of them mostly use horizontal bottom and timescale as a vertical scale. The price is usually up to the side, and for someone who is just starting, these charts are the only ones that you should be interested in. The vertical line or the timescale can be expressed in minutes, days, or even weeks, so you will look at the one, which is suitable for your trading style. However, it is not unusual that you'd want to know what happens with the other time scales as long as they are around the values you chose. Experienced traders mostly look at the other time scales to get the bigger picture of what's happening on the market. Here, we will mention three kinds of charts, and we will suppose that they all have the same time vertical line and that they are all in the same currency.

CHAPTER 15

Buying Calls

Buying calls is a more advanced form of training than selling covered calls. But it's not that complicated, so let's dive in.

What You're Actually Buying

Remember that one option contract is for 100 shares, so you'll need to be able to buy 100 shares of the stock in order to exercise your right to buy.

Also, remember that an options contract has a deadline. If the stock price fails to exceed the strike price by the deadline, you're out of luck and will lose whatever money that you invested in the premium. In relative terms, the premium price will be small, so chances are if you are careful and not starting out by buying large numbers of options contracts, you won't be out that much money.

Your Goal Buying Options Contracts

The goal when purchasing options contracts is to buy a stock at a price that is lower than its current market value. In other words, you want the stock price to be significantly higher than the strike price so that you're enjoying significant savings in purchasing the stock. When evaluating your options, you'll need to take into account the added costs of the premium paid plus commissions. In some cases, commissions can be substantial, so make sure you know what they are ahead of time so that you choose a good strike price and exercise your options at the right time.

You're a Trader, Not an Investor

You may be mentally conditioned to think in terms of investing. An investor wants to build a diversified portfolio over a long time period that they believe will increase in value over the long term. A trader operates in the same universe but has different goals. You are after short term profits—not investments. You are not going to hold this stock. If you were interested in holding the stock, you would simply buy it at the lower price that is currently on offer. Your goal is to be able to buy at the strike price when the stock has increased significantly in price and then sell it immediately so that you can pocket the profits. Let's take an example. Suppose that XYZ Corporation is currently selling at $30 a share. People are expecting the stock to rise, and some people are really bullish about its short-term prospects. If you are an investor, your goal is to get the stock at the lowest possible price and then hold it long term. If you are using strategies like dollar-cost averaging, you might be buying a few shares every month without paying too much attention to what the price is specifically on the day you purchase. In any case, as an investor, you'll simply buy the shares at $30. As a trader, you're hoping to cash in on the moves of XYZ over the next couple of months. You'll buy an options contract, let's say its premium is $0.90 and the strike price is $35. Your cost for the 100 shares is $90. Then the stock price shoots up to $45. Since it passed the strike price, you can exercise your option to buy the shares at the strike price. You can buy them at $35 for a total price of $3,500. But remember—you're not an investor in for the long haul. You'll immediately unload the shares. You sell the shares for $4,500 and make a $1,000 profit. After considering your premium, your profit is $910. It will go a little bit lower after considering commissions, but you get the idea. The purpose of buying call options is to make fast profits on stocks you think are going to spike.

It's hard to guess when the best time is to really buy call options. Obviously, you don't want to do it when a major recession hits. The optimal time is during a bull market, or when a specific company is expected to hit on something big, that will suddenly increase its value in the markets. A good time to look is also when a recession hits, but it passes the bottom out period.

Benefits of Buying Call Options
In Particular

- Call options allow you to control 100 shares of stock without actually investing in the 100 shares—unless they reach a price where you get the profit that you want.
- Call options allow you to sit and wait, patiently watching the market before making your move. If your bet doesn't work out, you're only going to lose a small amount of money on the contract. In our example, if XYZ loses value, and ends up at $28 per share instead of moving past your strike price of $35, then you're only out the $90 you paid for the premium.
- Call buying provides a way to leverage expensive stock.

What to Look for When Buying Call Options

Now let's take a look at some factors that you'll be on the lookout for when buying call options. You're going to want to be able to purchase shares of the stock you're interested in at a price that is less than the price you think it will go up to. You need to do this in order to ensure that the stock price surpasses the strike price. Of course, it's impossible to know what the future holds, so this will involve a bit of speculation. You'll have to do a lot of reading and research to make educated guesses on where you expect the stock to go in the next few weeks or months. Second, you'll need to take into account the cost of the premium when making your estimates. For the sake of simplicity, suppose that you find a call option with a premium of $1 per share. You're going to need a strike price that is high enough to take that into account. If you go for a stock that is $40 a share with a $1 premium and a strike price of $41, obviously you're not going to make anything unless the stock price goes higher than $41.

Remember that exercising your rights on the options contract is not a path toward immediate money. You're going to have to turn around and sell it ASAP in order to profit. Of course, when you sell is a judgment call, as is when you exercise your right to buy. You're going to want to wait until the right moment to buy, but it's impossible to really know what that right moment is. This is where trading experience helps, and even then, the most skilled experts can make mistakes. For a beginner, the best thing to do is exercise your right to buy the shares and then sell them as soon as they've gone far enough past the strike price for you to make a profit and cover the premium. If you wait too long, there is always the chance that the stock price will start declining again, and it will go below your strike price and never exceed it again before the contract expires.

Open Interest

If you get online to check stocks you're interested in, one of the measures you will see is "Open Interest." This tells you the number of open or outstanding derivative contracts there are for that particular stock. Every time that a buyer and seller enter into an options contract, this value increases by one. What you want to do with open interest as a trader looking to make real cash from call options is to look for stocks that show big movement in the number of open trades. You're going to want to look for increasing numbers. This means that other traders have an interest in buying call options on this stock and that they're expecting it to go up in value in the near future. Of course, you're going to want to take an educated approach to this. Simply getting online and going through random stocks will be a waste of time; it might take you weeks to find something.

You're going to want to prepare ahead of time by keeping an eye on the financial news. Watch Fox Business, read the Wall Street Journal, and watch CNBC and read any other financial publications that are to your liking. Find out what stocks the experts are talking about and which ones they expect to make significant moves over the next few weeks and months. Keep in mind that these people and experts often make mistakes, so you're only using it as a guideline. You also don't want to focus solely on looking for stocks that are going to make moves; you want to keep up with company news. You need to keep your ears open for news such as the development of a new drug or the latest electronic gadget. Sometimes you might find out news about that before the stock begins attracting a lot of interest in the markets.

Tips for Buying Call Options

- Don't buy a call option with a strike price that you don't think the stock can beat.
- Always include the premium price in your analysis.
- Look for calls that are just in the money. These are likely to bring a modest profit.
- Call options that are out of the money might give you an option for a cheaper premium. However, the premium shouldn't be your primary consideration when looking to buy a call option. Compared to the money required to buy the shares and the potential profits if the stock goes past the strike price, the premium is going to be a trivial cost in most cases—provided, of course, the strike price is high enough to take the premium into account.
- Look at the time value. If you're looking for larger profits, it's better to aim for longer contracts. Remember that with any call option, you have the option to buy the stock at the strike price at any time between today's date and the deadline when the stock market price exceeds the strike price. Longer time frames mean you increase the chances of that happening. Even if the price goes a little above the strike price and dips down, with a longer window of time before the deadline, you can wait and see if it rebounds. Remember, if it never does, you're only out the premium.
- Start small. Beginning traders shouldn't bet the farm on options. You'll end up broke if you do that. The better approach is to start by investing in one contract at a time and gaining experience as you go.

CHAPTER 16

Covered Calls

What Is a Covered Call?

Also known as a buy-write, this describes the act of selling the right to purchase a specified asset that you own at a specified price within a specified amount of time, which is usually less than 12 months. It is a two-part strategy whereby someone first purchases stock then sells it on the share by share prices. The beauty of this type of option is that off the bat, the seller benefits by receiving a premium payment from the options holder. Risk is mitigated because the seller already owns the stock. Therefore, your costs are covered if the stock price rises above the strike price. If the trader chooses to exercise the right to purchase on or before the expiration date, you simply deliver as agreed and rip any additional benefits.

Stock is the most common asset used in this type of option.

If you choose to consider covered calls, you need to be willing to own the stock at your price even if the price depreciates. Remember that there is no guarantee that you will earn greatly on the stock that you have purchased due to the volatility of financial markets. Therefore, you need to be diligent in your focus on seeking good quality stocks that you are willing to own. You need to be able to still potentially benefit from that ownership if there are down periods in the market.

As the seller of a covered call option, you need to be also willing to part with that stock if the price rises. You cannot change your mind if the price of the stock goes up if you have already entered into an option with a willing buyer. You must exercise that delivery if the trader chooses to exercise that option.

The maximum potential profit of covered calls is achieved if the stock price is met at or above the strike price of that call at or by the expiration date. The formula for this is as follows:

Sum of the Call Premium + (Strike Price - Stock Price) = Maximum Potential Profit

The seller also needs to consider the break-even point at the expiration date. The formula for this is as follows:

Purchase Price of the Stock - The Call Premium = Break-Even Analysis

The seller also needs to determine the maximum risk potential. This is equal to the purchasing price of the stock at the break-even point. The seller also needs to be satisfied with the static rate of return and the if-called rate of return on the stocks. The static return is the approximate annual net profit of a covered call, assuming that the stock price does not change until the expiration date and until the option expires. To calculate this value, the seller needs to know:

- The purchase price of the particular stock
- The strike price of the option
- The price of the call
- The number of days until option expires
- If there are any dividends and the amount of these dividends

Calculating these factors leads to a percentile figure being determined. The formula for calculating this is:

(Call + Dividend) / Stock Price × Time Factor = Static Rate of Return

The if-called return is an approximate annual net profit on a covered call with the assumption that the stock price is above the strike price by or on the expiration of the option and that the stock is sold at expiration. To calculate this figure, which is also a percentage, the same factors need to be determined. The formula for calculating this is:

(Call + Dividend) + (Strike – Stock Price) / Stock Price × Time Factor = If-Called Rate of Return

The Benefits of Covered Call Options

The first benefit of covered call options is that the seller receives a premium payment, which can be kept as income whether or not the trader chooses to exercise the right to the option. This can be set up as a regular cash flow by serious investors in markets that are relatively neutral or bullish. The investor can set up a program for selling covered calls on a regular basis. This can potentially set up a monthly or quarterly income stream. The second benefit of covered calls is that they can help investors target a selling price for a particular stock that is above the current price. Lastly, covered calls have the additional benefit of limiting risks as the asset provides protection to the seller.

The Risks Associated with Covered Call Options

The first major risk associated with covered calls is that the seller can lose money if the stock price depreciates below the break-even point. This is a risk that anyone who owns stock takes on. The second risk is not being able to anticipate a huge price rise in the price of the stock. Stocks have unlimited potential for profit, but if the holder of the options for that stock chooses to exercise his or her right, then the seller has to hand it over to this person. This can lead to a great missed opportunity as the seller now has to hand over a tremendous asset in the transaction.

How to Create a Covered Call Option

The first step in creating a covered call is purchasing the stock. This is done by purchasing it in lots of 100 shares. Doing this allows you to sell an option for every 100 shares of stocks. The great thing about buying stock in this way is that you do not have to option all of them. For example, let's say that you bought 1000 shares of stock. You can sell 5 contracts, leveraging 500 shares, and earning 5 premium payments. You will hold onto 500 shares of stock even if the holders of the options of those 5 contracts exercise their right.

The last step is waiting for the covered call to be exercised or for it to expire. If the covered calls are not exercised, then you still get to keep the premium. There is always the option to buy the option back before the expiration date arrives, but sellers hardly ever do this. Remember that you have to be willing to part with the stock once you option it.

How the Covered Call Works

Covered calls work in one of three ways.

The Stock Price Goes Down

In this case, the covered call will be worthless on expiration. The bad news is that the stock price goes down, but the good news is that the seller gets to keep the premium and so still earned from the transaction. The decrease in the price of the stock is simply the nature of owning stocks. You should have accounted for this before you made the purchase. Remember that you need to be willing to own that stock no matter what, so choose wisely. Note, though, that the profit from selling the call can help offset this decrease in the price of the stock. The stock price may fall before the expiration date. This is not a cause to fret because you are not indefinitely locked in this position. Even though the stock price has gone down and the call value went down as well, this is an opportunity to buy the call back for less money than you sold it for.

The Stock Price Does Not Change or Goes Up Slightly

This is not a losing scenario. While the covered call will expire as worthless, the seller still keeps the premium for the option. If you see a slight rise in the price of the stock, while the holder of the option is unlikely to exercise the right to gain that, the seller benefits from it nonetheless, even if the rise is marginal.

The Stock Goes Above the Strike Price

If the stock goes up above the strike price by the expiration date, the holder of the option will exercise the right, and the seller needs to sell the 100 shares of stock. It is a hard pill to swallow if the price of the stock skyrockets even if you already reconciled a willingness to part with the stock before but comfort yourself with the fact that you gain maximum profit from the transaction.

CHAPTER 17

Differences and Similarities between Day Trading and Swing Trading

A fundamental question to start with is this one—what are you looking for as a day trader? The answer here is quite easy. First, you must look for stocks that are following a predictable trend. Then, you need to trade them in one single day. You don't need to keep them longer than a day. If you purchase stocks of Amazon (AMZN) today, you should not hold the stocks overnight and sell them tomorrow. It is no longer day trading if you hold on to your position. That one is called swing trading.

As a day trader, you need to understand the difference between day trading and swing trading. The latter is a type of trading in which you hold the stocks over a certain period of time, usually from one day to several weeks. This is a different style of trading, and you must not use these tools and strategies that are ideal for day trading if you want to follow the swing trading style. Remember, day trading is a business (Rule 2). Swing trading is also a business, albeit a totally different type of business. Imagine owning a meat processing plant and a hamburger chain.

Both businesses involve food, but these are not similar. They operate with different revenue models, market segments, regulations, and time frames. You must not confuse day trading with other trading styles just because the trades are performed in the stock market. Professional day traders close their positions before the stock market closes. Many traders perform both swing trading and day trading. They are aware that they are running two different businesses, and they are trained to manage the risks of these two types of trading.

One of the main differences between swing trading and day trading is the style of choosing stocks. Many traders do not day trade and swing trade the same stocks. Swing traders often look for stocks in established companies that they know will not lose their value in a few weeks. But for day trading, you can trade any stock you want, including companies that are predicted to go bankrupt. Day traders don't care what happens to the stocks after the market closes. As a matter of fact, many of the companies that you day trade are quite risky to hold overnight because they may lose much of their value in a short period of time.

Before you begin to trade, you need to determine how active you want to be. How much time do I have at hand, and what are my current responsibilities? Your answers to these questions will help you to decide if you want to trade daily or if you want to buy and hold for some days or weeks.

The active traders are divided into two groups: the day traders and the swing traders. Both groups have a similar goal of making profits from short-term or long-term trades. However, there are major differences between the two that you should understand and make your decision on your best choice depending on your level of technical expertise, time frames, and your preference.

Basically, day trading is a form of trading where your long or short position is entered and exited on the same day—opens and closes within 24hours. Day traders get into positions based on quantitative, fundamental, or technical reasons. Day traders don't grasp their positions overnight. Swing trading, on the other hand, is a long-term investment where the trader buys or shorts securities and holds them for some days, weeks, or months. Unlike day traders, the swing traders do not intend to take trading as a full-time job.

Also, you do not need to have lots of capital to swing trade, while day trading follows the 'pattern day trader rule.' This rule is what governs any trader that makes more than four trades in the same security over five business days. This trader is referred to as "pattern day trader" based on the premise that the trades represent above 6% of the trader's total trading activity in that period. A pattern day trader must also have a minimum of $25,000 equity in their account on any trading day.

Day Trading

Being a day trader can be very beneficial; however, it has its inherent risks. A day trader needs to realize that there may be times where he may encounter a 100% loss.

Day trading, more than some other type of trading, requires quick and right choices on positions and estimating the entry, exits, and stop-losses. The trades are fast and must be amazingly precise. Day trading imperatively requires being available and comprehending whatever occurs in the market at every point in time. Even though it doesn't imply that one should trade every day or consistently, the evaluations need to be done frequently. This type of trading takes more time than swing trading. However, it can be satisfying all-day work.

Day trading is better for people who have a passion for full-time trading and possess discipline, decisiveness, and diligence. For one to be successful as a day trader, he needs to have an in-depth understanding of charts and technical trading. Day trading can be stressful and intense, and so, traders need to be able to control their emotions and stay calm under fire.

Swing Trading

A swing trader identifies swings in currencies, commodities, and stocks that occur over days. Unlike day trading, a swing trade may take up to weeks to work out. Swing traders have more persistence concerning their trade opening. As the positions extend to the second day, there is potential for enormous benefits on a single trade, yet there are fewer trading opens generally. Anyone who has the investment capital and knowledge can give a shot at swing trading.

Swing trading requires less technical investigative abilities and progressively focus research and information on macroeconomics. The entry focus does not need to be that exact, and the planning isn't so pivotal since the moves which swing traders are expecting to get are bigger.

Swing trading doesn't require the trader to put in much time as frequent technical evaluation and consistent sitting before the screen is not necessary. It is usually a stress-free and low-effort job. The swing trader can have a separate full-time job as he does not have to stay glued to his computer screen all day.

Swing traders usually require time to work out. The more time a trade is open for days or week, the more the chances of having higher profits than trading multiple times daily on the same security. Margin requirements in a swing trade are higher since positions are held overnight. Compared to day trading, whose maximum leverage is four times one's capital, swing trading is often two times the trader's capital.

Day traders need to understand and utilize stop-losses and target levels to their benefit. While there is the possibility that the stop order will execute at an unfavorable price, it is still better than having to monitor all your open positions constantly.

As is usual with all types of trading, a swing trader can also experience losses, and because the traders hold the positions for a longer time, they may experience more significant loss than the day traders.

Swing trading does not require the use of state-of-the-art technology. You can swing trade with one computer, and any needed trading tools.

Because swing trading is usually not a full-time job, the traders have other sources of income and have reduced chances of burnout caused by stress.

When should you go for day trading?

The points below have summarized the ideal situation for you to be a day trader:

- You are disciplined, diligent, and strong-willed.
- You are willing to make small profits daily by making small trades.
- You have the minimum capital requirements stated by FINRA rules for pattern day traders and SEC, if and when they apply to you.
- You are knowledgeable and have the expertise to make high profits.
- You are not easily stressed, and you can manage stress.
- You are committed to studying current trends and can take needed action at the speed of light.
- You never have a dull day, and you are out for excitement every minute.

When should you go for swing trading?

The points below have summarized the ideal situation for you to be a swing trader:

- You lack extreme levels of technical understanding

- You do not want to go full time into trading. That is, you don't desire trading as your only source of income.
- You do not like stress and will instead go for something that is not as risky as day trading.
- You do not fancy constant monitoring of market activities.
- You are patient and can wait for weeks to months while studying the movements of the market.
- You have a full-time job and can't spare time for day trading activities.
- You do not have plenty of money to invest.

CHAPTER 18

The Basics of Technical Analysis

The technical analysis or chart analysis includes all assessments and trading decisions that are primarily based on the analysis of the price development. In this chapter, we present the essential basics of chart analysis. The principle is relatively simple: a security rises, falls, or stays on its course. The apparent reasons for the individual behavior of security can be of various kinds. The procedure for analyzing security can be just as varied. A fundamentally oriented analyst examines the reports of the audit firms, the profit and loss accounts, the regularly published balance sheets, the ability of the management, the dividend policy, the sales, the competitive situation, the utilization of the production. And that's not all. He also tracks the orders and communications from the Ministry of Economy and Finance; he monitors price statistics, production indicators, and much more. It is a lot of work that offers a lot of discussion material.

Taking into account the above and many other factors, the fundamental analyst rates his security. If the security is listed below its estimated value, he sees this as a buying opportunity. Let's say he buys his security because he thinks it's undervalued. Let us further assume that despite the most varied arguments for rising prices, the security still falls, and it continues to fall.

Just why?

Let us search for an explanation together: Certainly, the fundamental data play a role in the supply and demand constellation. Undisputed! But many other factors influence this constellation. Very often, even have a considerable impact. You can already imagine which factors will put the course out of its position. Right, it's investor behavior. Investor behavior determines the price.

In our example, the stock is mostly sold by investors, and the market price reflects the fears, presumptions, and moods of those investors. Even the analysis of the stock exchange fundamentalist does not change this because the stock exchange is not logical. A stock market price reflects the moods of hundreds of thousands of people. Rational moods, irrational moods!

A stock market price reflects the needs of investors; they elude logical analysis. And yet: All of these factors ultimately express themselves in a rational event: the trend. This is the price that buyers and sellers agree on and make a transaction in the relevant security. So simple is what ultimately comes out of such a complicated process. And that's what matters: the trend. The trend contains all the information that is decisive for us. It is also said that the trend "pre-interpreted" all relevant information. The stock exchange market looks to the future and forms its price based on the expectations of investors. While the fundamental analyst is most likely still busy analyzing the current state of a company, the one with the technical approach evaluates investor expectations.

The fundamental analyst is probably going through the balance sheets again this minute; he thinks he must have missed something. The stock market makes it much, much more straightforward: it has already compiled all the vital information that the fundamental analyst could even take into account. Google share can be mentioned here as an example. For years, fundamentally-oriented commentators have rightly pointed to the exorbitantly high valuation of Google shares. For example, Google was worth as much in 2006 as the DAX groups BMW, Bayer, Commerzbank, Lufthansa, and Infineon combined. According to fundamental evaluation criteria at the time, and evaluation beyond good and evil, even if one had anticipated very high expectations regarding further business development.

The pricing of the Google IPO in the $100 range was already considered excessive. That didn't stop the share from rising 375% to $475 high in less than two years. Already at $100, Google's stock was a short for many fundamental analysts, as was $200, at $300 and $400. However, the share price continued to rise. In less than ten years since the IPO, the share has increased a whopping twelve times. And there is no end in sight for the rally.

Should one shorten the share simply because of the argument of fundamental overvaluation, i.e., sell it short? No way. This is shown in this example. As a day trader, you would have burned your fingers almost throughout the entire "lifetime" of the stock. The mistake of "value-shorting" made so many fundamentally-oriented market participants during the Internet boom at the end of the 90s and suffered significant shipwreck. Simply because the price-moving effect of the "none" fundamental factors was underestimated.

So far, so beautiful, but how does this help us in this course?

Well, there's an undeniable phenomenon. And that means: courses move in trends. And these trends tend to continue until the supply-demand constellation changes. And even more: The difference in the supply-demand constellation goes hand in hand with specific patterns, so-called chart formations. And these formations, as well as the trend, can be analyzed.

Fine!

And the best thing is: these analyses have always proven to be relatively reliable. And they will continue to do so in the future because the only constant on the stock exchange is investor behavior. And that will not change because man will not change in terms of moods, hopes, doubts, greed. So, we have a suitable tool, namely the price trend in a chart, to make forecasts—pictures that we can say that say more than a thousand words.

The Basic Concept of a Trend

In chart analysis, a trend is a price movement that runs in the same direction over a longer period. Filtering out trend phases to be invested in them is the primary goal of chart analysis.

The trend concept is indispensable for the technical approach of market analysis. And this market trend is significant because we align our transactions with trends.

The Trend Has Three Directions

You shouldn't think of these trends as straight price movements. Instead, trends run in forms that are characterized by jagged movements.

These jagged movements almost look like successive waves. These waves include highs and lows. The direction in which these waves move shows us the trend of the market.

There are three trends in total: upwards, downwards, and sideways.

Let us take a closer look at examples and characteristics of market trends below.

Figure 1 shows the patterns of an upward and downward trend. An upward trend is characterized by a series of successively higher lows and higher highs. A downward trend is precisely the opposite of an upward trend.

Figure 1

This has a characteristic series of lower highs and lower lows. As you can see, it is not difficult to describe an upward or downward trend. What remains is the sideways trend that you see in Figure 2. A sideways trend is constituted by a series of equally highs and lows.

Figure 2

Many investors assume that a market is either up or down. However, it very often moves sideways in these so-called trading ranges, repeatedly interrupted by upward and downward trends. The unique thing about such sideways trends is that supply and demand are in balance. Such market phases are also called trendless, which is not entirely correct, but this term is often used.

Let us look again at the three trend directions shown: upwards, downwards, and sideways. It is not difficult to associate that we should buy in uptrends; after all, we assume that a trend will continue until it reverses. Accordingly, we should sell short in downtrends and do nothing at all in sideways trends.

The Three Classifications of a Trend

In addition to the three directions that a trend can have, it is categorized again. These categories divide trends into long, medium, and short-term trends. Long-term trends last over a year and are also called primary trends. Primary trends are not straight, but (in the case of an upward trend) consist of upward movements and corrections. These upward movements and corrections are medium-term trends, also called secondary trends. They usually last from three weeks to a few months. Figure 3 shows the scheme of primary and secondary trends. The diagram in Figure 3 shows a longer-term upward movement and a longer-term downward movement.

Figure 3

Longer-term upward and downward movements consist of three medium-term upward and downward movements, which are each interrupted by two corrections. These numbers don't always have to be right, but you should consider them as a guide.

You must understand the direction of a primary trend. This is because rallies are strong in these long-term upward movements and the reactions, i.e., the corrections, are weak. It is different in long-term downward movements: the reactions (corrections) are strong here, while the rallies, on the other hand, are also strong, but short-lived and sometimes difficult to predict. If you have an idea of the long-term trend, you are better prepared for the nature of the medium-term rallies and corrections.

Medium-term trends can, in turn, be broken down into short-term trends. These short-term trends are also referred to as tertiary trends. They have an even shorter "expiration date" and usually last less than two to three weeks.

Now that trends have been categorized, a few critical points need to be mentioned.

Purchases are appropriate for an investor when the primary trend is in the early phase of turning up. Liquidations are advisable for the investor when the primary trend is at an early stage in which it is turning downwards.

As a trader, you should make sure that you position yourself in a long-term upward trend so that you buy the beginnings of medium-term upward movements. About our categorization, the medium-term trend is of particular importance. It is used for most trend-following approaches for positioning.

The break of a tertiary downward trend in a secondary upward trend would accordingly be used for purchases. So you are acting in the direction of the primary trend and have, so to speak, tailwind from this long-term upward trend. This is another reason why the trend is your friend.

Trading in long-term downward moves is more complicated.

You should also act in the direction of the overarching primary trend, i.e., the medium-term downward movements. In other words, it makes sense that you sell the rallies short. This is easy to say, but generally not that easy for traders who have not yet gotten to know a bear market and are used to bull markets.

There are many reasons. On the one hand, the entry into the reversals of the medium-term upward trend is not as easy for inexperienced people as within a long-term bull market, on the other hand, rallies occur very suddenly and in an extremely dynamic form.

They sometimes become independent, that with the very simple tools of technical analysis you do not have a suitable forecasting tool to master these price movements.

Ultimately, however, it must also be stated here that a good trader acts in both directions of the market and that a bear market is particularly beneficial to him.

One aspect of the temporal classification of trends has to be mentioned, namely that this classification is only an approximate guideline.

Because in reality, we are dealing with countless forms of trend duration, for example, with trends that only last a few minutes, to trends that last for several decades, even centuries.

Chart traders often make use of the described classification of a trend. This also helps traders to communicate with each other.

If one of the chart traders mentions that this is a tertiary trend, the other chart trader knows what is meant, namely a short-term trend with duration of less than two to three weeks.

In practice, misunderstandings often occur because chart traders with different analysis intervals also have different views about long, medium, and short-term trends. For example, it may be that for one trader, a two-hour trend is already a primary trend, but for others, it is a tertiary trend.

CHAPTER 19

Tips and Tricks in Stocks

Almost everyone is searching for a shortcut, which leads them to success. It's human nature, we always look for miracles that can change everything. When it comes to the stock market, people are scared of losing their investments. They find ways that could become beneficial for them to secure their investments and make a profit. Avoiding loss in stocks is not an easy task, and even sometimes, experienced traders fail to achieve their goals. With time by learning more and more about stock market behavior is the only way to get success. There are some pro tips and tricks for investing in stock exchange which every trader should know:

Invest in Index Fund

One of the most important tips for investing is to invest in an index fund instead of looking to invest in individual stocks. It also depends upon your goals, but investing in individual funds is not a good approach. If you are taking stocks on a serious note, then investing in an index fund in a specific sector can be a great way to build your portfolio. It also helps to focus on one thing. There are some important points to remember while investing in an index fund. These are expense ratio and assets in total.

Focus on Mutual Funds

It is a well-known saying that putting all eggs in one basket is always the worst choice. When you are planning to buy some stocks shares, do remember not to invest in single stocks. Always find good growth mutual funds and put your money in it. This approach is the most secure one, but it seems boring and time taking. But many people love to focus on mutual funds. This technique helps to minimize the chances of losing investment.

Timing the Market

Many beginners think that there are sometimes when the selling or buying of stocks can make them profits. They all end up losing their money. Learning market volatility is not an easy task. Some experienced traders also believe that timing the market is not a good way to dominate in the stock market. You have to experience market fluctuations and sell or buy stocks accordingly. There is no best and worst time to buy or sell stock shares.

Set Goals

Setting up goals is always the best method that every person should follow, which leads to success. People without goals are like blind people. Before diving into the stock market, first of all, you should set the goals of your investments. When you have set a long term plan, then you will have a better understanding of what to do and how to reach the destination.

Five Golden Steps of Trading to Learn

- Setup: A setup is composed of a high probability pattern to follow on the chart. It also ensures the reason why you are considering a trade. You need to track them to make sure that how consistent they are.
- Strategy: There must be a way to trade the setup and the perfect plan for it, which seems to be working. Beginners should always work on the strategies and spend time on it.
- Entry: Entry can make a big difference. If you enter the right way, then you will end up making a profit. On the other hand, the wrong entry will lead you to make run out of money.
- Stop: There should always be a stopping point when you are going through live trade. This whole thing should be pre-planned, and you should know why you are going to stop.
- Profit Target: When things start getting right in your favor, you sometimes make bad decisions. Instead of regretting later on, make decisions to set a profit target.

Have a Balance of Investments
There are three types of investments, which are low, high, and moderate risk investments. All these investments have some pros and cons. Keeping a balance between these three risky investments can be a wise approach. If you are just starting, then prefer to invest in low-risk investments. As soon as you get some experience, move to the moderate and then high-risk investments. Low-risk investments can make you small profits, but instead of losing all of your money in high-risk investments, consider low and moderate risk investments.

Think for Long Term
We always look for short term methods which can make big profits. But in reality, these things are nothing. So always plan for the long term. Try to invest your time in learning the behavior of the stocks to make more profits in the long run.

Buy Value Stocks
Value stocks mean stocks that are established with minimum variations. If you want to get success in the stock market, you need to learn the volatility of the stocks. Buying value stocks can make your investments much safer and secure. While looking for value stocks, consider their earning ratio and price to sales ratio.

Diversify Investments Among Sectors
No one can predict the stock market uncertainty. A sudden change in the country or even abroad can affect the stock market. This sudden change may be a political activity, a storm, a disaster, or any unusual thing. Diversification of investments among sectors is a proven way to minimize the chances of losing investments.

How Much Risk Can You Take?
Before start trading, you should make your mind clear that how much risk you can take. There are some pros and cons of this strategy.

This strategy helps to have a better understanding of your game plan. Whether you are going for long term or you have made your plan for the long term in both cases, you need to be clear about how much risk you can bear.

Control Your Emotions
One of the key activities to achieve your goals in the stock market is to be patient. The stock market is considered one of the most uncertain market. No one knows what will happen in the next minute. People lose millions in seconds. To control your emotions at that time is a hard task. But to become a mature trader, you must have the capability to see your pockets running out of money. With a relaxed mind, you can set a plan B and C to get things in the right direction.

360 Degree View
Experienced traders always dive deep into learning more about stocks every day. This is the reason because of which you gain more and more experience. Whether you are buying or selling stocks shares, always be completely aware of what you are doing. You must be clear about what its outcomes will be. There must be some strategies for the sudden uncertainty to keep you stable in the market.

Automate Stocks
Automating your stocks is a key activity to gain more experience in the stock market. It also helps to build your security and play on the safe side. If you are not willing to do it manually, then Robo-Advisors are always there to assist you.

When you have a habit of regular investments, then you also avoid timing the market strategy.

Say No to Leverage
Leverage simply refers to start investing in stocks by borrowing money. There are many ways to borrow money. For example, you can also borrow from brokerage firms. Some people who are new to the stock market use this method to start their stock market journey.

There are bright chances of their failure because of high risks involved. This strategy can work for you when you have gained much experience in stocks.

Choose One Sector

Investing in one sector can be a better approach. Professional traders always invest in one sector. There are many advantages to investing in one sector. If your focus is on one industry, you will learn more in a short time. You will also start getting familiar with the fluctuations in the industry.

Risk vs. Return

Simply, more risky investments always have chances of big profits. On the other hand, less risky investments have small profit margins. So, you have to be clear with your game plan that how much return; you are willing to have. People always make foolish mistakes and go for high-profit margins and lose their money. So instead of regretting at that time, invest in between high and low-risk investments.

Buy Low Sell Higher

This is the most well-known method which almost all the traders apply. But some people get wrong with this strategy, and instead of making a profit, they end up with a loss. One of the most important factors to consider while buying low price stocks is to calculate their standard deviation.

If the stocks in which you are interested in buying have a 15% standard deviation, you are good to go. It will be a better strategy if your stock standard deviation falls below then 15% in a short period. There are bright chances of that specific stock that now it will go up.

Final Word

Many people believe that stocks are a scam, but if you set up things in the right direction, then these stocks can make you more profit than any other business in the world. All you need is not to focus on investing your money in the stock market, but you need to invest your time to learn the stock market. No one can ever predict with 100% surety about the stocks.

But by gaining more experience, you can understand the behavior of stocks and learn about the fluctuations. Before going for the live trade, consider all the above-mentioned tips and tricks for investing in the stock market to make your journey in stocks successful.

CHAPTER 20

Important Trading Rules to Follow

There is more to options day trading than just having a style or a strategy. If that was all it took, then you could just adopt those that are proven to work and just stick with them. Yes, options day trading styles and strategy are important, but they are not the end-all-be-all of this career.

The winning factor is the options day trader himself or herself. You are the factor that determines whether or not you will win or lose in this career—only taking the time to develop your expertise, seeking guidance when necessary, and being totally dedicated allows a person to move from a novice options day trader to an experienced one that is successful and hitting his or her target goals.

To develop into the options day trader you want to be, being disciplined is necessary. There are options day trading rules that can help you develop that necessary discipline. You will make mistakes. Every beginner in any niche does, and even experienced options day traders are human and thus, have bad days too.

Knowing common mistakes helps you avoid many of these mistakes and takes away much of the guesswork. Having rules to abide by helps you avoid these mistakes as well.

Below, I have listed 10 rules that every options day trader must know. Following them is entirely up to you, but know that they are proven to help beginner options day trader turn into winning options day traders.

The Rule for Success #1 – Have Realistic Expectations

It is sad to say that many people who enter the options trading industry are doing so to make a quick buck. Options trading is not a get-rich-quick scheme. It is a reputable career that has made many people rich, but that is only because these people have put in the time, effort, study, and dedication to learning the craft and mastering it. Mastery does not happen overnight, and beginner options day traders need to be prepared for that learning curve and to have the fortitude to stick with day trading options even when it becomes tough. Losses are also part of the game. No trading style or strategy will guarantee gains all the time. In fact, the best options traders have a winning percentage of about 80% and a losing average of approximately 20%. That is why an options day trader needs to be a good money manager and a good risk manager. Be prepared for eventual losses and be prepared to minimize those losses.

The Rule for Success #2 – Start Small to Grow a Big Portfolio

Caution is the name of the game when you just get started with day trading options. Remember that you are still learning options trading and developing an understanding of the financial market.

Do not jump the gun even if you are eager. After you have practiced paper trading, start with smaller options positions, and steadily grow your standing as you get a lay of the options day trading land. This strategy allows you to keep your losses to a minimum and to develop a systematic way of entering positions.

The Rule for Success #3 – Know Your Limits

You may be tempted to trade as much as possible to develop a winning monthly average, but that strategy will have the opposite effect and land you with a losing average. Remember that every options trader needs careful consideration before that contract is set up. Never overtrade and tie up your investment fund.

The Rule for Success #4 – Be Mentally, Physically, and Emotionally Prepared Every Day

This is a mentally, physically, and emotionally tasking career, and you need to be able to meet the demands of this career. That means keeping your body, mind, and heart in good health at all times. Ensure that you schedule time for self-care every day. That can be as simple as taking the time to read for recreation to having an elaborate self-care routine carved out in the evenings.

Not keeping your mind, heart, and head in optimum health means that they are more likely to fail you. Signs that you need to buckle up and care for yourself more diligently include being constantly tired, being short-tempered, feeling preoccupied, and being easily distracted.

To ensure you perform your best every day, here a few tasks that you need to perform:

- Get the recommended amount of sleep daily. This is between 7 and 9 hours for an adult.
- Practice a balanced diet. The brain and body need adequate nutrition to work their best. Include fruits, complex carbs, and veggies in this diet and reduce the consumption of processed foods.
- Eat breakfast, lunch, and dinner every day. Fuel your mind and body with the main meals. Eating a healthy breakfast is especially important because it helps set the tone for the rest of the day.
- Exercise regularly. Being inactive increases your risk of developing chronic diseases like heart disease, certain cancers, and other terrible health consequences. Adding just a few minutes of exercise to your daily routine not only reduces those risks, but also allows your brain to function better, which is a huge advantage for an options day trader.
- Drink alcohol in moderation or not at all.
- Stop smoking.
- Reduce stress contributors in your environment.

The Rule for Success #5 – Do Your Homework Daily

Get up early and study the financial environment before the market opens and look at the news. This allows you to develop a daily options trading plan. The process of analyzing the financial climate before the market opens is called pre-market preparation. It is a necessary task that needs to be performed every day to asset competition and to align your overall strategy with the short-term conditions of that day.

An easy way to do this is to develop a pre-market checklist. An example of a pre-market checklist includes, but is not limited to:

- Checking the individual markets that you frequently trade options in or plan to trade options in, to evaluate support and resistance.
- Checking the news to assess whether events that could affect the market developed overnight.
- Assessing what other options traders are doing to determined volume and competition.
- Determining what safe exits for losing positions are.
- Considering the seasonality of certain markets are some as affected by the day of the week, the month of the year, etc.

The Rule for Success #6 – Analyze Your Daily Performance

To determine if the options day trading style and strategies that you have adopted are working for you, you need to track your performance. At the most basic, this needs to be done on a daily basis by virtue of the fact that you are trading options daily. This will allow you to notice patterns in your profit and loss. This can lead to you determining the why and how of these gains and losses. These determinations lead to fine-tuning your daily processes for maximum returns. These daily performance reviews allow you to also make determinations on the long-term activity of your options day trading career.

The Rule for Success #7 – Do Not Be Greedy

If you are fortunate enough to make a 100% return on your investment, do not be greedy and try to reap more benefit from the position. You might have the position turn on you, and you can lose everything. When and if such a rare circumstance happens to you, sell your position and take the profits.

The Rule for Success #8 – Pay Attention to Volatility

Volatility speaks to how likely a price change will occur over a specific amount of time on the financial market. Volatility can work for an options day trader or against the options day trader. It all depends on what the options day trader is trying to accomplish and what his or her current position is.

There are many external factors that affect volatility, and such factors include the economic climate, global events, and news reports. Strangles and straddles strategies are great for use in volatile markets.

There are different types of volatility, and they include:

- Price Volatility, which describes how the price of an asset increases or decreases based on the supply and demand of that asset.
- Historical Volatility, which is a measure of how an asset has performed over the last 12 months.

- Implied Volatility, which is a measure of how an asset will perform in the future.

The Rule for Success #9 – Use the Greeks

The Greeks are a collection of measures that provide a gauge of an option's price sensitivity in relation to other factors. Each Greek is represented by a letter from the Greek alphabet. These Greeks use complex formulas to be determined, but they are the system that option pricing is based on. Even though these calculations can be complex, they can be done quickly and efficiently so that options day traders can use them as a method of advancing their trades for the most profitable position.

The 5 Greeks that Are Used in Options Trading Are

Delta

This Greek defines the price relationship between an option and its associated asset. Delta is a direct translation of a change in the price of the associated asset into the changing of the price of an option. Call options deltas to range from 1 to 0 while put options deltas range from 0 to -1. An example of delta as it relates to a call option is a call option with a delta of 0.5. If the price of the associated asset increases by $200, then the price of the call option will increase by $100.

Vega

This Greek is a measure of the sensitivity of the price of an option to the implied volatility of the associated asset. Option prices are greatly impacted by the volatility of the associated asset prices because greater volatility translates into a higher chance that the price of the associated asset will reach or surpass the strike price on or before the expiration date of the option.

Theta

This Greek is a measure of the sensitivity of the price of an option to time decay of the value of the option. Time decay describes the rate of deterioration in the value of the contract because of the passage of time. The closer the expiration date becomes, the more time decay accelerates because the time left to gain a profit narrows. Therefore, the longer it takes to reach an options' expiration date, the more value this option has because it has a longer time period to gain the trader a profit. The theta is a negative figure because time is always a diminishing factor. This figure becomes increasingly negative; the closer the expiration date becomes.

Gamma

This Greek measures the rate of change of the delta of an option. At its most basic, it tells the likelihood of an option reaching or surpassing the strike price.

Rho

This Greek is a measure of an option's value compared to changes in interest rates. Options with longer expiration dates are more likely to be affected by changes in interest rates.

The Rule for Success #10 – Be Flexible

Many options day traders find it difficult to try trading styles and strategies that they are not familiar with. While the saying, "Do not fix it if it is not broken," is quite true, you will never become more effective and efficient in this career if you do not step out of your comfort zone at least once in a while. Yes, stick with wanting work, but allow room for the consideration that there may be better alternatives.

CHAPTER 21

Advanced Strategies in Options Trading

Here, we'll see some propelled exchanging methodologies.

Long Straddle

In a long ride, you'll, at the same time, purchase a put and require the equivalent hidden stock. You're likewise going to need a similar strike cost and termination date. This method is something that can be used with a profoundly unpredictable stock. That way, you have the chance to benefit regardless of what direction the stock moves. Before we perceive how this functions, how about we step back for a second and review how we decide if an arrangement will be gainful. We are taking a gander at this from the purchaser's point of view. In a call choice, you're going to benefit when the stock surpasses the strike cost. Be that as it may, you should make sure to remember the premium for your estimation. In the event that you think a stock will go higher than $54, however, you're paying a $1 premium for each offer, at that point, you should put resources into a considered choice that has a strike cost of at any rate $55. In a put choice, it's a similar game, however, you're trusting the stock will go underneath the strike cost. Along these lines, for our new situation of purchasing a call and a put at a similar strike cost and termination date, we will purchase a put with a strike cost of $55. For straightforwardness, we will remain with a $1 premium. Presently you have to know the net premium, which will be the total of the premium from the call choice + the premium from the put choice, for this situation, $2.

You can get a benefit when one of two conditions are met:

Price of basic stock > (Strike cost of call + Net Premium). In our model, you will make a benefit when the measure of the fundamental stock is higher than $55 + $2 = $57.

Price of fundamental stock < (Strike cost of put − Net Premium). Utilizing our model, you'll see a benefit when the cost of the hidden stock is under $55-$2 = $53.

The most extreme misfortune for a ride will happen when the agreement lapses with the hidden exchange at the strike cost. All things considered, the two agreements terminate, and you're out the premiums paid for the two alternatives. A long ride has two make back the initial investment focuses. These are:

- Lower breakeven point: Strike cost − Net premium
- Upper breakeven point: Strike cost + Net premium

Recollect you purchase the two alternatives with a similar strike cost and termination date.

How about we take a gander at a straightforward model. A stock is exchanging at $100 an offer in May. The financial specialist purchases a call with a strike cost of $200 that terminates on the third Friday in June for $100. The speculator additionally purchases a put with a strike cost of $200 that terminates on the third Friday of June for $100.

The net premium is $100 + $100 = $200.

Presently assume that on the expiry date, the stock is exchanging at $300. The put lapses as useless since the stock cost of the fundamental is far over the strike cost of the put. Be that as it may, the financial specialist's call alternative lapses in the cash with an inherent estimation of 100 x ($300 - $200) = $10,000. Less the premium, the financial specialist has made $9,800. Then again, assume that the stock drops in esteem, and on the expiry is exchanging at $50. This time, the call alternative lapses as useless. The speculator can purchase 100 offers at a cost of $50 each for an all-out expense of $5,000. Presently he can offer them to practice the put choice at $200 an offer, so he nets $20,000 - $5,000 - $200 = $14,800.

This is an imaginary model, so whether the numbers are practical or not, so much isn't the point—the fact of the matter is that the financial specialist will benefit regardless of what befalls the stock cost.

Choke

The term choke is an adjustment of the ride. For this situation, you likewise, at the same time, purchase a call choice and a put choice. Be that as it may, rather than getting them at a similar strike value, you get them at various strike costs. For this sort of system, you will purchase somewhat out-of-cash alternatives. This is utilized when you feel that the fundamental stock will experience noteworthy unpredictability for the time being.

You will accomplish a benefit with a choke when one of two conditions are met:

- Price of hidden stock > (strike cost of call + Net Premium paid) or
- Price of basic stock < (strike cost of put – Net premium paid)

As a rule, the strike cost of the put is set at a lower esteem. Benefit is controlled by one of two prospects:

- Profit = Price of fundamental stock – strike cost of call – net premium
- Profit = Strike cost of put–the cost of fundamental stock – net premium

Bear Spread

A bear spread is beneficial when the fundamental stock value decays. Like the above methodologies, a bear spread includes the synchronous acquisition of more than one choice; be that as it may, in a bear spread, you purchase two alternatives of a similar kind. On the other hand, a call bear spread includes selling a call with a low strike cost and purchasing a call with a high strike cost.

Bull Spread

A bull spread is intended to benefit when the cost of the fundamental security has an unassuming cost increment. You can do a bull spread utilizing either call or put choices.

Hitched Puts

A wedded put is essentially a protection strategy like that we portrayed before. You purchase a stock, and a put alternative simultaneously, so as to shield yourself against potential misfortunes from the stock.

Money Secured Puts

In a money made sure about put, you secure the conceivable acquisition of stock by having cash in your investment fund to cover the buy. This will permit you to buy stock at a rebate, if you have enough cash in your record to really purchase the stock. To put it plainly, you compose a set alternative and put aside the money to buy the stock. Money made sure about put is done when you are bullish on the basic stock yet trust it will experience an impermanent downturn.

Rolling

Rolling an exchange just implies that you are all the while finishing off your current positions and opening new ones dependent on the equivalent basic stock. When rolling a position, you can change the strike value, the span of the agreement, or both. You can move forward, which intends to expand the termination date for the choice. A move up implies that you increment the strike cost when you open the new agreement. A move up is utilized on a call alternative when you accept the fundamental stock is going to increment in cost. At the point when you are exchanging put alternatives, you utilize a move down. All things considered, you close your alternative and revive it with the equivalent fundamental stock; however, with a lower strike cost. A higher strike value implies that the new position will be less expensive. When moving, you're going out so as to cutoff time. When rolling a call, you're trusting that the stock will ascend in cost. For this situation, you're moving to an out of the cash position. The cost of the new call will drop. With a put, the inverse happens, and the cost of the new put will increment.

CHAPTER 22

Strategies for Making the Best of a Bad Situation

Good strategies of any kind of options trading are the major key to any kind of success that is about to be unfolded in any activity. Strategies are normally laid in the trading plan and should be strictly implemented in every options trading move that is likely to be involved. Let us wholly venture into the best strategies so far in options trading.

- **Collars**. The collar strategy is established by holding a number of shares of the underlying stock available in the market where protective puts are bought and the call options sold. In this kind of strategy, the options trader is likely to really protect his or her capital used in the trading activities rather than the idea of acquiring more money during trading. This kind is considered conservative and rather much more important in options trading.

- **Credit spreads**. It is presumed that the biggest fear of most traders is a financial breakdown. In this side of strategy, the trader gets to sell one put and then buy another one.

- **Covered calls**. Covered calls are a good kind of strategy where a particular trader sells the right for another trader to purchase his or her stock at some strike price and get to gain a good amount of cash. However, there is a specific time that this strategy should be utilized, and, in a case, where the buyer fails to purchase some of the stock and the expiration date dawns, the contract becomes invalid right away.

- **Cash naked put**. Cash naked put is a kind of strategy where the options trader gets to write at the money or out of the money during a particular trading activity and aligning some particular amount of money aside for the purpose of purchasing stock.

- **Long call strategy**. This is the most basic strategy in options trading and the one that is quite easy to comprehend. In the long call strategy for options trading, aggressive option traders who happen to be bullish are pretty much involved. This implies that bullish options traders end up buying stock during the trading activities with the hope of it rising in the near future. The reward is unlimited in the long call strategy.

- **Short call option strategy**. The short call strategy is the reverse of the long call one. Bearish kind of traders is so aggressive in the falling out of stock prices during trading in this kind of strategy. They decide to sell the call options available. This move is considered to be so risky by the experienced options traders believing that prices may drastically decide to rise once again. This significantly implies that large chunks of losses are likely to be incurred, leading to a real downfall of your trading structure and everything involved in it.

- **Long put option strategy**. First things first, you should be contented that buying a put is the opposite of buying a call. So in this kind of strategy, when you become bearish, that is the moment you may purchase a put option. Put option puts the trader in a situation where he can sell his stock at a particular period of time before the expiration date is reached. This strategy exposes the trader to a mere kind of risk in the options trading market.

- **Trading time**. It is depicted that options trading for a longer period is much value as compared to a short period dating. The longer the trading day, the more skills and knowledge the trader is likely to be engaged in as he or she is likely to get the adequate experience that is needed for good trading. Mastering good trading moves for a while gives the trader the experience and adequate skills.

- **Bull call spread strategy**. In this kind of strategy, the investor gets to purchase several calls at a particular strike price and then purchases the price at a much higher price. The calls always bear a similar expiration date and come from the same underlying stock. This type of strategy is mostly implemented by the bullish options traders.
- **Bear put strategy**. This strategy involves a trader purchasing put options at a particular price amount and later selling off at a lower price amount. These options bear a similar expiration date and from the same underlying stock. This strategy is mostly utilized by traders who are said to be bearish. The consequences are limited losses and limited gains.
- **Iron condor**. The iron condor involves the bull call spread strategy, and the bear put strategy all at the same time during a particular trading period. The expiration dates of the stock are still similar and are of the same underlying stock. Most traders get to use this strategy when the market is expected to experience low volatility rates and with the expectation of gaining a little amount of premium. Iron condor works in both up and down markets are is really believed to be economical during the up and down markets.
- **Married put strategy**. On this end, the options trader purchase options at a particular amount of money and, at the same time, get to buy the same number of shares of the underlying stock. This kind of strategy is also known as the protective put. This is also a bearish kind of options trading strategy.
- **Cash covered put strategy**. Here, one or more contracts are sold with 100 shares multiplied with the strike price amount for every particular contract involved in the options trading. Most traders use this strategy to acquire an extra amount of premium on a specific stock they would wish to purchase.
- **Long or short calendar spread strategy**. This is a tricky type of strategy. The market stock is said to be stagnant, not moving, and waiting for the right timing until the expiration of the front-month is reached.
- **Synthetic long arbitrage strategy**. Most traders take advantage of this strategy when they are trying to take advantage of the different market prices in different kinds of markets with just the same property.
- **Put ratio back spread strategy**. This is a bearish type of options strategy where the trader gets to sell some put options and gets to purchase more options of just the same underlying stock with a similar expiration date and a lower price.
- **Call ratio back spread**. In this strategy, the trader uses both the long and short options positions so as to eradicate consistent losses and target achieving large loads of benefits over a particular trading period. The essence of this strategy is to generate profits in case the stock prices tend to elevate and reduce the number of risks likely to be involved. This strategy is mostly implemented by bullish kind of options traders.
- **Long butterfly strategy**. This strategy involves three parts where one put option is purchased at particular and then selling the other two options at a price lower than the buying price and purchasing one put at an even lower price during a particular trading period.
- **Short butterfly strategy**. In this strategy, three parts are still involved where a put option is sold at a much higher price, and two puts are then purchased at a lower price than the purchase price, and a put option is later on sold at a much lower strike price. In both cases, all put bear the same expiration date, and the strike prices are normally equidistant, as revealed in various options trading charts. A short butterfly strategy is the reverse way of the long butterfly strategy.
- **Long straddle**. The long straddle is also known as the buy strangle, where a slight pull and a slight call are purchased during a particular period before the expiration date reaches. The importance of this strategy is that the trader bears a large chance of acquiring good amounts of profits during his or her trading time before the expiration date is achieved.
- **Short straddle**. In this kind of strategy, the trader sells both the call and put options at a similar price and bearing the same expiration date. Traders practice this strategy with the hope of acquiring good amounts of profits and experience various limited kinds of risks.
- **Owning positions that are already in a portfolio**. Most traders prefer purchasing and selling various options that already hedge existing positions. This kind of strategy method is believed to incur good profits and incur losses too in other occurrences.

- **Albatross trade strategy**. This kind of strategy aims at gaining some amounts of profits when the market is stagnant during a specific options trading period or a pre-determined period of time. This kind of strategy is similar to the short gut strategy.

- **Reverse iron condor strategy**. This kind of strategy focuses on benefiting some profits when the underlying stock in the current market dares to make some sharp market trade moves in either direction. Eventually, a limited amount of risks are experienced and a limited amount of profits during trading.

- **Iron butterfly spread**. Buying and holding four different options in the market at three different market prices is involved in the trading market for a particular trading period.

- **Short bull ratio strategy**. Short bull ratio strategy is used to benefit from the amounts of profits gained from increasing security involved in the trading market in a similar way in which we normally get to buy calls during a particular period.

- **Bull condor spread**. This is a type of strategy that is designed to return a profit if the actual price of security decides to rise to a predicted price range during a specific trading period impacting good chunks of profits made to the options trader and a limited number of risks involved.

- **Put ratio spread strategy**. This strategy entails purchasing a number of put options and adding more options with various strike prices and equal kind of underlying stock during a particular options trading period.

- **Strap straddle strategy**. Strap straddle strategy uses one put and two calls bearing a similar strike price and with an equal date of expiration and also containing the same underlying stock that is normally stagnant during a particular trading period. The trader utilizes this type of strategy for the hope of getting higher amounts of profits as compared to the regular straddle strategy over a particular period of the trading period.

- **Strap strangle strategy**. This strategy is bullish, where more call options are purchased as compared to the put options, and a bullish inclination is then depicted in various trading charts information.

- **Put back spread strategy**. This back-spread strategy combines both the short puts and long puts so as to establish a position where the ratio of losses and profits entirely depends on the ratio of their two puts that are likely to be experienced in the market.

CHAPTER 23

Selling Options

If you have 100 or more shares of a particular stock, you can sell covered calls against your shares. This is a common strategy used by people to earn money off their shares, but you always face the risk that your shares will be called away if the option is exercised. One strategy that can be used is to sell out of the money calls when you don't expect the share price to rise to the strike price of the call option over the lifetime of the contract. For example, Facebook is trading at $190.25 a share. You can sell a $210 call for $0.64, so for all 100 shares, one option contract would net you $64. This is for an expiration date of 30 days. Or you could take a higher level of risk and sell a $195 call for $4.05, which would give you a premium of $405 per option contract. If you had 500 shares, then you'd receive $2,025 in premiums. Not a bad passive income, and all you have to do is hope that the share price stays below the strike price.

If the share price closes in on the strike price, then you will be faced with a dilemma—risk having the option exercised if the share price rises above the strike price, or you can buy back the option and cut into your profits. With a few days left to expiration, the option you sold may be worth $2.05, so you could buy back the five options you sold, and you'd reduce your net profit to $1,000.

You could go further out, even selling LEAPS. In that case, the premium paid is much larger. A Facebook LEAP with a $195 call that expires in 18 months has a premium of $30.58, so selling five contracts for your 500 shares could bring in an income of $15,290. Of course, there is a higher risk that the share price will rise above the strike price over an 18-month period than there is over the short term.

The one principle to keep in mind selling covered calls is that you could lose your shares if the option is exercised. With that in mind, you should only select a strike price that is of a higher amount than what you had paid for the shares. That way, if you are forced to sell the shares, then you are not taking a loss doing so. That can make losing the shares easier to deal with. So if we had purchased our shares at $200 a share, we would not select a $195 strike price because that represents a potential loss, which would be given by the price we paid for the shares minus the strike price and then less the premium aid, in this case, $200 - $195 - $4.05 so we'd end up losing $0.95 on the trade. If you had purchased the shares at a lower price, say $190 a share, then the $195 strike would make sense since if the stock price rose and the shares were called away, we'd still profit by selling the shares.

Protected puts are the put version of a covered call. The risk with a protected put is that the shares will be "put to you," and you will have to buy the shares, so you will be required to have enough capital in your account in order to cover the purchase. Of course, the trick to selling options is to pick a strike price where you think the option will expire worthlessly. There is always the risk that you are wrong, but if you think the share price is going to rise for Facebook, to use an example, you could sell a protected $190 put for $4.95, earning $495 per contract. If the share price rises, the options would expire worthlessly, and you would keep the premium and profit from the deal.

Selling Naked Puts

Selling naked puts is a popular strategy for traders that are given level 4 status. If you can get this level from your broker, you can consider this possibly profitable strategy. Of course, the key is choosing the right strike price.

When a put is "naked," that means it isn't backed by anything. However, you are still required by law to fulfill your obligations should the option be exercised, but one way that traders avoid this problem is by buying the options back if there is a chance they would be exercised. Time value may work in your favor, which will make the options cheaper and so you can buy them back and still profit.

Another consideration is to choose a relatively low implied volatility, which reduces the chances that the stock will move much over the lifetime of the option. But that is a trade-off as well, as implied volatility that is a few points higher can result in a large increase in the premium received for selling the option.

Consider IBM. The stock price is at $139.20, but you could sell a 30 day $135 put for $2.44, or $244. You could even sell in the money puts. A $145 put would sell for $748; if you sold five contracts, that would be a 30-day income of $3,640. Selling in the money puts could be risky, but beneficial if it was believed that IBM shares were set to rise in price. If the price rises above the strike price, then the options will expire worthlessly.

Selling LEAPS, while it carries a higher risk for a long time to expiration, gives a higher probability that the option will move in the amount, also allows you to sell at high premiums. A $130 put for IBM expiring in 18 months would sell for $13.20, so selling five contracts would give you a premium of $6,600. Bid-Ask spreads can be large for LEAPS, and the volume is probably small. For this particular option, we find that the bid-ask spread is about 80 cents, which isn't too bad, meaning selling it might not be that difficult. Daily volume is small at 10, but the open interest is 1,282. Experienced traders often recommend an open interest of 500 or higher since that indicates there are enough people buying the contracts. The risk with naked puts is that you will be forced to buy the shares. Again, if it looks like that might turn out to be the case, you can buy the contracts back. Selling out of the money options that expire in the near term can leave you in a better position since the options will probably expire worthlessly, and you will be able to keep the premium without having to buy back the options. If you have to buy the shares, the loss would be the share price minus the market price. But of course, you'd have to get the capital to buy the shares as well. So if you sold a put option on IBM with a strike price of $138 expiring in 6 weeks, it would sell for $3.70. If the share price dropped to $136, you'd have to use cash to buy the shares at $138, and possibly lose $2 a share by selling them—or you could simply keep them and wait for the price to go back up. Plus, your loss would be offset by the premium, so your break-even point is the amount of the strike price minus the premium paid.

Selling Naked Calls

You can also sell naked calls. This means that you sell call options without owning the shares of stock. The risk that the option will be exercised means that you would have to buy the shares at a higher market price and then sell them at the lower strike price. So the key here would be to sell out of the money calls at strike prices that you doubt the stock will reach over the lifetime of the option. The same strategies can be used, and if it looks like the share price is rising, you can buy the options back to avoid being assigned. Looking at IBM, some modest out of the money call options 30 days to expiration have good prices. A $141 call, which is almost $2 out of the money, is $3.55, so selling one contract would give you $355. Suppose that a stock was trading at $195 a share. You could sell a call with a 45-day expiration with a strike price of $200 for $4.46, or $446. If we find that the share price has risen to $197 with 10 days to expiration, the calls would now be priced at $1.88, or $188. So you could buy them back and still have a profit of $258 per contract, avoiding the risk that you would be assigned if the share price kept rising. Of course, at $3 out of the money, you might wait. When the price of the share rises to $199 with seven days left, the calls would be $218, so you'd be cutting a little more into your profits. But if it dropped $1 the next day, then the call option would only be worth $1.58. Remember, when you sell options, you make money on the time premium. Or put another way, time decay is your friend. Out of the money, options lose value rapidly as the expiration date approaches. The biggest risk with selling naked call options if you can't buy them back is having to buy the shares at a high price and then selling them at a loss to honor your obligations. Supposed that a stock is trading at $95 a share, and you sell a call option that has a $100 strike price. If the stock breaks out and, say, rises to $130 a share, someone might exercise the option. Since you sold the call naked, you'd be forced to buy the shares at $130 and sell them at the $100 strike price, losing $30 a share, which would be partially offset by the premium, which might be around $1 per share. So selling naked calls can be profitable, but carries a lot of risks as well. The key to selling naked calls successfully is picking the right strike price and choosing a stock that you don't believe is going to be having price movements that are large enough to cause the option to be in the money.

Broker May Force Sale

Note that options that expire in the money may be automatically exercised by most brokerages. So you will not want to let an option expire in the money unless you are prepared to buy or sell the shares as required.

CHAPTER 24

Tips for Success

If you are interested in embarking on the journey of earning money through options trading, there are a few issues to address before getting on board. Here are some of them:

Know When to Go off the Manuscript

While sticking to your plan, even when your emotions are telling you to ignore it, is the mark of a successful trader, this in no way means that you must blindly follow your plan 100 percent of the time. You will, without a doubt, find yourself in a situation from time to time where your plan is going to be rendered completely useless by something outside of your control. You need to be aware enough of your plan's weaknesses, as well as changing market conditions, to know when following your predetermined course of action is going to lead to failure instead of success. Knowing when the situation is changing, versus when your emotions are trying to hold sway is something that will come with practice, but even being aware of the disparity is a huge step in the right direction.

Avoid Trades that Are out of the Money

While there are a few strategies out there that make it a point of picking up options that are currently out of the money, you can rest assured that they are most certainly the exception, not the rule. Remember, the options market is not like the traditional stock market, which means that even if you are trading options based on underlying stocks buying low and selling high is just not a viable strategy. If a call has dropped out of the money, there is generally less than a 10 percent chance that it will return to acceptable levels before it expires, which means that if you purchase these types of options, what you are doing is little better than gambling, and you can find ways to gamble with odds in your favor of much higher than 10 percent.

Never Get Started without a Clear Plan for Entry and Exit

More important than setting entry and exit points, however, is using them, even when there is still the appearance of money on the table. One of the biggest hurdles that new options traders need to get over is the idea that you need to wring every last cent out of every successful trade. The fact of the matter is that, as long as you have a profitable trading plan, then there will always be more profitable trades in the future, which means that instead of worrying about a small extra profit, you should be more concerned with protecting the profit that the trade has already netted you. While you may occasionally make some extra profit ignoring this advice, odds are you will lose far more than you gain as profits peak unexpectedly and begin dropping again before you can effectively pull the trigger.

Read

At least one manuscript per week. It will teach you a lot of things, especially secrets. It will also provide you with a deeper understanding of the risks and rewards involved.

Trade for Income, not Wealth

If you do this thinking that you will be getting returns at 120%, you should reconsider. While one or two investments may yield such returns, the vast majority of options will not.

Start with Enough Capital

One of the first things that you need to make sure that you are set with is enough capital to help you get into the investment. Capital is the amount of money that you can place into your account to help pay for any of the transactions that you choose, and that can be used if you end up experiencing a loss while you are trading. You should always leave a little bit of money in your trading account. This is going to help you out when you are in the middle of a trade and can make it easier for your broker to keep working on trades without having to worry about a delay while your fund's transfer.

Avoid the Really Big Risks

Good options traders don't like a ton of risk, and they don't understand why they should take a big gamble just so they can get a tiny chance at a big payday. Rather than going after things like this, they are going to work on some trades that are high gain but lower in risk.

Be Sure to Diversify

Diversification is of the utmost importance. Having a portfolio that is not adequately diversified is a rookie mistake; however, many professional investors prefer not to diversify because of the way money is run in the United States.

Try Not to Panic

People don't make money from panicking in stressful situations. You will always encounter better times to leave or make a move rather than moves brought about by nervousness or panic. This is the downfall of a lot of people who are interested in investing but can't seem to master the craft.

See the Positive about It and Find Opportunities

The following time you notice there is a situation with trading that has brought a lot of panic on, you should immediately take the opposing side. Some of the best trades you can make involve the trade having been cleared out from people panicking and using their market orders, without understanding that the doors for exiting are not as large as they believe or assume. This doesn't mean all of the merchandise that people leave out of panic is worth investing in over long periods. Usually, when the market or stocks get socked, there will be a bounce-back that lets you leave in a better position than you would have if you went along with what everyone else was doing when they left too fast.

Trade at the Right Times

Since you are going to learn how to avoid big risks when you are an options trader, you are going to learn how to be very careful about your timing when it comes to entering and exiting the market. You have to be able to read the market the right way so that you can learn the best time to do both of those tasks. These investors have spent their time doing some research, and they know how to look at the big picture, rather than always calling up the broker and hoping that they can trust that person.

Learn How to Be Focused

There are quite a few people who have an idea that options trading is super easy, and then they jump in and become overwhelmed by what they are dealing with. If you are not used to this kind of investment, it may seem a bit hard to deal with in the beginning.

If you find that you are a person who is not able to easily focus on the task that you need to, then it is easy to have trouble with options trading because you are missing out on things. A trader who can maintain their focus for a long time is more likely to get more out of this trading style.

Never Follow the Crowd

One of the worst things that you can do is try to follow the crowd and hope that will work out well for you. Many beginners find it easy to look to the experts for advice, and then they will follow exactly what that expert says without doing any of their research or trusting their judgment. There is nothing wrong with getting advice from an expert, but your plan is not going to be the same as theirs. You are the only one who has an idea of your limits and your goals, and while you can listen to the advice that others give you, it is important to think for yourself and pick out a plan that works for you.

Keep It as Simple as Possible

Options trading is a complicated market by definition. You do not need to perplex things any further. Keep your strategies as simple as possible, use the simplest technical analysis tools, and manage your money in the simplest way possible. The rest will fall in place on their own.

Do Not Overtrade

When you start dealing with inexpensive options, it will be very easy to lose track of what you are trading with. Keep the number of contracts at a manageable level.

Pay Attention to Rankings

Especially if you are dealing with spreads and particularly if you are a novice, qualification rankings are available to consult at all times. An option that is not ranked high is not a good option, and it will probably cost you money.

Be Consistent

Before you ever make any trade, you are going to want to have a clear idea of the strengths and weaknesses of the various stocks in question as well as the best point to enter into a trade and at what point you are going to want to exit the trade if things go poorly, and also where you will exit if things ultimately go as well as you could expect. Once you have made a plan, it is important to stick with it even if your emotions are making a compelling argument for going in another direction instead. It is important to always trust in your plan as it was made during a period when you were thinking as rationally as possible, giving in to your emotions at this point is akin to gambling with your investments.

Keep the Mood of the Market in Mind at All Times

Fundamental and technical analysis is all well and good, but they will only take you so far before you run into instances where the market seems to balk at the logical choice and move off in an unexpected direction. This typically happens when the will of the market goes against the status quo thanks to an unexpected outpouring of support from traders who are thinking with their guts instead of their brains. The best way to go about doing this is to keep tabs on what the major players in your market of choice are up to, as this will typically act as a litmus test when it comes to the feelings of the market as a whole.

Keep a Trading Journal

While it might seem to be a waste of time at first, the fact of the matter is that keeping a journal of all of the trades you make can be an extremely effective way to analyze what you are doing right, as well as what you are doing wrong when it comes to options trading. While one type of analysis or the other might pique your interest when it comes to trading at the moment, keeping a trading journal will allow you to look at your trading results from a more analytical perspective once you have gotten a little more distance and perspective on what it is that you are doing.

To get the most out of this process, you are going to want to keep track of each trade you make along with the date, the state of the market, and the underlying asset that you were basing all of your trades on, whether the trade ended up being profitable or not and your emotional and mental state while you were trading.

These tips should be enough to get you started. As time passes by, you will learn what options to look for and what to avoid. Remember that seasoned traders are considered those who have spent years on this business, not just a few months.

CHAPTER 25

Predicting Directions

The world is full of uncertainty, and the stock market responds accordingly. Sure, financial instruments are based on the so-called fundamentals like monetary policy, interest rates, and equity essentials like sales and taxes. We have a stereotype of market makers as being steely-eyed, cold, and calculating automatons. They are not. They are human beings and are as emotionally involved in the market as an investor, 'man-on-the-street,' or anyone else. Emotions often affect the market based on the sometimes irrational response to this uncertainty. Recent events like the BREXIT outcome are examples of that emotional reaction.

The Basic Academic Economic Theory assumes that investors act rationally, i.e., a manner that best satisfies their economic interests. In the real world, markets do not always act rationally because human beings do not always act rationally.

Certain internal events will affect market performance like the end of quarter movements by fund managers to establish positions to make their quarterly reports look better. You can also observe drops in stock prices and indexes on Fridays, as holders get ready for the weekend by taking profits. Predicting market moves is sometimes like reading tea leaves, with a similar amount of hocus-pocus and mystery. However, successful investors learn or develop a sense of where the market is going and when.

There are five things an investor must do to succeed. They are pretty obvious, but we need to keep them in mind. The first is the Fundamental Analysis. The second is the Technical Analysis. They are sort of the 'meat and potatoes' of trading. Perhaps more important are the next three, Intuition, Patience, and Attention.

Intuition

Intuition can lead to many really good investments. Some years ago, a family was making regular vacation trips from Michigan to Florida. They soon noticed a new restaurant chain along the interstate highway called Cracker Barrel. Whenever they stopped at one, they had to stand in line, and the food was very good and at good prices. As they made more trips, they noticed that more and more Cracker Barrel restaurants were opening, all with the same waiting line. They invested in CRBL and watched the stock rise, from their entry price of about $5.00 to today's trading range of $150 to $175. That decision was an excellent example of intuition in trading. CBRL had identified a niche and filled it with good service and products.

L'eggs is a similar story. Consumers quickly reacted positively to the quality of the product and the catchy advertising, introduced in 1969. Those L'eggs plastic egg-like containers were a hit with crafts workers and carried the stock of Hanes to new highs. Many investors noticed that L'eggs was the right product at the time, was good quality, and had an exciting marketing promotion. This is the essence of the Intuition component of successful investing. Look for products that are satisfying a market niche, have good quality, and are well received by consumers.

Patience

Investing in the market, whether by buying and selling stocks themselves or by trading in options, requires patience. Sometimes an investor gets nervous and makes an irrational move just out of uncertainty. Traders must learn to be patient. No market moves so fast that the trader cannot make the proper trade in response to some change. Remember, options trading is not for the faint of heart. Nervous responses to extraneous conditions can wreck a well-planned strategy.

Attention

There is also no substitute for paying attention to the market and your positions. No, you do not have to spend every hour of every day watching the big boards. Remember that trading options are not a 'set it and forget it' activity. Traders can build very solid portfolios and make a handsome profit, but like any other job, the trader has to be current, not just in the market moves but also in global news and reports. Some resources have delightful features like daily free videos on changes in the market and outlooks from their experts. Keeping current is essential. Some traders will close out all positions while they are on vacation, and then resume trading when they return. And since most people use portable computer devices, laptops, tablets, smartphones, and so forth, they can spend time even on vacation, trading, and investing. Either way, you choose to do it, remember that options trading requires the investor to pay attention. Make that commitment before you start.

There are many tools available to traders and analysts to predict what is going to happen, at least to some extent. There are two schools of thought on the subject of market predicting; technical and fundamental methods used by informed investors. Most traders use a mixture of the two.

Fundamental Analysis

Fundamental analysis looks at several indicators to determine, at least as an estimate, of the direction of the economy, various industry groups, and individual stocks.

It begins with the general trend of the entire economy, both national and global. That old saying about the flapping wings of a butterfly in Africa causing a hurricane in Florida suggests that no national economy exists in a vacuum. There is an enormous interaction between them and among them. When the general economy rises, just like the tide, all individual boats rise, but not necessarily equally. Similarly, when the economy contracts, all sectors contract, but not equally. Some sectors will contract more than others.

In an expanding economy, sectors like technology, biotech, electronics manufacturing, and cyclical industries like major appliances and automobiles tend to expand. Here are some more cyclical industries:

- Heavy equipment
- Discretionary consumer goods
- Machines and tooling
- Restaurants and hotels
- Airlines

Typically, these stocks have a high Beta (β), meaning they respond quickly and strongly to fluctuations in the national and global economies.

Non-cyclical industries are those who are relatively safe during downturns, sectors like utilities, consumer staples, energy, and retailers. Counter-cyclical are those that can even thrive in economic downturns, like discount retailers, auto parts retailers, and big-box building suppliers.

Importantly for options traders, option prices respond to the volatility and trend of the underlying stocks, so traders need to pay close attention to the economic cycle and the sectors of interest to them.

When an investor or options trader has identified the economic trend, i.e., expanding, or contracting, she will then focus on a sector of interest like durable goods, finance, or hospitality, to name just a few. Within that sector or industry, she will then examine the individual companies, looking for those who will lead the way. She will do this by evaluating the company's business model, business plan, management quality, and firm financials. Assessments of business models and business plans can be gained from resources like analyst's reports, annual reports, and public commentary. She will examine management quality by looking at results, internal business indicators like return on investment, return on sales, and debt levels compared with market capitalization. She will read and understand the various documents like the balance sheet, the income or profit and loss statement, cash flow positions, and debt positions for the firm she is interested in. Most of this information is available online and through public documents, including annual reports. Documents like annual reports, of course, are written by insiders and may not be completely objective. Various industry analysts and experts may offer more objective insights. These are available through brokers and online sites.

Technical Analysis

Many investors base their trading decisions on technical factors that look at past performance with knowledge of present and past economic conditions. This analysis is dominated by examining charts that reflect stock performance over some time. Using these charts, they can estimate upcoming stock moves and therefore act on those forecasts by buying and selling options. The following charts describe some important market moves that any options trader needs to know. The Symmetrical Triangle in Chart 1 shows a stock that is trading within a diminishing range. The upper line represents a resistance line, and the lower is the support line. As the price varies between these converging lines, it is often an indication of a coming breakout. With a breakout to the upside, the options trader will buy calls to cover a long position in anticipation of the upside swing. On the other hand, if the pattern shows a likelihood of a breakout below the support line, the trader might choose to buy puts in anticipation of the drop in market price.

Chart 1: Triangle Pattern

Triangle patterns can also be pointed upward or downward, showing a general tendency for the stock to rise or fall.

Chart 2: Triple Top

Chart 2 shows a condition called a triple top. The horizontal dotted line below the chart is the support line, and the upper dotted line is the resistance line. The chart shows the market price breaking out low. This is an occasion to sell puts. The pattern could have broken out upward, crossing the resistance line. Notice that that chart can also be inverted, making a triple bottom. These charts indicate the direction of the stock and tips the options trader off to trade in either puts or calls.

Chart 3: Head and Shoulders

Chart 3 shows a pattern called 'head and shoulders.' This is slightly different from a triple top pattern in that the middle peak tends to be higher. Head and shoulders patterns can breakout either up or down. Either way, it presents an opportunity for options traders. The dotted line shows the recent support line. This pattern happens to break out down, but it very well could have broken out upward.

Bollinger Bands

Bollinger bands are probability bands around a moving average line. These bands are usually set at either 1 or 2 standard deviations from the historical stock prices, the closing prices for each day. Movement outside the Bollinger Bands indicates a change in the underlying stock reflecting market changes. Breaking through the Bollinger Band acts as a signal to the options trader to take action.

Many other technical indicators are valuable to options traders. The various resources will provide excellent education and insights into both fundamental and technical analysis techniques. Most investors and traders use both fundamental and technical analysis, and the combination is a personal preference. Just make sure you are familiar with the various indicators and what they can tell you. Be careful to use the correct tools for each condition. There is no "one size fits all" tool; each trader has to develop her system of analysis. The key to success is Intuition, Patience, and Attention.

CHAPTER 26

Trader Psychology

Trading with Emotions

It is common for traders to have their emotions and feelings jumbled up when day trading, from the highs and the lows they experience from the market. This is a far outcry from the confident self that a trader usually poses before the markets open, bubbling up with excitement over the money and profits that they intend to make. Emotions in trading can mess up and impair your judgment and your ability to make wise decisions. Day trading is not to be carried out without emotions, but rather as a trader. You should know how to work your way around them, making them work for your good.

A clear, levelheaded, and stable mind should be kept at all times, whether your profits are on the rise, or whether you are on a losing streak. This is not to mean that as a trader, you are to disconnect from your emotions. One cannot avoid emotions, but when confronted with the real market scenarios, you have to learn how to work through and around them. The personality type of a trader plays a huge role in determining which kind of a trader they are. The cautious traders are mostly controlled by fear when opening up trades, while the risky type is on the greed motivated bandwagon. Fear and greed are such huge motivators that they go a long way in the layout of losses and profits.

Greed

A trader may be fueled to earn more money by checking their balances in their accounts and seeing it be as of a low level. While this may be a motivator to work hard, some traders take it too far, wanting to earn a lot of money right there and then.

They make mistakes while trading that has reverse effects than the intended ones. Such mistakes include an overtrade, taking unnecessary risks, among others.

Taking Unnecessary Risks

Greed for more money will seek to convince the trader to take risks that are not worth so as to achieve a certain financial threshold in the trading account. These will most likely end up in losses. The risky traders may take risks such as high leverage, that they hope will work in their favor, but at the same time may have them making huge losses.

Making an Overtrade

Due to the urge to make more and more money, a trader may extend over long periods of time trading. Commonly these efforts are too naught, for overtrading through the highs and the lows of the market put a trader in a position where their accounts can be wiped off as a result of greed. Not putting into account, the time of trading and plunging into opening up trades without having done an analysis will most likely result in a loss.

Improper Profit and Loss Comprehension

Wanting to earn a lot of money within a short period of time will have a trader not closing a trade that is losing, maintaining the losses, and on the other hand, overriding on profit-making trade until a reverse in the market happens, canceling out all the gains made. It is advisable to maximize and specialize in a successful trade and close a losing trade early enough, avoiding major losses.

Fear

Fear can work in both directions, as a limit to an overtrade, or also as a limit to making profits. A trader may close a trade so as to avert a loss, the action motivated by fear. A trader may also close a trade too early, even when on a winning streak in making gains, in fear that the market will reverse and that there will be losses. In both scenarios, fear is the motivator, working in avoiding failure a success at the same time.

The Fear to Fail

The fear to fail in trading may inhibit a trader from opening up trades, and just watch as the market changes and goes in cycles when doing nothing. The fear of failing in trading is an inhibitor to success. It prevents a trader from executing what could have been a successful trade.

The Fear to Succeed

This type of fear in trading psychology will make a trader lose out his profits to the market when there was an opportunity to do otherwise. It works in a self-harming way in the market scenarios. Such traders in this category fear having too much profit and allow losses to run, all the while aware of their activities and the losses they are going to make.

Bias in Trading

There are several market biases that a trader may tend to make that may be as a result of emotions play, which traders are advised against. In the psychology of trading, these biases may influence a trader to make unwise and uncalculated trading decisions that may prove to be loss-making ones.

Even when the trading biases are in focus, as a trader, you have to be aware of the emotions in you and come up with ways to keep them in check and maintain a cool head in your trading window. Together with the main reason behind all of them; fear. They include the bias of overconfidence, confirmation, anchoring, and loss.

Bias in Overconfidence

It is a common occurrence with traders, especially new traders, that when you make a trade with huge profits, you get in euphoria in the state of winning. You want to go on opening up trades, with the belief that your analysis cannot go wrong, boiling down to the profits and gains you've made. This should not be the case. One cannot be too overexcited and overconfident in the analysis skills that you believe you cannot make a loss. The market is a volatile one, and therefore the cards can change at any given time, and when they do, the over-excited and overconfident trader now turns into a disappointing one. Get your analysis of the market right before opening up any trade, regardless of the last trades, whether they were a loss or again.

Bias in Confirming Trades

In trading psychology, the bias in confirmation of a trade you have already made, justifying it, is one of the factors that waste a lot of time and money for traders. This type of bias is mostly associated with professional traders. After making a trade, they go back to evaluating and analyzing the trade they just made, trying to prove that it was the correct one, whether they sailed according to the market. They waste a lot of time digging for information that they are already aware of. They could also be proving that the mistake they made in opening a wrong trade and making a wrong move was a correct one. Nevertheless, the bias in confirmation kicks in when a trade they made turns out to be correct, and that strengthens their resolve in their researching skills, plunging them further in wasting time in proving to themselves already known facts. They could also lose money in the process, and it is thus advisable against this form of bias in trading.

Bias in Anchoring on Obsolete Strategies

This type of bias in the psychology of trading applies to the traders that rely so much on outdated information and obsolete strategies that do more harm than good to their trading success. Anchoring on the correct but irrelevant information when trading might make the trader susceptible to making losses, a blow to the traders who are always lazy to dig up for new information on the market. Keeping up with the current events and factors that may have an impact on the market is one of the key aspects of having a successful trading career. Lazy traders will tire of keeping tabs with the ongoing economic and even political situations whose influence is exerted on the foreign exchange market. An example of this is that some traders will have a losing trade, but their hope is that the markets will reverse their assumptions based on obsolete information and strategies. Carry out extensive research, mindful not to be too much time consuming, to ensure you make trades in accordance with the right data.

Bias in Avoiding Losses

Trading with the motive to avert losses usually boils down to the factor of fear. There are some traders whose trading patterns and their trading windows are controlled by fear of making losses. Having gains and making profits is not a motivation to them when fear hinders them from opening trades that could have otherwise been profitable. They also close pas trade too early, even when making profits in a bid to avert the losses, their imaginable losses. After carrying out a proper and detailed analysis on the market, go for making profits without being deterred with the bias of avoiding to make a loss, for that just holds many traders own. Come up with a plan for your day trading to deal with doubts on the trades you are to make.

Psychology Affecting Traders' Habits

Psychological aspects affect habits in trading, the mistakes, and the winning strategies that a trader comes up with. Explained below are the negative habits that many traders make, with the influence of psychology on their habits.

Trading without a Strategy

With no trading strategy and plan, a trader will face challenges with no place to refer to the anticipated end result. A proper strategy should be drawn by a trader to be a referencing point when facing a problem in trading in the market. It should be a clearly constructed plan, detailing what to do in certain situations and which type of trading patterns to employ in different case scenarios. Trading without a strategy is akin to trading to lose your money.

Lack of Money Management Plans

Money management plans are one of the main aspects of trading, and without solid strategies in this, it is difficult to make progress in making gains in the trades opened. As a trader, you have to abide by certain principles that will guide you in how to spend your money in the account in opening up trades and ensuring that profits ensue from that. Without money management plans, a trader would be trading blindly with no end goal in mind, risking the money in non-profitable trades.

Wanting to Be Always Right

Some traders always go against the market, placing their desire of what manner they would like the market to behave in. They do not follow the sign that the market points to, but rather they follow their own philosophy, not doing proper analysis and always wanting to be right. Losses ensue from such psychological habits. When the trading window closes, the market will always overrule the traders. Thus, a trader's want to be always right against the market is overruled.

CHAPTER 27

Money Management

What Is Money Management?

Money management is how you handle your finances, your savings, your expenditure, and investments. It is making sure you can survive a financial crisis. It means planning a budget for your long-term goals and also making investments that will help you to successfully achieve your goals. When you manage your money, you will be able to make wise purchases. Otherwise, you will always complain of having less amount of money no matter how much your income is. It can also be known as investment management. Money management is more about risk. When you have better money management skills, you will reduce the risk. You must understand all the areas of money management to be able to avoid any risks. Plan with a negative bias, always ask yourself "what-if" scenarios, take action, and plan. When budgeting for money management, make sure you are spending less than what you save. Excellent money management will help you monitor your spending before going beyond your budget. By doing this, you will secure your savings. You will be able to invest if you make the right decisions. Avoiding taking on more risks will help you reach your financial goals. The strategies you use in your investments play a significant role in your success. When you decide to invest, the first important thing to focus on is the risk involved, and you can avoid it. Here are some of the basics, advantages, and disadvantages of money management.

The Basics of Money Management

Money management is a wide term that involves solutions and services in the entire investment industry. You can now have a wide range of resources in today's market and also phone applications to help you manage all your finances. Investors can also seek services from a financial advisor for professional money management. Financial advisors work with private banking and even brokerage services to offer money management plans involving services like retirement and estate planning.

The Advantages of Money Management

Better Tracking of Your Money

When you have a reasonable budgeting plan, you can track how you use your money, and you can monitor every expense. This is a significant benefit to you, as you can spend less and end up saving more money. Monitor your expenses for some months and then change your budgeting by removing the less required expense and allocate that money to your savings plan, a retirement plan, or a vacation fund. Excellent money management will help you stay on track; you will be able to pay your bills on time, will be able to stay within your limit, and avoid bank account overdraws. Poor money management can put you in bad debt quicker than a blink of an eye. You can prevent those nasty fees charges when you go over your limit. By having an excellent budgeting plan, you will avoid overspending.

A Good Retirement Plan

Better money management and savings plans will help you in the long term. You will be able to secure your future and have an excellent retirement plan. With better money management skills will give you a better retirement plan for you. No matter how much you save, even when you save and invest a small amount of money, it will provide you with a more significant amount for your retirement later in life.

Peace of Mind

Proper money management brings you peace of mind. Having bills on the counter and having no idea on how you will pay the bills or not having the money to purchase something that you needed. All these issues can be difficult to face each day. Managing your money wisely and experience all the benefits of sound money management, you will enjoy peace of mind, and you can provide for yourself and your family, too.

The Disadvantages of Money Management

Rapid Changes

With the rapid changes in the financial world, it is required to change your management plans every time. It is sometimes challenging to adjust your planning to incorporate the fast-changing situations. Unless your plan can help to adopt the new techniques, it will be limited.

Time-Consuming

Managing your money can sometimes be a time-consuming exercise. It requires you to make the estimates as accurate as possible. However, you can use software and mobile applications to assist you with planning, and this may reduce the time you will take if you were not using the technologies. And if you have less knowledge about money management, it will take you more time to achieve this.

Inaccuracy

When planning, you make a lot of assumptions in terms of estimation of your expenses. Any shift like economic downturn or the change in the currency rate or interest rates can change your estimates in your planning.

Why Is Money Management Important?

Money turns to wealth when it is well-managed. It is an instrument which is used to pursue wealth. For wealthy people, having and spending money does not bring them happiness, which gives them joy is having a steady income, and they can go on achieving their goals—and being able to leave a legacy to their loved ones. Money management focuses on your habits, and your decision making can have affected the outcome in your long-term strategies. In pursuit of wealth, there are many powerful elements such as debts, risks, and taxes that can take away all the hard work you have put in to achieve your goals. This is a life skill that everyone must learn. You don't have to be financially savvy to start managing your money. There is plenty of information available to help you better understand your finances. The following are the importance of money management:

- **Establishing clear goals**. Have a clear approach to your decision in money management to build your wealth. Making the best decision will bring you closer to your goals. Also, set some clear and realistic goals which you want to achieve and set a time horizon for achieving them. Setting up clear goals will help you track where you are, and this will help you see your progress towards your goals. Some people give up earlier due to not being able to see their progress. You can be able to see your progress and stay encouraged if you break your goals into short term milestones. Finally, have clear and quantifiable goals to help you to make clear decisions. Abandon any choices that will not get you closer to your destination.

- **Controlling your cash flow**. Spend less than what you earn will help you accumulate wealth. You can't be financially successful if you are not tracking and monitoring your expenditure. Drawing up a spending plan and religiously following the plan might seem trivial, but it's central to the success of the wealthiest people in the world. If you own a business, your goal will be to find ways of increasing your monthly profits, which you will use to invest in for more growth. You will learn how to prioritize your spending when you have a solid money management plan and also by making the right decisions, which will bring you closer to your goals.

- **Budgeting**. Creating a household income budget is an essential part of personal money management. Budgeting will help you better understand your cash flow, thus giving you a clear understanding of your current financial situation.

- **Debt management**. There is proper financial education to help you understand consumer debt and how it works. There are also financial advisers and credit counselors who provide advice on how you can review your debts, your loan terms, and how you can pay off the debt quickly and stress-free.
- **Managing your risks**. Your risk exposure increases as you continue accumulating your wealth. You might think that wealth can make life easier, but it does not. The ignored reality is that it can make life more complicated. Getting a bigger house, expensive cars, and lavish lifestyles. These bring financial exposure and the potential to lose if all is great.

Have a risk management assessment in your money management plan with also protection strategies to help prepare you for the unexpected. Some of the unintended exposure include:

- Income loss due to illness or accident
- Death of the breadwinner in the family
- Asset exposure to liability claims

Money management will provide you with a 360-degree view of your financial status, and having financial discipline will assist you in overcoming these obstacles. With a solid money management principle, you will have better control of your financial goals.

- **Being tax efficient**. Paying taxes is a responsibility; however, there is no obligation to paying more than necessary. Most people are not aware of how much taxes they are paying and the results of the unnecessary taxes and how it affects their wealth accumulation abilities. Money management does not focus on what you make but what you get after paying your taxes. Tax characteristics of your investment and your overall portfolio must be considered. The first thing to consider is the account location, the money allocation on different types of accounts based on respective tax treatment. Secondly, the asset location, wherein you allocate different types of investments among the different types of accounts on the tax treatment—for example, allocating your least tax-efficient assets to a tax-deferred account such as 401(k). The taxable accounts can hold in a tax-efficient investment such as low turnover funds. This will give you more options for distribution of income in the more tax-efficient retirement, thus enabling you to accumulate more wealth faster.

CHAPTER 28

Trading Errors and Mistakes

When you trade options, you generally get profit when the stocks go sideways, up, or down. Option strategies are a great way to get good gains and protect them while avoiding losses as well. You can control significant parts of stock with small cash outlay, but all of this sounds too good to be true, as there is a catch associated with this.

You can lose more than what you invested initially in little to no time while trading options. This is why it is crucial to move forward with ample care and caution. Many times, even expert traders make simple errors that lead to grave results.

Options and trading them can help people gain a lot of profit. It is necessary to trade the options correctly and avoid any potential mistakes that can lead to a huge loss. It is recommended to have a list of common mistakes that happen when you try to become an advanced trader. Many of these mistakes are similar to the mistakes that are made by new traders. This is why many traders tend to lose their entire account right after they start. But most of these errors are simple enough to avoid them. Let us have a look at the variety of errors and mistakes that you should avoid while trading options. You should always keep these things in mind, as they will help you to earn a lot of profit while avoiding loss as well.

Avoid Short Time Frames

In the past few years, many options brokers have begun to provide a large range of time frames. Nowadays, many brokers offer users options contact periods that are extremely small; in fact, many brokers also offer a minute-long contact period. These periods generally attract new users who do not have experience of trading. But they can also attract experienced traders who are on a lookout to get rich quickly. If the statistics are consulted carefully, it is clear that this novel approach is a fad that can lead to huge problems. Markets are impossible to predict, and no one can deduce what the market will do in the next minute or so. This is why these options contacts should be avoided at all times. Do not go after them, as they will surely lead to a loss.

The market is difficult to predict even in the broader frames such as months and weeks, but in the case of longer time frames, traders can generally assess the dominant trends. They can also make a stance that understands and reflects the condition of the options market.

Use Conservative Leverage Levels

Another error that can be avoided with ease is using extreme amounts of leverage. This generally takes place in many variations. For instance, some traders who find themselves in a loss begin to look for new strategies that can make up for their losses. When traders add new positions at higher or lower levels (depending on the direction of the original trade), it is generally known as doubling-up. This term is often considered to be a polite and diplomatic version of 'adding to a loser,' which again describes the same phenomenon.

Many other mistakes can be observed when traders use very little margin in positioning. This brings out the potential for significant profits, but it can also make a trading account vulnerable to extreme losses if the market fails to move in the correct direction. These are some of the many reasons why it is always better to avoid chasing quick profits and work hard instead. It is recommended to use a conservative but functional approach that will limit the leverage levels on an average scale.

Use an Economic Calendar

Many trading failures can happen when the trader uses an economic calendar before creating and establishing new positions on the market. It is crucial to understand that for any tradable assets, there always exist relevant events that may result in shocking and surprising volatility in the prospective prices. These events generally change based on the type of asset that is currently being traded. For instance, the people who are trading stock options, or are dealing with stock benchmarks need to a have a proper understanding of when the major earning reports come out. In most cases, this results in volatility inequities. It can be quite impossible to point out the direction in which this volatility works and towards which direction it will move in the future. Due to this, it is generally a smart plan to wait for important news events to go away before you decide to establish positions on the market. Normally, most of these events are scheduled in advance, so it is recommended to have an economic calendar handy. It will prove to be a great asset for all traders if you use it proactively.

Focus on Liquid Assets

This is contentious advice for some people, but it is recommended to focus on liquid assets. Many options traders seek opportunities in assets that are not as frequently traded as others. It is possible to make a significant profit using these types of trades. But if you want to continue with a conservative outlook and reduce the chances of risks, you should consider liquid assets. Liquid assets will help you avoid risks and still gain profit. Liquid assets are the most commonly and frequently traded assets. These include stock benchmarks, blue-chip stocks, silver, gold, oil, and forex majors such as EUR/USD, USD/GBP, USD/JPY, and AUD/USD, etc.

Always Have an Exit Strategy

When you enter the world of finance and trading, you need to learn how to control and manipulate your emotions. This does not mean that you should forgo all your emotions and become a fearless entity. Instead of doing that, you need to create a plan and stick to it as much as possible. You need to have an exit plan.

It is necessary to have a plan B or an exit strategy before you decide to start trading. If you plan to put a lot of money into trading and do not have an exit plan, you may suffer monumental losses. It is crucial to have an exit strategy for people who use American-style options trading. It is necessary because, in this style, the traders are allowed to close the position before the expiration of the contract happens automatically. No trade can provide your 100% chances of success because the market changes all the time and is volatile. This means that traders need to prepare themselves for all kinds of scenarios, especially when the markets do not follow the planned or expected trajectory.

You may have never used an exit strategy before and have still fared well in the past, but there is nothing worse than losing a lot of money just because you cannot get out of the market. The most successful options traders are the ones who have a plan prepared for every possible scenario. To begin this, you need to check and develop an exit strategy before the market starts to work against you.

You need to create a downside exit point, an upside exit point, and all your timeframes for all other exits when things are going your way.

It is recommended to form an upside exit plan and a worst-case scenario downside exit plan as well. If you reach your upside goals, you should clear your positions immediately. Do not act too greedy. If you reach your downside loss step, clear your positions immediately. Do not let yourself suffer more losses by gambling your options by waiting for the price to come back.

Many people tend to avoid this advice because the circumstances change frequently. But don't do it. Make a plan and stick to it as much as possible. Many traders make a plan and then forget it and follow their emotions instead. It may work a couple of times, but it may eventually lead to huge losses.

(OTM) Call Options

Purchasing OTM or out of the money calls outright is a difficult way to earn money through options trading, while this option may sound great for beginners and some experts because they are extremely cost-effective and seem efficient. Buying them cheap allows you to put money on a lot of things. Many people think that this is a safe option because it coincides with the pattern that people who indulge in equity trade are used to this. This patter i.e., buying low and selling high, is present almost everywhere. But if you plan to use only this strategy, you will limit yourself significantly and may start losing money regularly.

Try selling the OTM call option on a stock that you own already. This should be your first strategy. In trading terms, it is known as a covered call strategy. The best thing about the covered call strategy is that the risk factor is not a result of selling the option when the option is covered by a stock position. It also has a lot of potentials to help you earn money on stocks when you want to sell the stock when the price of the stock goes up. This strategy is great because it can it allows you to 'feel' how OTM option contract prices fluctuate all the time, especially when the expiration is approaching rapidly. In such cases, the stock prices fluctuate as well.

A drastic risk is situated in owning the stock, though. Selling the call option does not produce capital risks as such, but it will limit your upside. This means that it will create an opportunity risk. Another risk is when you plan to sell the stock upon the assignment when the market rises. Your call then becomes exercised.

Misunderstanding Leverage

You will be surprised to know that even a lot of advanced traders fail to consider the leverage factor option. Many people tend to misuse this option that the contracts offer because they do not realize how much risk they are taking due to it. They often tend to buy short-term calls.

It is recommended to become a master of leverage. It should be your priority, especially for beginners who are looking to enter the advanced strategy. If you generally trade 100 share lots, instead of considering a lot of shares, stick to one share only. Similarly, if you generally trade 400 share lots, stick to 4 contracts. This is a decent starting amount. If you fail to succeed in these sizes, then you will surely fail in the bigger sizes as well.

Not Being Open to New Strategies

Change is necessary, and accepting change can help you become an overall successful person. Many options traders believe that buying out-of-the-money options or never selling in-the-money options is bad should never be done. These may seem like a childish strategy until you get caught in a trade that is moved against you.

All experienced options traders have gone through this in the past. This scenario can be quite difficult, which is why many people try to break their rules and work against it.

CHAPTER 29

How to Become a Millionaire with Options Trading

Highly Profitable Trading Strategies for Any Market Condition

Most investors and traders at the securities markets often aim to buy low then sell high and make a profit. However, options traders are the key layers in any market. This is because they can earn large amounts of money regardless of market conditions. The options traders can make money in any market environment, even where there are no trades up or down. The reason is that options contracts are flexible in different ways. This versatility is what makes them such powerful market tools for continued profitability. Here are some profitable approaches that you can adopt.

Writing options

One of the best ways of winning at options is to write options. You can write some pretty sophisticated strategies which are capable of earning your top dollars. As a writer, you get to earn what is known as a premium. This is money that you earn even if the investor does not eventually use it. It is very possible to write profitable commodities-based options regularly. Speculators can come up with profitable options that they believe will fare well in the options markets.

The Straddle Strategy

This is another approach that can help you get rich with options trading. Options mostly involve the buying of security that then turns profitable when the underlying commodity moves in a particular direction. It could be up or down but all that is necessary is a movement. A straddle is a great choice of options investment vehicle because it does not desire a specific outcome as is the case in other situations. With a straddle, you can purchase both calls and put options with the same expiry dates and at similar strike times. The straddle strategy can be successful if and only if the underlying security of the option sees movement in either direction just so long as the movement is sufficiently large to cover the cost of premiums in both directions. Speculators can write straddle options if they believe that it is going to do well in the market.

The Collar Strategy

We also have a strategy known as the collar strategy. It is considered a pretty challenging options strategy to understand. However, a seasoned speculator can write one for you but only if he owns the underlying asset.

By owning the asset, he can take the risk.In this instance, the best option is an out-of-the-money put option. This is beneficial because should the commodity price go down, then the losses will only be minimal as it is a put option. However, should the commodity move upwards, then the trader will make a tidy profit.

The Strangle Strategy

The strangle strategy is in some ways similar to the straddle. This is because they both include the buying of a call and put option as well as the same expiration date. The only difference is that they have different strike prices. For speculators, it is possible to use the information available to enter a low-cost position.When a trader or speculator opts for this strategy, they choose a low-cost entry because either or both of the options contracts may be bought out-of-the-money. As such, it may not be worthwhile exercising the right afforded by the shares. Both the straddle and strangle can be written by a speculator or even the trader.

So, what is the Most Profitable Options Strategy?

We have now looked at quite a several options trading strategies all of which are profitable and easy to execute. There are more than 40 different variations of options trading techniques. This makes it a pretty difficult job to determine the most profitable options trading strategy.A lot of the time, traders try to find trades that will not lose their money. Also, there is a lot of varied opinions out there about the best and most profitable strategies. Fortunately, most options trading strategies offer very attractive returns with huge margins being quite common.

However, it can be a risky venture, so it is advisable to proceed with caution even as you seek to become a wealthy millionaire.

Options Trading is Quite Profitable

Some express concern about profitability as well as risks posed by options trading. Fortunately, it has been proven, over the years, to be quite profitable.Trade-in options provide you with leverage which offers you the inherent right to control a huge number of shares. This kind of leverage offers returns far greater than what selling stocks only can offer.

If you can make use of the leverage afforded by stock options, then you stand a great chance of making huge profits. These are profits made from just minuscule movements of the underlying stocks. By identifying the right strategies, then you will be able to make money regardless of the prevailing market conditions.This means making profits even when there is no movement in the market. However, with some strategies, you may lose money if you make a wrong move. Therefore, sufficient care needs to be taken to mitigate against any such losses as they can be significant.

The Most Profitable Options Trading Strategy

It is advisable, to begin with, the most basic options trading strategies first. This is the way most options traders start. By using these simple options trading strategies, you stand to make huge returns on your investments and trading skills. It is very possible to enjoy a 100% return on investment within a couple of days and sometimes even in just a couple of hours.

You can also find plenty of websites and advisory services that provide advisory services and trading assistance to traders. Some trades may fail. But it is also likely that most of your trades will be successful. Therefore, a good strategy, or approach to this challenge would be to ensure you place multiple trades on each occasion. Ensure that your strategy will win you money even though one or two trades may lose some money.

Consistently Profitable Strategies - Selling Puts & Credit Spreads

There are some studies conducted by credible institutions that the two most profitable options trading strategies are selling credit spreads and selling put options. The study found that the profits from such trades are consistent and regular over a long period.

However, the study found something else. The study reveals that buying call options and put options is more profitable in the long run even though it is not as consistent. You stand to make 7% - 12% per month on the total portfolio which is about 84% to over 144% per annum. Considering that the techniques used are very simple, easy to apply, and require the most basic of technical analysis, then your chances of making stress free money are very high. You can expect to win over 80% of your trades if you come up with the right trading plan.

Overall Best Options Trading Strategy

According to finds, it is widely accepted that you will make the most profits selling puts. If you invested a lot of your trading resources into selling put options, then you stand to make a lot of money consistently and with very little risk of loss. The only challenge with the selling option is that it has certain limitations. This is because selling put options works best in a market that trends upwards or is on the rise. You can complement selling puts with selling ITM puts for long term contracts. These are contracts that last 6 months or longer. They will make you tons of money simply because of the effect of time decay.

Also, when you sell, as a trader on the options market, credit spreads, you will be able to take advantage of the market in both directions. This means you will profit from an upward as well as downward market trend. This is great as even smaller traders can make some money regardless of experience. Therefore, always remember not to search for the size of the profits.

When searching for the most profitable and successful options strategy, focus on factors like;

- Ability to come up with a reliable and safe plan
- Have a plan that generates regular income
- Associated risks are low
- Technical requirements are manageable

Sell Naked Puts is one of the most lucrative ways of making money trading options. The return on margin is almost as lucrative as selling credit spreads. However, it does not carry a similar level of risk. In short, anytime that you sell a put option, then you make it possible to purchase a stock at a price of your choosing.

A Closer Look at Naked Puts

It's the end of June and XYZ stock is at $50. However, the market is fluctuating and you prefer to buy this stock for $45. What you need to do at this stage is to sell a $45 put option for $2. You can put the expiration date on this option as the third week of July. Once you post the option, you will immediately receive $200 into your trading account. Now should the XYZ stock price fall below $45, you will be required to purchase 100 units. This will cost you $4,500.However, you already have $200 in your account so the cost of buying the shares is reduced by this amount. If you sell a put option each month for the following six months, you will receive a total of $1,200. This will drastically lower the cost of buying XYZ shares. However, if the stock starts rising, you will not need to buy it but will keep selling the put option. While there is a slight risk due to liquidity issues, this strategy is quite a winner and can lead you to immense profits in just a short while.

ROI or Return on Investment

The Term ROI stands for Return on Investment. ROI is a measure of performance and is used by both investors and traders to measure the effectiveness and efficiency of an investment. This includes your trading capital. ROI deliberately endeavors to measure directly the total return derived from a particular investment.For instance, if you invest a total of X amount on a particular trade and then received a return of Y from this investment, then ROI will endeavor to indicate the performance of your investment amount and what you received for your efforts. If you want to calculate the rate of return of an investment, you will need to know the total return which is then divided by the investment amount.

One of the most important aspects of your investment portfolio is its profitability. You need to regularly monitor your investments which are best achieved using the ROI or return on investment. It is advisable to work out what each dollar invested has generated. There is a formula for working out this figure.

R.O.I = (Profits – Costs) / Costs

Even then, investors need to understand that the ROI depends on numerous other factors such as the kind of investment security preferred and so on. Also, note that a high ROI implies a higher risk while a lower figure means reduced risk. For this reason, appropriate risk management must be undertaken.

Conclusion

So here we are at the end of this guidebook on trading options. They can be extremely profitable, but learning to trade them well takes time. You can choose to use indicators to determine your entry points. I'm all for this approach but remembers that over the long term, you're better served learning the basics of order flow and using them. There is no shortage of options strategies you can use to dramatically limit your risk, and depending on the volatility levels, you can deploy separate strategies to achieve the same ends. Contrast this with a directional trading strategy where you have just one method of entry, which is to either go short or go long, and only one way of managing risk, which is to use a stop loss. Spread or market neutral trading puts you in the position of not having to care about what the market does. In addition, it brings another dimension of the market into focus, which is volatility. Volatility is the greatest thing for your gains, and options allow you to take full advantage of this, no matter what the volatility situation currently is.

Options can be a bit hard to get your head around at first since so many of us are used to looking at the market as a thing that goes up or down. Options bring a sideways and a different vertical element to it via spreads and volatility estimates. More advanced options strategies take full advantage of volatility and are more math-focused, so if this interests you, you should go for them.

Said that, do not assume the complexity means more gains. The strategies shown in this book are quite simple, and they will make you money thanks to the way options are structured. They bring you the advantage of leverage without having to borrow a single cent. You can choose to borrow, of course, but you need to do this only if it is in line with your risk management math. Risk management is what will make or break your results and at the center of quantitative risk management is your risk per trade. Keep this consistent and line up your success rate and reward to risk ratios, and you'll make money as a mathematical certainty.

Qualitative risk management requires you to adopt the right mindset with regards to trading, and it is crucial for you to adopt this as quickly as possible. Remember that the implications of your risk math mean that you need not be concerned with the outcome of a single trade. Instead, seek to maximize your gains over the long term. The learning curve might get steep at times, but given the rewards on offer, this is a small price to pay. Keep hammering away at your skills, and soon you'll find yourself trading options profitably, and everything will be worth it. How much can you expect to make trading options?

Well, I said that I'm not keen on putting numbers to this sort of thing. Generally, good options trade can expect around 50-80% returns on their capital. As you grow in size, this return amount will decrease naturally. However, to start with, these are beyond excellent returns.

Always make sure you're well-capitalized since this is the downfall of many traders. You need to be patient with the process. A lot of people rush headfirst into the market without adequate capitalization or learning and soon find that the markets are far tougher than they thought. So always ensure the mental stress you place yourself in is low and that you're never in a position where you 'have' to make money trading.

I wish you the best of luck in all of your trading efforts. The key to success is to simply never give up and to be resilient. Reduce the stress on yourself, and you'll be fine. Here's wishing you all the success in your options trading journey!

Made in the USA
Las Vegas, NV
04 January 2024